Joining Loose Ends

Joining Loose Ends

How a long walk revealed a new life

Keith Badger

Rescope Publishing

First Australian edition published 2017
www.joininglooseends.com

Published by Rescope Publishing (a division of The Rescope Project, a registered charitable organisation based in Australia)
www.rescopeproject.org.au
All profits from the sale of this book will be dedicated to furthering the work of The Rescope Project

www.keithbadger.com

Cover art created in Melbourne, Australia by Sarah McConnell
www.sarah-mcconnell.com

Internal illustrations created in Shrewsbury, England by Jason Davenhill on the back of recycled scrap offcuts of RAF flying charts

ISBN: 978-0-6482012-0-5 (Hardback)
978-0-6482012-1-2 (Paperback)

Printed in Australia by Griffin Press on paper certified against the Forest Stewardship Council® standards.
(FSC promotes environmentally responsible, socially beneficial and economically viable management of the world's forests.)

A catalogue record for this book is available from the National Library of Australia

Lives are lived through relationships and neither the walk nor this book would exist without Debby and the love we share.

Contents

Civilisation has always been a project of control, but you can't win a war against the wild within yourself.

– Paul Kingsnorth, Dark Mountain

LAND'S END 2010
LONDON
FLAT
CARDIFF
COAST
HEARTLAND
DYKE
DUBLIN
BELFAST
the WAY OUT
the WAY IN
EDINBURGH
BORDERLANDS
GLASGOW
WEST WAY
INVERNESS
GLEN
THE HIGH ROAD
JOHN O'GROATS 2010
LAND'S END
BEFORE
ORKNEY ISLANDS

Chapter 1 - BEFORE

Five days before – to Thurso, Scotland

Swathed in clouds Scotland may be wet and wild, but up here at 35,000 feet it presents no threat. When the pilot calmly announces we're starting our descent though, Debby looks at me nervously and sheepishly I smile back. She is a strong woman, but I've brought her on an expedition our friends say is crazy and I know the doubt she harbours. In this modern world vacations are meant to be framed in luxurious comfort with Caribbean sun, turquoise infinity pools, loungers and cocktail umbrellas to distract us from the real world. I'm the one who wants to do the opposite. Let's throw ourselves into months of physically demanding trekking through some of Britain's most exposed countryside, I said. Debby has had to live with this daunting prospect hanging over her. Now, the idea is about to become our daily reality.

The clouds part and I peer down through the window at steel grey rocks scourged by elemental forces, wind and water their ever-present tormentors. This geography will not soften for our passing, it's us who will need to adapt to its demands. I lost Barbara my first wife to the ravages of an unrelenting illness, but to break another on the anvil of my stubborn desire would be unforgivable.

People ask me why we're doing this and I still can't be sure. The germ of something had settled on me 20 years ago when I first heard the notion of a walk across England. It was impossible at the time as Barbara's breast cancer had begun its insidious journey through her bones. But the idea of moving across Britain by foot must have called to something deep in the humus of my DNA. The illness claimed Barbara a decade ago and the seed remained dormant. I hadn't realised though that once an idea enters the mind it often does not die with the passing of time. Ignored and seemingly forgotten it can lie inert awaiting its season. During marital rebirth and the extended time of nurturing and weaving five teenagers from different upbringings into a family, we renovated an old Victorian home. Life was full of busyness and the seed remained quiescent. If spring had erupted in my personal life, the conditions were not right for such a fanciful project to sprout.

Eventually life settled and as our new family bonded, an innocuous newspaper article about a Coast to Coast walk had sparked that deeply buried memory into life. After so many years the idea quickly flowered and within months we boarded a plane from Melbourne on Australia's east coast to connect with a single carriage train to England's north-western edge. It was our first serious long-distance walk and we followed the footsteps of England's foremost long-distance walker, Alfred Wainwright. We set out with puffins circling the red sandstone bluff of Cumbria's St Bees and two weeks later descended into the steep-sided little town of Robin Hood's Bay on the bleak Yorkshire coast.

We arrived on 22nd May, 2009 and that evening Debby and I were sat in a bar under gaudy yellow lighting bathed in the walkers' satisfied brew of exhaustion and elation. Surrounded by a din of conversation and raucous laughter, the thick grimy atmosphere was of the type found in many of England's small pubs on a Friday evening. We were there to celebrate an ending, but an outlandish idea was about to lurch into my life. A dramatic new beginning was afoot. I'm used to thoughts flitting in and out of my head like midnight bats seeking an attic rafter to hang from, but this one arrived like a mammoth. It lumbered out of the mists of time to stand proudly centre stage and defied me to look away. Whatever spell was cast that evening, the idea that materialised has come to dominate my life.

It is the English custom at the end of a long walk to go to the local pub where a book awaits to immortalise the achievement. You enter your name and there's space for reflections or comments, profound or otherwise. Besides the person following you to the book, nobody probably ever bothers to read these comments. However, at the time it feels like an honour to have the opportunity. The task is a tradition to be respected. On that evening after a 20-mile day, Debby had felt neither the strength nor inclination to move from her seat and had asked me to order her a stiff drink with some food. As far as the record book went, she said I could write a comment for the both of us.

As I manoeuvred through the press of people towards the bar, I was feeling good. The fact I was about to turn my life upside down and forever change its direction was the farthest thing from my mind. We'd walked about 220 miles in a couple of weeks and I felt chirpy. The sheer exhilaration of all those miles of magnificent countryside, all that weather, all those sights and sounds, had been heady stuff. Something had been released inside me and I wanted more. I'd told Debby, as she made her painful way down to the harbour-side pub from our guest house at the top of the cliff, that I felt like I wanted to turn around and walk back to the start. Debby had told me in no uncertain terms that I was mad and to stop being so 'Tiggerish'.

At the bar I ordered a second pint and asked for the Coast to Coast book to sign. As I took out my pen I wasn't expecting anything strange to happen. The words that flowed didn't come from any conscious intention, but just seemed so right. I will never know who was writing, but as soon as the pen finished its work, I became embarrassed. These words were not for public viewing and I quickly turned to check no one was furtively watching ready to laugh over my shoulder. Thankfully, people were blissfully unaware of me and the stake I'd just placed in the ground. I gazed down at the book and the words stared back up, daring me to turn away. In my confused state I quickly closed the book and returned to the table. Debby looked at me:

'So, what did you write in the book?'

'Er, just that we've today finished the Coast to Coast walk.'

'What nothing else?'

'Oh yes, um, yes, I, er, wrote "Now for Land's End to John O'Groats!"'

'You've written what?!'

A quest is born…

At that moment, I had no idea how long such a walk would be, or indeed if it were even possible. I'd heard that celebrities do the walk for charity with a full back-up crew taking the shortest possible route along main roads. If we were ever to attempt this walk, I knew we would be alone and would want to stay well away from roads. As an English Australian who had only moved to Melbourne about 20 years ago, this was the country of my birth and I'd clearly had an experience to reconnect me with my roots. However, something more fundamental in my psyche had been awakened and I could feel its pull defying resistance. Whatever instinct was unleashed, by the time we were back home in Melbourne the idea seeded in that pub had taken root and its inevitability has consumed me.

Of course, a crazy unstructured concept is not enough of a reason to take on such a major venture. Nonetheless, the idea once conceived would not go quietly away. Here on the plane to Inverness I still find it hard to believe what has been set in motion. I've often wondered just what it was about that walk last year that I found so stimulating. By the time it ended, something hard to understand had happened. Cold soaking rain, bruising terrain and nightly exhaustion seemed to have inflated my spirits and made mere physical aches an irrelevance. However, one thing was clear I was smitten like a 16-year-old, who couldn't get enough. I had reached the end and wanted more. If walking across a country where the land is narrow had been good, then surely the logical next step should be to cross it where it is longest.

As we returned from our walk, so the idea had returned with us. In fact, it became our constant companion whether we talked about it or not. It lay there dominating our subconscious, defying us to ignore it. There was no way we could just reject it. The sheer scale of such an adventure and people's excited reaction quickly led us to understand how remarkable it could be. On the one hand, this larger than life idea glowing inside us brought a special warmth and nervous energy that was scary yet stimulating; on the other hand, the challenges seemed daunting. I knew we would face the inevitable sarcasm of living down to friends' expectations if we were simply to give up on it. No, we'd created something that could not be idly dismissed. For better or worse it had hold of us and to either take it on or cast it out would require great effort.

Over those first few weeks back in Melbourne we would find ourselves drawn to discussing the idea and looking for simple reasons not do it. We canvassed all manner of potential hurdles that might enable us to forget it and still preserve our pride. We talked of the time it would take and whether we could afford that. We had a large home with two of our children still living there. Would we have to disrupt their lives by accelerating their independence? And if so, could we find a house-sitter able to take over our responsibilities for such a long time while we were half a world away? Then there was the personal physical challenge this would represent. It would be well beyond anything we had ever done before. Would it perhaps cripple us?

The fact we'd only completed one well-established walk requiring moderate physical ability with professionally managed accommodation bookings, meal arrangements, bag carrying services and the like didn't unduly worry me. I always say everything will be OK and practice will make possible if not perfect. Was I being naive? Of course, but that's my normal approach. I've lived by the dictum that if we don't let our dreams have a day out in the real world we become lesser people for it and the world loses an invaluable experience. At the start all big ideas need protecting and nurturing. With wind under their wings they can sometimes fly, but with wet blankets laid over them early on, they most certainly never will.

It took several months before we made the decision to commit to this walk, but we did so knowing it would turn our lives upside down. It seemed to be such an all all-encompassing challenge we knew we'd have time for little else. At the start we had no idea just how much work would be needed in the planning and preparation. Determined not to become overawed by the prospect, we threw ourselves into it with gusto using a technique for working on big projects which has always held me in good stead. Simply focus on what is known and get on with that. There are always unknown things at the start. Over time they will present themselves and when they do, that's when they are meant to be tackled and the plan can simply be expanded to include them.

Apart from preparing for the physical challenge, such a grand adventure would involve an enormous planning and logistical exercise. This was especially so given the route we were considering. We were not aware of anyone taking on this walk in the 'slow' manner we envisaged. We would want to keep off the roads and follow country footpaths. However, that would require path-finding beyond anything set out in guidebooks. And as someone who had never used a compass seriously, this meant risk. Would we be safe? Also, there would be the issue of the large amount of supplies we would need during such a journey. How could we possibly walk with the level of supplies we're used to having available on a day to day basis? Some backup would be required, but how could we organise it?

So, the hurdles surfaced and although some appeared daunting, nothing became an absolute knockout. The key really was, did we want to do it enough? I could not articulate what was happening inside me, but knew that this idea had taken hold and was putting down strong roots. I did know that we were very fortunate to even be able to contemplate such a venture. At 57 I was in pretty good health and able to free up my time. Debby was a little younger and in prime health. We had many interests and lived busy lives, but understood we were truly the masters of our own destiny. We had the luxury of the time and resources to be able to take on this venture if we set our minds to it and were sufficiently determined to see it through.

It's taken a year to be ready to board this plane today and launch the quest in earnest. We've worked out the best way to tackle the adventure is in reverse, starting at John O'Groats on the far north-eastern edge of Scotland and walking 'downhill' so to speak, to Land's End at England's extreme south-west tip. Having spent almost the entire year thinking about, planning and preparing for the walk, it has already had a major impact on our lives. We now know that where a direct road route would mean a walk of about 870 miles, we are about to embark on a considerably longer challenge. Taking the scenic route, we will follow some iconic footpaths, but also a variety of smaller ancient footpaths for which Britain is famous. Our goal is to complete the walk while enjoying the journey. We have no plans to rush or beat records but simply hope to wander and wonder our way across about 1,500 miles of Britain's countryside.

With a thud we're on tarmac and the noise of roaring engines quietens. Inside the airport our first, totally unexpected setback arrives. A year of planning and disruption, late nights sleepily plotting millions of footsteps onto detailed maps, researching hundreds of potential accommodation options in obscure B&Bs and hostels, weeks of trudging through Melbourne's streets carrying backpacks full of bricks, and now all I can do is stand here in Inverness airport's uninspiring baggage hall, shaking with frustration. The overweight suitcase containing all our supplies for several months trekking has not appeared on the luggage carousel. It appears our belongings have gone on their very own adventure leaving us stranded. I turn away from the polite baggage supervisor. I don't want polite, I want somebody I can be angry with. We'll be on a four-hour train journey soon to Scotland's far north coast and then tomorrow a ferry across to the Orkneys to acclimatise. Telling me I'll have to wait at least two days for our case makes me want to scream: 'What part of "that won't work", don't you understand? We're about to start the journey of a lifetime which has already consumed the life we've known and you are not listening!'

Debby steps in. She calmly gives the supervisor tonight's address and phone number while moving me out into the grey streets of Inverness in search of distraction. We both know coffee, food or second-hand bookshops are most effective in these circumstances, but to immediately find all three under one roof seems a miracle. Leakys, with its mezzanine café an enticing bubble of steamy warmth and inviting aromas, overlooks a huge array of captivating, dusty books in a converted old church. It appears to be nothing short of a spiritual experience, but with heart-warming chicken soup thrown in for good measure.

Refreshed and calmer, I push the list of our carefully accumulated kit contents out of my mind. I buy a change of t-shirt, just in case, and board the afternoon train for our first sight of Scotland's highlands. The flyspeck stations are impressively quirky, as are the four young men we meet on the train. They are about to cycle from John O'Groats to Land's End in ten days at 80 miles per day. A certain cockiness seems to disappear and they become a little subdued as we explain our plan to walk it the long way in about five months.

Immediately we arrive in Thurso, I become aware the walk will provide other gifts. I've never been here before nor met my cousin-in-law Robert and his wife Rachel. Immediately Scottish hospitality is on show, including a half tumbler of single malt whisky which Robert assures me is the regulation local 'home measure'. A delicious three course roast dinner follows, before Robert produces his fiddle to summon up tunes that evoke the romance of this land. As my consciousness disappears into nightfall, our suitcase turns up by express courier and suddenly things are back on track.

Now I understand our new reality. One slip-up could undermine this whole adventure. A long string of accommodation reservations could unravel in an instance. No matter how much planning has been put in there is always something that can bring it undone. Travelling as we are means we're more vulnerable than I like and nothing can be taken for granted, neither the weather, nor the meals we may encounter. Tomorrow we go to the Orkney Isles for our first brief walking experience in this country before setting out on an extreme adventure. Will the weather see us stranded in the Orkney Isles, or some bad food confine us to a guest house loo before we even get into our stride? Even if we fail to complete our walk I already sense we'll create great memories and meet some wonderful people along the way. Before turning out the light in this strange bed, I realise there'll be over 100 more strange beds before we find a way back home.

Four days before – to Stromness, Orkney Islands

The day starts as every day should, with a bracing walk down to the sea. Melvick Beach is just about as far north as possible on the Scottish mainland. I pull on my Speedos, walk out into the chill waters of the Pentland Firth and dive under the swell. My body comes alive. Nothing lifts my spirits and provides succour like the vibrancy of immersion in this elemental liquid. Light streams from above the surface refracted down into all manner of unseen and unimaginable life. As an 'Iceberger' in Melbourne I swim with friends all year round in Port Phillip Bay. The water temperature falls to around eight degrees in the depths of winter and yet we still swim in Speedos our 1,400 metres standard 'no brainer' course. As a slow swimmer, I come out half-frozen after about 35 minutes but my day is set up. It's my heart-starter and my meditation.

I guess some form of demanding workout has been part of my life for a long time. However, I've attempted nothing on the scale that now confronts us. This idea of an extreme walk has been bubbling within me, not just as an epic adventure, but also as a really strong physical challenge. Can we walk across all sorts of terrains, in all kinds of weathers, over huge distances, day in, day out for several months? And what's more, can I do it while carrying a 20kg backpack? Within the Iceberger group there are many wise individuals and I've learned much. The camaraderie is cherished as much as the swimming and through the friendly competitive culture I've been encouraged to go beyond my normal limits.

A few years ago, I set myself a particular daunting swim challenge for a full month of winter that hadn't been attempted before. I managed it, but as some of my colleagues then went on to ever-increasing physical demands I wondered at the wisdom of it. Andrew, an accomplished doctor quietly reassured me,

'Keith, our bodies are capable of so much more than we use them for.'

The phrase was immediately etched into my psyche. So, if we're not using our bodies for all we could, it makes sense to take on challenges to get the most out of our lives. Perhaps then, just perhaps, this idea of a gruelling walk is indeed a sensible idea. At the very least it won't harm anyone else or do any damage to the world. If we do it, we'll probably change nothing at all other than give ourselves all the elements required for a grand story.

During all the preparation I've grappled with a lurking misgiving that we might not make it. All manner of things could go wrong, some of them completely out of our control. But first and foremost, what if the physical demands are beyond us? If this happens we'll be exposing ourselves to public ridicule. Not that anyone would criticise Debby, of course. No, if we fail, then I will probably become a laughing stock. I will be criticised for putting my dear wife through such tribulations for no good reason. The fact Debby has now entertained this challenge will in no way shift the blaming and shaming of me by a friendship group that thrives on such little weaknesses. That great Aussie mateship ethic, which saw all my friends turn out to support me during the tough times of personal family tragedy, can quickly become the searching scrutiny of friends embedded in a competitive culture looking for some opportunity to go one up. Many would delight in putting me down for this ridiculous misadventure.

Before we left Melbourne a *bon voyage* dinner had been arranged. I realised then, it's not battling through icy waters that toughens us up, but the psychological demands of a group whose motto is 'strength through humiliation'. There is no doubt I have certainly been the subject of much 'strengthening activity' recently. The pinnacle was a 'FOK' dinner which I chose to believe stood for 'Friends Of Keith' but others suggested was a more crude travel instruction. They were fed up with all this grand adventure talk and made it clear I was setting myself up for anticipated humiliation. The host even started taking bets on the odds of me breaking down before half way. My already stubborn personality simply became even more determined.

Walking out of the stinging, dark water I dry myself off with white fingers and hope today's air temperature might rise above the 12°C typical summer high hereabouts. Melbourne is a full four degrees warmer than that and it's winter there. We head off for the appropriate antidote – a huge breakfast of salted porridge accompanied by full Scottish fry-up including the local butcher's black pudding, the best I've tasted.

It's one-fifteen in the afternoon as the ferry severs our tenuous hold on the Scottish mainland. A 90-minute journey stands between us and Stromness, a place immortalised from childhood memories of shipping forecasts. For such a wild stretch of water the seas are kind to us and in the brooding calm my mind drifts to images of Viking longboats sailing through here for 400 years when the Orkneys were part of Norway. Almost too soon we enter the little harbour through a collection of brightly coloured boats. While at rest in a lifeless sea under a solid grey sky, their pastel colours lift the dour tone of the hard grass moorland and hills beyond. We find our modest guest house and then head off to dinner at the local hotel with no expectations. And sure enough the evening lives down to our fears. The experience brings back memories of 1970's food overcooked and swimming in rich creamy sauces. No matter, this is a day to savour and tomorrow our serious walking preparation starts.

Three days before – to Kirkwall

It's time to blow out the cobwebs and do some walking. Skara Brae, recognised as a World Heritage Site for its well preserved 5,000 year old human settlement, seems an obvious jaunt. We arrive six hours later, tired and frustrated, and we've only covered 14 miles. This is a worry given the bigger challenges that await us. Over the last six months we've worked on our fitness, but I considered we were already in pretty good shape. Debby has recently qualified as a yoga teacher and I have my daily swimming. However, once we committed to this adventure we did step up the preparation and took regular morning walks to include our only local hill. Of course, Point Ormond is only about 20 metres high and the lack of anything sterner did concern me. Still, we bought pedometers and made sure we were getting some miles under our belts.

At least once a week, rather than pick up car keys, we would go about our business by foot. We'd walk 10 or 12 miles, usually going into the city, to a football game at the Melbourne Cricket Ground or to a cinema in another suburb, and then walk home. In short, we moved around on foot whenever we could. It took up more time, but we came to love it and got to understand and appreciate our city and the streetscapes. Often we would carry backpacks, mine with bricks or a large pumpkin inside to build up weight-carrying confidence. Of course, all of this further cemented the image of us in our friends' minds as a couple who clearly had a screw loose.

I've chosen to overlook our only real attempt at hillwalking. We visited the New South Wales coast and walked up Tilba Tilba's Mount Dromedary. It was only a two hour climb, but coming back down Debby's knees became very painful. She recovered quite quickly, but while watching her struggle down I kept thinking that we'd need to be doing things like this day in, day out. Debby talked to her body saying, 'Come on that little bit there is struggling, all you other parts need to work harder to help us get through until we can all rest'. Even I began to worry about her level of eccentricity at this point, but somehow the pain would soon be forgotten and she would happily carry on. She is such a strong person and just kept repeating her mantra, 'Everything will be OK, just take one step at a time.'

At the end of the day, we've done what we could, but as Jason our foot specialist said, 'The only way you really get fit for walking, is by walking.' I wonder now if I've relied on that concept too much and just assumed when we set off that everything will come good. Certainly, today it's taken us much longer than sauntering around Melbourne's leafy streets. We've had to scramble over wild terrain, including large unstable stones on remote beaches. Debby's water camel pack leaked and when I slipped, gouging a finger on rusty barbed wire, I realised just how easily an accident could bring our journey undone. It seems vulnerability will be our permanent companion. Yet marvelling at the birds thronging above the rock stacks from the Yesnaby cliff edge, all my worries seem to lift.

On the spur of the moment I take out a small notepad and jot down a type of haiku. It seems like a good way to keep track of memorable moments along the way. I've never even read haiku poetry and certainly have no idea of the rules. I've never tried to be an artist, let alone write a poem, so the urge surprises me. I wonder if I'm beginning to let go of inhibitions to express myself? Perhaps feeling part of nature's wide expanse is giving me the space to create? I decide on my very own form of haiku and set just one rule – there will be seven words. I breathe in deeply from the cliff edge and write:

Seagulls soaring
Clouds subsuming,
All is up.

On paper it looks disappointing, but fortunately Skara Brae itself is impressive. Here are the clear remnants of the home of a family group that lived hundreds of years before the Egyptians built their pyramids. Yet it feels so familiar. Their needs were so similar: to eat, cook, clothe and live together as a family. They had to manage without all the technologies we've developed, but also they didn't have all the wants which have become our needs in the consumer society we inhabit. As we trudge into the visitor centre for a well-earned hot drink, I wonder how much better off than our forebears we really are. I smile as Debby asks for a weak latte. There's a look of bewildered confusion on the face of the old lady as she turns from the machine: 'I just push the button dear and it comes out as it is.'

Meanwhile, sitting at a table patiently waiting for us are Phyllis and Colin. They are our logistical support team from London and have flown up to Scotland to see us off. We've deposited a large suitcase of neatly packaged and itemised supplies at their home and as needs arise they will mail things 'Poste Restante' for us to pick up at post offices along the way. After so many planning discussions they've entered into the spirit of the adventure completely. Such dedication and encouragement is just the support all adventurers gain strength from.

As I stir the caramel-coloured milk masquerading as coffee, I become aware of something odd. Our trusty support team are trying hard to keep tabs on us, but without success. They have in these few short days assumed some responsibility for us and we are instinctively referring to them as 'Mum and Dad'. What is it about the relationship one has with people called Mum and Dad? You love them, but feel you have to continually assert your independence from them. By evening we enjoy a hearty pub meal and as Colin and I appreciatively sip Scottish hand-drawn real ales, Debby questions whether this adventure is just an excuse for a grand pub crawl.

Two days before – to St Margaret's

A rattling window disturbs the night and from three onwards, broad daylight floods our room through a flimsy curtain. Only two more sleeps to go and I hope they will be better. Kirkwall has some history and we give rein to our growing sense of excitement to play tourist. St Magnus Cathedral dates from about 1150 AD and was built to commemorate a Viking chieftain treacherously killed by his cousin. It is fascinating to marvel at this impressive building knowing it only exists due to such a heinous act. We walk out of town reflecting on how good can even come from the most brutal acts. The wind blows constantly, and in time its nagging persistence clears my mind.

Crops growing
Wind blowing
All leaning over.

The decision to go ahead…

One minute everything is fine and then suddenly Debby is down with a grazed knee. I go to help her up, full of words of concern. Getting her breath back and letting the shock recede, she shows her customary pluck and sets off again. We don't say anything, but I feel the familiar discomfort which has arisen several times over the past few months. When we first returned to Melbourne with the idea for this mammoth expedition I had simply answered Debby's concerns with, 'but why shouldn't we do it?' And she would look back at me and say, 'I just don't know'. These exchanges brought home to me that no matter how much this idea may have taken root in me, unless it was also growing in her, it would die. The health, time and resources I have are all great advantages, but my relationship with my wife is the foundation on which all else is built. I wanted to do this walk with Debby or not at all. So, I told her the decision would be hers alone and stopped talking about it.

Of course, during this time of self-imposed restraint I still pondered how I would feel if Debby decided we shouldn't go ahead. Whatever was growing inside me was taking on the features of an almost mythical adventure. Could this possibly be my own *Lord of the Rings* story and if so, would I be more like Gandalf or Frodo? Or perhaps this was my search for the Holy Grail? Did I see myself as some modern day Jason, contemplating how to go out after the Golden Fleece? Memories of heroes battling animated skeletons in old films I'd rushed to see at the Saturday morning cinema in my youth came flooding back. If we give ourselves over to wild imaginings I'd told myself, surely a grand adventure could stir within anyone. This could well be mine and I would be very reluctant to let it go without good reason. Yet, I had handed over *my precious*, my ring of destiny was in Debby's hands.

So, days and weeks went by while I tried to get comfortable with my larger-than-life project being beyond my control. Friends would ask, 'You talked about a long walk, when are you off?' And I would try to be nonchalant: 'Oh I'm not sure we're going to do that now.' Occasionally Debby would raise it and I would reassure her that I was happy to put it off unless she really wanted to embrace it as her own challenge. I knew that if I asked her to, she would acquiesce. But I also knew the love we had for each other was something I couldn't take advantage of. This walk would demand great sacrifice and it was impossible to contemplate being soaking wet and cold with her thinking: it's not my challenge I'm only suffering this pain because of him. No, however much I wanted to do this, I would never impose it on Debby. Quite the reverse, I needed to protect her from her own strong tendency to do something through her love for me.

So, I waited, and waited. Then I began to overhear Debby talking about the walk and its challenges and people would ask why I was thinking of putting it off when Debby was so keen on it. Finally, as we sat in the spring sunshine one late November day, Debby spoke:

'When you asked me to do the Coast to Coast walk I thought you'd gone mad and I'd never make it. When we did it, I realised for all the hardships it was at the same time wonderful. I'd done more than I thought I ever could and created a whole lot of powerful memories that would stay with me forever. Now you've given us this new idea and I find myself talking about it. The idea's growing inside me and I think what have I got to lose? I might not make it, but if I don't have a go, I'll never know. I hate to miss out on an adventure, so not only am I prepared to give it a go, but I'd be disappointed if we didn't.'

All I could do was hug her, tell her how much I loved her, and say,

'Well then, we'd better get to work.'

With that, the planning started in earnest and we shared the tasks. Debby took the three H's leaving me with the three M's. Debby's jobs were Home – a bed for each night, Health – creating and managing the first aid kit, and Humour. Despite my encouragement Debby was concerned she could not be responsible for such a critical role as the provider of Humour. My tasks were Money, Maps and Meals. To organise the funds, be the map creator and pathfinder and select the places to eat and foods to buy along the way. Thinking ahead it's clear finding good food all the way through Britain will be a tough ask, and if Debby thinks she'll let me down on Humour, it's likely I'll do even worse on Meals.

The afternoon gradually disappears into weary acceptance of the new life we've chosen. We reach St Mary's feeling tired and hungry but I'm struck by the uplifting effect of a freshly mown roadside:

Smell the grass,
Newly dead
Bringing life.

Then it's as if we've entered an obscure time-warp – back to a Europe at war with itself. The Churchill Barriers in Scapa Flow were built to stop German U-Boats attacking the British Fleet stationed here. In bizarre contrast, a nearby chapel had been fashioned from two Nissan huts by a small group of Italian prisoners-of-war. Full ceiling paintings that wouldn't have looked out of place in a Roman church were created from a postcard sent by their leader's mother. The place is inspiring and the serendipity which saw its creation makes me wonder what we may discover about ourselves over the next few months.

Our practice is nearly over as the time for the real thing is fast approaching. Tomorrow morning we'll take the ferry back from the Orkneys to John O'Groats and the prospect of fair weather for our trip appears a good omen. I'm not normally superstitious, so perhaps it's nerves that make me interpret even the weather forecast as a portentous sign of the fates being either for or against us.

One day before – to John O'Groats

One day to go and any thoughts of not making it back to the mainland for our date with destiny have evaporated. A calm one-hour ferry trip and we're at the start. We check into an unremarkable pub annex with no heating. Now we're ready to pay due homage to the long-distance walk rituals. I've always believed in trying to respect the rituals of any undertaking and long-distance walking certainly has a few. In many ways they may be considered silly, and yet I've found they bring out the full taste and richness of the experience. First, there is arriving properly. To come to a place for the first time and immediately leave it behind feels a little disrespectful. By spending a few days in the Orkney Isles I feel we've done justice to acclimatising to the local conditions. Not only have we introduced ourselves to the weather and scenery, our companions for the next few weeks, but we've also partaken of the culture, history and people who breathe life into this area. And that's not to mention the fine malt whisky we've sampled.

The next task is to sign in at the register of End-to-Enders and we head downhill to the John O'Groats harbour to find the Journey's End Cafe where it's kept. We congratulate the only other person making an entry, a Melbourne man who has just completed a fast direct walk in the 'uphill' direction. This strange coincidence puts me off my stride and I cannot find appropriate words to record the gravitas of our adventure. I scribble something inane and close the book.

Now we must select something to carry with us on the journey. Typically, this is a stone or pebble when walking from one coast to another, so we head to the beach. The ritual requires at journey's end the pebble be flung back into the water to symbolically signify completion. Debby quickly selects a small stone in her usual efficient manner. For me the choice is more difficult. After all, this stone will be my companion every day for several months and I don't want to get bored with it. Every day I want to feel good about taking it out of my pocket at nightfall and be able to take comfort from the feel of its smooth surface in my hand in times of difficulty along the track. Obviously, with hundreds of thousands of pebbles to choose from this all takes time. I finally pick up two. The second, I promise to carry for Phyllis, our 'Mum', in recognition of all the support she's providing. As I look at these random pieces of stone, I wonder whether we'll reach Land's End together, and if so, will I be able to fling them back into the sea?

The other great ritual that now seems to have developed around travel, including long-distance walking, is 'The Blog'. A blog can be anything from a personal journal, to a way of keeping in contact with friends. Originally, I did not intend to write one, but a friend suggested it and others seemed keen. So, I've agreed, but I still have no real idea what's involved let alone what level of commitment it will require. Given my natural tendency to record the more arcane details of experiences, I have an uneasy feeling writing a blog may turn out to be a more momentous decision than I yet appreciate.

Although this is officially our last rest day before the adventure gets underway, I insist we start the walk this afternoon with a 600-metre stroll from the very tip of the harbour to the pub. I've always been a stickler for doing the right thing. In a swim, I'm known for rounding or touching every pole in the course regardless of whether anyone else sees you. I've always felt in cutting corners you commit the worse form of injustice to yourself, the person you can't hide from in the mirror each morning.

Back at the hotel in a comfy armchair I realise such rest will henceforth be a luxury. As of tomorrow we'll have more than an idea to contemplate, we'll have a grand project to tackle. The challenge has been with us for a full year in the planning now, but at the beginning I had no idea all it would entail. My thoughts were more of the romance of such a grand adventure when I unleashed the walk to friends in my Christmas letter:

'Walking is an opportunity to slow down and smell the roses… A chance to breathe in the fresh air on the hills and come alive in the presence of the elemental bracing sea winds, an opportunity to take communion with nature and meet the people who live in tiny villages along the way… a rare chance to rediscover a life connected to the seasonal swell and fall, the true, gentle rhythm of life, or perhaps just an opportunity to discover some real ales in quaint pubs, eat steak and kidney pud without feeling guilty, visit tiny 1,000 year old churches and stay in historic inns and B&Bs with eccentric owners. Whatever drives you, come and join us along the way.'

Planning and preparation…

But as we prepared, the romance slipped under all the hard work required. One particular challenge revolved around our home. We believe it doesn't help to let kids hang around in the parental abode too long, so we gradually worked through the issues to help them down the path from our front door to create their own homes and Ree, a dear friend, came to house-sit. Much of my time then was spent in very familiar ways. Although I approached the planning with some trepidation, I felt I could rise to the challenge, especially knowing that Debby was there to back me up. I had qualified as an accountant without giving it any great thought, but had come to understand I was well suited to the profession. Spreadsheets were just so much fun and they were the perfect tool for the meticulous plans required for such a massive logistical undertaking. To organise something of this size and scope needed quite a few big spreadsheets, and I was the man for it!

The sheer scale of the mapping challenge was the most daunting. I had to develop a route to cover about 1,500 miles with sufficient detail to trace every small 'right-of-way' out in the countryside. Walking the Coast to Coast had given me an insight into the huge difference between looking at a dotted line on a map and finding and negotiating a real track through wild moorlands, mountains, valleys, forests and farms. Every field we would cross. Every hill we would scale. Every river bank we would follow. All would need to be identified. In total I had to come up with a route map that could guide the placement of somewhere between three and four million consecutive footsteps.

My vision from the start was to forge what I considered would be a unique nine-stage approach and keep us off roads and in nature as far as possible. This would include some of the great British treks. In Scotland I wanted us to walk The Great Glen Way and the much-revered West Highland Way. In England, if we could come down the east side of the country, there was the foreboding yet compelling prospect of The Pennine Way, often described as the toughest footpath in the country. Then I wanted to get back to the west to follow the Dyke created by King Offa back in 700 AD to separate the Welsh heathens from the English. To finish such an adventure I always knew we must follow a path built right into the rocky cliffs of this island nation. We wouldn't be able to do the whole of The South West Coast Path, but we would be able to complete the full Atlantic coast section.

However, whereas I could find information about these major trails, there was a much bigger problem. Little footpaths needed to be stitched together to cross the in-between sections and these are set to represent a full third of the journey. I've consulted Ordinance Survey maps, which show the myriad footpaths and rights-of-way. It's a wonderful feature of the UK that footpaths criss-cross the whole country. Some are thousands of years old, predating Roman settlement. They were enshrined in law as public ‘rights-of-way’ by King Richard The Lionheart in the 12th century, and people have used them ever since to move about their daily business. Nowadays their use is more recreational and I’m aware the Ramblers Association supports their preservation against those who would have them closed off. We already know some landowners organise significant deterrents to keep walkers from their properties, but ultimately a determined walker can’t be stopped.

In these times where personal ownership of land is prized and people are encouraged to live increasingly private and isolated lives, it is easy to understand why a farmer or landowner might want to stop people walking across their land. Paths frequently go right through farms, crossing ploughed fields through the middle of mature stands of crops, or past the very doors of the cowsheds and farmhouses. Yet the rights were laid down before the farms were established, and so the walkers’ rights-of-way are preeminent. Such arrangements sound eccentric to my Australian friends, but they stand as a stark reminder that our modern world seems to have lost track of the importance of human connection with the landscape. In the rush to build monetary wealth we tend to downplay community rights and elevate a fear of outsiders. I’ve come to appreciate walking along these paths as a fascinating and refreshing antidote.

The work had seemed endless. Hour after hour, week after week, month in month out, step by step the route gradually took form, from the top of the country to the bottom. To now have with me a map for our whole walk including every little footpath required to connect the five major well-established long-distance paths while keeping us off tarmac roads and embedded in the British countryside, is pretty rewarding in itself. Of course, only time will tell whether the tiniest dotted lines on maps which may be critical to our journey, will be passable on the ground and not heavily overgrown or fallen into disrepair.

Stitching together a route was one thing, but I wonder if I've correctly anticipated the conditions we'll experience and hence how appropriate will be the distances I've set for each day's walk. In part this has been determined by the availability of accommodation. Right from the start we knew it would be impossible to carry camping equipment. We needed to be able to assure ourselves of shelter for the night. A bed, regardless of its comfort, and some sustenance, whatever the quality of food, were the essentials we'd need. So, I've had to direct our steps to the farms, hamlets, villages, towns and even in a couple of cases cities, to find a bed. Where we've already got accommodation booked our route is now marked with the directions to the very door of the hostel, B&B or pub we're staying in. After all, there's nothing worse at the end of a long day, feeling exhausted, only to get lost finding our bed for the night.

We quickly discovered that accommodation can be very scarce in remote spots, particularly in the first half of our journey. We are about to tackle three major British footpaths in the peak season. We needed to know we were going to have a bed at the end of our long walking days. The prospect of having to sleep under hedgerows in pouring rain was not something we could countenance. So, we decided to book some accommodation in advance and Debby took on the challenge in her typically efficient manner. Once she started, we realised the areas where we would likely have the most difficulty were down the Pennine Way, two months from today. To book accommodation this far out meant locking in our timetable from the very beginning. Every stop along the way up to that point effectively had to be set in stone.

By the time Debby had finished she'd secured beds for our first 70 nights. So tomorrow, we'll set off with reservations for the first half of the walk. Looking at her quietly resting this afternoon I am full of admiration for her dedication. She has researched many hundreds of options and made bookings at all manner of hostels, basic B&Bs and pubs. Spreadsheets were methodically completed in the detail I demanded, with the full address of each establishment, together with detailed directions of how to locate them, the tariff rates agreed and any advance payments handed over. I'm sure this was not in her mind ten years ago when she read my letter proposing we spend the rest of our lives together.

The evening approaches and I feel a little nervousness creep up on me. It's time to celebrate tomorrow morning's departure. Colin and I go to the bar to share two large single malt whiskies at a badly inflated price. Could this be an example of the Scots getting their own back on us English for past atrocities? Whatever, there is no better drink sitting in northern Scotland to toast the beginning of our challenge. The girls join us for a basic dinner and by the time we go to bed the sun is still an orange fireball, a reminder midsummer is only two days away. It's half past ten and once again pulling the thin curtain has almost no effect. The sun still streams in and I wonder how we'll ever get our eyes closed with such formidable excitement pending? Sleep descends within seconds.

INVERNESS
RIP
LAST
WOLF
The HIGH ROAD
MELBOURNE 10470
JOHN
O'GROATS
2010
LAND'S END 874

Chapter 2 – THE HIGH ROAD

Day 1 to Wick

It's six-twenty and finally the journey begins in earnest. I think we're ready, but I'm stirred up, the emotions are hard to decipher. I know that Sunday 20th June 2010, a day otherwise destined to slide into oblivion, will not go quietly. Whatever happens now, this day will live forever as a bookend to an expedition that just might dwarf any of my previous life experiences. There's nothing to be done now, no more preparation, just a few more minutes of peace while Debby dozes peacefully in the strong daylight.

Eye patches
Ear plugs
Purring peaceful oblivion

I knew the weather was never going to be great. Strong northwesterlies and misty rain are forecast, but nestled in this small room it doesn't seem to matter. Today will be different, though. We don't have the option of looking out the window and saying: 'Ah, not a good day to go out, let's wait until tomorrow.' That excuse won't be an option for several months. The change brings a tremor of excitement, a sense of liberation to engage with the raw outdoors. I don't know what awaits us out there, but I've a compulsion to find out.

I sprinkle a few of our favourite Earl Grey tea leaves in a characterless mug and we begin our preparation. We move quietly with the sense of a special event in the making. At breakfast we sit with people oblivious of us and our great sense of purpose. In a world where the media routinely stream news of endless reality events, we're no more than the latest trivial addition to the day's mundanity. It's our beloved support team who are perhaps more excited than we are.

Things move quickly now and I check out before we step across the threshold to feel the day. With just a simple daypack on my back my immediate thought is, we're frauds. Is this really such a great challenge if we're here with a backup crew for a simple walk down the road to Wick? I let the idea go. The road is deserted and we establish an imaginary start line. Surely something more momentous should be happening, perhaps a brass band playing or crowds with banners and flags waving. That may all be going on in our minds, but the reality is we're just an odd couple in a bleak setting with a plan for a long walk. *The sooner we get on with it the better,* says a voice inside me.

'Mum and Dad' anxiously take photos and give advice to 'be careful on the road'. Of course, they're just doing what mums and dads feel they have to do and we feel we know better. It's nine on a Sunday morning and we start walking. I'm happy to let go of this place, the poor night's sleep, lousy room, breakfast buffet with empty juice and milk jugs and no muesli. Hardly an auspicious start. I look around. It feels surreal after all the importance and drama we've invested in this venture. After all the detailed research and planning, here we are, just walking, one foot in front of the other. Nothing so special, simply moving through the landscape the way our bodies were designed to do.

Before I can deepen my contemplation, driving rain forces a switch from mental activity to the physical. The downpour is not unexpected but still comes as a shock, and my fingers quickly go numb. Our waterproofs are holding up well and it's a delight to discover a map pocket built into the front of my jacket. I've been moaning for six months about the lack of pockets in this supposedly specialist walking jacket. This incident has quite made my day, a good omen. I stride along feeling happy while Debby murmurs quietly under her breath something about little things pleasing little minds:

'If you can't find a pocket on your chest what chance will we have finding our way across thousands of miles of open country?!'

The landscape we're walking through is a surprise, no uninhabited barren moorland, but fields of sheep and cattle. Large houses and castles are dotted around, some more intimidating than others. Gazing across to the forbidding grey of the North Sea it's easy to understand how unaccustomed we city dwellers would be for the challenges of life up here.

Waves lapping
With steely determination
Wind reigns

I can't find any footpaths to Wick that would get us off the road. So, rather than explore the unknown on our first day, we stick to the straight road. There'll be plenty of time for getting lost later. The road also offers its own particular joy. Every time a rare car appears, we raise a hand in recognition of our fellow human and are rewarded with a wave back from the driver. There is something heart-warming about this small token of a shared human existence and I wonder why it only happens in these remote spots? Obviously there are too many people in cities to wave at them all, but why is it once we get behind the wheel of a city car, we shed our humanity and regard fellow humans as enemies out to frustrate us?

Maybe it's because we're road walking, but for some reason I begin to think about how I've come to be here. I'm a city boy after all and never thought connection with the countryside was in my veins. It certainly wasn't in my mind growing up in a South London council flat. My life was more about congestion, concrete, cars, and nervous nightly returns home through the red-light district on my doorstep. Choosing accountancy as a profession took me even further into the artifice of counting illusory riches rather than nature's gifts. Suddenly, in my late 50's with a family reared, a successful career achieved, a wife lost to cancer, another loving partnership established, everything seemingly in balance, bubbling up from somewhere deep inside comes this yearning for something more meaningful. An urge to go further and engage more fully with life.

I still find it hard to believe I've initiated this adventure. But, despite my jaundiced thoughts about affirmations, I do live my life by one very important one: *Everything will be OK because it always is.* This is the rock upon which my life is moored. I've learned that just as self-esteem provides the courage to chase life's potential, so not being afraid in a society with dark undercurrents of fear and dread can be empowering and liberating.

I grew up as an acutely shy, lonely young man despite the benefit of my parents' unqualified love to sustain me. In time I came to realise I had all the nourishment needed to go into the world to find what I could offer it. I took my skills, but also my weaknesses and vulnerabilities, in the certain knowledge it was all right to do so. In sharing my inadequacies, I was surprised others seemed to respond positively and let go of the burden of their own human frailties. To my surprise, being at ease with myself warts and all in a society driven by competitive forces didn't seem to hold me back. Quite the reverse, in a world riven by doubt, people seemed to respond better as they could be at peace with themselves.

Debby suddenly brings me back to the here and now, pointing to the 'Welcome to Wick' sign. The first 16 miles are on the pedometer. It's nearly three and we go straight to the café for a recovery coffee – at least it's called coffee. By dinner we're still hungry and the owner of our little hotel provides encouragement. Enthralled by our adventure, he asserts: 'More people should do this.' Laying my head on the pillow his comment brings a warm glow of encouragement to carry me off into peaceful oblivion.

Day 2 – to Lybster

It's shortly after six when we wake. I slowly pack the case for our support team and realise it will soon be more challenging when I have to squeeze it all in the backpack. It's nine again as we walk out on the day's path. Is this a routine beginning to establish itself as a frame for our days? I feel a quiver of resistance. I've rebelled throughout my life against the demands of others and the confines of routines. Perhaps it's only-child stubbornness? I still remember digging my heels in to drop out of university despite my well-intentioned headmaster's encouragement to stick with a course he chose for me. It took a year to get out and I knew my parents were worried sick, but I wanted to be free to explore the world.

My stubbornness meant I had to survive hard, soul-destroying, temporary labour work. Washing fetid bottles on the night shift at the Canada Dry drinks factory, single-handedly unpacking container trucks of chemical drums, day shifts following within an hour of the end of my night shifts, finally, my body beaten, I understood labouring was not my forte and took an office job. This change proved crucial and I found new ways of working with people and ideas that provided a foundation for a successful career. So, if resisting routines and maintaining flexibility has been my credo, surely I shouldn't cast it off on a grand adventure like this. Yet Debby insists:

'It's the discipline that sets you free, Keith.'

Well we'll see, but with each night's accommodation booked for the next 70 days and various commitments to meet people along the way, this is clearly not starting out as the liberated, spontaneous adventure I'd once imagined.

The morning is sharp cold and our exertions bring white breath clouds through which we look up at a sullen grey sky. The harbour lies quiet, almost empty. It's hard to believe 150 years ago Wick had the third largest port in Scotland with a thousand herring boats. I wonder where all those people and their appetites are now? Being Scottish, they needed sustenance to get through the tough conditions and Wick had 45 pubs to help. I've read the locals would consume 500 gallons of malt whisky a day. Today, Wick's 8,000 inhabitants' greatest claim is the world record it holds for the shortest road in the world. At just six feet nine inches Ebenezer Place has space for just one building, the one housing the bar we sat in last night.

The temperature is slowly rising as we leave the harbour. I look enviously at Trinkie's natural rock- formed ocean swimming pool where I told everyone last night I was going to 'bravely' swim. Seeing it now in misty rain on a murky morning, the 100 metres of rocks between the path and any swim appear treacherous. Breaking a leg this early on would not be smart and Debby gently reminds me of our greater goal, Land's End. I forego the swim and swallow down my dented pride.

The footpath soon proves a worthy distraction. At the edge of the cliffs we look down on heaving seas and wonder how the Old Man of Wick Castle was built right into these rocky crags 860 years ago? I could imagine pirates coming ashore, stashing their stolen booty into the weathered coves. Distracted by our imaginings, we suddenly find the path has disappeared. We're on a goat track perched precipitously on a rock edge. I direct Debby over a barbed-wire fence for the relative safety of a bog. Two miles of trudging with feet submerged in a brown sponge is an early warning to pay closer attention to the path. Before we reach the road the bog introduces us to our first taste of the Highland midges, or rather they have their first taste of me. We know these miniscule biting creatures are likely to be regular annoying companions for many weeks ahead.

Walking for three hours this afternoon I realise I'm grumpy. Straying into the morning bogs and extending our hike to nearly 20 miles has not helped my mood and I rely more heavily than normal on Debby. Although tired she is unperturbed and has energy left to work her quiet magic supporting me. It's four-thirty as we reach our destination and I badly need the tray-baked chocolate slice at the little Harbour Cafe. One of the benefits of long-distance walking is the appetite you bring to every opportunity for food. Another is the weariness you bring to bed at nightfall.

Day 3 – to Dunbeath

Over breakfast we bid farewell to the support team. It won't be the same without their camaraderie and I try not to dwell on the thought of carrying my 20kg rucksack for the first time tomorrow. Before leaving we spend an hour touring the gardens and sheds our hosts have created. We see beautifully turned timber works, vibrant fresh produce growing in the garden and an extensive handcrafted train set that runs through it to the far duck enclosure. Andrew, our host, is living his passion, his work a labour of love evidenced by the detail crafted into each engine, carriage and piece of railway track. For now, my inspiration has simply brought us here to bear witness to his endeavours. However, it's made me think of the tremendous latent potential locked up inside us all if we were to unleash our passions.

Walking off into a thick mist is surprisingly agreeable. It restricts our view but eliminates the midges. I'm not feeling in the best of form and whether it was the long, heavy sleep last night, or the malt whisky nightcap, I'm happy not to be pestered by insects. The prospect of tackling the tortuous, long, steep Berridale hills tomorrow with a full load on my back feels daunting. There's no way out though, so I simply put my head down and walk while Debby does her best to lift my spirits.

Mist drifts
Horizon gone
All at sea

This main road into the north is gradually becoming busier and, without a path, more dangerous. Trucks steam past less than a metre away. We try to make light of it and ignore them but you can't hide from the fear. Despite today being a short walk we still stop for afternoon tea at the Laidhay Croft Museum and Tearooms. Two enterprising older women run the tearooms and leave us in no doubt about serving arrangements. When I ask for a cheese scone with soup I am told to 'Get it yourself'. Although out of line with modern service conventions, this curt treatment is somehow more natural and likeable. I may not have stomach for the coffee, but I warm to these characters who have a good business going in this obscure spot.

Tonight's farm stay is better known locally as the Ivy Heart House. An enormous 106-year-old heart-shaped ivy covers the gable end facing the road. Here is evidence of another labour of love. When they planted and nurtured what is now a gnarled weather-beaten specimen, the original owners bequeathed something very special not only to the house's future occupiers but to everyone in the community and passers-by like ourselves. It's impossible to behold without smiling. I marvel at the sight and wonder what I've done to leave a legacy to benefit the future? Certainly, there is little likelihood this walk, even if we can complete it, will leave any trace for future generations. Already our footsteps are disappearing into the misty meandering threads of an uncertain memory. Thank heavens for the blog, even more reason to pay attention and make the days count!

Day 4 – to Helmsdale

It's six and now we face the foreboding prospect of a longish day, 16 miles, including the Berriedale and Brae hills of local infamy. Our first day carrying full backpacks and the scale of the problem comes home as I try to pack up. It's a struggle to stuff everything into bulging packs. We stagger them into the bathroom to confront the stark reality. The scales show I'm going to have to lug 23.5kg while Debby has 11kg. In total we have about 50 percent more weight than we'd planned. I've been lulled into a false sense of security having the support team with us. We'll need to shoulder our burdens today and hope we can send some surplus back to London tomorrow.

Mary our host kindly distracts us from our concerns over breakfast. She recounts the harsh winter conditions this past year when snow fell, the temperature dropped to about minus 20°C and everything remained frozen for the best part of two months. The wild animals suffered terribly and many deer died because they couldn't scratch through the icy surface for food. A number of their bodies were found by the roadside. It was one of the harshest winters Mary could remember at the farm in half a century. As a city-dweller it's impossible for me to understand the arduous experiences Mary has had to endure. This walk is taking us into the lives of more people than I'd imagined. I had expected we'd engage with flora and fauna in the open countryside, yet here I am again paying witness to another rich human life. It's only the first week of this walk and already we're connecting with a wide variety of characters and their diverse life paths.

We drag ourselves from the breakfast table, struggle to hoist packs on backs and set off. We'll follow the A9 road all the way today, and with no footpath it's immediately quite dangerous. Cars and trucks whizz by shuddering with violent noise. We distract ourselves by developing a categorisation system for car drivers. The large majority appear considerate people who, when we raise our hand to wave, reciprocate. They try to give us space by pulling out given how very little room there is for pedestrians. Other drivers make no such effort. These 'miserable bastards' just ignore us. Nevertheless, the 'utter bastards' are an even more threatening species. They seem to delight in leaning in on us as they speed by. Forced off balance, we can only grasp at the stone walls for security.

Before the day is out a further category bursts on to the scene. The 'unimaginable bastards' come at us from behind in the same direction we're walking. These drivers choose to overtake as they approach us. Coming from behind at speed we have no warning and it's hard to believe they're not trying to kill us. Today's ultimate demon driver overtakes alongside us, his double log transporter coming within inches of cleaning us both up. Once we've stopped shaking, I wonder why these drivers, humans like Debby and I, don't sense the link between them and us. Somehow insulated inside that metal hulk they seem oblivious to our kindred nature. Yet, once they park and walk back into the world as a human, they are invariably as friendly and hospitable as any. Debby says my challenge is to remember these experiences and maintain a considerate spirit next time I'm behind the wheel. Somehow, I know she will be right there helping me remember when the time comes.

The journey today is a long slog. At 17°C with no mist and layered clouds however it's the best weather we've had. The long slow ascent out of Dunbeath takes a full two hours to the top of the Berriedale Braes, followed by a long sharp descent down to a hidden flyspeck of a village. A small memorial stands erect by the stream and I read the sad inscriptions of those lost far away in world wars. The names are separated into lists drawn up to carefully identify from which of the two villages these poor souls bravely ventured forth. Here today, I wonder if the distinction is important.

Brae or Berridale?
Men lie dead,
Elsewhere

From here, we gird ourselves for the long slow ascent back up and then press on with another road slog. Under the relentless demands of my pack and the heat I almost collapse, staggering out into the middle of the road. I hide my discomfort and light-headedness from Debby and we carry on for about another hour. The classic Highland scenery with its wild open moorlands comes to the rescue, breathing new life through my weariness. Soon a sun-dappled forest beckons us in for lunch. Can there be any greater bliss than throwing off shoes and socks to massage tired feet in greenery? A very average block of cheese with oat cakes and egg sandwiches feels like a royal feast.

We arrive at our night's pub with the crucial England-Slovenia World Cup game set to start. I rush upstairs, drop the backpack and throw off shoes and socks in favour of my new rose-coloured flip-flops. Ordering a pint I wonder why the four somewhat surly Scotsmen are reluctant to talk to me. By the end of the match, with England's insipid 1:0 victory secure, it becomes obvious these dour Scotsmen see me as some sort of pseudo-Englishman. They struggle to support their fellow Brits and delight in telling me how Scotland was the first team to beat England after they had won the World Cup in 1966. They do finally warm to me and gently but firmly make it clear that wearing pink thongs in a public bar in Scotland is not a good idea.

Day 5 – to Brora

It's early, just twenty to six. Already I relish being able to simply lie in bed soaking up rest. Every part of my body – limbs, muscles, tendons, even skin – can relax into the bedding, but I sense a deeper process at work. It's as if every molecule of my being knows it has been putting in an increased effort and is now seeking this comfort. A sublime sense of peace settles over me in the stillness. I watch the shafts of bright sunlight refresh the room, gradually circling through me, bringing lightness of mind. The diary calls for yesterday to be written up, nothing must be forgotten. After breakfast, we go straight to the Post Office to dispatch four kilos of surplus stuff to London.

It's a temperate 17 degrees, and surrounded by nature at peace with itself, I tell Debby, 'Bliss is back.' We realise we both much prefer to walk in the morning. I'm more relaxed now and can better appreciate the journey and the joy to be had in every moment. With a quieter mind, all my sensing channels seem open to experience the day. It feels like joy is pumping around my system. Nothing dramatic needs to happen, I just have to be open to let the natural habitat in. The speckled patchwork of clover blossom and yellow gorse flowers amongst the heath is almost overpowering. The colours seem to swirl around more vividly than normal. I can taste the salty air on my lips and smell the deep earthy fragrance on the breeze. It's as if I'm losing the compulsion to simply arrive and tick off the day's journey. Slowly it's dawning on me, we're on a long walk and striving for pleasure in completion is misguided. Why try to arrive quickly when the pleasure and joy are found along the way?

It's day five and as Debby says, 'it's all falling into place now.' It seems to have been easier for her to cope with the journey. She's getting the job done in her customary efficient manner. It has been more difficult for me. I've been grumpy and questioning whether I really want to do all this walking. But not today! Today, we are both feeling strong and walk-hardened. Neither of us is showing any signs of physical damage – perhaps just a slight concern about putting on weight due to all the extra eating!

As the morning slips by though, my thoughts turn to lunch. Our leg muscles tell us how much energy they're burning up, and it seems wrong to deny them nourishment. At first, there's no obvious stopping place, but we're freer now, liberated from the norms society fences us in with. We deftly hop over a gate from the road into a rough field and enter the embrace of a bucolic setting framed by the competing blues of sea and sky. We throw down packs, shed shoes and socks, and while insects move about their business through the grasses under our feet, we let go of the trials of exertion.

Lunch of fields,
Sea, sky
How fulfilling!

In the afternoon the Moray and Aberdeenshire peninsula comes into view, the first major variation in coastline since we set off, and we can see our walk defined in tangible landscape terms at last. The sense of progress feels significant, perhaps more than it really is. Today's 16 miles means we're now over 75 miles into the journey. Amid the satisfaction though there is another odd sensation. Could it possibly be grief for the days already lost?

At day's end a piece of seemingly trivial information remains with me. We passed a stone memorial noting the place where the last wolf in Britain was said to have been hunted to extinction around 1700. No doubt this would have made Scottish King James VI happy. In 1577 he had made it compulsory for all to hunt wolves three times a year because of the damage they were believed to do to cattle herds. So why is it that 300 years after the last wolf howl sent nightly shivers down people's spines, a debate is now underway over whether to reintroduce wolves to the UK. Surely, we need to make up our minds about such things. All that effort to get rid of them seems a bit silly if we then find we need them.

Walking seems to bring such contradictions into sharper focus. I remember our walk last year finished in the brooding moorlands of Yorkshire. Vast uninterrupted views had drawn our eyes towards the coast near Whitby, Captain Cook country. In Australia, Cook is an iconic figure, but just as many praise him as an intrepid adventurer, others loathe him as the forerunner of the white man's settlement of 'Blackfella's country'. Opinions like these can polarise communities and make reconciliation seem impossible. More contradictions were evident on the moors walking past young grouse. They were enjoying the protection of devoted minders, yet were being reared to be ready for death as the essential ingredient in England's summer shooting tradition, 'The Glorious 12th'.

As I get older, contradictions like these remind me that simplistic black and white solutions, although appealing, are often more complex. It seems like life used to be so much simpler. Something was either right or wrong, either good or bad. Now the complexities of differing opinions and perspectives seem to have grown. I built a career around defining black and white objectives, achieving clear goals and finding solutions to fix problems. Now I find I'm confronted with shades of grey at every turn. Somehow, I know I'm probably just beginning to peel back the onion skins of my world and seeing it as it really is. This is now the discomfort I suspect I'll have to live with for the rest of my life.

Day 6 – to Cambusavie

We are quickly discovering every breakfast brings a different experience. The people running B&Bs are as varied as the undergrowth beside the paths we tread. Today we enjoy a comedy as Malcolm burns the toast and Sally burns the kippers. Both set off the fire alarm and ensure we're fully awake to enjoy a delicious breakfast and ritual exchange of life stories.

After breakfast we check our packs. I'm now carrying a fairly trim 21kg and Debby a manageable 9.5kg. We may need to reduce further when the tougher footpaths and hills of the Pennine Way come into view. We head straight to the Brora beach and within half an hour I'm in my element, breast stroking into the deep blue water that has a bite beyond the sun's power. I draw myself into the sea's sparkle. One hundred metres out a colony of seals bobs attentively in a safety cordon and watches my progress. This is a magic the world holds, if only I can tune into it. It's probably not much more than ten or twelve degrees in the water, but when I reluctantly return to the beach I warm up quickly. My soul soothed, this is the best morning yet.

Our path meanders along open grassland with the coast on one side and woodlands edging a meadow to our right. By eleven-thirty Dunrobin Castle stands before us. Home to the Earls and Dukes of Sutherland for a thousand years, I'm impressed by the sense of deep association with forebears this place represents. Why are we thinking of selling the family home to downsize now the kids have grown up? Of course, most suburban homes are not built to have as long a life as this castle, and in the global swirl of travel and migration we tend to think nothing of regular moves. Yet I know I'm on this journey in part because of the sense of connection I feel with the place I've come from. Perhaps the merry-go-round of travel hides a loss – our human craving for identity framed in place. We always seem to be searching for somewhere else without knowing where we're from.

Just as the walk gets into a reflective mood it gives us an unexpected lesson. In the castle a bird of prey display is starting. The combination of grace and power these birds exude is arresting, but more so the passion of their keeper who has dedicated his life to these magisterial creatures. Here again we meet a man pursuing the love of his life. My storybook imagery struggles with the concept that the most deadly of all these hunters are not the speedy hawks and falcons, but the well-loved, wise old owl. When an owl collects a mouse held just behind someone's ear without being heard, it brings a completely new meaning to the term 'silent and deadly'. The sage trainer ends,

'If you want to know what's happening in the environment, study these birds. They're the top of the food chain. If they're doing well, everything down below will be.'

His words resonate, but I feel the disquiet of yesterday's information about our extermination of Britain's keystone species, the wolves. With the apex predator gone what's that doing to the integrity of the food chain?

It would have been easy to spend the whole day at Dunrobin. However, the life of a long-distance walker only permits brief stops. Back on the woodland coastal path I find myself on another journey. The pungent beach smells have transported me back to the late 1950's of my childhood. There were rare day trips away from Streatham Common station to the Brighton and Whitstable seafronts. My mind fills with memories of the steam train's milk-run depositing me with soot-spattered cheeks for early morning walks with mum and dad on desolate weather-beaten pebbles a lifetime ago. The particular seaweed smell on this beach must be stored deep in my English cells, together with the cries of the circling seagulls. They are so different and more demanding than the Australian birds. My senses are receptive channels, rekindling powerful visions of long ago.

Another childhood memory surfaces and I recognise it's the one that's been niggling my conscience about this grand adventure. As a working-class boy from south London, born into post-WW2 rationing, I'm the product of parents who were used to managing with limited resources and yet still able to enjoy their modest lifestyle. We lived a council-supported working-class existence, but once or twice a year were able to afford a treat – a big joint of beef for Sunday roast.

For most of my childhood dad had been a window cleaner, but before that a merchant navy man with a reputation for standing up for the rights of his fellow sailors. Mum was a nurse, who considered her profession a calling and refused to become matron in order to remain at her patients bedsides. Both of them had believed in their work as a way of helping others. They were good people and tried to support family, friends and neighbours when they had the chance. Both were very cautious though of people with money and grand ideas. Dad would certainly never entertain the idea of owing someone money – even taking out a £500 loan to buy a house was something he rejected. So, as for taking time off for a 1,500 mile walk, I don't think so!

This is the background nagging away, making me think this adventure is perhaps a bit too grand. And certainly too selfish! After all, what would this walk ever achieve? It wasn't likely to make the world a better place. In short, it's a completely self-indulgent project with no noble purpose to justify it. This is the type of thing people with too much time and money and little care for others attempt. I remember before we left someone said, 'Why don't you do it for charity?' My response was a firm no. It would make the enterprise a fraud. This idea arose as a personal challenge, plain and simple, and it couldn't be cloaked in some other guise.

I ruminate on this uncomfortable thought while we pass by landscape I may never see again. Fortunately, a surprisingly tasty cauliflower soup in Golspie assuages my concern. With our physical needs replenished the afternoon passes comfortably and by five we've safely negotiated another day.

Day 7 – to Tain

First up today are the Cambusavie curves, another treacherous, narrow, winding piece of locally renowned road. Once the challenge is safely overcome, my mind drifts as the light rainfall runs off into roadside runnels. My morning's midge bite survey revealed the itchy raw marks of a dozen bites. Debby has none. The contrast is somewhat more irritating than the bites themselves. Never mind, I'm feeling good, but I wonder whether the little luxuries we packed are really necessary. The small pinch of almost weightless Earl Grey tea leaves each morning is well appreciated, but do I really need the half dozen books? They were chosen carefully in Melbourne with my friend Clifford at his Grumpy Swimmer bookshop. Certainly without his guidance Bruce Chatwin's 'Patagonia' would never have entered my life and I'm relishing it. Surely the books are vital!

The day passes uneventfully. We stop at the Glenmorangie distillery to learn some of the finer points of malt whisky production. Most endearing is the 'angels share', the two percent annual evaporation of this fiery nectar. Today was always going to be a short day, just 14 miles, and by four we arrive at the B&B. At this point the day's harmony breaks down. The landlady displays zero understanding of service and we're hit by a verbal barrage. She has the joint disabilities of never stopping for breath and never listening. If things aren't bad enough, she seems to have induced Asperger's in her down-trodden, terse hubby. He only opens his mouth to berate guests for flouting unknown rules. When I finally get to ask about internet coverage, they delight in telling me there will be none available anywhere in town tomorrow because it's Sunday. Our first rest day and we've chosen this place!

Just as one stranger can bring down our spirits, so another can put right the damage. Over dinner at the local hotel not only is the meal good, but Robert the manager listens to our plan and says, 'Good on you – that's really great. I could never do it, but you'll make it, I have every faith in you!' Silly how such bonhomie can so revive our spirits. One week down, 100 miles under our belts and probably less than 1,500 miles to Land's End now – of course we'll make it…

Day 8 – in Tain

After seven days developing a routine of getting up, packing, breakfasting and walking off, it seems odd to have a rest day. It may be Sunday, but I know I mustn't switch off and rest. The bloody blog must be written and in this internet-free zone I'll have to record my thoughts in longhand. Not sure which is more arduous, walking or blogging? At breakfast we talk to a quiet retired little man. He's nice enough, but I question his sanity when he says he's been coming to this area for 40 years and regularly boards here. I begin to feel distinctly uneasy when he tells us he always drives the same route from Winchester in two hour stages with 45 minute stops at the same service centres for a WC visit and coffee. We promptly leave the breakfast table only to discover our landlord has been in to check we're not breaking any of the unwritten rules. This stay could undo the benefits of a week's peaceful walking.

My gloom lifts quickly under the influence of spirited staff at a café serving reasonable coffee. I sit with my thoughts and write. Later in a seedy pub we watch Germany convincingly eliminate England from the World Cup. Why do I still support this team after all these years? One year of glory in 1966 has left nothing but pain since. More rewarding is a chance encounter with Ernie and Patricia from Sutherland in southern Sydney. It's surprising how many Aussies you bump into over here. Soon after that famous day England made World Cup history against Germany, this 63-year-old welder bought a £10 ticket to Australia. He was 21 and says it's the best £10 he ever spent. As if to prove it, this is his first visit back. Another human seed taken root far from home.

This discussion gets me thinking about the unexpected twists and turns of my life's journey to Melbourne. It was a business relocation with the opportunity to run something. I had always found corporate life exciting from the very start. Others perceived I had a talent with numbers and people and I relished the opportunities that brought. Business was such a different environment from anything anyone in our family had experienced. I was free to make it all up as I went along and soaked up the sense of invincibility that came with youthful zest. As the sap rose through my veins, so promotions had flowed quickly from junior clerk to Financial Controller.

The joy of youthful romance had brought the settled family life I relished. I married Barbara in the month of my 23rd birthday, and within five years we were living a hedonistic lifestyle in a grand apartment behind Paris' Champs Elysees. The high ceilings and marble-adorned fireplaces encouraged far too much champagne consumption and promoted an appetite for *foie gras*. Our first child, James, was conceived in Paris and then another promotion meant spending a couple of years as a young family in Lagos. It had been surreal thrust into the fierce tropical heat and humidity of one of Africa's most teeming hubs of humanity. As a 30-year-old embarking on fatherhood amid the dirt and dysfunction of the Nigerian capital while my compatriots were going to war for Maggie Thatcher in the Falklands, made everything seem out of kilter.

When I left my Wild West experience with the African oil exploration industry, I returned to London. The Brixton race riots were rolling out near my childhood home, but by now I had moved on to more elevated surroundings. Perched amongst the genteel finery of an apartment on top of Richmond Hill, I had the Thames and a former Sovereign's hunting estate on my doorstep. Training for half marathons, I used to crunch through snow-covered paths past startled deer in Richmond Park and considered my good fortune complete. As our second child Ed was born, I threw myself back into the corporate maelstrom joining a big American conglomerate in the automotive industry. The International Finance Director role was stimulating, but it was the chance to morph from bean-counter into general management that really grabbed me and changed my life.

At 35, I was still hungry with ambition. The chance to relocate to Melbourne to become Australian Managing Director and CEO at such an impressionable age was the turning point from which there was to be no return. I took on full responsibility for rapidly expanding a business and providing leadership to hundreds of people in a sprawling undertaking. This proved the final adrenalin shot to a career on hyper-drive. I embraced it all enthusiastically and the rewards flowed in a heady mix of celebrations and material success. This was indeed giddy stuff for the son of working-class parents from a blue-collar council estate. I had escaped into an unfathomable world and my frame of reference had changed forever. If I had awoken one day to find Alice introducing me to the Queen of Hearts and explaining I had fallen down the rabbit hole I wouldn't have been surprised. It was as if something dreamt up in the 1960's counter-culture had become my new reality.

Like Ernie, we embraced Australia enthusiastically, and Barbara quickly dubbed it the 'world's best kept secret'. Melbourne was sunny, full of fun and recognised as the world's most liveable city. My career blossomed. Endless growth meant I had grown well beyond anything I could ever have imagined. Just when it seemed life was to be a perpetual merry-go-round of detachment from anything deeper, my dear wife brought me back to Earth. Not yet in our forties, she broke down one day and admitted to a lump in her breast she had been hiding from for nearly a year.

It is remarkable how swift change can be and how all-encompassing the effect. A short number of days passed as we waited with apprehension while medical specialists carried out their investigations. When we sat with the doctor for that most feared result, I knew I had returned from the rabbit hole of Wonderland leaving Alice and her fantasy companions behind. My reaction was to get very angry that the world of comfort, love and success was being brought to an abrupt brutal ending. The future seemed to have been wrenched from my control. Fate was intervening to stop the heady pleasure-filled existence we inhabited, and as the giddiness subsided, I was confronted by unimaginable desolation. A likely death sentence had been handed down for my life partner and soul mate. The love of my life was to be ripped from me, changing forever the destiny of our family.

It's hard to comprehend how a life path can bring such deviations, let alone how I can now be on a trek I don't understand with a new soulmate. It may not have been a particularly remarkable rest day, but the blog diary is fully written and before turning out the lamp I give a nod to the memories Ernie the welder from Sydney has stirred up.

Day 9 – to Culbokie

Eyes open to the watch registering five-thirty. It's early, but today will be significant, our first without knowing where we'll sleep. By the time we step away from the B&B it's without any sense of regret. Tain does offer a departing gem though, a great little crusty loaf for just £1. With yesterday's ham, sweating cheese and fruit in the bag I know we're now well set for lunch. We walk off down a tiny back-road to Alness and both feel the energy surge to move at a fair old clip.

The magic of the day arrives early as we disturb a lone deer in the forest. The doe eyes blink at us and our hearts flutter. Walt Disney has seeded my childhood with romantic imagery, yet as the sight buoys my spirits so my head fills with questions. This is a splendid creature, but in living its life some would say it's no more than part of a forest-destroying plague that's a direct result of the demise of the wolves. Then again, hunters would be delighted to be here now and reach for their gun. What's right? Is it Walt Disney, the hunters, or is this just another creature on its life path? Clearly the black and white simplicity has disappeared into a multitude of grey textures to once again stir my tranquil mind. We walk off as the vision of a venison casserole pops into my head.

I'm enjoying myself immensely today. It feels like I'm running away and leaving life behind. But is it running away from life or running full-tilt at life? Is it going on an adventure from life or making life an adventure? While I consider this conundrum, Debby just gets on with the task at hand and we walk without much break for over four hours. The Scottish tendency for rain continues and it looks set in for the day. It's one o'clock, lunchtime, and we're in Alness, a solid 13 miles under our belts already. The high street might not be the most exciting culinary setting, but munching our homemade sandwiches makes us happy. Penknife-sliced bread, sweating ham and stale cheese, all's perfect save for the plastered finger from my loaf-cutting injury.

We duck into Heidi's for a coffee and homemade cake dessert and this proves serendipitous. We've had to cancel tonight's accommodation reservation as the Cromarty ferry isn't operational and that's meant a route change. The girls at Heidi's recommend a place run by 'a lovely lady', nine miles ahead. It's a long way on top of our morning's exertions, but we decide to try. When we arrived in Alness I thought Debby couldn't tackle another mile, but now she looks strong, caught up in the challenge of reaching this mythical lady's B&B. My attitude is different today. Rather than paying attention to our journey's sensory experience, I'm driven by the incredible power of completion. We're fired up, single objective to just get there. Seems I need both these elements, the yin and yang, sometimes taking the time to enjoy the journey and sometimes just going for it.

The rain falls and our pace slows as we trudge along the verge of the busy A9. We bring out the iPod's for support and while Debby tunes into the Forest Gump soundtrack, I select a random playlist of my rock and pop favourites. It starts well, 'Only the Good Die Young' spurs me on, but I soon completely tune out of my surroundings as Jim Morrison smoothly drawls 'Riders on the Storm'. The tinkling rain soundtrack blends with the light rain falling on me and I'm back in the early 1970's. I feel 20 again, unable to contain my air guitar and drum solos. God knows what the drivers going past think. Debby tries to get me to look at a stream babbling by the roadside, but then gives up and doesn't bother to warn me as I walk straight into a thicket of thistles in my shorts. Not to worry, I've got 'Light My Fire' to inspire me: *The time for hesitation's through, no time to wallow in the mire.*

When I trip over a tuft of grass and fall face first, I'm grounded back in the real world. The turf is forgiving and there's no damage, but I know we're both very tired. We need a reviving drink before the last push, yet there's no sign of relief along the road ahead. Spookily, the iPod randomly throws up another Doors song and Jim Morrison hollers 'Roadhouse Blues'. Just then, emerging from the next bend is a Farm Exhibition, shop and restaurant. We gratefully take a 15 minute break to down fizzy pear juice. With that we strike out for the last push. By the time we climb up to Culbokie and I slip the 20kg off my back we've nearly done a marathon, and even if Andrew does think our bodies are capable of so much more than we use them for, I reckon I've pushed mine nearer the limit today.

The B&B is a haven of gardens and summer evening birdsong. Although we've driven our bodies to be here, we're politely informed there's another mile to dinner at the pub. After dinner we digest the day's exploits. Today was the second longest day we've ever walked and certainly the longest with full packs. We were motoring all day and I never seemed to feel the backpack. We were fired up and that gives me the confidence to believe we just may be able to tackle this challenge. As we turn out the light and snuggle into the comfort of bed sleep quickly conquers consciousness.

Day 10 – to Fortrose

With yesterday's sense of achievement still vibrating we have no need to rush today and so take stock of our bodies before getting up. Once again, rest has worked its magic. All the aches and strains, scratches and bruises seem to have receded leaving mere memories in the body to accompany the more colourful ones etched into our minds. Even my early midge bites are receding and fading quicker than new ones take hold. Porridge and poached eggs are the perfect accompaniment to an hour of deep and meaningful conversation with our host Jane. She's lost two husbands to tragic accidents over the past ten years and it's inspiring to hear how hard she's worked to restart her life with this B&B.

Sharing personal stories and thoughts on life like this is a pleasure and privilege. The conversation ebbs and flows like the waters of the Cromarty Firth below. I recount the nine year journey I travelled with Barbara as she fought the symptoms of breast cancer, and Jane insists on giving me a book about a Scotsman who lost his wife to breast cancer. As part of his trauma and recovery he went off to follow in the footsteps of Robert Louis Stevenson's *Travels with my Donkey*. Given Stevenson's book is already a favourite of mine I smile at how the synchronicity of it all plays out.

This is our best weather yet. Sunshine, occasional clouds and a low 20's temperature, suggest today's short ten miles will be a doddle. On the one longish Black Isle hill I decide to give up the mantra taught by Mike, an early mentor. While running half marathons he would call out 'Attack the hills!', before leaving me for dead. My new one is, 'Love the hills – they help expel weakness from the body.' Perhaps my new more Zen-like state is influenced by Debby. She often stops me now to point out features I don't usually tune into. Gentle breezes ripple through fields of young cereal crops, their spontaneous patterns like water unflustered by purpose moving across a lake.

Lunch is a tightly gripped sandwich, sitting squeezed between a ramshackle hedgerow and the tiniest of muddy lanes. Behind us a large field of newly sown wheat attracts a murder of crows. We assume they're crows and not a death of ravens. Why are these collective nouns so dark and funereal? Such are the questions which now confront the long-distance walker. We walk on at the pace of the countryside and I feel my eyes are open to it as never before.

Later, over dinner in a whisky bar, we sample two of the 200 different varieties of malt accompanied by Jim the owner's life story. An American from Philadelphia, he's a long way from his natural environment. We exchange stories and admire his 15-year-old dog with a diamante collar. Both Jim and dog appear comfortable in their skins. This obscure outpost was for him the ideal place to raise his nine-year-old son, so he set himself up as a landlord seven years ago. This walk of ours seems so humdrum when I reflect on his decision to turn a life upside down. I caress another malt and muse over what other lives I could have invented if I'd been more adventurous.

Day 11 – to Inverness

I can feel that tingle of excitement stir as I get up to make tea. Today will bring our first ending. By tonight, we should reach Inverness and finish Phase One of the trip. But first, breakfast. In a sun-filled room we look out at the glare reflected off ripples the breeze gently coaxes across the Inverness Firth. We could be in the Mediterranean. Another stranger enters our life when Bill unpacks his family's life story. After bringing up five children in Inverness, he and Gillian moved here to renovate this place and create their dream B&B. Again the recurring theme of lives relaunched.

Gillian tells us to follow a disused railway path rather than the busy main road. It's a great improvement and I wonder what Dr. Beeching, the former Chairman of British Rail, would think? I still remember the fury which raged as a child when he published the controversial report that was the basis for enormous cuts to the extensive country rail lines of Britain. Even 50 years later the debate still has the power to make some people's blood boil. Beeching became despised and synonymous with all that was bad about cutting public expenditure at the expense of village life. At least we can take pleasure today from a footpath bestowed by these cuts.

Two hours brings us near the tiny village of Munlochy. A roadside bench is too good to pass up. It's been positioned for million-dollar views down the Moray Firth, and with the juice from a crisp apple trickling off my chin, I smile at Debby. We feel like royalty. We're becoming hooked on simple pleasures and they cost nothing, so why not?

Some significant hills come and go through the morning, but we cover our distances quickly. The Black Isle woodlands and farmed landscape gradually disappear. A new experience looms. The North Kessoch suburb of our first city fast draws near. We put the inevitable off, throwing down our packs. It's one o'clock and we take shoes and socks off to cool our feet before pulling a simple lunch from the pack. I feel self-conscious suddenly. Across the river Inverness is looking back at us. Are the inhabitants inspecting us under furrowed brows concerned our smelly bare feet and unwashed clothes will bring down the tone of the place?

Completion drives
While the life journey
Ambles.

Re-energised by lunch, we now have to acclimatise to city life. The transition is slow at walking pace, but the contrast stark. The last few miles are through a drear industrial area to penetrate the town centre. It's a dispiriting walk. Is this our sad destiny, to clothe cities in development bereft of any beauty? I'm surprised at my reaction. As a Londoner I've experienced much worse suburbs. Yet arriving here from the vibrant natural world it just feels flat and grimy. It's been built without imagination. There is none of the layering and texture we are beginning to take for granted. We've become accustomed to brush through vibrant foliage, delighting at filigree webs threaded between fresh leaves and flowers that quietly absorb raindrops. All that peace and beauty is exchanged for this tawdry mess. I know we humans are better than this. Nature's harmony may elude us, but her creations can inspire us to nurture the beauty our spirit craves.

At the B&B Bob proves a cheery host and so our spirits revive. We enter his world. A film producer with his studio in the garden, he's someone who genuinely belongs in the hospitality industry and seems to enjoy meeting us as much as we do him. On the way to John O'Groats we left our back-up shoes and some other supplies in Inverness with Linda. She and husband Robert are friends from another life. I could never have imagined when we met 30 years ago as I got out of my first rattling ten-seater turboprop flight to Nigeria's Warri oilfields that one day they'd look after my shoes. This really is proving to be a walk that just keeps giving. Not a day goes by without the opportunity to catch up with old friends or enter the lives of new ones. For now though duty calls, and we go straight to a serviceable small internet café run by a charming young Polish woman to blog and blog and blog.

Day 12 – in Inverness

The sound of rain on a rest day means it's perfect blogging weather. At breakfast our host Mary explains, 'It's July 1st and in July it rains!' Mary used to be a nurse, the kind who can lift a patient's spirits. She recounts the story of when Bob asked her where she wanted to celebrate their ten-year anniversary. She chose walking the West Highland Way, just down the road. To make it the perfect anniversary experience they did it in July and it rained every day. Yes, these are our kind of people.

We slip into fragrant clean shoes and send the pair that got us here with memorabilia collected along the way to 'Mum' in London. The shoes will rest and be refreshed to return hopefully for our arrival in Glasgow. Now it's time for a serious focus on the blog. There's barely time for a coffee. Well, to be truthful there's always time for a coffee but not for all the time spent searching for one that might offer something resembling Melbourne's rich dark comfort shots. After a disappointing cup we use two computers at the internet café for almost the entire day. During a brief interlude we take tea with Shirley and Willie, a cousin of my cousin we've never met before. This journey begins to feel like it's more a walk between people's lives than places.

At eight in the evening we stagger bleary-eyed into the street. I throw 'M for money' caution to the wind and buy two large malt whiskies at the nearest bar. We've earned them. During today we've formed quite a bond with the young Polish woman who runs the internet café. As we wrote up the story of our walk, so we listened to the story of her life, and Debby was in her element offering counsel on her favourite subject, romance and human relationships.

Phase One is now successfully ticked off. One hundred and fifty-five miles completed. I know we've only just started, barely ten percent of the way to Land's End, but it feels like we're walk-hardened already. And we're coping well with the somewhat heavier-than-planned backpacks. Every day we learn more about the nature of our challenge. And now the big stretch of road walking is behind us we have the exciting prospect of striding out along the country paths for which Britain is renowned.

Perhaps more than anything else, this beginning has revealed a fuller understanding of the impact the blog will have on our journey. At first, I was disgruntled, begrudging the time spent keeping the detailed handwritten notes required. Then there was the frustration of seeking places with a computer and internet coverage. Uploading photos takes so long and writing up my memories and musings even longer. It's become obvious that to do justice to the blog there'll be no time for much else than walking and blogging.

However, gradually my frustrations with the blog have receded. I questioned why we were devoting such effort to connecting in absentia to friends and acquaintances. Then it dawned on us: it's not actually for our friends. It may perhaps only have been their 'hits' and the blog's perceived popularity which kept up our early commitment to it, but we now understand we're documenting something special in our lives. The blog has become a friend on the journey. By plumbing the depths of our minds at day's end and trying to put shape to our experiences, we're finding we have richer memories of this trip than any before. There's no longer any doubt: the blog is for us.

Something else has become a lot clearer during these first couple of weeks in Scotland. We've found ourselves more taken up with the stories and lives of the people we've met, than with the flora and fauna of the places we've passed through. Of course neither of us has a background in natural science, so in some ways it's not surprising we've become more involved with our own species than other life. More than this though, we both have a fascination for the human condition and are learning so much from talking to people in very different walks of life. There is richness in this diversity that's compelling and hard to find in the daily routine back home. With four months' walking ahead, I can feel the excitement bubbling in anticipation of meeting more lives.

It is perhaps a feature of my accounting mind, but I was always going to track the full distance we walked on this adventure. We bought two pedometers, but before reaching John O'Groats I'd lost mine. Slightly unnerved, we've only had Debby's to rely on throughout this first phase. I bought a new one on arrival here in Inverness and with relief synchronised it to Debby's before going to bed last night. It felt scary to awake this morning and find her pedometer had died overnight. The detail I pride myself on recording was so nearly lost. I'm not a great believer in fate or being watched over by a god, though I accept there is much mystery in the world far beyond my comprehension. Debby dismisses my feelings of unease:

'Such is the power of the universe to protect us, Keith.'

I was tempted to unleash my logical mind and argue, but decided to keep quiet. OK, with about four more months to go there'll be plenty of opportunity for the Universe to pull out all the stops for us.

BEN NEVIS
FORT WILLIAM
GLEN
FARAWAY TREE
LOCH NESS
INVERNESS

Chapter 3 – GLEN

Day 13 – to Drumnadrochit

At last, today we come to grips with our first official footpath. The Great Glen Way follows the Great Glen Fault from Inverness on the east coast to Fort William on Scotland's western edge. The idea of walking for five days towards the Atlantic Ocean along a series of brooding mystical lochs has whetted my appetite in the way our early days of road walking never could. Today we will cast off the city and its bitumen roads for a trek through the wild Highlands to Drumnadrochit.

Our friend Linda lives in 'Drum' as the locals call it and is walking with us today. She starts us off on a longer route following the canal towpath to the loch at Dochgarroch. It feels like a simple morning stroll between the two waters of the Caledonian Canal and the River Ness. It seems odd to build a canal alongside a perfectly serviceable river, but I let the thought go as we begin a three-mile climb through thick forest. It's the first time I've found wonder in closely planted pine trees. Their massed presence holds a hushed, dark, brooding energy. The life force within the forest is shrouded from our view but I can feel its power. I almost expect Rob Roy to step out from the shadows.

Then, everything changes. From forested hill to dramatic moorland and faraway peaks, it's classic Brigadoon country. We have the certainty of a gravel path underfoot now and can appreciate the scenery, the Highlands of our imagination. Glimpses of the mighty Loch Ness appear and I try to comprehend just how much the two cubic miles of water it contains really is. At 600 feet, it's deeper than the North Sea and holds more water than every lake and reservoir in England and Wales added together. What Australia's east coast would give for a body of fresh water this big! Our spirits are high and we happily embrace the forceful wind as a deterrent to the midges.

By early afternoon with 12 miles under our belts, we're pushing through unformed dirt tracks and come across a basic painted sign in low brush pointing toward 'Rory's Café'. Linda marches us through the undergrowth into an incongruent fantasy land with yurt, colourful chickens pecking over the uneven ground, four Husky dogs, black pigs and a rough wooden lean-to café. Next, we meet Sandra who, with her husband Howie, has created this unique place. Over the next hour, I struggle with the implausibility of finding people offering sustenance to walkers in such a harsh environment. The quality of the plunger coffee, hot chocolate and soups is irrelevant given the warmth of the welcome and genuine hospitality. Perched on rickety chairs under a crude shelter, however surreal it maybe, I realise it's a haven.

They tell us stories of how they bought this Abriachan acreage as a massive bog and drained it, collecting the water for their use. Shame that Howie hand-dug the ditches before buying a mechanical digger! Pine martens, wild cats and stoats try to steal their chickens when not protected in the 'Chicken Alhambra' henhouse. However, during last year's severe winter they even provided food for the predators. What it's like in winter using their outdoor loo is beyond me. It's a real gem though, with a Coca-Cola ice bucket for the toilet pan labelled 'Pissing on Capitalism'. These three locals all support the Loch Ness Lifeboat station and as we say goodbye I'm left to ponder the disconnected life I lead in my city, unaware of community needs. Part of me wants to stay here and experience the hard reality of their lives. With a head full of uneasy thoughts, questioning the comfortable anaesthetised existence I lead back home, we walk on.

The rain comes when we finally snatch lunch after three o'clock. The wind has dropped and the midges take advantage of a late lunch circling my legs. Another stiff two hour walk brings the day's 19 mile trek to an end.

Day 14 – in Drumnadrochit

We blog all day with just a brief respite to bear witness to the centuries-old struggle for supremacy between the English and Scots at the Urquhart Castle ruins. Observed through the lens of history the ebb and flow of human attempts at domination seem so pointless.

Day 15 – to Invermoriston

We bid farewell to Linda and Robert with new memories built on the foundation established in Africa 30 years ago. Scotland is famous for all its lochs and we soon find out where all the water comes from. The weather forecast was for rain and wind everywhere, all day. Still we're not prepared. We walk up the first hill and it rains. No matter, I think, this is nothing we haven't had before. The rain keeps coming at a steady drenching pace, penetrating any gaps in the gear, pouring over our faces and down our necks. Debby's kit is holding up pretty well, but my jacket has quickly given in under the onslaught. My chest is soaked and pockets with map and guidebook have puddles inside them. I can't remember rain like this since leaving Nigeria.

On the long uphill track, silent dense forests surround us and my thoughts seek refuge inside. *Why are we doing this? Should we be doing it? Why have I exposed Debby to such an experience? How can we possibly keep going for another four months in conditions like these?* The waterfall before my eyes is relentless. After two hours we pause for a handful of trail-mix to offset the damp chill then carry on along a strenuous track where pine forests give way to open moorland. Never flat, our footsteps rise and fall constantly and, if possible, the rain gets heavier. Debby craves a rest and when the rain eases briefly, we stop to eat voraciously. Within 20 minutes we're back on our feet trudging through a renewed deluge.

The afternoon downpour seems even heavier, the worst we've experienced. At times, the wind hurls its full power at us. Perhaps it's my stubbornness, but I find myself smiling at the sheer stupidity of our self-imposed wretchedness. Debby seems to have fallen under the same spell: 'Keith, I love you for bringing me on this adventure,' she yells through the wall of water, and we laugh like kids at the sheer madness of it all. Under steel-grey skies the merciless downpour continues and all we can do is plod on.

When we walk into Invermoriston after five and a half hours we're greeted by the young woman running our B&B with, 'No, we don't have any heating on to dry your clothes, it's summer!' We strip off, towel ourselves dry and get straight under the bedcovers for warmth. Later on, over dinner at the pub, I think about today. We've endured a forceful challenge yet are enlivened and stimulated. It was wonderful to feel the power of the Highlands and to engage with it on its own terms, not reduced to human picture book frames. With no real protection, we were immersed in a world I normally look out at through a secure window. Only this morning I read Bruce Chatwin's comment from *In Patagonia*:

> I haven't got any special religion this morning. My God is the God of Walkers. If you walk hard enough, you probably don't need any other God.

Now I understand those sentiments. The forces thrust upon us today were larger and more powerful than anything within my control.

Perhaps this adventure will bring new spiritual insights into my otherwise orderly material world.

Day 16 – to Fort Augustus

After yesterday, today looks like it might be a pleasant, short stroll, perhaps even an anticlimax. Light rain comes and goes. First up there's St Columba's well, honouring a missionary from 580 AD who converted the pagan Pictish King Brude to Christianity by making his doors fall open. The legends are fascinating, but the well isn't, so we keep going. More impressive is a great double span stone bridge built on natural rock in the middle of the stream by one of Britain's most famous engineers, the young Thomas Telford. It's a striking example of a worthy creation commissioned by an eminent businessman who, by the time it was finished, had gone bankrupt. Nothing much seems to have changed over the years. Capitalism after all, is founded on competition and produces at least as many casualties as beneficiaries.

Walking today is much easier. We leave the little village uphill along a fairy-tale woodland path. Off to our right are massive densely packed dark green Scots pine trees. The Caledonian Forest is Scotland's rainforest yet today it's only five percent of its original 1.5 million hectares. The facts are uncomfortable: the elimination of wolves has produced more deer and in combination with widespread land clearing, the introduction of sheep and demand for timber, it means we humans have decimated much of the forest's glory. Of course the trend has been going on for years – we even built an aluminium smelting plant on Loch Ness 115 years ago. I don't like to think about the damage we're doing and turn instead to peer into the thick-treed interior.

It's as if night has fallen. A carpet of thick downy moss is draped over everything below. My eyes slowly become accustomed to the dark, drawn in where the mossy ground is peppered with particles of weak light from a watery sun. Somehow, this small plant dominates the setting, capturing the light and engulfing all. Despite their majesty, the huge trees can only look down forlornly as the moss envelops them. The quiet darkness appears calm and inviting and we take comfort from it. The trees have been growing here for 6,000 years, yet nothing I've read mentions the moss. I'm sure it's been here longer and humans would have scraped it from the trees cut down a thousand years ago to build the boats that went off to the Crusades.

As the day unfolds we're presented with some travel brochure views of Loch Ness. However, it's only in the early evening that we can walk to the edge of the Loch and stand in awe. The power pent up in sky and water seems tangible, the might of the hills invincible. No wonder people have been inspired to write and create legends in this setting. I know I instinctively crave this beauty. Our hearts filled, we return to our B&B wondering if the spectral shape glimpsed through swirling mists was Britain's highest mountain, Ben Nevis.

Day 17 – to South Laggan

We both awake this morning from a night filled with vivid dreams. Perhaps Loch Ness had infused our subconscious with mythic imagery. Breakfast brings another chance to enter the lives of others. Our hosts share the story of their emigration to South Africa and return 18 years later. Now they work at this B&B for eight months of the year and travel in the winter months to be with their adult offspring in Durban and Adelaide. It seems everyone we meet is living a unique life and there's no such thing as a norm. If that's true, and the world is made up of nearly seven billion diverse individuals, I wonder why we often go to such great lengths to try to conform?

It's colder today and for five miles we stroll by the side of the canal with a dry wind to quell the midges. At Cullochy Lock, Debby insists her hot feet need a break. I'm reluctant but we stop and sit on a bench, eating bananas, looking down the canal with just the lock-keeper and one boat for company. The surroundings are peaceful, green-brown hills flank the steely water and a raked gravel path winds past a pair of whitewashed silent houses. I slip into a reverie of nothing and everything. I'm conscious of the breeze on my skin. Clouds rise and fall overhead, never quite revealing the mountaintops lurking close by. A sense of bliss brings tears to my eyes and I blink with embarrassment at such pleasure. This country is getting into my system.

Later we stop for lunch at Loch Oich. Shoes and socks come straight off and I'm so relaxed I watch a long-legged yellow-backed spider run up my leg. It seems even my arachnophobia has been turned off by this walk. This land is clearly working its magic on me. In the afternoon, gentle woodland soothes us as we stroll at peace along a muddy path. This track is on the old Fort Augustus to Invergarry railway line. Trains used to run on this line until it was abandoned in 1911, a casualty of treacherous rivalry between competing railway companies. The people who built the line couldn't do a deal to run it through to either Fort William or Inverness at either end. Today, the sense of human folly and wasted resources brought about by competing egos, stands in stark contrast to the might of the natural landscape and elements hereabouts. Meanwhile, we walk on falling in love with Scotland.

Settling down for the night, I calculate we've now set a record. We're 219 miles from John O'Groats, the longest walk we've ever managed. Thank heavens we've still got plenty of this adventure to go before we have to re-enter our old lives.

Day 18 – to Gairlochy

Our first night in a hostel and we have to make our own breakfast. No eggs, just a small bowl of muesli with half a chopped apple. As we step out, we're immediately confronted with a fierce headwind. It's so strong I lose my footing and the heavy backpack almost takes me down. Perhaps I did need some scrambled eggs? For two hours, we trudge along Loch Lochy looking up at the imperious high-sided valley. Despite the evocative forestry setting our weariness grows, and when a small promontory into the loch appears with a sheltered pebbled beach, Debby wastes no time. Shoes and socks off she chills her red-hot feet in the black waters. Taking her lead, I strip off and breaststroke out into the welcome embrace of the ancient dense liquid. The water temperature is probably low double digits, the perfect antidote for my over-heated body. My gaze drifts out to the farthest hilltops before the smallest of creatures brings me down to earth. The dreaded midges descend and even Debby is not immune. She attracts her first two bites of the trip, but it's nothing to the damage wreaked by the fun these insects appear to derive dive-bombing my freshly shaved head.

The weather plays around with us today in typical Highland fashion. One minute we're learning to love the winds, the next we marvel at never-ending changes of light in the sky. The cloud cover runs through every shade of grey before an occasional flash of sun followed by sudden downpours. Debby continues to suffer overheated toes and her shoes come off for unplanned stops. I urge her on as punishing taskmaster and refuse to listen to her pleas for an early lunch. Walking close to the loch with rough country on either side the rain begins to fall more steadily. Debby spits out:

'Why do you always spend so long looking for just the perfect lunch spot? I'm tired and hungry and need to stop now!'

With that, we round a corner and right there, about eight feet above this lonely one-track road, the most idyllic setting appears. I simply point and smile. Debby bites her tongue. The elaborate root system and gnarled trunk of a huge Scots pine towers over us. It looks old enough to have witnessed the final Jacobite uprising of 1745. We scramble up to sit under the broad dry canopy of its heavy old branches on a luxurious carpet of soft brown pine needles.

With packs off, we breathe deeply and gaze out at stunning views across the water back up towards Laggan Locks. I feel myself being drawn into the scene, moving out across the water's brooding surface past the far-off banks to scale hills running up into ever-changing swathes of clouds. Meanwhile, Debby has relaxed. She is on her own enchanted flight of fancy. This tree has triggered childhood memories and she regales me with tales from her favourite book, Enid Blyton's *The Folk of the Faraway Tree*. It's almost as if Moonface and Mrs Wash-a-lot are here having lunch with us. Lunch reveals unsuspected cultural differences too. We bite into pork pies and I say nothing as my eyes roll into my head as proof enough the experience is sublime. Debby, on the other hand, grimaces and complains her mouth feels like it's been instantly coated with cold fat!

After lunch, the rigours of the day quickly take effect. I see a sign for the Clan Cameron Museum and suggest we visit for a break. We persevere up a mile-long driveway to find ourselves immersed in a place which has born witness to just how tough life really can be. Winston Churchill commissioned this estate during WW2 for training the earliest Commandos. Many of them died here as a result of the decision to always use live ammunition on manoeuvres. Hearing this puts our challenges into perspective and we slink off without complaint. At four-thirty, we walk into Gairlochy, the day's walk done. I feel footsore and weary, yet the pedometer shows I've walked just 27,455 steps for today's 15 miles. It makes me even more aware of Debby's strength. Last week she notched up 50,974 steps on our day into Culbokie.

After dinner as the evening draws to a close, the blog update takes longer than it should. My eyes continually stray from the computer screen to drift outside into the natural grandeur of this remote place.

The River Lochy, one of Scotland's finest salmon rivers, flows briskly by, and out beyond that the rising sides of the great Beinn Bhan mountain tower up 800 meters. The final birdsong goes out of the evening. Mists flow silently down the hillside and clouds circle overhead as summer darkness falls. Somehow, this landscape is infiltrating my being. Its tiny feelers are finding receptors beyond my consciousness. I feel changed, different in ways I cannot fathom. I close down the computer and breathe deeply into the calm comfort of black night. Another day is zipped-up and put to bed. In this Highland setting, thousands of miles from where I now call home, I gaze into a nothingness that is dense and full of meaning, yet beyond my understanding. It is beginning to dawn on me that this journey is far more than simply a walk through my old country.

Day 19 – to Fort William

I make tea and gaze up at Beinn Bhan, its early morning presence partially hidden under a cloud-wreathed peak. I pull myself away from the view and go to shower. I get a shock. A large blood boil has grown overnight on the back of my knee. Closer inspection reveals the dreaded tick has got into me and is busily sucking my blood. We've been told it's critical if a tick enters the body to remove body, head and teeth to avoid them breeding and spreading disease. Debby takes the tweezers, but explodes it, blood everywhere. There is much discussion over breakfast about what to do next. The potentially toxic teeth need to be removed. Our host produces a scalpel that he uses for model making and offers to help. I look at this man, a civil engineer by profession, and consider whether this is a good option. Somehow, I doubt his facility for delicate surgery and ask Debby to take up his blade.

We hastily re-arrange our room into a version of a MASH field surgery. Debby casually sterilises the knife in boiled water and I wince at her incision. She can find no further sign of the tick so I'm left to worry about the lump which remains under the skin. Unsettling visions spring to mind of graphic scenes from *Alien.* Will Sigourney Weaver have to fly in to eliminate me? In the meantime, the mere 2mm scar is disappointing and will do nothing to earn me any bravery Brownie points with the Commando Unit up the road.

It's ten by the time we re-join our track. I sense this is late, despite the day appearing short and easy on paper. The weather quickly confirms our mistake. Soon we're battling fierce headwinds and intermittent heavy showers. Heads bowed, we batten down the hatches, zip up everything we can and just keep going. Eventually we arrive at Neptune's Staircase, a dramatic series of locks, the longest in the whole of the UK and testament to our tremendous human capacity to alter geography. Starting here on the west coast, the Caledonian Canal was created to enable water transport to navigate a relatively benign 60-mile trip through to the North Sea. To start the journey though, a combination of eight locks had to be built here to lower boats 64 feet.

It has been blowing a gale and we're soaked from the heavy rain, but we can see the outskirts of Fort William ahead. Relief soon gives way to disappointment however, as the official route into Fort William follows a long coastal path loop of four more miles. We lean into the wind and press on along the foreshore, on through some houses, on over a bridge, and on along a tiny path through trees. We're quietly resigned to our destiny of just plodding on. Then, when the strong wind has almost dried us out, the heavens open again. We know better than to complain and with heads down, completely drenched, simply march on. As we walk in the solitary confinement of our own minds, Debby announces:

'Walking is like parenting. Often, as a parent, when you are tired out, uncomfortable and in need of rest, you keep on – doing whatever needs to be done to look after the little loved ones. You always feel good when it's over, and they're happily asleep in their beds, full tummies, stories read and peace reigns at last.'

I feel a bit grumpy, but Debby carries on:

'It's just like that with walking. It's windy, it's raining, we've already walked far enough and it's longer than we thought, but hey, we're not there yet. So, we have to simply keep on going until we are. And, when we do arrive, we'll feel good.'

Eventually we do arrive and in the main street of Fort William some higher being, perhaps Chatwin's god of walkers, truly smiles on us. The first café we come across is undoubtedly the best we've found in Scotland. I'm modest about my knowledge of most things, but do consider myself something of an aficionado of Melbourne's gift to the world: the flat white coffee. I know a good one when I sip one. Friends would attest to the importance of two well-made coffees to my daily mood. The freshly roasted beans, the grind and pack of the coffee, the cleanliness of the espresso machine, the temperature of the water, and the way the rich coffee dribbles out to be covered by perfectly heated milk with a *crema* that sits plump on top, this is the sublime pleasure I've foregone to make this adventure possible. Today though, I can relax, dry out and relish the achievement of our arrival here.

In completing the Great Glen Way, Phase Two of our grand adventure has concluded. More important than the 250 miles completed, I'm beginning to understand the walk has become a teacher. The lessons are somewhat opaque though and I'll need time to unpick and interpret them.

Scotland has offered one lesson that's already clear though and that concerns the weather. This truly elemental force of nature is often reduced to a newspaper forecast of temperature and conditions, a mere footnote to enable us to negotiate our orderly lives with the least inconvenience. I now understand just how much we miss. The weather creates the landscape in which we engage with life. Scotland is defined by its weather. The Scots weather has a personality that has its clan roots in the Highlands. A moody male personality that epitomises the tradition where clan means family and the clan leader is its father. The weather is the leader in Scotland, a fierce, powerful, dour, and taciturn Victorian father. Certainly, he's not to be toyed with. Reserved, often hiding part of himself from us and prone to dramatic outbursts, he's sometimes playful in revealing by turns his moods and holding out promises of better conditions ahead, but then abruptly withdrawing them. He's a stern taskmaster, demanding total compliance, acceptance without question, but never harming if one acknowledges his complete authority and right to rule.

Once you bow to the weather's supremacy, it's as if you've been welcomed in as part of the clan family. Each day by stepping out on the track with my belongings on my back regardless of the weather conditions, I'm demonstrating my fealty to this weather lord. I've come to understand complaints or attempts to avoid his demands tend to simply make matters worse. More than this though, I'm also gaining a real insight into something fundamental in my makeup. Here I am, almost every day facing up to physical challenges well beyond anything I've been used to. Not only do I make no attempt to resist them, but I'm also not finding the routine unpleasant. In fact, I never think twice about the need to get back on the track each morning, and despite that daunting lift of a 20kg pack onto my back, I shoulder it without complaint.

So, here is a basic tenet of my outlook being overturned. I've learned to consider manual labour and physical exertion as something to be replaced by mental activity. Yet, here I am relishing the physical challenges that confront me. I read Robert Louis Stevenson's *Travels with my Donkey* before I left home but until now had no real understanding of why one paragraph called out to me:

> For my part I travel not to go anywhere but to go. I travel for travel's sake. The great affair is to move; to feel the needs and hitches of our life more nearly, to come down off this featherbed of civilisation and find the globe granite underfoot and strewn with cutting flints.

It may be too early to reflect on the implications for my future life, but I already know that in stepping out from the sanitised, insulated civilisation to experience these hardships, I feel my life is richer and more connected to something grander than mere human constructions. It's obvious this country and even this weather is getting into our blood. A love affair has enveloped us and it will be very hard to leave the Highlands behind.

Day 20 – in Fort William

It may be called a rest day, but there are a full list of chores to do. First stop though is the local hospital emergency department as a second tick has surfaced, hanging off the back of my calf. I suppress the idea an alien has entered my body and is already spawning infants. The nurse reassures me the entry site looks clean and not swollen. A fact sheet explains that I need to watch for Lyme disease. When I ask how I would know if I had contracted it, I'm told I would come over feeling very tired. As that's now my normal state Lyme disease would probably pass unnoticed. A bigger immediate problem are midge bites. My otherwise glowing healthy skin is spotted with several nips around the lower legs, back, shoulders and head and even one on my lip. Debby is not squeamish and will still kiss me, but the unfairness of the midges still rankles as she has only two insignificant bites.

The rest of the day is spent preparing for Phase Three through to Glasgow along the West Highland Way. We walk around with heavy tops and wet weather gear as the rain falls incessantly. It's midsummer and all of 14 degrees, but despite this, we're excited. The prospect of further immersion in Scotland's Highlands drama is appealing, although tempered by the nervous realisation that whatever state of fatigue we reached this past week will likely be surpassed. The Great Glen Way is described as a doddle by comparison.

WESTWAY
GLASGOW
LOCH LOMOND
RANOCH MOOR
BEN NEV
FORT WILLIAM

Chapter 4 – WESTWAY

Day 21 – to Kinlochleven

Opening the curtains, it's a clear bright day with no sign of the forecast deluge. Is this a good omen? The West Highland Way is particularly rugged and exposed and it would be good to be spared the weather's worst. The walk is one of the world's most famous and adored trails, the beauty of its landscape considered the equal of anywhere in the world. It's a pilgrimage for mountain lovers and it will be our path from the Highlands' wilds to Glasgow's city centre. It's also our only opportunity to use a bag-carrying service. I have debated whether to do this, but Debby had strong views: 'It's your British upbringing again, making you feel things must be hard if they are to be worthwhile.' I meekly signed up. However, any delight I feel being freed from physical burden is tempered by a mental anguish that now labours our footsteps.

Leaving Melbourne we knew that our son Matt's partner Kathy was very ill and having chemotherapy for a form of mesothelioma. It's tragic when anyone contracts such a disease, but when it strikes a beautiful vibrant young woman in her late 20s it's all the harder to bear. No matter how much we may have run away from our life, it's still there in all its brutal reality. Kathy was quite stable when we left home, but updates suggest she's deteriorating rapidly. The final tragic stanzas of this shocking illness are playing out to an ending now as inevitable as it will be unconscionable. Nothing in our rich surroundings can anaesthetise us from the sorrow we feel for Kathy, Matt and her family.

We climb out of Fort William on a long stony uphill track and meet John, an uncomplicated fellow who's also undertaking a John O'Groats to Land's End (JOGLE) walk. He's 43, and this walk has been a life's ambition. He's worked 25 years for one manufacturing company near Sheffield, but threw it in to do this walk. He has a different, shorter route planned, but we may see more of him before our paths diverge. Today the weather smiles on us and we're able to gaze at Britain's tallest mountain, Ben Nevis, at its spectacular best. This clear view only happens a dozen times a year and our heavy hearts lighten. For the next few hours, we walk an undulating path through wooded mountainsides and deep valleys and fall into quiet contemplation while our spirits feed on the beauty.

Ben Nevis magnificent,
Dimly seen
Through Kathy

We lay out our feast on a tree stump. Pork pie, Scotch egg, cheese and salami sandwiches, tomatoes, fruit – never was a more scrumptious meal prepared and no dining room could outdo this lightly wooded clearing. The greenery glows under a friendly sun and deer come to graze beside us. It's as if we've strayed into the Elysium Fields. Mother Nature's splendour soothes our weariness before we press on to Kinlochleven. By the day's end, we still feel relaxed and peaceful. We've walked 16 miles over six hours with fine weather and yet within half an hour of arrival the skies open and rain sets in for the night. Debby had asked the Universe for the rain to hold off and once again proved her power to create.

Day 22 – to Kingshouse

Today we'll cross our highest point in Scotland. We know the scenery will be dramatic and probably the weather too, as it's rained all night. However, we've just heard the sad news we most feared. Early on this Sunday morning in Melbourne, Kathy, the young woman who had captured our hearts and become part of our family life, has passed away. It's been such a brutally short illness that we struggle to contemplate her life force already gone from the world.

As the grief sits with us, we begin to understand another stark reality. This adventure has separated us from our family. Debby just wants to be with Matt right now. To hold him as only a mother can and comfort him at a time of trial he shouldn't have to experience at his age. We talk of putting the walk on hold to return for the funeral. But that's a decision for later. Kathy was born in the UK and today we will carry her spirit to its highest mountains.

No packs today
Instead
We carry Kathy.

We walk off in bleak conditions for a midsummer's day. Our hearts are heavy and it feels like the sky is shedding tears of rain while the harsh winds remorselessly buffet us. My hands lose all feeling as if I've been swimming too long in Melbourne's midwinter bay. Given the weight of emotion and the weather, it's hard work pushing ever onwards uphill, but we have no option anymore.

As the track remorselessly saps energy from our tired muscles I think of Churchill's recurrent insistence during WW2 to KBO or 'Keep Buggering On'. It's a real strength of my British heritage that I know I can do that and when the chips are down Debby can call on her 'Aussie Battler' spirit. It's late afternoon when we arrive at the remote inn in Glen Coe. I'm asked to sign the registration form but simply hold up buckled white fingers, useless for the task. We agree I'll sign in at dinner.

This old pub in the middle of nowhere sits on a valley floor with a backcloth of mountains. Deer come to graze outside at twilight and bring a magic to lift sad hearts.

Dear she was
And
Deer she is

I tell Debby I think I've just jotted down my last haiku and will leave it there out of respect to Kathy.

Day 23 – to Bridge of Orchy

Yesterday's arduous weather has washed the sky clear and we walk uphill in peace. The valley is still known locally as the 'Glen of Weeping', but today it's hard to imagine the appalling massacre over 300 years ago. On a late winter's evening 38 men of the Clan MacDonald were murdered in their own homes in Glen Coe by men to whom they had offered hospitality. Forty women and children also died of exposure after their homes were burned. The atrocity is considered the most heinous of many murderous acts carried out between Highlanders and supporters of the British sovereign. Even though the people killed were later found to be innocent and an enquiry found the perpetrators guilty, they were never brought to justice. Our capacity for inhumanity seems boundless in the struggle to contain the evil irrational siblings, fear and greed. The high weathered mountainsides we pass through are built from some of the oldest volcanic rock in the world. Even in the context of the cauldron subsidence which created this setting 380 million years ago, I still can't let go of the human violence that will forever stain the landscape.

The relentless pummelling of rough stone tracks gives reason to pause. We gaze out over Rannoch Moor, which my book says is

Britain's largest uninhabited wilderness, just 50 square miles. We're on a 300-metre-high plateau and the moor is covered in bog, lochans and streams. Robert Louis Stevenson described it in *Kidnapped* as 'A wearier looking desert a man never saw', but today there's a magical sense of stillness here. This otherwise desolate place, surrounded by mountains, defies any inhospitable image. I sense in the moment we bring something to the landscape. As Nan Shepherd with her lifetime devotion to the Scottish Cairngorms wrote in *The Living Mountain:*

> Here then may be lived a life of the senses so pure, so untouched by any mode of apprehension but their own, that the body may be said to think. Each sense heightened to its most exquisite awareness is in itself total experience. This is the innocence we have lost.

I wonder about this idea of wilderness. Just how large would such an area be in Australia? Hell, everything is bigger. I've been to a cattle station at Anna Creek in South Australia which is over 9,000 square miles, as large as Wales. This modest-sized moor though makes me feel uneasy. Are we destined to completely eliminate wildness from our lives and rely purely on money and technology for stimulation? We're blessed to have this experience and stop to paddle in a stream before lunch. We've seen no shops for two days, but the stale food we're carrying is just fine for our needs. The world may be dominated by shopping as its chief recreation, but the wilderness has filled our hearts and lungs. We feel refreshed, set free and more alive than ever.

Of course, even here, Thomas Telford built a road 200 years ago and now walkers like us traipse through. We appear doomed to play out the Catch 22 of eliminating the natural world in our search for the wilderness so important to our psyche. I start the afternoon trek feeling disturbed about the fragility of what I'm seeing.

After six hours' walking we're ready for a hearty dinner. John, our fellow JOGLE trekker joins us. For someone in his 40's to throw away 25 years' job security for a long walk had at first sounded a bit imprudent. However, reflecting on Kathy's tragic fate and the rapidly disappearing wilderness, his decision appears more sensible. We all have ideas and dreams of grand projects or simple follies which call to us. Yet we're taught to prize discipline and control. The chance to weave richer patterns into our lives is so often shelved to hang in abeyance awaiting a break in the shackles of routine. But routine is an intolerant taskmaster. Questions thrown up by this adventure circle like buzzards ready to pull apart my ordered life. Even though I still don't understand what has called me to be on this journey, I already know it's one of my best decisions.

Day 24 – to Crianlarich

The morning's trail meanders gently beside a little railway line. The track loops through an old tunnel and onwards down a valley, between gradually smaller hills. Under our feet water still runs through the stony path from yesterday's downpour. Kathy continues to travel with us as a silent companion, her youthful energy extinguished, her life's potential unfulfilled. My reverie is shattered as two RAF jets fly straight towards us, looking no more than 100 metres overhead. They're contour flying down the valley and appear to waggle their wings as if to remind us to stay alive to our surroundings.

Our day unfolds 700-year-old-legends from history's picture book. A Robert the Bruce battlefield is followed by the ruins of an important Augustinian priory dedicated to Ireland's Saint Fillan. For us though everything appears tinted sepia by the sad scene we know is playing out at home in Melbourne.

We reach our B&B after five and have walked 18 miles. On arrival, we go through our customary medical check and Debby says, 'I'm feeling good, but I got a midge bite on my ear.' I wish I could be less irritated by her good fortune, but know the warm, still conditions haven't favoured me. The midges have targeted my head, and in particular a half-circle of shaved flesh exposed through the back of my baseball cap. No bigger than an old florin, it has attracted particular attention from these annoying insects. Running my fingers over a close grouped set of three, I wonder if the third creature shouted '180!' as it struck home like a top darts player.

Weariness deepens over dinner, but there is a satisfaction in writing in the journal that we've broken the 300-mile mark today.

Day 25 – to Inverarnan

The wind howls and rain splatters noisily on the windows of our room. It's the sound we least like on waking. What's even worse is the forbidding heavy grey sky. It looks like the weather will be with us all day. When we do step out into the onslaught, I reassure Debby we have a short walk and can afford to go straight to the famous Crianlarich railway station tearooms. We dawdle over steaming hot chocolate and scones. With hands wrapped around hot mugs and warm tummies digesting their treat it's hard to convince one another we should move.

At eleven, we know we have to leave. Bending heads and flexing muscles, we go straight up a stiff long muddy hill while the rain teems down. Along the track though I realise forests are at their best in the rain. The water runs and drips from every branch adding lustre to their greenery. Their vitality is contagious and we too come alive. We force ourselves to keep going up the hill and both get a buzz, a sense of achievement from pushing ourselves to reach the summit. I look across at Debby and her smile reminds me I'm blessed to have a partner who's enjoying this experience as much as me.

The demanding uphill stretch gives way to an easier undulating track along the River Falloch. Here we confront one of those quaint British oddities, a sheep creep. This old stone tunnel is designed to enable small animals to pass under a railway line. Not four feet high, it's assumed people can also use it to cross the line. On a soaking muddy day it's no mean feat to manoeuvre my six-feet-two frame with bulky daypack through to the other side. I grizzle and curse and my demeanour doesn't improve when Debby smiles and skips through.

I can't be downhearted for long though and soon we're laughing in the presence of a large number of small birds. They sing out as they dart hither and thither, seemingly expressing their delight in this countryside. They look to be contour flying like the big RAF jets of yesterday, except are more nimble, closer to the ground and all together more skilful. Of course, they've been born to it! I wish I had a greater knowledge of the birds, but even though I lack the labels to name them, nothing can stop me marvelling at the lesson they provide in their exuberant embrace of life.

The rain eases and we leave the track to find a picnic spot by clambering up on large rocks at the headwaters of the famed Falls of Falloch. After all the rain the river is in spate and the white froth of the waterfall lightens the dank wooded banks and grey mossy rocks. It's a woodland idyll and although our food is mundane that's irrelevant in such a setting.

In sharp contrast, our destination is a pub more interested in garish touristy humour than its patrons' wellbeing. The place is full of stuffed creatures, stags' heads, a bear, a wolf, a two-headed lamb, and all manner of other odd birds and small animals considered worthy of the taxidermist's life after death. No doubt, it's a tremendous example of the British tradition of eccentric collecting, however it leaves us cold and we retire early.

Day 26 – to Rowardennan

The first seven miles today are considered the toughest of the West Highland Way, so by eight-forty we're out on the path. Path is not the right description – it's more like a rushing stream in the pelting rain. With nearly a months' walking under our belts, I wonder why the walking feels so hard. It must be too early for our still cold limbs. Inevitably we're presented with a steep hill climb and as we ascend, the teeming rain shows no more sign of concern for our wellbeing than last night's pub. Debby's wet weather gear again keeps her drier than me. I silently endure pocket puddles and a wet t-shirt. We move ever deeper into woodland scenery though and that provides an antidote to the hardship. It may not make me any drier but at least my spirits float to the surface. I now understand the sheer variety of greens we experience could only be possible in the rain. We are seeing the scenery in its natural form, lush and dripping wet and nothing can match it.

Within an hour, we're giggling uncontrollably and hugging. Our first view of Loch Lomond quite literally brings us to a halt. Seen through swirling mists and torrential rain, it looks the product of a flamboyant magician's wand. Loch Lomond is so damn impressive. The statistics only tell part of the story. At 44 square miles it has the largest surface area of fresh water in Britain; it's 24 miles long, up to 5 miles wide and 190 metres deep. Gouged out by a glacier 1,000 years ago, it's dotted with 38 islands. The people of central Scotland draw 450 million litres of water daily from Loch Lomond and the water level drops a mere 6mm. A quarter of all Britain's flowers grow on its banks and 200 species of birds and 19 species of fish call it home, including the giant pike. However, leaving all that aside, here today for us, it is simply jaw-droppingly gorgeous. Our spontaneous reaction is to gasp at such loveliness. Once again we confront the power of nature's beauty to nurture souls and inspire in ways no technology ever could.

The walking is now progressively more challenging. We have to work along a narrow track by the loch edge negotiating rocks, elaborate tree roots and sometimes squeezing through narrow passages between boulders. With the rain coming down and everything under our feet slippery, I'm again confronted by my vulnerability and the tenuous control I have over my safety on this walk. The slip I fear comes and I pull a muscle as I pirouette and right myself just in time. All the work I've done to improve my poor sense of balance over the past six months has saved me from crashing on the sharp rocks and I give silent thanks to Lance, my dear friend and yoga teacher.

Debby and I talk to distract ourselves from the danger. Even after four weeks alone together, we still find new things to talk about. Today Debby explains the eight limbs of yoga, but the ancient wisdom can't hold my mind. It's the small white butterflies that captivate me as they merrily flit from plant to plant despite all the rain. I guess if my lifespan was just one day like theirs I'd be determined to make the most of it, regardless of the weather.

My focus returns to the walk just as we arrive at Inversnaid. A bizarre Fawlty Towers-like establishment, it's massive and quite out of place in this remote spot, but it is the only lunch option. We join a group of seniors from a coach tour and wonder what they make of us drinking soup while sweaty vapour rises from our damp bodies.

The afternoon passes more easily as the rain holds off. Waterfalls have been unleashed to cascade down the hillsides beside the track, while a mist holds sway over the Loch. I have gazed out across the pristine water all day and felt its calling. Finally, I give in to temptation, strip off and plunge into the cool, clear dark water to swim into another world. Instead of observing the landscape, I'm now in a deeper visceral relationship with it. The joy of immersion quickly disappears though as I climb out on the bank. My almost naked body is now the preserve of the dreaded midges. In the humid conditions they immediately cloud around me. I quickly towel off and dress. Just when the risk seems to have abated, I'm brought unstuck from a different quarter. Insects are not to blame now, but my species. We've entered the world of day-trippers and one has left a broken beer bottle at the water's edge. I curse and attempt to staunch the blood streaming from my big toe.

In the evening a monster blogging session is necessary and it's midnight when we creep wearily into bed. Our B&B hosts are exceptionally friendly and my thoughts about our fellow humans have mellowed. Not only did they provide a computer, but also at ten o'clock a bottle of malt whisky and two glasses appeared with the instruction to help ourselves to a nightcap.

Day 27 – to Drymen

Gusty winds and heavy cloud cover provide an exhilarating backcloth to our world today. We're on a pedestrian big dipper and our lungs and muscles work hard. Foot placement and sense of balance are critical on the tiny waterside tracks, but the beauty of Loch Lomond's woodland cloak is a constant distraction. The sight of a red deer quietly feeding in the bushes only yards away brings us to a sudden hushed stop.

The afternoon is more demanding. Three hours of climbing through forests stops briefly when a helicopter makes a dramatic rescue. A walker has broken an ankle and we try not to think about the risks we may face before Land's End. The afternoon slowly disappears as feet and muscles grow sore. Debby is clearly knackered, her face lined with exhaustion and perspiration. She won't stop though and somehow soldiers on to Drymen.

When I finally take off my shoes at the B&B, I find a large green caterpillar crawling up my sock. My usual reaction would have seen the creature swiftly put to the sword. Now I'm more philosophical and calmly pick it off my foot to take back to the garden. I see myself as a form of bug-magnet. My flesh provides nourishment for various insects, evidenced by a wide collection of impressive bite marks. I now have a new vision of myself. Like the hero in the film *Avatar*, I figure I must have some sort of deeper spiritual connection with these creatures. When I share the thought with Debby, she asks me if I've been secretly drinking.

I shower and lay on the bed before dinner, aware of a sadness settling over my fatigue. We've walked out of the woods, so to speak. Drymen has a post office and a few shops, the first town of any size that we've been in for over a week. It means we're back in what's known as civilisation. However, the walk down the banks of Loch Lomond today opened my eyes to how uncivilised our society can be. We're only about one hour from Glasgow and the tourism here is much more intense. Attracted to the post-card scenery, my fellow humans descend in droves discarding their waste before heading home. Debby has been filling a plastic bag with pieces of rubbish as we've walked the West Highland Way. However today, confronted by the sheer volume of track-side debris, she gave up. Instead we simply tried to gaze out over the loch and ignore the plastic bags full of rubbish dumped behind trees. Of course, I've seen such sights before, but now it prompts melancholy. We've spent weeks absorbing the breath-taking splendour of the natural world and it irks me how people can be so thoughtless.

Day 28 – to Milngavie

We are out on the track at nine sharp. I grab an anaemic taste-less drink purported to be coffee and wonder why I bothered. Still I'm determined nothing will get me down this morning, the last day of the West Highland Way. The weather lord seems to be in a supportive mood and the heavy rain abruptly stops leaving a mild day. On a country lane, meandering over a small bridge I spot a fly fisherman standing out on rocks under a tree. He appears to be in a state of deep meditation, connected by the finest of threads to the river flowing fast beneath his feet. There must be a parable here. I've heard it can cost £150 for a day's licence to fly-fish in Scotland, and even then any fish caught have to be put back. So, is it all about pitting wits against the slippery muscular flash of a salmon just to tell it I'm smarter than you? Is this all part of reassuring ourselves we're the superior race on this planet?

After an hour, a trackside café appears. This is a sure sign we're entering the world of people. I try my luck with a second coffee. It's passable and for a brief time it's as if we're home. It's a Saturday in this world and I pick up the newspapers, the first I've seen in weeks. To my surprise, the news seems strangely petty and unimportant relative to the life experience we're having. With yesterday's rubbish encounter still fresh in my mind, I say to Debby perhaps we should give up on civilisation and keep walking forever. Debby casually reminds me,

'Keith, nobody is more addicted to prowling city lanes in search of daily caffeine hits than you. Where do you think you'll find those in nature's wilderness?'

I silently take up that conundrum with my pack and we walk back to the track. The walk is tiresome and the weather plays games with us. Our wet weather gear comes on and off regularly, increasing Debby's tiredness. By one-thirty, we're desperately searching for a lunch spot. Approaching a built up area it's not easy to find idyllic picnic spots. Bright red specks, glossy and damp amid the wayside greenery, come to the rescue. Wild raspberries are a delectable pick-me-up for the weary traveller. Clearly all is not lost when city coffee culture is absent.

We walk into Milngavie about four and sheepishly take photos together at the Obelisk signifying the end of the West Highland Way. We've re-entered civilisation now. For the last hour, we've negotiated suburban types walking their dogs and couples sauntering under umbrellas. The umbrella seems a strange artefact after we've confronted regular downpours this past month under nothing more than a jacket hood.

With a plate of homemade sausages and mash and a pint under my belt, I think about what we've learned from the West Highland Way. There's been everything from thousands of years of human history to arcane features of the natural world. I can now recognise the pink berry-infused pine marten spoor and it gives me a warm sense of satisfaction that a south London boy has acquired this knowledge even though I'm not sure exactly what I'll do with it. It's ten, and slipping under the bedcovers I know the West Highland Way landscape, with its demands, drama and delights has left an enduring mark etched deep inside both of us that will infuse our dreams.

Day 29 – to Glasgow

It seems odd the West Highland Way has stopped here. We stand on the cusp of one of the great cities in the world but have been dumped unceremoniously in a tawdry suburb. It feels as if we'd been heading into London and found ourselves in Tooting where I first learned to swim. Never mind, today we'll do justice to the history and grandeur of this city by walking right into its heart.

It's late morning when we bid farewell to Milngavie. The path is surprisingly meditative, not the endless rows of suburban housing I'd expected, but green countryside, cows grazing and a peaceful river meandering by our side. The river Allander leads into the Kelvin where it flows along a winding path into Glasgow's centre.

After an hour the path is completely overgrown. I feel we are cutting our way through some remote wilderness like Indiana Jones and pay no heed to the insects around my calves. It didn't occur to me that wearing shorts could prove perilous walking into a major city.

Many signs of Glasgow's imperious past are on view along the riverside. The city was once known as the second city of the British Empire. Its fortune originated with the tobacco trade and its port became the entry point for most of Europe's demand from the West Indies. It went on to become the pre-eminent centre of the shipbuilding industry producing 80 percent of all the ships made in the country. Steam trains were also almost entirely manufactured by the city's highly skilled workforce. The signs of this success are still everywhere in the great buildings and churches. But best of all for us is the marvellous collection of bridges we pass by. It's a grand city which we feel we're entering along a country backwater.

Too soon, we are at the mighty River Clyde. Although elated to be here, the 14 miles we've walked have once again left Debby exhausted. So we call Shona and Gerry who are complete strangers to us. Morag, a good friend in Australia, has volunteered her sister to put us up in Glasgow and we've tentatively accepted. We're not used to asking for help, but any doubts disappear when they arrive. They whisk our bags into the car and we are ready to go home for a well-earned rest. However, they have other ideas.

They proceed to take us on a walking tour of their city. We walk a couple of miles seeing the sights and soaking up their enthusiasm. New energy flows into us and we realise this is a good idea. By the time we reach home for the evening we feel we've done justice to this great city. Nourishing food and convivial conversation carry us through to bed and utter exhaustion around eleven. I'm barely able to turn out the light before all knowledge of the day departs into dreamy oblivion.

Day 30 – in Glasgow

Sleep is so blissful for walkers. After walking for nine straight days across 130 miles, it feels otherworldly to wake and look out the window to see rain pouring down. I know we deserve this lie-in in the dry, snug comfort of a warm family home. Yet somewhere inside me, there's a tiny prickle of disappointment that I won't be engaging with the elements today. This month has taught me the contradiction in the way we organise our lives and frame our ambitions. I've grown up within a system that encourages people to move away from physical activity as something core to daily life. Technology and the way work is organised all lead us to a more sedentary life. Physical or manual work has been silently branded as being in some way demeaning and uncouth.

I learned early it was more fashionable and I'd be better respected if I worked behind a desk. Physical effort was something to be tacked on to a busy lifestyle. In a gym or out on a running track a sophisticated image can be maintained by using the latest gadgetry and wearing state-of-the-art hi-tech clothing in trendy colours. Yet on this walk, I've come to realise I not only benefit from daily physical exertion, but need to feel some pain and exhaustion as an essential part of it. Moreover, I need to do it within nature's profusion of life. And as nature has welcomed me in, she hasn't given a damn what I'm wearing. For now I'll enjoy listening to the rain outside as Thomas Merton did:

> The rain surrounded the cabin ...with a whole world of meaning, …Think of it: all that speech pouring down, selling nothing, judging nobody, …washing out the places where men have stripped the hillside …Nobody started it, nobody is going to stop it. It will talk as long as it wants, the rain. As long as it talks I am going to listen.

In preparing for the day, we get quite a shock. We know we have been eating more than normal and wondered whether we had put on weight. Checking on the scales this morning, we get the answer. Debby is two kilos lighter than when we started and I am down to 81kg, the lowest weight I can recollect. To think I've happily lived my life for the past 20 years around the 91kg mark, only to drop so much weight during the last few months in training, preparation and a month of actual walking. Anyway, whatever's happening to our weight, we are ready to do justice to the groaning breakfast table laid out for us.

The rest day is once again anything but. By the time breakfast is over we've done another two loads of washing, re-waterproofed our jackets and over-trousers and completely reorganised our pack contents, retaining just what we need for the next phase. A 4kg box with our change of shoes is put together ready to post to Kirk Yetholm in preparation for the start of the Pennine Way. Another 1.5kg parcel awaits dispatch to our support team in London.

The day ends in companionable fashion, sipping malt whisky. It's doesn't seem out of place here in Scotland to sit in front of a log fire with a warming drink in the middle of summer. The hospitality of our hosts is remarkable. Strangers until yesterday, they've welcomed us into their home, showered us with kindness and shared their lives with us. We've felt mothered, chauffeured and supported at every turn. Through their eyes as Glasgow residents, we've come to understand this city in a far richer way than if we'd arrived as tourists. We have the walk to thank for this. Our quest is being passed on through friendship networks and we find the web of our lives expanding in wonderful ways. Our need for help has provided the excuse for people to become interwoven in the fabric of the adventure. It seems people want to share their lives with us and provide help where they can. And at a time when loneliness and isolation are prevalent in today's more self-centred society, it's a joyful antidote.

KIRK YETHOLM
ENGLAND
BBC
EILDON HILLS
MELROSE ABBEY
BORDERLANDS
EDINBURGH
GLASGOW

Chapter 5 – BORDERLANDS

Day 31 – to Bothwell

The alarm goes off early. Time to relax while we pack slowly and prepare our minds. It feels like the end of each phase of the walk brings a sense of achievement, tempered by a sense of loss at its passing. This morning another new beginning awaits. I can feel the excitement to get out on the trail again and disappear into the forgotten byways of this ancient landscape.

Our fourth section will be quite different. I look at my journal: it's 20th July. We've been walking for one month and covered 385 miles. However, until now, we've followed roads or two very famous footpaths. From today, we'll set off through the Borders with no well-established route or guidebook. This will be a different challenge. I've had to cobble together a pathway across southern Scotland where no particular walking route exists. It's involved much detailed map work, poring over tiny dots on the smallest scale maps I could find. As I stitched together these flimsy threads before leaving Australia, I wondered whether they would actually exist in the landscape of the real world. I also worried about how wise this deviation would be. Over the next ten days, the route will lead us over 150 miles almost due east. That's in pretty much the exact opposite direction to our ultimate destination. However that is the only way we can get to the start of our fifth stage, Britain's first national trail and the one still considered its toughest.

When the primordial sludge of this adventure first surfaced in my mind, it was already framed in the shadow of the Pennine Way.

Of all the UK's great walks, this has the most fearsome reputation. The prospect of its challenge had drawn me in, the candle for my moth-like fantasy to flap around. Today, that prospect seems as intimidating as it is exciting, but it's too late to change plans. We turn to the east today and set our sights on a small village near the English border called Kirk Yetholm. For centuries it was the headquarters of the Scottish gypsies, but now it is the gateway to Britain's pre-eminent trail along the backbone of northern England.

We say our goodbyes and by the time we reach the Clyde riverside I look for inspiration to wash away my early lethargy. But today it's just another large grey sullen city watercourse which once channelled power into Glasgow's pulsating industrial heart. Gradually the city centre disappears amongst leafy green trees and parks that now clothe the suburbs. Suddenly we're shocked to see a runner who's staggering after a fall. Blood pours from the wounds to his arm, hands and knees. We rush to his aid and in a flash Debby is in 'H for Health' mode. With backpack off she calls on her first aid skills. I pour the contents of my water bottle down the man's nasty puncture wound while Debby applies disinfectant to the worst of his cuts and bandages his arm. We give him water and a boiled sweet with strict advice to go straight to hospital where he'll clearly need stitches.

We walk on, feeling good about our Samaritan-like intervention, but vaguely disturbed that most passers-by just carried on with their day ignoring the man's distress. The contrast with the hospitality we've received on this trek could not be more stark. It's as if we're now conditioned by society to fear strangers and close down our natural instinct to help fellow humans. As we walk on a feeling of shame creeps over me that in another life back home I would probably not have stopped.

The Clyde Walkway flows beside the river and takes us out of Glasgow through a show-book of its former industrial glory. By two o'clock we've passed 21 bridges and lost track of time marvelling at these wonderful feats of engineering. Unfortunately, we've arrived in Dalmarnock which is not marvellous and we feel uneasy. It's now a major construction site, and as we enter the grey, run down streets, rain begins to fall heavily and a small dog attacks Debby's leg. Looking for somewhere to eat will have to wait. We push on, walking hard, and avoiding eye contact. Of course, I grew up in a worse council estate than this and most people around here would probably be helpful. Is our reaction another consequence of the way we're conditioned by strident media voices to demonise those less fortunate and create fear? We're told the refugees and asylum seekers are dangerous and deserve their fate, but seemingly, we can't compartmentalise our empathy, so just turn off our humanity altogether.

We reach the relative calm and safety of a huge cemetery and Debby puts her pack down amidst the memories of lost lives. With the river in front of us, we're back on our path. Half an hour is all we can afford but as we move on a patch of wild raspberries stops us briefly. The fruit is particularly sweet and we try not to think about what rich nutrients influence their taste, squeezed as it is between river and cemetery. The afternoon path leads us into countryside amidst waist-high grass, trees of all varieties and a carpet of pastel wildflowers any Persian rug merchant would be proud to offer. A fragrant scent accompanies our footsteps while the Clyde, a watery serpent, remains a loyal companion.

Our energy levels wear away with the afternoon. A mere 30-metre hill almost brings us both to a stop. The path descends into a dark damp tightly-wooded path across slippery 100-year-old bricks. We cross the Rotten Calder, a small tributary of the Clyde, on a treacherous path pit workers used daily to reach the coal mines. My state of fatigue is nothing to what those wretched men must have experienced to follow their destiny and create Glasgow's industrial might. It's past the time I'd expected us to finish and we're worn out. This seems to be an early warning these smaller footpaths may be more challenging than I'd expected. Another patch of wild raspberries and the enchantment of Bothwell Woods lighten our footsteps, but we can't do justice to the 13th-century castle despite being intrigued to know more about someone called Archibald the Grim who restored it.

We arrive at six with Debby on her last legs and after a hot bath and simple bowl of pasta we both collapse into bed and deep sleep.

Day 32 – to Carluke

The alarm rouses us and I blink in disbelief. We've slept nine hours. Debby went to bed exhausted and in a bad mood. Now it's my turn. Perhaps the long sleep has drained me, but I'm too tired to write up the diary or prepare for the day's walk. Nothing is right in my world, and to make matters worse Debby is positively chirpy. I take time to read the newspaper with breakfast.

I read about the world's new breed of leaders. David Cameron is visiting the United States in his prime ministerial capacity for the first time. He's taken Barack Obama a piece of graffiti art as a present and a couple of pairs of pink and purple Wellingtons for his children. They appear such modern charismatic statesmen, but I wonder if they will do any better than their predecessors in understanding the depth and complexity of the challenges in this modern era. Global economic and geopolitical issues will likely see realpolitik set them at odds, rather than working together to embrace more joined-up policies.

Setting aside global political challenges our first challenge is to negotiate a path through a nature reserve. The vibrant colours and sounds of small birds are a tonic. A small mammal darts off the path ahead, but I can't identify it – such is the blindness of a city dweller. The variety of sights in meadow, marshland, scrub, woodland and wetland is a heady mix, and my lack of labels for what I pass in no way limits my enjoyment.

By midday there's a spring in my step. More wayside raspberries, intoxicating scents, colourful wildflowers, chirruping birds and infinite lush greenery have lifted my spirits. Better than any multivitamin tablet, I'm feeling refreshed and completely re-energised. The vast array of greens in nature seem infinite. I feel sure we'll one day acknowledge we can no more count the variety of delicate shades of colours around us, than identify the tiniest particles at the Large Hadron Collider or calculate the number of galaxies in the Universe. Although we may not be willing to accept limits to our ability to understand and statistically quantify the universe, I'm learning from this walk we can open our senses to wonder at the splendour of the world and the mystery of the universe in which we are embedded. Perhaps one day we'll find this is the unique gift we bring to a fathomless cosmos.

Suddenly I'm brought back from musing on the infinite to a large bull standing directly in our path. Peter, our friend and livestock expert, had warned me, 'If you meet a bull, don't engage in eye contact with the beast'. Head down and eyes averted we cross the field, hop over a stile and look back. The bull is completely unfazed and unmoved.

We recover our poise over lunch and then zip up rain jackets, pull on over-trousers and march on into teeming rain. For close to four hours the rain never stops. We follow the riverside, occasionally sliding on muddy paths while I struggle to understand the path's direction. There's no one else walking, which suggests people have yet to discover the Clyde Walkway.

The river looks its best in the pouring rain, fed by a number of small streams flowing rapidly. Whereas in the centre of Glasgow the Clyde is a mighty, serene, elder statesman, confident of its power, we've watched its size diminish as we walk back towards its source. This morning we've seen it transform, like 'Benjamin Button', into a virile, almost swaggering young man, smaller but carrying all before it. Now as we approach Cambusnethan Priory, it's become a teenager, running merrily either side of roots and small obstructions, bubbling with the inconsistency of an adolescent.

The afternoon wears on and my search for the point to bid farewell to the Clyde begins. The General Roy memorial is our target, a mile off the Clyde Walkway on the road to Carluke. In the absence of any clear landscape markers to confirm the route-map I've drawn, I pull out the compass. My hero Shackleton steered a small boat by dead reckoning through the storms of the Great Southern Ocean, and even though I've no experience of such things, the incessant rain focuses my attention. I direct Debby to a path more in hope than with any confidence. Soon after joy drives out the cold and wet as we arrive at the memorial. How fitting that we're here at the birthplace of the man who took up the challenge of producing a map to enable more effective policing in the 1750's. His work established the network on which Great Britain's treasured Ordinance Survey maps are founded and without which our walk would have been impossible.

By the time Debby and I trudge up a long lane into the eastern outskirts of Carluke we are thoroughly saturated, but have completed another 19 miles.

Day 33 – to Biggar

What a depressing sight. Rain is pouring down outside the bedroom window. We linger over breakfast while our hosts Ann and Alec worry about the first section of our route along the A721. A deviation they suggest would probably add three miles to an already long day. I look for excuses to delay a decision and listen to Alec expound on the different cattle-rearing and birthing techniques he practises with his mixed herd. The rain, as if bored of waiting for us to come out and play, moves on. Immediately we rise, hoist our packs, still damp from yesterday, and pass out into a cold, dank morning landscape. First stop is Kilncadzow which we're told is pronounced Kill-kaggie. There's a great bakery here and the women who run it think the walk we're doing is sensational. They spur us on with their enthusiasm while we buy filled rolls for lunch. We decide speed is of the essence, so ignore the alternative route to take our chances with the traffic.

In time the road falls away, Carstairs is behind us and we enter the open countryside we crave. A meandering river frames the foreground and the Southern Upland hills appear as backcloth. We've made good time, but by lunchtime I'm very tired. The rucksack has worn my shoulder sore and it appears we'll have a longer day than I'd planned. While I conjure up bad omens about the dead badger we saw this morning, Debby says she's worried about how tired I look:

'Debby I think I've come down off the featherbed of civilisation and am feeling the flint under my feet right now...'

At this stage of the day when the chips are down, we simply know we both have to get there, and the best way to do it is in our own way. So, we revert to our natural pace and I let my longer stride take me ahead of Debby. We've agreed a system on days like this where I'll forge ahead and then wait up ahead for her to catch up. By mid-afternoon, I decide emergency measures are necessary and turn on my iPod. Debby has begun reciting yoga sutras and chanting and her pace has quickened. Immediately, everything seems easier. A sort of yogic serenity has fallen over us and it appears to be spreading out over all the beasts in the fields and the birds in the trees.

Meanwhile, I'm transported to another time zone, where a young Paul McCartney croons 'The Long and Winding Road'. Once again the random tracks on my play list seem intuitive and Bob Dylan belts out 'How Many Roads Must A Man Walk Down Before They Can Call Him A Man?' I don't know how many he thought, but it can't be as many as I've walked down today.

Somehow we get to Biggar, and our arrival brings to an end another 19-mile day. That makes 55 miles in three days, our longest stretch so far. We feel in celebratory mood at dinner despite the now routine pub menu. I write up the diary before stepping out under a deep cloud-free blue sky to blink in unaccustomed sunshine.

Day 34 – in Biggar

We share our rest day with a woman who huffs and puffs through a respiratory ailment while posting several hours of Facebook updates in this small dingy internet dungeon. Occasionally I look up from the blog to peer through a small window at the sun. I suspect the weather god is looking down with a wry smile having laid on the most beautiful sunny day since we set out.

Day 35 – to Peebles

A railway trail along the bubbling Biggar water leads us down to the Tweed to start our day. The first five miles into Broughton are perfectly flat, another rail trail benefit. These smaller paths are not as well known and we can be alone with ourselves and find the peace intense. I listen to the breeze gently stirring the emptiness until Debby says, 'Keith, we are worshipping at the church of nature.' That reminds me of something I'd read about one of the first BBC outside broadcasts. A cellist, Beatrice Harrison, had played to the accompaniment of nightingales in the woods where I courted my first wife Barbara near her home in Oxted, Surrey. Lord Reith had summed it up:

> Milton has said that when the nightingale sang, silence was pleased. So in the song of the nightingale we have broadcast something of the silence which all of us in this busy world unconsciously crave and urgently need.

The route gets progressively more difficult to follow. At times it seems to disappear altogether and we have to hack our way through undergrowth. Before leaving the hotel, I had decided to remove the bottoms of my trousers, anticipating fine weather. This was a bad decision. Although the weather is close to perfect, we're now passing through prodigious nettles and thistles that give my legs a severe exfoliation. In the distance there are hills, but not like those of the Highlands. These are rolling hills that create a landscape of extraordinary beauty. All blues and misty greys threaded through with small patches of blurred yellow farmland. They do not look forbidding or harsh, but gentle, as if we're being enticed to run into them. Now I'm falling in love with a softer version of Scotland.

It's two by the time we lunch at the side of the Tweed. This famous salmon river will dominate the next three days of our walk and provides a pleasing distraction while we rebuild energy. After lunch, the afternoon becomes a succession of classic walking challenges. We have an unexpected river deviation, an impassable railway trail, a stint on a B road, a tiny 'sheep creep', and the obligatory shoes soaked in the ooze of wet excrement while negotiating a field of sheep. At times, our movement sends up ducks in a frenzied flurry of wings and quacking, but eventually they learn we're not shooters. We regularly pause to forage luscious wild raspberries and by four o'clock when I tell Debby we've 12 miles behind us but still a fair way to go, she calmly assures me: 'I'm a bit tired but I've certainly got another five or six miles in me.'

There are days when walking is good and days when we simply trudge for hour after hour. There are days when the weather and countryside improve a walk or punish us. Today is a walk of joy, one for the true believers. We've no sense of drudgery, our footsteps are cushioned by the grassy banks of the Tweed and our mood buoyed by the gentle ever-changing sights, scents and sounds. The Borders appears an area at peace with itself, and we've been invited into its inner sanctum today.

It's late, six-thirty, when we walk into our B&B. Within half an hour we unpack, shower and slip into our evening attire. It's very easy to dress for dinner, because they are the same t-shirts and trousers we wear every evening. It may have been another 19-mile day, but I notice we're moving with ease. As Debby says, the body has a wonderful recovery system. The strains and stings, bruises and blisters, aches and abrasions, all disappear as the body regenerates and repairs itself.

Day 36 – to Innerleithen

Despite yesterday's big walk we struggle to sleep. The blocks of Imperial Leather soap in the old communal bathrooms of this B&B may add a certain nostalgic charm, but if the bed's no good, everything else is irrelevant. At check-out I wonder why the elderly white-haired but steely-eyed woman, who looked every inch the consummate Scottish landlady, added up the bills in German. We will never know the answer and are promptly out on the pavement just after nine. Tomorrow we'll be walking through a remote area, so first we need to stock up on supplies.

It's Sunday and my urban heritage tells me we should be having a café experience before setting out. 'Surely, I've earned it?', I say to Debby, but she's unmoved. The quiet grey deserted streets are not encouraging. Every café we pass is still closed and only one has a sign 'Open 10am Sunday'. Even I can't justify a 45-minute delay for what would inevitably be a bad coffee. With grumpy resignation, we go to the local Co-op, stack up on unenticing food and cross to our track on the south side of the Tweed. After a while, Debby's keen eyes spot an information board showing a better riverside walk along the north side of the Tweed. By the time we have retraced our steps to cross back over the bridge the town clock is chiming ten,

'Debby, how fortunate, the café will be open!'

With resignation Debby humours me, and when we walk into the café it's like we've walked onto the set of a TV sit-com. It dawns on me it's exactly like being in our local Melbourne café with the swimming group. The owner has a gruff Scottish accent and a penchant for sarcasm. In the course of the first ten minutes of opening, in come half a dozen men of a certain age who sit themselves at different tables. They act like mates but would never own up to it, and there's little doubt this is the highlight of their week. They come here for the camaraderie, to throw sarcastic jibes at one another and be exposed to friendly humiliation. So very British and a reminder of my love for the Icebergers. We've stumbled into a precious experience, a chance to be part of something rarely acknowledged by men: the true spirit of community. We stay longer than we should to soak up this wonderful cameo of Scottish manhood and blokes bonding. It's nearly eleven when we get back on the trail. 'The coffee was pretty poor,' I acknowledge to Debby, but the delicious oven-warm fruit scones have left us ready to tackle anything.

I thought we had a mere two hours stroll today, but gradually realise I've seriously underestimated the effect of our route change. This will nearly double our walking distance. Although still a short day, it's a feature of walking that no matter the distance, disappointment creeps in when it takes longer than expected. I duly become frustrated long before we walk into Innerleithen. Only Traquair and its magnificent house, the oldest continuously inhabited house in Scotland and one visited by 27 Scottish kings, slowly vents my irritation.

Day 37 – to Galashiels

Breakfast at eight and I think it's time to try poached eggs. I should know better. The egg white is so undercooked a grey white watery fluid runs over the toast from the point of my knife. I gag but was brought up in Britain and pride myself on a capacity to cope with any bad cooking despite the culinary delicacies I've grown accustomed to since. With no reason to delay further, we hoist packs and step out on the road, tingling with excitement.

Today the Southern Upland Way awaits, part of a lesser-known long-distance footpath that crosses Britain from coast to coast. The sight of these hills has been a temptation and we're looking forward to testing our muscles and feet on the paths that run through them. This should be great preparation for the Pennine Way, now less than a week away.

After one hour I'm reminded just what hillwalking with full backpacks is all about. We negotiate a stiff uphill winding track through small Christmas trees to reach the 400 metres mark. Next we're on Minch Moor, close to the 567m summit and a brief snack at eleven-thirty. Now the route traverses high hills on an undulating stony track known as the Old Drover's Road. Our peak is the Three Brethren, a charming if obscure name for three impressive ten-foot-high stone cairns. We arrive and find another couple, the first people we've met today. They are locals from Melrose and the friendly discourse ebbs and flows until it finally turns down the well-worn runnels to food experiences. What could be more natural than to meet people at the top of a mountain and discuss where to get good food when we descend?

The weather has confused and challenged us all morning. A fine misty rain has dampened our bodies if not our spirits. Distracted by our new friends, we're caught out as the rain suddenly becomes intense. Hasty goodbyes are exchanged and with no shelter we unpack jackets and trousers in the rain and place them over our already sopping t-shirts and shorts.

We know there'll soon be a major descent down to a small hamlet called Vair where we've been told there's a tearoom. Much as we try to conjure up a quick descent, the track stubbornly refuses to conform and keeps pulling more undulations from its magician's hat. Finally, sanity reigns and the path begins to turn down even though the rain does not. With nowhere to shelter all thought of lunch is suspended. We reach the bottom and find the tearooms are only open at weekends. Today is Monday. However, the rain is abating and an opening leads us down to the Tweed. The setting is grand and by three we're scoffing oatcakes, sweaty cheese and rolls crudely stuffed with a tinned version of the magnificent fish that inhabit this illustrious Tweed.

It's five when tonight's landlady, Ann, greets us with the kind offer to wash our smelly clothes and dry sodden shoes. We shower and sprawl on the comfortable bed while the tremors of exhaustion slowly fade from our bodies. We've been sucked dry by today's 17 miles. Sliding into bed at ten my only concern is the close proximity of the Town Hall clock. Surely it won't chime all night?

Day 38 – to Melrose

We can't be sure what happened at one o'clock, but we know for certain the Town Hall clock chimed every other hour of the night. Somewhat bleary-eyed we go downstairs for our customary eight o'clock breakfast. After we've eaten Ann kindly offers us free use of her computer. We've a very short six-mile day, so that means plenty of time to bring the blog up to date. At ten she has to leave, but insists we should stay in the house and go whenever we want. She has entrusted her home to us and I'm beginning to realise such acts of generosity of spirit are the fabric of community life.

On a sunny day it's a disappointment to put dry feet into shoes still sodden from yesterday. We walk down Galashiels High Street to pay our respects to yet another Robert Burns Memorial, but I'm distracted by the odour rising through the damp uppers of my shoes. With resignation, I accept my new role for the day: *the man with the smell.*

Never mind, the Southern Upland Way is a great path, exactly the type of lesser-known adventure we love. Every great long-distance path combines two key characteristics: dramatic landscapes coupled with a broad selection of interesting places to visit along the way. This trail has both in spades and cuts across the grain of the country, unveiling a great variety of different geography, everything from coastal cliffs to high woodlands, rolling hills, mountain streams, gorgeous valleys and abundant wildlife.

Although Galashiels and Melrose are adjacent towns just a two-hour walk apart, they could not be more different. The former has all the big shops locals use, while Melrose is a more elegant place. It's steeped in history and teeters on the edge of being a tourist haven, but holds the line as something more appealing. I waste no time changing from my smelly shoes. Today has given me an inkling of the judgement I can make about others less fortunate. I briefly experienced the daily world of a homeless person who can't clean or change old clothes and it wasn't any fun.

There's a rich river of history that flows wide and fast in places like Melrose. The Abbey we'll save for tomorrow, but I learn the Old Drover's Road we walked yesterday has been in use for hundreds of years and was the main route across southern Scotland in the 1200's. Edward I had travelled across it when invading the northern kingdom he tried so hard to conquer, while Sir Walter Scott's mother rode along it in a coach and six, with several footmen to regularly lift the coach free of gorse and heather, to attend evening balls in Peebles.

From Melrose we look out at three different hills that we'll pass through tomorrow. These Eildon Hills are considered the most distinctive landmarks in the Scottish Borders. As we've been walking our minds have been opened to a richer experience than just observing the landscape. We've begun to understand the background and importance of Britain's great store of legends. The ghost of King Arthur is said to live under these hills, and another says they were split by a wizard from one giant hill. Thomas the Rhymer, a genuine historical figure was said to have met the Fairy Queen beneath a tree on the slope of the Hills.

I've read about the legends and come to understand there's no reason they should be dismissed any more than Aboriginal Dreamtime stories are in Australia. In the technological world we inhabit they may seem fanciful at first, but legends make for powerful stories and are at the core of much of our belief system. The grand myths are not to be taken at face value, but opened up and considered at a deeper level of meaning. As Lawrence Boldt said in his 1992 book *Zen and the Art of Making a Living:*

> It is not as fact but as metaphor that the mythic stories speak to us. To approach myth as fact is to miss the point. Similarly to view your life as nothing but the facts is to miss an opportunity for a marvellous adventure, a conscious encounter with the universal energies and dilemmas of the human drama. In this encounter we take the hero's journey, we experience life as art, we put the soul into our work.

Debby and I need to determine our own understanding of the myths and legends which emanate from the paths we navigate on this journey. However, whatever else I discover, I know I'll be keeping a sneaking lookout for Thomas the Rhymer's Fairy Queen tomorrow when we pass through these hills.

Day 39 – to Ancrum

The patter of rain on the window welcomes us to a new day. It's remarkable just how much rain appears to fall in Scotland in summer. For a moment longer I lay back in the comfort of bed. Maybe it was the weather that drove our Scottish friends, Morag and Ed, to Australia. It's through their friends we were referred to this great B&B. Such is the intricate web of life I seem to have woven. Somehow we smell out kindred spirits who can enchant and bring meaning to our lives.

I could never have known 29 years ago where this friendship would lead. In the splendid foolhardy manner of youth, I'd agreed to relocate with a pregnant wife to Africa. I'd already travelled through many of the diverse countries on the continent, but Nigeria was different. I never told Barbara what life would be like in the grime and oppressive heat of the tropics, let alone enmeshed in the urgent press of humanity, corruption and fear that were Nigeria. Yet, these are the conditions under which friendships are forged. As testament to that, here I am living a different life with a different wife, travelling on a different passport – almost a different man – and yet the friendship forged in the oil fields of Port Harcourt with Morag & Ed has endured and deepened.

By nine-thirty we're at Melrose Abbey. It's a magnificent old ruin, yet still a powerful sign of Melrose's importance in times gone by. St. Aidan of Lindisfarne established a monastery 1,400 years ago, but it was the Scottish King David I who encouraged Cistercian Monks to found their first monastery here in 1136. By the 1330's Melrose Abbey became so important it was chosen as the burial ground for the heart of Robert the Bruce. The Abbey had become one of the richest in Scotland as a direct result of the notoriously austere Cistercian monastic lifestyle. Medieval abbeys, like Melrose, were actually factories of prayer, and noblemen would pay monks to pray for their souls to improve their chances of reaching heaven. Prayer was a commodity and the more devout an Abbey the more it could charge for its prayer because it was expected to be more effective.

It's a reminder of the powerful influence of the monotheistic religions and their promise of a heavenly afterlife. People talk of the undue power money wields today, yet here it was in play a millennia ago corrupting the ethics of spirituality. Things are probably worse now, but much of today's wealth is held by monolithic companies and it's become commonplace to criticise the morals of their leaders. I feel uneasy about the small role I've played in this saga as so much of my life was spent in the pursuit of building corporate wealth. However, by establishing public companies with a very clear, single obligation in law to maximise the financial wealth of their shareholders, society has made it clear how they want companies to function. The people running companies have no option to consider their own moral preferences. The single financial imperative makes any wider morality impossible. I worked diligently with my colleagues to minimise the taxes paid in desperately poor countries with never a thought for the local peoples' needs for tax revenues to pay for the support infrastructure these communities badly needed. We extracted the natural resources and made as much money as we could for our shareholders with the simple belief we were doing the good work we were paid for.

Ever the practical one, Debby cuts short my ruminations pointing out that I'm standing in the pouring rain looking at an old ruin and it's time we left. Today we join St Cuthbert's Way, designed to shed light on the life of this man who had a religious calling at the age of 16 and became Bishop of Lindisfarne. Today's first hill is a real heart-starter. We gain 300 metres in height in less than half an hour. The path is no more than a slim track sheathed in the fresh bloom of purple heather and despite the demands on our muscles, we feel our spirits rise with our bodies. Next, a slow spectacular winding descent to the River Tweed brings us into the midst of beauty. We breathe in the peace with nothing other than a silent fly fisherman for human company.

Lunch today is special. It's one anybody who was a child growing up in 1950's England would understand. I experience a form of ecstasy, almost akin to a St. Cuthbert miracle. We sit on the banks of the Tweed in dappled sunshine. I pull out a crusty old grain roll and eat it with a tin of the original Fray Bentos corned beef accompanied by Branston pickle from a sticky plastic bag – a meal fit for a condemned man's last supper. Just how London's post-WW2 food rationing memories are embedded into my psyche, I cannot begin to understand. However, they're there and it's impossible to describe the pleasure this meal provides. Debby doesn't understand it at all:

'Fray Bentos is *gruesome*, it tastes just like the Camp Pie that I spent my childhood trying to avoid.'

I smile and let such small aberrations in her character pass by with the gentle bubbling of the Tweed.

After lunch, we stroll along rough paths through woodlands along the Tweed Valley. We stop for a paddle and then join Dere Street. Although no more than a country footpath now, this is one of Britain's oldest Roman roads. We're 17 miles into the day and our muscles are beginning to complain, but we still make the detour into a field to gaze at old Lilliard's stone. It commemorates a brave fighter who fell at the battle of Ancrum Moor in 1545. Apparently Lilliard has transformed from a man into a woman over the centuries. Legend has it she was a brave Scottish fighter who had her legs chopped off and continued to fight on her stumps. This may be myth, but it reinforces the heroism of thousands of woman on both sides of the border who endured 300 years of wars. It's unfortunate, but for my generation it immediately brings to mind the Monty

Python sketch of the knight who cheerily fought on as his limbs were hacked off.

Day 40 – to Morebattle

This B&B wasn't good and by nine we're only too keen to walk out the back gate and struggle along a barely navigable sheep track to re-join St Cuthbert's Way. Summer seems to have finally arrived on 29th July. Deep in sun-dappled woodlands, this former Roman road makes for good soulful walking. There's not a lot to listen to except the gentle rustle of leaves on the breeze, the odd insect buzzing as it busies itself with its daily chores and that distinctive British bird-song evocative of lazy summer days. After an hour, I see a hand-written sign pinned to a tree pointing to Woodside Garden Cafe. We decide to take a look and step into a 200-year-old walled garden. A couple of women in their 50's have taken five years to create this haven from an overgrown mess, their initiative spurred by the life-threatening disease one of them contracted. Buoyed by sensational cake we walk on, and without warning Debby breaks into a sprightly version of Robin Hood riding through the glen. She's happy and H for Humour is bursting out.

In the Borders we're never far from a river and today it's the Teviot. A little suspension bridge crossing brings a flutter of vertigo before the woodland enchantment falls away and we're left with wide-open arable farmland. We follow hedgerow boundaries of oats, barley and wheat taking the time to read signs designed to help improve understanding between farmer and community. We learn of the importance of birds, animals and all the other small insects and creatures critical in promoting healthy, nutritious crops. The patches of wildflowers left around the edges of crops are colourful and together with long hedgerows and beetle banks alongside ditches, provide homes for voles, otters, newts and frogs. It's good to appreciate how this web of life works, and the hedgerows, some ten feet high and just as thick, look magnificent, amongst the healthiest we've seen.

The Cessford Castle ruins are more impressive than the map foretold. It's hard to believe its only inhabitants now are sheep. The Bishop of Ross once said of the Kerr family who built it in 1450:

> They do not concern themselves whether it be from the Scots or the English that they rob and plunder.

Perhaps time has brought just deserts. We decide to lunch here with the sheep and a few hundred thousand thrips swarming over our food.

Forty minutes later, we walk into Morebattle. We drop our packs and saunter down the pretty main street to find a bench to sit on in the late afternoon sun. I take out the journal to write the blog longhand while an industrious group of community-minded women arrive to tend the village planters and hanging baskets. Their pride brings colour and vitality to this sleepy hollow. Despite its fearsome name, Morebattle's Anglican origin, 'dwelling by the lake', seems apt in today's repository of calm.

Day 41 – to Kirk Yetholm

Fortified and full of the joy that springs from all being well in the breakfast world, we walk out of the village at nine. Today should be a doddle, just six miles, but it includes three peaks, a small introduction to the mighty Cheviot Hills. Within minutes we're on the first hill ascending rapidly. Leg muscles sing out under the strain. Lungs gasp for air and then settle into the higher work rate. Our reward opens up as the Borders landscape is revealed. Humans have softened the harsher brush of bottle-brown and green grasses. The fields are planted in pastel shades in an interlaced patchwork that disappears into a grey sky at an indistinct horizon. Five hawks soar overhead moving at speed and I can only marvel at the highly developed senses which enable them to recognise a tiny fieldmouse treat.

We press on up to Grubbit Law, the views distracting our attention from our resistant leg muscles. Thirty minutes from the river and we've climbed 300 metres. The imposing peaks of the Cheviots in two days' time however will be far more challenging than these mere molehills. The final peak of the day is Wideopen Hill. At 368metres it's the highest point on St Cuthbert's way, exactly halfway along and over 30 miles from Melrose. To the east stands the mist-shrouded romance of Lindisfarne, the Holy Island where we once negotiated the causeway which disappears at high tide. Our encounter with St. Cuthbert is fast coming to an end. He's only a bit player in our grand adventure. We've bigger fish to fry with the 250 miles of the Pennine Way in prospect.

We're early and no one's home at the B&B so we sit in the back garden and I scribble in the journal. The peace is disturbed frequently by something that reminds me of a croaking frog. Later I'm told the noise comes from a mole-scaring machine – another contraption we've needed to invent to reach the giddy heights we call civilisation. Later we celebrate the conclusion of Phase Four of our walk. With 540 miles under our belts there's no better way to toast our arrival in Kirk Yetholm than by emptying the remaining dram of Caol Ila malt from the hip flask.

Day 42 – in Kirk Yetholm

The last day of July has arrived, bringing with it another brief marker in my life, my 58th birthday. The blog has kept us in closer contact than normal with a wide circle of friends and on this rest day I take time to enjoy good wishes from around the globe. During these six weeks on the marathon trail I've gained some new perspectives on what we're doing. We created this adventure for ourselves as a personal challenge. I hadn't thought too much about how we might affect others, or indeed, they us. When I mention it, Debby says:

'Keith, you're a collector. Our bookshelves can't hold all your books and you've got boxes of memorabilia stacked in the back-room. You collect people the same way.'

Our walk has clearly fired the imagination of friends, families and some complete strangers met along the way. We've had introductions to people on their doorsteps and departed the next morning with more names added to our list of friends. People seem fascinated by what we're doing. Some are envious, although most think we're completely mad. The blog has played a much bigger role than I ever could have imagined. I'm staggered by how many 'hits' we get. People seem to be engaged in our adventure, reading and commenting on it, including some we've never met. The blog may at first have been a heavy, time-demanding burden, adding to the tiredness that threatened to swamp my sanity, but it has now become our greatest companion. I can no longer imagine being too tired to write the blog any more than I could imagine voluntarily giving up our quest.

We always expected we might get one or two people to join us for the odd day or even to spend a week walking with us. However, we'll have company for much of the Pennine Way. There's no better birthday present than the arrival this evening of Debby's daughter Kate and her Swedish partner John. They set out from Stockholm before four this morning to reach this obscure spot in one day. They will be with us for the first week and then an Australian friend will join us. Together we'll no doubt create stories and share laughs that are sure to deepen our friendships and lay down rich memories for years to come. Apart from those joining us on the Pennine Way, others have committed to walk with us as we head south. And with each new person we know we'll gain new insights into ourselves. As one of our friends has already remarked, accompanying us is like walking with a giraffe and a rabbit. Me with a long loping stride and Debby, legs working overtime, scurrying along to keep up.

I slip into bed and contemplate the daunting prospect ahead. The first two days of The Way will cover over 30 miles of some of the highest hills in Britain, including a vertical climb of about one mile. The troublesome statistics roll around in my head before I let go of the day. Debby continues to ponder our fate until one in the morning.

The WAY IN
HAWES
TAN HILL
PATH
PENNINE WAY
CROSS FELL
HADRIAN'S WALL
KIRK YETHOLM

Chapter 6 – THE WAY IN

Day 43 – to Trows

It's early and I pull back the night-time blanket of sleep slowly. The toughest challenge of our adventure lies beyond this room waiting for us. We've walked through much hardship these past six weeks, and although we might nod and smile when people describe us as accomplished long-distance walkers, the Pennine Way has forged a reputation which suggests nothing we've experienced has prepared us for what awaits. I pick up our Trailblazer guidebook again:

> Of all the long-distance trails in the British Isles the Pennine Way… along the backbone of northern England, is pre-eminent... and it's arguably the hardest.

But it was the typically blunt words of that doyen of long-distance walking, Alfred Wainwright, in his Pennine Way Companion that snared me:

> The Pennine Way offers you the experience of a lifetime… to do it at "one fell swoop"… entails the greater hardship and privation… but is the more challenging….It is a tough, bruising walk and the compensations are few. You do it because you want to prove to yourself that you are man enough to do it.

This morning the words sound daunting, especially as we're not only going to attempt the walk in 'one fell swoop' but after already walking 541 miles over the last 42 days. Of course, it's largely the physical challenge that makes any adventure exciting and sharpens the mind. The uncertainty of outcome and prospect of overcoming obstacles is what makes it worthwhile. These mere two-dimensional words can never truly relay the experience of an outdoors beyond any human control. Surely, the aesthetic beauty and texture of the landscape will be uplifting? I want to believe that, but I understand now it's the vagaries of a temperamental weather god as much as the bruising terrain that will determine the impact of the next month on our physical and emotional wellbeing. An encounter with nature in the raw is outside the door and we'd better get on with it. I throw off trepidation with the bed sheets, just another 'day one' on the adventure.

At breakfast I admire John tame his mighty Swedish appetite with four slices of black pudding, and by seven-fifty we're out on the track walking in crisp sunshine. Perhaps this near perfect weather is a final offering from St. Cuthbert? The walking is certainly the toughest yet, mostly stiff uphill climbing, but the inevitable wind is manageable. We chose the high route; on a day like this it would be cowardly to do anything else. After Whitelaw Nick and White Law Peak (430m) we cross that all-important stile that takes us from the wilds of Scotland into English civilisation. Next comes Black Hag before we break the 500-metre mark. The Schill (601m) is our next challenge. The backpack weighs heavy and the memories of 42 days exertion in thighs and buttocks nag, but I keep moving. 'One step at a time' is the mantra Debby has instilled.

A brief morning tea stop at the mountain refuge hut and we're off again. Hearts beat faster and lungs work harder, but somehow the body's chemistry is playing out in background mode as we gaze in wonder. It's said the Cheviots are a range of nameless, never-ending hills and we seem to be right in the centre, high up with a 360 degrees panorama across them all. The North Sea provides a far-off eastern horizon. Here today anything seems possible. A sense of invincibility has been released from some place where I guess potential is usually locked up to protect us from failure and embarrassment. Occasionally we simply stop and listen to the rich silence of wind blowing across the few low shrubs and grasses that clothe these hills. John identifies tiny plants with pale yellowy-red berries that he tells us are cloudberries, an expensive delicacy in Sweden.

Next is Auchope Cairn (720m). The map contours almost join and the rocky ascent is so steep I struggle and stop several times to rally breath and energy. When I step into the summit cairn I drop my rucksack but can't bring myself to look back at Debby. I know she's still halfway back down the mountain and once again I feel the weight of the quest I've saddled her with. Time passes, but when she arrives with Kate we regroup and are caught up in the exhilaration of achievement. Concern to get off the mountain safely this evening means we press on and soon pass our highest peak. Next, an old drover's road, Clennell Street, provides a lunch stop. The food is welcome, but as usual it plays second fiddle to the nourishment of our surroundings.

After lunch we reach Russell's Cairn (620m) and then leave the Pennine Way. A little winding track leads down to a spot of peaceful nothingness called Trows. Here we sprawl on the grass in weak sun to await the woman who runs the only hostel in this remote countryside. A bumpy half-hour drive back along the tiniest of single track country lanes brings us to our basic accommodation. We make up our own beds on arrival and feel like we could go straight to sleep, but hold on for a simple dinner. I turn out the lights at nine and quickly release my grasp on the day.

Day 44 – to Byrness

It's a long weary climb up a winding rabbit warren from deep sleep before I can blink my eyes open in early morning light. Total exhaustion is hard to throw off. My proven routine of placing one foot out of bed onto the cold floor makes progress possible. This hostel is functional and the host to be applauded for her commitment to keep this northern end of the Pennine Way open to non-campers. However, there are no luxuries here to encourage dalliance. Cardboard boxes of cardboard loosely disguised as cereal are purchased for 40p each from the storeroom. The accompaniment of cardboard slices of toast at 25p each is fitting and we pay the extra for tasteless nutrition-free jam sachets. Debby decides to go with the 'healthy' option, a double pack of instant porridge. By the time she has burned it on to the bottom of a saucepan, it is equally inedible. Fortunately, one of the other walkers, enamoured of Debby's new short hairstyle, immediately offers to wash the pan up for her. We quickly retreat feeling he will certainly be a late starter.

We want to walk every step of the way on our grand adventure and are soon being driven back to yesterday's pick-up point at Trows. Forty-five minutes after drop-off we've forged our way back up to Russell's Cairn. With muscles warmed, we stride out freely along a chain of inspiring hilltops. Mozzie Law (552m), Beefstand Hill (562m) and then we avoid a steep-sided valley to pass over Lamb Hill. Once again a mountain refuge hut provides the excuse for morning tea, and more of Kate's enormous homemade Swedish-style muesli bar. There are three other walkers at the hut, one a very experienced fell runner. He's a relatively quiet introvert, not surprising really considering the dribble that hangs untended from his chin. A couple of women in their 60's are pounding the Pennine Way out in two weeks. One of them recently lost her husband and decided on this to raise money for the Marie Curie Foundation. She seems hell-bent on grinding herself into the ground to experience the suffering her husband endured.

We descend to Dere Street, the Roman road encountered on St Cuthbert's Way. The imperious attitude of these Romans is evident in the way they built this road straight through a formidable range of hills. It crosses the Borders and ends up in Perth, the extent of their empire in central Scotland. Even for them control of the unruly Highlanders was a step too far and they eventually pulled back to Hadrian's Wall. The misty rain doesn't trouble us, but our flagging limbs need a break, so we eat our lunch supplies at Coquet Head.

We didn't expect bogs up high in the mountains, but it's the bogs that define the day. Three unlikely adventurers, more the inspiration for Jerome K. Jerome's *Three Men in a Boat*, than the biblical Three Wise Men, are unlikely heralds. One still has mud on his backside where he'd sunk in a bog to his waist. They tell of their experience and leave us to cautiously descend Byrness Hill. Debby has the worst bog experience going in the thick brown sludge to her calves. By the time we scramble over wet rocks into the hostel it's nearly five. Once we've showered I wonder how long we can stay awake. The 17-mile day was tough, and once dinner at six is called I know it will be difficult to make further meaning of the evening hours. Before eight I head to bed and quickly give up my grasp on 2nd August. I know all too soon another day and 19 more miles of trudging will present itself.

Day 45 – to Bellingham

We sleep long and at breakfast move like zombies. The four of us sit with the indecipherable contents of eight more small cardboard boxes. I promise Debby I'll be less critical of the food I'm given in future, but she knows me too well. Before leaving, I pay Joyce the modest £27 bill we four have accumulated for breakfasts and lunches over two days. We bid farewell with congratulations for her dedication. She has forged another version of life in this remote setting, one of great value to the few foolish souls that chase adventure here. She calls out one last piece of advice: 'Take the other path, it'll cut 300 metres off the journey.'

It should have been easy, but the simple route change throws out my navigation. On an obscure forestry path with no signs or visual reference points, the dense plantation makes route-finding well-nigh impossible. Half an hour is lost before we find a dour, hard-packed, flint-covered track through forestry commission land, much of which has been clear-felled in the past five years. Once the forest recedes a more interesting footpath winds off to the left. Finally, we turn our backs on the Scottish border and will have to content ourselves with England now.

We may have become footsore on the unforgiving flint-topped track, but at least we could walk on it without slogging through water and mud. We're now consigned to walk in conditions ranging from wet and muddy to deep bogs that suck feet downwards. At first we're fussy about where to put our feet, but once they are wet and deep brown, that's an irrelevance. We just plod on, following old stone walls in the search for a particular piece of stone to indicate an old property boundary. Wide open moorland opens up and we catch a final glimpse of the North Sea. It's one when we reach Padon Hill's Pepperpoint cairn and I ask two fencers about track conditions ahead. They smile at my wretchedness, 'It just stays boggy.' These men are putting up 1,000 metres of fencing in this hostile rocky country. Debby catches up and proudly announces she's walking to Land's End. The fencers smile again, 'You've got a wee bit further to go.'

One large rock offers seating for four and we eat lunch. We become transfixed at the sight of three sheep scratching themselves on rocks 50 metres away. Not only have our bodies become tired, but our brains, stilled by the walk, seemingly find such small entertainment fascinating. The afternoon fare is moorlands, more bogs and finally a walk through the heart of a farmyard and down into our village of Bellingham. The pedometer shows 19 miles for the day, which means 53 miles in three days. Stooped backs and lined faces are evidence of our weariness.

A small bakery draws our attention like small children to the brightly-lit windows of a Dickensian sweet shop. At our B&B, Ken brings us a pot of tea to drink in the garden. It seems kindness personified until I realise Ken wants to keep the stink emanating from our shoes and socks out of the house. Ken and Joy take two large bags of our dirty clothes straight to the washing machine and we head for a restorative dinner at the pub before the curtain falls on another day.

Day 46 – in Bellingham

The rest day we've dreamed of with nothing to do but blog.

Day 47 – to Once Brewed

The weather is lovely and the memory of a bad night's sleep is sloughed off as we start out along the North Tyne riverside path. The old brick bridge leads us across open land and up to the local radio relay station. Up over Shitlington Crag and down through a field where muck has been spread thickly, we pass Shitlington Hall. The accompanying putrid smell suggests a truly prescient person named the area.

Suddenly I am brought to an involuntary standstill. My eyes are drawn to the east towards Redesmouth and Countersspark Wood. It's as if my body is reacting to some instinctive urge. It's telling me to live here, to wake every morning and absorb this radiance through the rich sun haze. The way the fields are quilted into one another, the different colours of gold and innumerable greens appear as translucent as the finest gossamer silks. I just stand and stare. The physical response within my chest is overwhelming. My heart swells, body lightens and I sigh audibly, standing motionless in the presence of beauty. Here is deep peace and my heart pumps joy for blood. Eventually I drag myself away and move on, but I know I've just had another very special moment which has left its mark deep inside me. It's as if a voice is speaking: 'Keep walking, Keith – there is beauty if you open your eyes to it.' Is this what Ikkyu's ancient Zen wisdom speaks of,

> Every day, priests minutely examine the Law
> and endlessly chant complicated sutras.
> Before doing that, though, they should learn
> how to read the love letters sent by the wind
> and rain, the snow and moon.

The miles pass and we grab 20 minutes rest before descending into waterside country searching for a bridge to cross the Warks Burn. More energy is used up to battle through an overgrown path and on to a pretty little woodlands bridge. Now the track turns boggy and progress is harder still as we enter a forest. The feel of dark sludge coating feet as it seeps from age-old bogs into our shoes is repugnant. A familiar brown tidemark inches up our socks. No doubt tonight we'll make another forlorn attempt to relieve shoes and socks of their filth and putrescence. As the thought passes the rain comes down to drench us before we can get the wet weather gear on.

Tumbling out of the thick forestry plantation we find ourselves on Haughton Common, a remote stretch of open land bearing no resemblance to what we city-people call a common. One landmark stands out, an old drystone-walled sheep fold, now home to half a dozen trees. We make a beeline for it and shortly after two throw ourselves onto the grassy ground and proceed to lay out around us a cornucopia of Bellingham bakery's bounty.

After lunch, we suffer the consequences. Our body temperature has dropped and with full stomachs our weary limbs resist the effort required. The walking feels tedious, like we're simply ticking off the miles. However, we know there's something special ahead. At Rapishaw Gap we reach it, Hadrian's Wall. The excitement of reaching one of the world's great landmarks is somewhat offset by the fact we've joined the tourist route, now a constant part of life along the old Emperor's great edifice. We can see about 20 people along the first mile-stretch of wall, and although we wouldn't normally think of that as crowded, it's 20 more than we've seen all day.

Our final objective today is to find the Twice Brewed Inn at Once Brewed. Odd names that stem from an incident in 1710. General Wade found the local ale on this staging post between Carlisle and Newcastle so weak he advised it should be brewed again. And so the pub's name was born. Many years later when the village Youth Hostel was opened by its patron Lady Trevelyan, she said she hoped her cup of tea would only be brewed once and not twice like the General's ale. And so two otherwise trivial events have left their indelible mark on this landscape.

Day 48 – to Slaggyford

Debby opens the curtains: 'Look at all these lovely shades of light grey, a real cotton wool sky.' By the time our backpacks are on, we walk out with heads bowed under pelting rain. Within 15 minutes we're back at Hadrian's Wall. Like so much Roman construction, it runs dead straight traversing all manner of natural obstructions. This part of Northern England lies on a geologic fault line and high rocky crags mean our path constantly rises and falls. The path is easy to see but the endless climbs and descents make for arduous walking. Within an hour, our muscles tell us they would rather not be doing this. A deep pain in my right buttock is not a good omen.

It's rugged countryside and at Winshields Crags we walk over the wall's highest point (345m). The sheer enormity of human enterprise is impressive. Seven feet wide, on a ten-foot-wide base with defensive ditches alongside, it spans over 60 miles of remote unwieldy geography. The Emperor Hadrian conceived the Wall when he visited Britain in 122 AD. The Roman Empire stretched 1,500 miles from here to Iraq in the east and 900 miles south to the African Sahara, yet it was only here he determined the necessity for a stone wall. The 'barbarians' – known as Picts at the time, but soon to be known fondly by the English as the bloody Scots – needed to be kept out at all costs. The scale of this folly is remarkable. It was considered a short-term success but eventually fell into disuse and much of the stonework was taken away to build more useful farmsteads and roads. Just like in Berlin, nothing as transient as a wall can ultimately hold back a human tide.

We arrive in Greenhead for a well-earned lunch. I check the pedometer and see we've hit a memorable milestone. We've completed 621 miles from John O'Groats, equivalent to 1,000 kilometres in Australian terms. Compared to Hadrian's Wall, is this a success or perhaps another example of the futility of human effort? Our walk has had no effect on the world and when we are finished it will have changed nothing. Perhaps the difference between success and failure is just the mental frame we construct to judge it by. And does any of this really matter, anyway? Right now the most obvious results of our adventure are the pain in my buttock and the toothache I've carried for a week. Meanwhile, apart from hot feet, Debby seems to drift on serenely.

Whether it was all the mental consternation or enjoying a longer lunch, we are now behind schedule. The guidebook's gloomy prediction is for another six and a half hours' walking. We think we can improve on that, but given it's already well past two, the pressure is on. The afternoon now typifies much English long-distance walking. There are several large tracts of open common land at places such as Wain Rigg and Blenkinsopp Common, waist-high grasses and bogs of the deepest black sludge. At times, when weariness seems ready to bring us down, I think of others who have achieved far braver and more challenging exploits, and particularly the millions of starving, homeless and ill-used across the world whose lives are steeped in hardship through no fault of their own. We walk largely in silence just to get through this long day and finally tumble down onto a disused railway line, the old South Tynedale Railway, for the last mile into Slaggyford. It's seven and we've walked over 21 miles. We're exhausted, but our greatest concern is the shocking smell coming from our shoes.

Day 49 – to Alston

Through the skylight, I can see and hear the rain steadily fall. We're a week into August, high summer, but still England refuses to recognise it. The conservatory on the back of this converted chapel is chilly in the pouring rain, but the breakfast on the other hand is warm and hearty.

When we build up the courage to set out the contrast is sharp. The rain has stopped and the chapel gardens are full of sun and freshly-washed colour. The dozen white doves are not amused though and burble their admonishment as we walk through shod in noxious-smelling shoes. Today is a short walk, about seven miles, and because it is so insignificant, I've written it off mentally as not being worth the challenge. Every five minutes I look at the watch: *are we there yet*? An hour passes and in the absence of any hills there's nothing to get the lungs going or warm the muscles. We feel weary at every step; like teenagers made to get up early by unreasonable parents, we're recalcitrant walkers today.

The rain comes and goes and I feel annoyed. *If it's going to rain, let it rain without stopping and then we all know where we stand.* More importantly, we'd know what gear to wear. The rain continues to be uncooperative, showers gently creep up on us from a light drizzle. The first misty rain doesn't warrant the effort of stopping to don wet weather jackets and trousers, but imperceptibly our clothes become wet and then the rain picks up a notch. In a frenzy we remove backpacks and put wet weather gear over already wet clothing. We feel wretched, but when the backpacks are finally buckled back in place the rain subsides. It's the ultimate turn of the screw by a sarcastic weather god. I try to second-guess his next move. 'Keep the gear on, the rain will soon be back,' I tell the team. Heat spreads discomfort through the body from armpits to groin. I give up and in frustration take off everything to release heat and body odours. No sooner is the wet gear packed away and backpacks strapped on than the rain falls. Expletives flow involuntarily from my lips. Perhaps Peter's departing words before we left Melbourne were right:

'Keith, when you arrived in Australia, you were very proper. We called you the "Voice of the BBC". You didn't swear then, but your language has really deteriorated over the last few years.'

At approximately 1,000 feet, Alston is the highest market town in England. We arrive under a half-hearted sun that's making the stink from our putrid feet worse.

Later, in clean clothes, we find the village a delight. We buy tomorrow's lunch supplies before the rain catches us off-guard. Back in the room we drape more clothes around to dry and it occurs to me we've probably enough food to feed any stray Roman legions that may have been left behind at Hadrian's Wall.

In bed, I begin to think of the challenges just around the corner. Tomorrow is Sunday, a short day, but on Monday with full backpacks we'll have to tackle Cross Fell, England's highest peak outside of the Lake District crags. The guidebook says we'll have to go up over one vertical kilometre that day. I haven't been able to get this day out of my mind since we arrived at Kirk Yetholm. This is the day when an adventure becomes something else, something truly fearsome. Cross Fell is dangerous and in bad weather people have died attempting the traverse. This will be something far outside the comfort zone of my typically cosseted life.

Day 50 – to Garrigill

There's no rush as we only have a short walk. The important business today is to say goodbye to Kate and John. It's always special to be able to spend time with adult children on any occasion, but to be able to do so here, removed from all the day to day distractions, and engage together in an adventure is particularly satisfying. Such experiences are the foundations of family memories and traditions, to be pulled out and relived over dinner tables of the future. We don't intend to rush the moment. I insist John's final English breakfast is memorable and watch with admiration while he ploughs through eggs, black pudding, hash browns, fried bread, sausages and all the trimmings before giving all his Scandinavian stamp of approval. Final turgid coffees are drunk and then suddenly they're gone and we're alone again with our quest.

I scheduled the short walk to Garrigill to reduce tomorrow's arduous, long trek and this is a delight. It's hard to believe we'll have to scale Cross Fell in 24 hours. I teeter on the edge of confronting the prospect, but no, not yet. Cross Fell may well be our greatest challenge, but there's nothing I can do with the fearsome prospect of that peak now that will be of any help when we tackle the real thing. Whatever awaits us is not for today, so I cast the thought out. We simply press on along the South Tyne river with peaceful rolling farm scenery to each side. Occasional decayed reminders of the mining that took place in this area a century ago mark the landscape, but otherwise prolific patches of pastel-coloured wildflowers accompany us and their gauzy sheen lightens our path before we're engulfed in their fragrance.

Now my feet have stopped and I'm once again rooted to the spot. The power of mind over body is lost. I'm called to gaze at the distant hills by some force that seems to flow through me, yet comes from outside my body. Even though it's beyond my understanding, I'm beginning to recognise it's one of those rare moments where I'm suddenly totally at peace as part of my surroundings. All the human busyness of the world seems to have disappeared and I feel completely alive in the stillness. It feels like my body has become an aerial tuning into the wonder Mother Nature beams at me. All I need do is be fully conscious and present in the moment. Perhaps this is what Joseph Campbell meant:

> We are so engaged in doing things to achieve purposes of outer value that we forget the inner value, the rapture that is associated with being alive is what it is all about.

The pub is boarded up when we arrive and so Margaret our host runs us back to Alston for dinner. We chat to another End-to-Ender, who at 54 is cycling the route for the second time. He's doing it to demonstrate to his fiancé and friends that he's fully recovered from being in a coma for six weeks after being knocked off his bike by a bus. And so another fascinating human specimen is added to the catalogue we've compiled on our journey. The life stories people weave can appear stranger than fiction.

Margaret's husband Bob collects us and on the short journey back I find we've much in common. He's also ten years into his second marriage, lost his wife to breast cancer at a similar time to my loss of Barbara, and scattered the ashes at a remote beach she loved in north Scotland, called Auchmelvich. Not only had I scattered Barbara's ashes on a remote beach down the Great Ocean Road on the other side of the world, but by chance I'd discovered the tiny Auchmelvich gem and swam there a few years ago. Things get really scary when Bob and I discover *Local Hero* had been both our wives' favourite film. Once again I'm made aware of the richness of the stories and connections that await us when we take time to be present with our fellow inhabitants on this planet. Telling and listening to stories seems to tap the very essence of our shared humanity and helps us feel complete. As walkers, we move more slowly and can connect more easily with other people's lives in the same way we're connecting with the countryside we inhabit.

Day 51 – to Dufton (via Cross Fell)

Today might be just another Monday to most people, but lying here I know it will be more than simply 9th August. We've walked for 50 days to be here ready to face the biggest challenge of our walking lives. The weather looks good as I open the curtains, but I know not to be deceived. We'll be at the mercy of notoriously unpredictable weather on the fell. However, despite all my book-reading about it, I have no real sense of what is waiting for us up there that gives it such a fearsome reputation.

It's after nine when we set off and although we appreciate the relatively bright morning, I know there are no guarantees these conditions will last. It does nothing for our confidence to begin the day on a path called Corpse Road, the route all dead bodies once had to be carried along to find hallowed ground elsewhere. Within 30 minutes, conditions change and we're soon leaning into a fierce headwind. Fortunately, I have my gloves. Our trusty chief of logistics in London had questioned why I requested them given the warm weather down south. Now they go on, together with the winter hat, all necessary accessories for walking in the northern English summer. For two solid hours, we trudge up Corpse Road into a nagging bleak wind. Swirling misty clouds come down creating a heavy dark atmosphere that cuts the visibility to less than 50 metres. I'm fearful of what's ahead.

Of course, it's been far harder for others. The lead miners used to walk up here to live for a week at a time, in basic huts with a few meagre supplies and dossing down several to a wooden pallet-like platform. After two hours, we reach one of these former shelters, Greg's Hut (600m). Inside, despite my waterproofs and padding, I can imagine the wretched conditions the miners had to endure. There are three other walkers here, the usual somewhat gruff older men who struggle to believe a young couple like us could possibly be doing such a walk. Debby's youthful hairstyle has clearly distracted them and the grumpiest begins to tell stories of the mining history. He's written a dozen books on the subject, including his current work in progress covering the mines in this 30-mile corridor of the Pennines. It's too obscure for us, so against their advice we forge our way back out into what has now become a pea-souper, thick-white and without form. The clouds have painted out our world and a white abyss swallows us.

The visibility is no more than 20 metres and closing in. We continue to climb into a fierce wind along a path that's become a mere goat track. We're looking for a rough stone cairn, the marker where we're to turn off to the summit. A modest cairn materialises, but on the wrong side of the track. This is not good. The signage on the Pennine Way has been unreliable so far, however, never would there be a more critical decision to take than the one that now confronts me. A mistake in this place and these conditions could have terrible consequences. Is this our cairn? I pore over the map and what little hillside I can see ahead. For the first time I take out the compass in earnest. I've carried it all these weeks and sense this will be a defining moment on the quest.

I feel fear welling up inside but know I must suppress it. I need to be able to rely on a clear mind to find the path without eyesight, using only compass and map. With that, I become aware of something odd happening inside me. My body surges with conflicting emotions, but my mind is demanding complete authority to act. There's an inner battle for supremacy raging within me the like of which I've never experienced before. It's as if my intellectual self is in combat with my emotional self. I think of the many people over the years who've died in this inhospitable place and how I'm not renowned for my practical skills. Any reputation I may have was earned behind a desk, yet here I am desperately trying to reach a connection with the hard earth of this mountain on which our lives could depend. I snap to attention, my mind takes control and, decision made, 'We'll turn here,' I say, as much to convince myself as Debby.

We head up over what appears underfoot to be open moorland with no sign of a path. There are three markers somewhere above us we'll need to find; a bell-shaped cairn 600 metres away, followed by a smaller cairn and finally a large cross cairn of rocks, the Cross Fell summit (893m). The ground deteriorates into a rough rock-strewn steep slope. With heavy packs we can barely stagger on. In these shocking conditions, I stop for a moment to take a photo of Debby to inject some sense of normality and allay her mounting concern. I step back until she is a ghostly outline, the visibility just eight metres.

We're now completely engulfed in white-out conditions. Debby is completely out of her comfort zone. She can barely control her fear and has handed me all responsibility for her safety. The buffeting winds are threatening to blow us over and we know there is a mist-shrouded edge to this peak somewhere close by. My Shackleton moment has come. If he could steer a longboat for days through Antarctic waters, surely I can do this. I set a direction, tell Debby to stay close and we walk blindly to a compass reading. The uncertainty nags away at me. What danger am I leading us into? The sensible decision would have been to stay back in the hut, but my ridiculous sense of a mission to get through this leg on schedule has overridden good sense. Did I turn at the correct stone pile? Are we walking in the right direction or simply wandering into potentially lethal oblivion? Sheathed in a white formless void the weight of self-recrimination is heavier than any backpack.

An outline of a cairn in the shape of a bell quivers, spectral and disconnected from the land directly ahead. My emotions surge in delight, but my mind takes hold to temper any celebration. *One down, but still two to go!* Again, I take a careful compass reading and set the line. We walk off into swirling whiteness detached from the world of substance we rely on. Other than the ground underfoot, there's nothing to see, no sky or horizon, none of the structure we live by. Then elation wells up, a faint outline of the next cairn is there, suddenly just a few metres away, veiled in mist. Again, emotions seek release, but fear holds them in check. There's still one more cairn to find. My body shakes with emotion; it still cannot trust the work of a logical calculating mind to reach this summit. The next line is set while I force myself to ignore my disturbed body's sense of impending calamity.

'There it is, Debby, right where I'd plotted it!'

I can't hold myself back from kissing the Cross Fell summit cairn while Debby clambers up and stands on it, raising her sticks high. We couldn't feel more elated than if we'd scaled Everest. The emotional maelstrom of walking into danger amidst thick fog only to arrive here with an amazing sense of achievement, euphoria and relief, and all the while ensnared in the turmoil of an internal battle, is beyond anything I've known.

Elation quickly subsides now as I realise we're left with the very real challenge of getting back down. We might have reached the summit, but we have to scale three further peaks before we can get off this mountain. We grab a quick snack from our back-packs sheltering behind a cairn marker. However, we take no more than ten minutes because I know we need the energy boost from the food but cannot afford the energy-sapping effect of standing in the driving freezing damp wind.

In the same fashion we found Cross Fell we push on. Two more cairns have to be picked out of the ephemeral landscape and then after crossing a rocky ledge, a path found to the next and final peak. And so, the next two hours focuses our minds, drains our emotions and exhausts our limbs. We do scale Little Dun Fell (841m), Great Dun Fell (848m) and the famous radar station that had been the last to make contact with the Lockerbie Jet before it was blown out of the sky. We walk on, often staggering, like late-night revellers after the bar calls last orders. We trudge through sopping wet bogs, and have to cope with ankle-wrenching uneven rocky ground.

Very slowly, we rediscover the world we used to know. One last peak remains to be conquered but then, just as suddenly as it arrived, the cloud lifts and we re-enter the world of substance and context with a blue sky overhead and a defined horizon. We see the Knock Fell 'Old Man' cairn ahead and know our mission is complete. The experience we've had up this mountain has been all the more confronting because we were removed from the tangible signs of reality we expect. Once our basic sense of vision was eliminated, in the cold wet conditions all our other senses seemed to disappear. After the internal battle that threatened to close me down, I already know this experience will not soon slip into the oblivion of so much of my lived life.

Safely down from the higher peaks, we can absorb the scenery with distant views across the tiny hamlet of Dufton and out into the Lake District. We finally sit exhausted at four to eat our lunch and try to make meaning of the experience we've just had. Our day should be over, but for once I see a Pennine Way sign. We dutifully follow its loop around to the other side of Dufton only to find ourselves at the farthest point in the village from our B&B. It feels like the day's final insult.

We walk up to our B&B at six and are met by the genial host who says, 'Hello, you must be the Badgers.' Immediately out from the lounge walks our friend Di, who has flown in from Australia. Of course, she has no idea of the experience we've just endured. She raises her cup of tea with a smiling face oblivious tonight of what she's signed up for. Debby's happy demeanour fades when she looks at today's map.

'For what perverse reason did you terrorise me today? We're headed for Land's End in the extreme South West, and I've just had to survive the terror of 19 miles on a mountain edge heading in exactly the opposite direction!'

Bed comes early, but I know however restorative tonight's sleep may be, the memories forged on the mountain today will remain.

Day 52 – to Langdon Beck

It's gone six and we're awake. For all yesterday's physical and mental exhaustion we must get ready to take on another day. The body's resilience is no longer the miracle it seemed a few weeks back and we fairly bounce down the stairs at eight, ready for a lively breakfast discussion with Di and other guests who include a former head of the BBC World Service.

Unusually, we set off under a radiant summer sky. First on the agenda is a 600-metre climb to High Cup Nick, an impressive U-shaped glaciated valley. To sit at its head and look down on the twinkling river of Maize Beck is considered one of the seven wonders of the Pennine Way. The walking is tough on stony ground that winds upwards for over two hours in a morning routine we tell Di will become her new norm. The spectacle when we arrive is every bit as good as we'd read. Memories of lavish animated documentaries help me visualise the mile-high glacier on its million-year journey to patiently grind through the granite and carve out this scene. Today a howling wind blows straight up the valley and although we find a small indent to gain some shelter, after ten minutes, our banana eaten, we turn our backs to the grandeur and move on.

The rain now begins to fall and the ground turns boggy. The excitement seems behind us and we settle in for a dour route march. The weather gradually gets worse, the temperature drops and the rain comes and goes in waves on the strong wind. We find shelter in the lee of a dry stone wall between the farm buildings and barn of Birkdale Farm. Surrounded by wet ground and in a howling wind I briefly remove my backpack, but don't sit down.

I try to lighten the girls' spirits: 'This is nothing compared to what some people around here had to put up with.' The trials that played out in these buildings were the subject of a documentary called *Too Long a Winter* in the 1970's. Hannah Hauxwell was a local woman who lived at subsistence level, relying on her one cow to produce one calf she could sell for £250 to cover her entire annual living expenses. She had no power and survived the harsh winters by putting on another coat. She became famous for her courage and innate wisdom of the natural world. The hardship she endured produced a staggering response from the British public who sent money and food parcels.

'However wretched we may feel today in these bleak wet surroundings, we're not doing it that tough.'

Debby shakes her head and tells Di about my British hardship fixation as we move off.

The weather gods decide it can be tougher and up the ante. The rain beats down and the temperature drops. It's far too late to put on wet weather trousers and when the rain becomes hail ripping into my legs, I just plod on and think of the tough times I've had swimming through the winter waters around the pier back in Melbourne. Just when things seem to have reached an exquisite level of wretchedness, the rain lifts its intensity again and torrential chill water works its way into every crevice. At this moment we're presented with the toughest assignment of the day. I've read of something imaginatively named, the Cauldron's Snout. It's the rock funnel at which water escapes Cow Green Reservoir and gushes down to feed the River Tees below us. We're at the headwater and have to climb down the treacherous slippery rocks by the side of this raging torrent to the riverbed. It's an unfair challenge for Di on her first day and looking down the side of the waterfall she's immediately taken out beyond the edge of her comfort zone.

There's no visible path and it's impossible to see where previous adventurers may have gone. Debby and I gingerly explore different options. Whatever fear we feel we know we now have a friend who needs positive encouragement. We daren't slip, if for no other reason than the insecurity it will sow in her mind. Di uses her sticks, hands, feet and bottom to gingerly work her way through fear. The sharp slippery rocks are a challenge, but it's her fear of heights that's so debilitating. Once we reach the river progress is still pitifully slow. We scramble over a boulder-strewn embankment with no discernible path. Eventually conditions improve. The rain falls away and the going becomes easier as we negotiate a final obstacle course of narrow stiles with our bulky packs.

Long hours in freezing wilderness have made it feel like we've covered a lot more than 16 miles. We're in a poor state, desperately needing to dry clothes, shoes, backpacks and bodies. However, when we fetch up at the only tiny outpost of humanity for miles to be greeted by a smile and the words, 'Ah the Badgers, we have some post for you', it brings tears to my eyes. Another small highlight is woven into the fabric of our adventure. Two letters with bold Australia postmarks are handed over. To know friends are still thinking of us and encouraging us on our journey brings a warmth no fire can muster. In these hurried days of emails and text messages, the craft of ink on paper mailed halfway around the world to coincide with our arrival at a flyspeck of a place is priceless. Before the evening wears itself into a torpid stupor, I glance down with a sense of satisfaction at the three pairs of soaking wet shoes resting quietly by the side of the pub fire. Only two other people are quietly drinking at the bar, but all is right with the world once more. Now is the time to sip drinks and chew over the day's experiences in search of meaning. The chill wetness and lethal slippery rocks beside an icy torrent stand in contrast to the evening's peaceful satisfaction of a day well-lived and tackled head on. Somehow, the extreme effort, discomfort and fear we confronted today has sharpened our sense of being alive. I take another draft of ale and smile; there could be no greater pleasure than to be here tonight in this lonely outpost. The yin and the yang has played out to produce a day of perfect harmony.

Day 53 – at Langdon Beck

This obscure little pub hidden away in a sleepy landscape is the perfect place for a rest day. We can simply rebuild our energy here while we gaze out at scenery that changes by the hour. Rain, clouds, mist and sunshine, revolve as if pulled randomly by some weather god from a giant dress-up box to clothe the countryside. There's no internet, so truly it's a day of peace and tranquillity.

Day 54 – to Baldersdale

Today is notable in the country calendar for a typically British reason. It's 12th August, known as 'The Glorious 12th', the day on which grouse shooting starts. Three men dressed in traditional English country field attire, plus fours, tweed jackets and check shirts sit at an adjacent breakfast table. We cast off thoughts of the senseless shooting of scatterbrained small birds by people who, from their fashion statement, appear similarly mentally challenged, and set off down to Cronkley Bridge over the River Tees. As Wainwright says,

> These little game hunters who measure their prowess with a gun would demonstrate it better with a walking stick doing the Pennine Way.

Our morning walking is an easy stroll along the riverside to the acclaimed High Force waterfall. There are a few sightseers here, more people than we've seen so far on the Pennine Way. I realise I've become addicted to the remote barren uplands and bog-covered moors and can feel growing frustration at the presence of casual tourists. In the wild landscapes I've been able to see beyond the human technology and artifice that seems to frame the normal world I inhabit. Whatever it is about this new world I can't define, but it's swept me up and exposed me to a richer reality.

After two hours, Debby takes time to soak her feet in the chilly waters of the River Tees. She dries off and the inevitable English summer rain begins to fall. With heads down, we walk for two more hours into Middleton-in-Teesdale. We pull out packed lunches on a bench in the middle of this small town, basking in a brief sunny interlude. Despite the relaxed environment and our happy demeanour, the potato patty sandwiches are unedifying. We throw them away and tell Di it's the first and last time she'll be given responsibility to order our lunch food. I'm still desperately hungry and eat a three-day-old pork pie gone grey around the edges. My stomach rumbles a warning. I don't know whether it's the sunny interlude or our general feeling of the joie de vivre from following the morning's babbling river and its abundant insect and bird life, but we visit a café and while away two hours in this village. The rain comes back with a vengeance and in full rain gear we march off.

We head in the wrong direction. I admit my mistake and we try again to reach the open moorland of Harter Fell. On the fell, I lose the path again and we double back. A little later, it happens yet again! Slowly we make progress and, crossing Grassholme Reservoir, we have the long tramp up over Mickleton Moor and descent past Hannah's Meadow to negotiate. The weather plays games and wet weather gear comes on and off regularly. It's six-thirty and still no sign of our B&B when I again take us down a wrong track. The arrival of a cloud of midges, or the English equivalent, does nothing to improve my filthy mood. By the time we knock on the door of Clove Lodge and fall into the arms of our welcoming hosts, it's nearly eight, our latest arrival in eight weeks.

Soaked, exhausted and with me grumbling through an apology about all the fundamental guidebook errors, we're enveloped by warm hospitality. It feels like our hosts have held out a large heated bath towel for us to step into and we're small children being towelled dry. Nothing is too much trouble for them. We thaw out in baths, and after a memorable late meal tired legs then take on their final challenge of the day. We climb up the one flight of stairs to bed. It's ten as we snuggle down and reflect on how many of today's 21 miles were unnecessary.

Day 55 – to Tan Hill

I arrive back in the real world from the deep sleep of the innocent, but mixed with some truly weird dreams. I decide to keep quiet about them, feeling a vague embarrassment at the thought of sharing the bizarre machinations of my subconscious. After all, I was brought up to believe hard-edged realism is the only worthy mental state. I throw back the curtains to expose this morning's hard-edged realism. Steely grey skies hold sway over noticeably colder air. All too soon, the inevitable rain begins to fall. Can't be sure at seven o'clock but this weather looks set in for the day. That means it'll be bleak on the moors as we head to England's highest pub.

Breakfast at eight brings physical sustenance, along with the sharing of some new life stories. I now hunger for these interactions which seem to offer a connection to the essence of what makes us human. I realise this conviviality is something I never consciously allocate time for in my busy life. There are two other guests, Amy and Nadine, Tibetan Buddhists who later today will start a one-week silent retreat. The conversation spills out to spirituality and I'm asked about why I call myself a deeply spiritual atheist. 'I think the need for a God is unnecessary,' I say. The French philosopher, Andre Conte-Sponville, tells a story in his *Book of Atheist Spirituality* about an elderly Catholic priest who came to talk to him after his presentation about a godless spirituality:

> 'I came to thank you,' he said. 'I enjoyed your lecture very much.' Then he added, 'I agreed with everything you said.'
> I thanked him in turn, but could not help adding, 'Still, Father, I must admit it surprises me to hear you say you agreed with everything I said. Surely you can't agree when I say I don't believe in God or the immortality of the soul!'
> 'Oh,' said the elderly priest with a benevolent smile, 'those are such secondary matters!'

Splendid subject matter on a full stomach and the discussion circles in animated fashion until Debby brings me back to the more hard-edged realism of the day and our need to move on:

'Keith, did I just hear you say you would be keen to attend a silent retreat?! If that's so why are breakfasts so long and the blog so drawn out?'

Duly chastened, I slope off to don the wet weather gear and pack for our next appointment with the outdoors. We bid fond farewell with Caroline's credo resonating in our heads, *we want people to arrive as guests and leave as friends* – a heart-warming thought as we walk out into the pouring rain.

This wretched day seems to infiltrate my very pores. We've been warned the path is vague and, in the gloomy conditions and heavy rain, even harder to navigate. I had an almost blemish-free track record before yesterday's debacle and I'm determined to regain my pathfinding stride today. I can sense the unspoken pressure of the girls' concerns for my navigational prowess as we head up onto Cotherstone Moor and across Race Yate. We hold our line well and despite ploughing through interminable bogs, find the descent of Knotts Hill pretty straightforward. The next moor challenge ends at a remote crossing of the A66, the only flash of civilisation we'll see today. I notice how uncomfortable it now makes me feel to instinctively grasp this word civilisation. It has positive connotations completely at odds with the concrete constructions that often accompany it's path and scar the landscape. Today this is a particularly bleak spot and we keep moving.

It's hard not to feel sorry for ourselves, drenched by driving rain and feeling footsore from all the bogs, but no matter I take out the compass, survey the scene and look for a faint track across Wytham Moor down to a bridge over the River Greta. Despite the wretched conditions, my line is true and a quiet glow of satisfaction begins to rekindle renewed map-reading confidence. We come out onto the gravel track leading us across the charmingly titled Frumming Beck.

Sleightholme Moor, our final challenge, appears boundless and featureless. It's cold and we plod uphill with feet routinely up to the ankles in bogs. The path is non-existent, but somewhere up ahead on the far horizon in the dark grey sky we occasionally glimpse the outline of a tiny building roofline, more House of Horrors than welcoming pub. I know this must be the famous Tan Hill Inn, located 528 metres above sea level and the highest pub in the British Isles. We walk and walk and walk and eventually arrive. This supposedly short 12-mile day has been spent almost entirely in bogs and we're exhausted, having taken just one ten-minute stop to stand in rain eating nuts and a banana.

Despite our dishevelled, mud-stained appearance, it takes more than five minutes to attract attention at the busy touristy bar. Once in our room, I look out the window and see what a truly dark, desolate spot we've walked into. For three days, we've only seen the one small village of Middleton-in-Teesdale as the Pennine Way has lived up to its reputation for staying off the beaten track. Looking at the scene I begin to feel an accumulation of tiredness. Lower back, right buttock, left calf, left Achilles, right arm upper and lower, and all the bones that comprise the weight bearing elements of the feet, all are signalling signs of fatigue from eight continuous weeks of walking.

Back down in the bar we sit by summer's obligatory roaring open fire and I sip a pint of real ale. The thoughts of hardship slowly drift off like the water vapour coming out of my sodden socks and shoes. Again, the travails of earlier generations put my efforts to shame. The pub dates back to at least 1586, its mission to service the coal miners. Hard to believe people were mining coal on this inhospitable moor back in the 12th century. The last colliery closed in 1945 and few now remember those times, although it's reputed the pub is haunted by many old ghosts, including a particularly fearful old landlady called Mrs. Peacock. I can't believe even she'll be able to interrupt my sleep tonight. Tiredness and full stomachs draw down the curtain on the day and we descend into the welcome restorative oblivion which any bed now so readily provides.

Day 56 – to Hawes

I awake after a disturbed night. Perhaps Mrs. Peacock's ghost was about after all, although my four o'clock visitation had more to do with the physical world as the half-rotten pork pie I ate a couple of days ago departed in a violent crescendo. Reluctantly I open the curtains. The dramatic moorland scenery is missing. All is sheathed in a dense white fog. It's more like a ski lodge than a haven for walkers. We go down to breakfast and the Tan Hill Inn reputation hits rock bottom. We have to cross the lounge room next to the bar and our senses are assaulted. A smell of stale alcohol combined with stinking body odour suggests a sad scene of jaded revelry. Naked and semi-clothed Rubenesque, bald men are beginning to stir and lay scratching themselves. The girls want to run for it, but we're trapped. The door to the breakfast bar is locked and so is the outside door. We retreat back upstairs just in time to stop two other disoriented guests who are trying to get into our room as the best option for their dog to relieve itself.

By the time we finally start the day's walk we have company. Kay is a friend of a friend of a friend who has heard of our quest and come to join us today, bringing valuable local knowledge. Walking out into the mist with Kay, I feel tired and achy. I certainly feel inferior to this remarkable woman who, though more than ten years my senior, seems to be effortlessly covering the ground. She is inspiring and a delightful companion and we're thankful for the chain of friendships that have led her here.

The walking conditions are bad across Stonesdale Moor. The ground is sodden and the rain falls steadily. After two hours we reach Keld, in Swaledale, part of the Yorkshire Dales, one of my favourite English national parks. We passed through Keld last year on the Coast to Coast trek. It's hard to believe only one year ago we let the walking bug enter our veins and infect our minds right here. Last year the conditions were freezing, but this time Keld appears in a different light. Today, we can rely on Kay's local knowledge and she steers us to a rare morning tea delight. A small shop that produces one of the best Eccles cakes I've had since I was an eight-year-old living within a two-minute run of the old Broomfield's bakery in Streatham Common. Quite why in this pretty, northern England village my mind has regurgitated that bakery, forever immortalised for their cakes and cottage loaves, is beyond me. However, as the rain falls heavily outside, we dally over morning tea and I let fond 50-year-old visions fill my mind.

A small track leads us up out of Keld, curving around Kidson Hill to the top. The rain continues and I look down to the Swale River below and out across the delicately interleaved slopes and hillsides around us. I feel that now familiar tug as the beauty of the landscape takes hold of me and I stop. I know I'll never be able to get enough. Looking across at the Coast to Coast footpath on the opposite hill running parallel, I know it was on that path when the tiny receptors in my body first became switched on to such joyous attractions.

Another two hours disappear before we reach Thwaite and a lunch break. Straight after, a stiff uphill track gets the blood flowing and the muscles warm. We keep going up to reach Great Shunner Fell (713m) by four o'clock. The weather has turned dry this afternoon and the experience feels strange. The scenery demands attention and we regularly stop to impress upon one another some view that might have been missed. The way the sun lights up a field in the distance, or water runs down to cut through a sharp gully, the sight of a particular drystone wall or even one of the rare breed sheep which have found a place in Debby's heart, all these sights and so many more halt us in our tracks. The Dales have been a delight. A showcase of gentle human influence that enhances the natural peace and beauty of nature's grand backcloth. Over thousands of years people have lived amongst these valleys, or 'dales', constructing modest stone-built villages and drystone walls to frame vibrant green fields and rugged-brown hillsides in traditional farming landscapes. Life may have been hard, but nothing feels violent or jarring about the human impact here and our walking seems easy in such inspiring surroundings. By six-thirty we reach Hawes, another 21 miles under our belts.

At the B&B I drop my pack and feel the accumulated tiredness surge. Our feet have been saturated all day and all we need is a welcoming host to comfort us. Instead, we get a woman lost in her own world, one she has framed with rules to defeat guests' needs. Right now, her rules are designed to stop us getting our clothes washed. With a rest day tomorrow, the scene is set for two days of frustration. The girls take control, and as Di whisks me off in case I should threaten physical violence, Debby uses all her persuasive powers to get a load of washing arranged. Later I delight in disobeying the rules to surreptitiously wash my underpants in the sink. This B&B is in a tiny suburb, a 15-minute walk away from Hawes. The prospect of an extra walk to dinner doesn't appeal, but the short stroll along a peaceful path by a field and down the side of an old churchyard works its magic to bring a smile back to my face.

Day 57 – in Hawes

Sunlight streams through the window, the air quivers and gradually consciousness returns. It's Sunday, a rest day, and I'm happy to just lie here watching the tiny threads of energetic squiggles and pulses concocted by my drowsy eyes play in the golden atmosphere above the bed. *Don't think, Keith, you've walked over half the Pennine Way. Just relax with mind in neutral and celebrate this tranquil moment of peace and comfort.*

EDALE
HEBDEN BRIDGE
M62
M62
PENYGHENT
MALHAM PAVEMENT
GNOME SWEET GNOME
GOBLIN HOLE
The WAY OU
TAN HILL
HAWES

Chapter 7 – THE WAY OUT

Day 58 – to Horton in Ribblesdale

Hawes is an attractive little town, but summer sun draws large numbers from the nearby industrial hubs of Leeds and Bradford. The day off has refreshed and energised us and we're ready to create new stories with old friends. Last night John and Sarah arrived and John will join us on the track today. They lived in the house at the back of our garden on top of Richmond Hill when my youngest son, Ed, was born. We were neighbours only briefly, but here they are joining us in Yorkshire 26 years later.

Once we get into our stride I can feel the early morning sun on my back. This has the makings of a day to remember. It's great to have a new companion with us. John brings a fresh pair of eyes to our quest and reminds us just how lucky we are as he comments on the beauty of a landscape new to him. We tackle Rottenstone Hill (580m) with lungs and legs alive to the challenge and then carry on up near the crest of Dodd Fell. Expansive views of Snaizeholme Valley open up to captivate us. The weather shows England at its best, and a cool breeze tempers the heat while the sun brings a golden lustre to our surroundings. The valley is wide and long and curves in a perfect parabola up the hills on either side. The gradients are soft green, like a massive playground, perhaps a skate-board park for giants and trolls. I can imagine them waiting for the anonymity of dark, when we humans have gone to bed, for their pleasure. Smiles never leave our faces as we meander along the ridge.

The sun makes a world of difference. The demands of the terrain are still there, but now we're on a long summer ramble, enjoying the scenery rather than sheltering from the weather. Debby calls for a ten-minute break at eleven to cool hot feet. The distant sight of the grand Ribblehead Viaduct draws our eyes. It was built during an era when beauty was a common element in engineer's creations. I'm not nostalgic for the romance of times past and the harsh lives many then lived, but I do wonder why so much modern construction ignores the importance of creating long lasting beauty.

This morning we've followed packhorse roads, tracks used for centuries to transport everything from animals and wool, to coal, iron, lead and stone. In many places they've become sunken 'hollow ways'. Names gain greater meaning as we move slowly through the landscape. Modern bitumen roads run far from here and these old byways are relics of another age, a portal through which walkers enter wide peaceful forgotten landscapes. I feel more in harmony with the world and our human place in it here.

We launch ourselves along an undulating downhill track to Ling Gill Bridge. On the other side of the 16th century grit-stone bridge, our path then follows the rim of a steeply wooded limestone gorge. On the Pennine Way another hill climb is never far away and this time its Jackdaw Hill. It's a mere 400 metres, but that includes a traverse along a drawn-out stony track that pulverises the soles of our feet and stretches and strains Achilles tendons and seemingly every other tendon and ligament in our feet, ankles and knees.

By day's end we've covered 17 miles. I'm weary and ready to stop, but the charity box someone has placed on the way in to our little village brings a smile. I have to support this charity, the sign on the box reads, 'It's not easy being a Badger'.

Day 59 – to Malham

Despite an unmemorable breakfast, the day starts on a bright note. Debby tries for the third time to call Australia with her British post office phone card and fails again. Time is short and my usually calm, unflustered wife is angry and frustrated as she comes out of the old red phone box. I try to help and suggest she has another go but Debby loses it 'My mind is full of exploding expletives!'

I simply smile and stride on whistling a happy tune. Meanwhile, the day looks a corker. Every type of scenery and challenge is expected on what is flagged as a classic walking day. Our customary early morning heart-starter takes us uphill along a walled lane where the imposing Pen-Y-Ghent stands defiant, its 696-metre lofty summit lost in swirling mists. A steep jagged dark grey rock path leads our footsteps ever upwards and slowly the cloud claims us too.

A full two and a half hours of climbing and rock scrambling brings us onto the summit. The view would normally be reward for our labours, but today we can only imagine what this damp shroud hides. We turn our attention to the challenging rocky descent. The Silverdale Valley lies somewhere deep in the white void below. The descent from this precipitous rocky escarpment is no child's play and Di is again forced to confront her fear of edges. As she does silent battle, we follow the chiselled rocks through to steep limestone steps. Gingerly we drop down through the mist and the valley opens up as the world we know returns. Wide untameable landscapes of tough grasses are dotted with random upsurges of limestone while occasional treed clumps and dry stonewalls purposefully attempt to delineate human boundaries.

We unexpectedly encounter a couple of day walkers in this remote setting. One of the two men about to climb Pen-Y-Ghent hails from Putney in South London which I briefly frequented in my teenage years. Immediately snippets of life stories are exchanged, the natural play between kindred spirits, reinforcing how enjoyable it is to spend time in the company of other adventurers. Somehow, we have more time to chat. This seems a contradiction given that walking requires more time to get to places and should encourage less dawdling and greater haste. Yet, time rarely seems short when walking. It's as if the seemingly inexhaustible list of things that we're conditioned to cram into ever-diminished free time has been let go. The frenetic pace we've become accustomed to consider normal, as deadline follows urgent deadline, is no more than a foolish addiction to the chimera that over-activity is the most sensible way to live in today's world. We've now adopted a much slower and less complex life pace, and in doing so our days seem filled with more time and greater richness and contentment.

We're now in the classic limestone country that Wainwright describes as the best walking on the entire Pennine Way. We can see Fountain Fell across the valley, our next challenge. Rising up from Silverdale the views grow bigger and the cloud lifts to give an uninterrupted view back to Pen-Y-Ghent. Halfway up Fountain Fell the panorama is so spectacular we stop for lunch. Debby and Di are worried we've still got a big climb ahead. I instinctively reassure them it's not as bad as it looks because we don't go to the 666-metre summit. When our climb stops a full eleven metres lower, I tell the girls I was right. They are not amused, but reluctantly acknowledge this second peak has made for an exhilarating day.

We assume that's the end of today's excitement, but this day refuses to let go. Down from the fell, the track's muddy but enchanting scenery more than compensates. The waters of Malham Tarn sparkle, a lake in a fairy-woodland setting. Here, the drama of the high crags and expansive valleys is replaced with the charm of an old wooded path where wild raspberries and strawberries poke out of the greenery to provide welcome tasty nibbles. Captured by the magic, we're oblivious to the sudden onset of a heavy shower as we walk up the drive of Malham Tarn House study centre. How lovely to think this was originally a shooting lodge but has now come full circle to be a centre dedicated to protect the flora and fauna from human influence.

Reluctantly we turn our backs on Malham Tarn, but walk off into common land with satisfied smiles on our faces. It's been a day of glory yet it's still not finished. Now the lush green landscape gives way to a dramatic dry stone valley known as Watlowes. Steep descents on rocky terrain couldn't make for a sharper contrast and conjure up images of trolls, goblins and supernatural beings scurrying around hidden caves. More delights from the day that keeps giving. And still it continues as we walk into another completely different setting. Now we clamber up on a giant cobblestone pavement of natural limestone that's been weathered away by eons of water moving over it. We're at the head of a vertical drop that's unnerving for Di and me with our vertigo. Debby goes to stand fearlessly at the very edge for the obligatory photograph. Waterfalls higher than Niagara Falls once cascaded over this very edge. We cross the grey pock-marked rock of this natural pavement, one last gasp of an adventure worthy of a week that's been shoe-horned into one bulging day.

A steep stone staircase finally leads down over a hundred metres to Malham. This day has been our best yet, a veritable feast of walking geology and scenery. The 17 miles lifted us up and brought us back down like no other. We were exhilarated and exhausted in equal measure and fed a banquet of the finest landscape Britain has to offer. Any one of today's six individual highlights would have blessed a day's walking.

We arrive at our accommodation in quiet reflective mood. It feels somehow appropriate to check into this old Hall with welcoming lounge, open fire, library and an honesty bar. It's from a different era, even a different world, as if we've entered a story where Frodo may appear on his hobbit travels from the Shire to Bree. After an enormous pub dinner, we collapse into the welcome embrace of sleep.

Day 60 – to Gargrave

I'm awake early and imagine lazy time downstairs in the comfort of the lounge with book in hand. Reality breaks into my reverie and I get up to make tea. Once we committed to this grand quest, all semblance of free choice for more restful daily pursuits was ceded to the greater demanding goal. Debby leaves before me, but when I walk down the hill of this pretty village to join her, the day brightens. Debby is fuming. The red telephone box has once again outwitted her attempts to call home. I try to calmly explain what she should have done, but all that seems to do is increase her frustration. I try to disguise my joie de vivre and focus on today's simple walk along the River Aire. The riverside track is occasionally muddy, but relaxing and peaceful. With almost no hills the short journey is no more than a morning stroll.

Three hours later we reach Gargrave. It's a rare treat to finish walking by lunchtime. We won't have to walk on a full stomach, so I order bread-and-butter pudding to follow my vegetable soup. For some reason, the pursuit of culinary delights from my childhood has become an integral part of this adventure. Markers of long forgotten experiences are being unearthed to remind me of special family meals. In this case a vision of sitting as a child at my nan's table while she lays down a mouth-watering crisp-topped bread-and-butter pudding straight from the oven. The dish disappoints but is possibly no more flawed than my memory.

Day 61 – to Cowling

Last night our journey's mum, Phyllis, came to join us for dinner with her sister Carol. Despite carrying a 20kg backpack, the logistics of walking week in, week out have been a challenge. 'Mum' has sent supplies as we've called for them and has taken care of the surplus and dirty things we've offloaded. Last night we handed over our worst dirty gear, including two pairs of trail shoes that have taken all the punishment the northern sector of the Pennine Way could throw at them. The evil-smelling shoes that went back to her from the Scottish borders are back freshly cleaned from a gentle machine-wash cycle.

We may be walking down the spine of England, but today we follow the bucolic heartland that's supported English stomachs for centuries. The landscape is populated with all manner of animals but no villages of note. In the absence of other distractions, the animals come to life. There are plenty of cows, occasionally banged up in a field with a wily old bull, and fields strewn with all manner of sheep experiencing various states of what Debby refers to as 'a bad hair day'. This is just the beginning though. There are apple-seeking horses, uninterested donkeys, and even free-range pigs snuffling and snorting through their plough-like snouts. The usual casual companions cross our path, indignant chickens strutting their colourful glory. The noble deportment of the White Sussex with their silvery black necks, hardy red-brown fowl, perhaps Derbyshire Redcaps, and a feathery fashion creation that could be a Dorking, betraying its Italian heritage dating back to the Roman roads we've walked on. Large numbers of ducks, in rich watercolour greens, blues and browns, leap lemming-like from the grassland into the river as we intrude on their day. And when we look down, out of the gleaming greenness, tiny frogs leap gleefully ahead. Are they scared of us, or showing us how to live life with more spontaneous zest? The girls are in their element and burst into a stirring rendition of 'Old MacDonald had a Farm'.

The only sign of industry today is the old Leeds-Liverpool canal towpath. A first-rate climb up to Thornton Moor is more challenging, and after lunch we pass through the heather to scale the grass-topped mound of Pinhaw Beacon (386m) on Elslack Moor.

Before today's modest 14 miles are done there's more uphill to negotiate, then a drop to ford Surgill Beck. The last part is heavily overgrown and challenges my navigational skills. At the bottom of a field in a higgledy-piggledy mess of scrub and trees, I locate the track and let out a cry, 'Yes!!'. Such are the small things that bring satisfaction and meaning to long-distance walkers. With that, we are through the gate, cross Gill Bridge and walk into Cowling, a rather depressing, old, drab mill town.

Day 62 – to Haworth

This may be a small house in an unremarkable street set amidst a grey lifeless town, but it has blessed me with deep reviving sleep. Today we must confront the foreboding wilds of the Yorkshire moors, so at least I'll be well rested. Better still, we're presented with a delicious breakfast in a tiny dining area. No matter the inauspicious little terrace house and its limited facilities, Susan and her husband are the B&B hosts we relish. Susan is a walker to boot (sic!) so understands our needs completely. It's a particular joy to experience people doing something with love. Their joy uplifts and energises us in a way the more money-orientated operators cannot comprehend.

It's pouring with rain as we put on our shoes in the small conservatory. The forecast is not good, the rain is likely to be our constant companion today. It seems somehow appropriate to be walking into the landscape immortalised by the Brontë sisters in bad weather. Jane Eyre and Wuthering Heights, the classic novels of thwarted passion and simmering unfulfilled lives, will surely resonate more strongly against a bleak windswept sodden backcloth. With Susan's kindly smile and warm wishes as encouragement, we head out into the rain, fully buttoned up in wet weather gear. Despite the conditions I feel invincible, a situation that lasts for about one minute.

From Susan's back garden it's a steep, uphill, muddy footslog. The rain pours down and with heads bowed we push our limbs and feel our lungs struggle to respond this early in the day. In these conditions it's hard to find the obscure route we need to a little bridge, followed by a steep uphill track used by shooters to reach the grouse butts at the top of this lonely moor. There's a grand sense of achievement when we do reach the top and a Pennine Way marker welcomes us back. We settle into trudging across a greasy, ankle-twisting, purple heather-covered moor. This is Ickornshaw Moor and a bleaker, more desolate spot in the driving rain would be hard to find. Meanwhile, I'm ruing the last rest day when I washed my wet weather trousers and removed all their waterproof qualities. It's hard not to shudder as soaked cold legs adhere to the sodden trouser fabric with each stride.

This moor is a long hard slog. One and a half hours of solid bog-tramping that seems to go uphill all the time. To encourage the team I instinctively yell out, 'On, On, On!' It's as if the rain has washed away 30 years and I'm back running with the Hash House Harriers in Lagos. Debby and Di look at me with incomprehension, concerned that perhaps I'm losing my mind. The cloud now lifts and the rain subsides. This feels better and we walk on through remote wilderness with wide views of purple, brown and green holding up the grey sky. The track has been indistinct all morning and so I feel another sense of triumph when the edge of a dry stonewall we've sought appears in the distance. This signals we have now crested Old Bess Hill and can begin our descent.

We've now entered Brontë territory. Tonight's destination is Haworth. Reverend Brontë brought up his three daughters, Emily, Charlotte and Anne together with his son, Branwell, in the old parsonage there. The poor reverend held out such great hopes for his son, but almost inevitably he was a great disappointment. Despite all that was lavished on him, he died early of drink and drugs. The sisters of course also died young and largely unrecognised for the books they wrote.

It's hard to comprehend today the different morals and standards the Brontë women had to confront growing up less than 200 years ago. In a time of male dominance, girls were certainly not expected to write influential novels. Even writing under male pseudonyms did not bring them the credit they deserved in life. Their stories were infused with the wild forbidding environment of these moors, and the emotions suppressed under genteel imagery. Another feature of Haworth's past was the high risk for people of contracting typhoid and dying young. Eventually it was discovered that rain ran through the hilltop graveyard into the town's springs, and thus the long-dead inhabitants exercised eternal influence on the town.

Haworth presents a striking contrast to other Pennine Way villages. It may no longer have corrupted water, but its essence has been corrupted by the popularity of the Brontës' works. The sisters' deserved acclaim has now come home to roost with a vengeance. Haworth is a major international tourist stopover. Thousands of Japanese visitors pay tribute here. Quite why the Japanese in particular come to scour such desolate English moorlands in search of Brontë photos and memorabilia is beyond me.

Before we reach the village Debby's weary limbs give way, and on a gravel track her feet slide from under her. She lands heavily on hands and knees. I help her up, bruised but fortunately no broken skin. Another lucky escape. This is our fifth straight walking day, about 70 miles of tough terrain without a break. Tomorrow is another longish day and I worry we're pushing our depleted energy reserves too hard.

Day 63 – to Hebden Bridge

Despite our tiredness, we feel a lot stronger and fitter than when we started out two months ago. One more day and then the luxury of two consecutive rest days awaits. While Debby showers, I shout to ask if she knows where my belt's gone. She assures me she hasn't taken it and then I realise my error. I'm walking around in Debby's shorts. My slimmer body speaks of weight lost humping a big backpack up hill and down dale. While I wonder if a new career as a male model may be opening up, I overhear Debby's caustic, 'poor deluded boy'.

Outside we're met by perfect walking weather, bubbling fresh air and a vivid clear blue sky overhead. The immediate hour-and-a-half uphill challenge adds zest to a day like this. Top Withins is our first goal. The old property's now a ruin, but still a magnet for Brontë worshippers. Despite no official evidence, it's commonly accepted this was Emily's inspiration for the Earnshaw home in *Wuthering Heights*. When we reach it, the old ruin feels soulless, and I'm more taken by its impressive companion tree. We've blown the cobwebs out of our bodies now and leave behind Brontë's fame-cloaked moor to plunge into a classic walking opportunity. The sun shines intermittently through scudding clouds and the relatively clear conditions offer 360 degree views under a massive sky reminiscent of the big Australian outback skies I love.

A kindly older Yorkshireman walks towards us and stops to chat. He tells us the walking is always good here no matter what the weather. When I mention my disappointment at Haworth he concurs and says it was once a real town, a place where people lived. 'There used to be five butchers' shops, but they've all gone now. Things have been spoilt by big shops and tourism.' He tells us people come from all over the world, but said the last couple of Japanese he chatted to had heavy Glaswegian accents. That seems to be a fair example of the incongruity of so much in this wild moorland setting. I've read our destination tonight, Hebden Bridge, in the dour Yorkshire moors, is considered the lesbian capital of England. What a wonderful reminder that the world is a richer place than we might otherwise imagine. Anyway, the affairs of mere humans can't distract us. The purple-sheathed slopes and moors roll out in all directions and every breath seems to capture something of life's essence.

We come down off the moor amidst some confusion over the correct path. There's a rare walker up ahead and I hold firm that he's taken the wrong track, the Pennine Way bridleway not the footpath. Small distinctions can be so important on this route. Our tiny path proves correct and we're led to a peaceful picnic spot set by two little bridges over Graining Water. We've dropped down into a small steep-sided gully. The determination of a diminutive stream is etched into this mighty landscape and is too pretty to pass up.

Despite the early hour, we stop for lunch and enjoy another opportunity to chat with a couple in their late 70's. They've come out from Leeds for a picnic, a tradition that appears to be an important but unspoken part of their romance. I'm impressed they can still manage the demands of the steep footpaths to get here, but it's also a reminder that even at such peaceful hideaways large cities are never far away in England. We listen attentively to their stories of how things have changed over the years and how far fewer people now attempt the Pennine Way. When I say our destination today is Hebden Bridge, they can only smile and in heavy Yorkshire accents say, 'Aye, there's weird folk as live there.'

Lunch over, we bid farewell to our romantic couple and head up to Clough Head Hill (400m). From here Hebden Bridge is set in a steep ravine some way off to the south-east. The Pennine Way has one of its vague moments at this point, but we persevere towards Colden Water and onto a woodland path dotted with wildflowers and enlivened by birdsong. Gradually we're led down the side of the ravine and find we've eaten up the day's 15 miles.

The bright lights of the mecca that is Hebden Bridge are laid before us. The town used to be known as the Switzerland of the North, and although it has now been regenerated with an influx of alternative people, or 'weird folk' as locals call them, we immediately feel welcome. A fine café and an organic baker demand attention for afternoon tea provisions and then we sit with our snacks in the bustling town square surrounded by vibrant small shops. The townspeople fiercely assert their independence from bland global retail brands which so often drive life from such settings. In maintaining the right to do their own thing, Hebden Bridge seems to have established a unique attractive personality.

Day 64 – in Hebden Bridge

Oh the bliss of a slow start and a long blog. Hebden Bridge is working its magic on me. Regular flooding has not deterred the rejuvenation of the town, and with the influx of artists in past decades it's not hard to see why it won the 2005 accolade of Europe's funkiest place to live.

Day 65 – still in Hebden Bridge

Muscles and joints tremble appreciatively at the thought of a second full day without walking or backpack. Even so, the walking bug is circulating through my veins and consecutive rest days make me feel vaguely uneasy and restless. We saunter around the lively streets and I seek the distraction of a slowly-sipped flat white. Outside the café the hillsides look inviting. My hands seem to itch for a walking pole. Whatever I've caught, its call is powerful. I take a second coffee and watch the light rain carelessly waft in and out of the streetscape, briefly glistening under shop window lights before merging with the pavement's resolute grey.

The shops provide some temptation and we replenish stocks. I add one more book for the journey, but even as I pay, a slight concern flickers. The book is extra weight just before we tackle the last three days of the Pennine Way. These coming days include the infamous Kinder Scout traverse on what will be our last day. Most Pennine Way walkers tackle the route in the opposite direction heading north, and the days we face stop many of them dead in their tracks before they've really got started.

It's nightfall and I sit on the bed to look out at a scene of rain painted luminous black by lamplight. I pull the curtains to bring the day to a close, and with no particular god to pray to I can only hope the weather will improve. The forecast for heavy rain tomorrow can't stop my slide into oblivion.

Day 66 – to Bleak Hey Nook

Disappointment rather than surprise settles on me as I pull back the curtains and contemplate teeming rain. So, ahead of us, the three days reputed to be the toughest walking on Britain's toughest path and the weather looks set to be against us! I think back to the lessons learned in Scotland. As we enter England's famous Peak District in these conditions, we mustn't fight the weather but simply acknowledge its dominance and accept what it demands of us.

As we set off the rain stops and a flash of sun briefly illuminates the path. 'We're in luck,' I say, 'Let's get takeaways for the path.' Within 15 minutes all sense of smugness is gone. We walk along the Rochdale canal and the dark sky opens. Rain comes down in a torrent to make a mockery of three heavily-laden fools trying to look bright while stooped over takeaway drinks cups being watered down from on high. What was I thinking? One minute I acknowledge the mighty power of the weather relative to my tiny human life and the next I imagine I possess a certain invincibility.

Thirty minutes of canal walking and we arrive at the inevitable turn uphill to extract ourselves from this deeply hidden valley town. For 75 minutes with heads bowed we watch our feet trudge uphill. If the path corkscrews relentlessly upwards, so the rain drives down pencil-straight under strong headwinds. Near the top Di lightens the gloom. She steps down off a stile directly into a large, steaming, caramel-coloured pile one of the resident cows has recently deposited. This selfless act lifts my spirits if not Di's. Such are the strange ways in which friends can bring support.

Stoodley Pike (402m) is our first peak. As we approach, I gaze up at the defiant stone edifice erected here to commemorate the defeat of Napoleon. It's a bleak unforgiving spot and we have to brace ourselves to stand against the gale-force winds. The 37-metre monument was put up by local men of influence who were keen to have their names associated with what looks to me for all its grand intent simply like a giant phallic symbol. It seems rich men of the 1800's were keen to be associated with large erections as we have come across many of them crowning the landscape. I wonder if this desire has evolved today into the urge to be associated with fast cars with stubby gearsticks.

The call of nature flushes away all musings about humankind's unquenchable thirst for recognition. I grin at the appropriateness of simply cocking my leg here to mark this place of faded grandeur as my territory for the day. It's no mean feat to relieve oneself in such conditions. I learned my lesson last year in Keld that turning one's back to driving wind to face a wall is not a good idea. That day as the wind rebounded off the wall I got a tepid, salty face shower. Older and wiser now I avoid a similar fate. Perhaps I am acquiring true bushman skills after all?

The foul conditions persist. Our shoes are soaked, as is every uncovered part of our bodies. We continue on, leaning into the wind. We have to fight our way down from Stoodley Pike to Withens Gate pass before rising up again to Coldwell Hill (398m). The boggy ground improves slightly and occasionally benefits from the intervention of a slabbed track. Although there are inviting distant green views opening up across Mankinholes in the valley below, it's hard to appreciate them in these conditions. I'm more distracted by the loss of feeling in my hands as the biting cold takes hold.

We descend into the South Pennine Moors with more bogs to traverse. What a sad sight we make embedded in this unforgiving environment. We plod into a frigid wind, feeling wretched. Three reservoirs need to be walked around, all nearly empty. I can't imagine why, given all this rain. It feels an insult to think nature has provided so little moisture this past year and is now determined to assert its whimsical authority and throw down a deluge. And this in so-called summer! We stop for ten minutes after three hours of hard labour to grab some nuts and raisins. There's no real relief though. We stand forlornly with packs on rather than go to the effort to take them off and then have to hoist and clip the sodden loads with raw, unresponsive hands back onto aching backs. With no prospect of a break in conditions we press on. I feel miserable and start to worry about how we'll get our meagre food supplies out with largely dysfunctional hands in heavy rain.

We round the last reservoir and walk onto the A58 road. It's one-thirty, there's no traffic, and I'm about to lead us across the road when I notice we're 50 metres from the White House Inn. I'd seen this on the map, but expected it to be a farm or private home. In our miserable condition, it's like a mirage. The smoke bellowing up from the chimney looks and smells real enough, and the welcoming pub sign seems authentic.

'OK, perhaps we can go in for a quick break, but only 30 minutes mind, as we've still a long way to go.'

I find I'm talking to myself, the girls are already inside.

Not only is the White House a real pub, but it is one of the best we've come across in all of Britain. We are welcomed by a cheery landlord who could have been Dickens' role model for Mr Micawber. Despite my advice, I'm the last one ready to leave, a full hour later. Of course, I had some excuses. It had taken me over ten minutes standing in front of a crackling fire to get enough feeling back into my hands to get money out to pay for our order. Sod the packed lunch, I thought, that can wait for tomorrow. My homemade steak and kidney pie with chips and vegetables was the best I've had for years. Just before we leave, a shell-shocked individual comes in to stand by the fire. He has a soaked Pennine Way guidebook and tells us he's an experienced walker who's been to base-camp Everest but has never encountered such bad conditions. His ashen face gives lie to the very real fear he's experienced out on the path today. We wish him well and in sober mood head outside.

First we walk up to Blackstone Edge (472m) and follow a drainage ditch that's several feet deep and in full flood. To stray off the path into that would be truly calamitous. The sign to signify our southerly turn to rise up on the Edge presents itself clearly amidst the shocking conditions. It's a simple stone marker, the Aiggin Stone, put here 600 years ago as a guide for travellers like ourselves. Sure of our path, we carry on up to the peak. The rain and wind continue to buffet us but it's the endless boggy conditions underfoot that do more to slow our progress. By now, we're less choosy about where we place our feet. We know every option will bring mud or cold water into our shoes. When I do stray slightly from the 'approved' bog into an adjacent bog the mud comes up over my calf. Not for the first time its slimy texture runs over the top of my socks to sheathe foot and toes. Just as we think the conditions can't get worse, Di calls out 'It's snowing!', and for a few minutes the rain becomes a snowy sleet. The rasping whiteness swirls around us as the wind howls driving frigid grit into our raw faces. Thank God it's summer – in winter it must be really tough up here!

We gradually work our way down from the peak, and as the conditions ease so we encounter something we used to call civilisation. It brings us to a dead halt. For weeks now, we've made our way through wilderness, isolation and the inspiration of Mother Nature's endless creativity. We've encountered modest roads and towns, but here the great industrial heartlands of Lancashire and Yorkshire press in so close it's surprising they don't engulf the moor altogether. Cities like Halifax and Huddersfield, Barnsley and Burnley, are all within an easy half hour drive, not to mention the huge conurbations of Sheffield and Manchester. Here today we bear witness to the inevitability of their demands. We stand and stare at what seems the greatest blight on the landscape, the M62 motorway.

The motorway assaults our senses. First, there's the acrid smell and bitter taste of the cars' constant discharge. Then the horrendous noise drives out all other sounds. And finally, the visual image of concrete and speed brutally scarring nature's patchwork. We are all struck dumb by the experience. Somehow, our human desire for personal, immediate transport is laid bare as a gross folly. Surely sane folk would not use thousands of tons of concrete to make paths for heavy chunks of metal powered by vast quantities of costly, destructive and increasingly scarce resources to typically move just one person? Yet this is the world I inhabit. I drive along motorways, so why am I reacting so badly to this one? Something has clearly moved in my frame of reference to let me see this reality.

We walk to the impressive footbridge and tentatively climb up above the din of speeding vehicles. I want to hurry but am quizzical about everybody's urgency. Most cars have one person inside. My accounting brain wants to comprehend how this equation works. Apart from all the money people pour into cars, I'd read somewhere that the petrol cars burn is quite inefficient. By the time we've drilled a barrel of oil from the earth's crust, refined it, transported it and filled our tanks, only a small percentage actually gets to drive the engine. And by the time we allow for the weight of the vehicle, only one percent of this precious resource called oil actually moves the human inside the car. So one percent of what comes out of the ground gets used for the purpose of moving us around in cars and 99% is wasted. Yet we risk disasters to drill several miles under the sea or use explosives under the land for our right to be wasteful. And still we cannot quench our thirst for energy. For all those years I worked in oil exploration I was blind to this. I thought we were helping the world modernise and that was worth the corruption it stimulated in the developing world and the damage inflicted on ecosystems. Perhaps Ralph Waldo Emerson was right when he said:

> The end of the human race will be that it will eventually die of civilisation.

For some reason right here on this bridge today I feel I can see the system for what it is. It looks like we're unsupervised kindergarten children having fun in wasteful and selfish ways with no heed to the damage we create. Heaven knows what it will take to reverse this trend of ever-expanding motorway networks and their flood of destructive automobiles, but surely something will have to change one day. We walk on and I'm troubled. What on earth can I do with these observations? I'll go back into this civilisation – my civilisation – motorway driving and all. Still, right here today it would be good to think that in 600 years the Aiggin Stone will still direct humans across the moor when motorways like the M62 are a mere derelict example of a period in time which humankind has grown up from.

Somewhat subdued and reflective, we climb quietly through the rocks of Green Hole Hill and up to the next summit, White Hill (466m). Despite our beaten-down condition, our minds refresh as the sky clears and for a moment we marvel at the 360 degrees views. We've entered the Marsden Moor Estate. In 1066 William the Conqueror first documented this remote moorland making it part of the 'Honour of Pontefract'. As big as 5,500 soccer pitches it was given to the Lords of Pontefract as a forested hunting estate. What the Crown giveth though, the Crown has a habit of eventually taking away. Around 1950 the estate came back into Crown ownership in lieu of death duties.

The afternoon is wearing thin and our energy disappears as we gradually work our way up the rocky side of Millstone Edge (448m). The wind is still buffeting us and we stagger on like punch-drunk boxers. The smiles on our faces are frozen in place, but we've lost the ability to make light conversation. At least the rain has stopped. We plod on through ground that alternates from boggy, energy-sapping land, to foot and knee straining rocks. A too-casual step and I slip over in a bog. The full weight of the backpack presses down on my extended left calf and back muscles. No major damage done, but I'm now experienced enough to know I'll be feeling the effects for days. It's the fag end of the day and my search for the bridleway to signify release from the day's travails becomes desperate. Relief from the Pennine Way's grip is elusive and with my pathfinding confidence shot I foolishly lead the girls on an ungainly scramble down goat tracks from the edge to our night's rest.

Immediately the door opens I know we've made a wise choice. There's no better summer welcome hereabouts than the blast from a central heating system on full. The aches and pains embedded deep in weary bodies from footslogging across 19 miles of tough terrain for eight and a half hours with just a one-hour break, immediately begin to ease. I feel embarrassed as tears fill my eyes. Just the thought of stopping and letting go makes my usual stiff upper lip become somewhat wobbly. Our host Eric says he's working on a roast turkey feast. I couldn't believe such pleasure could await us after all we've endured. I give silent thanks for the English obsession with potatoes. Eric says the turkey will be accompanied by three vegetables plus three potato dishes, mashed, roast and garlic sweet.

The cold and grime gently oozes from our bodies under the hot shower's exquisite embrace. Black sopping shoes are placed on radiators and then we settle in for a convivial evening of conversation. Eric tells us stories of two couples who have given up walking the Pennine Way in today's atrocious conditions. Another Australian Pennine Way walker, Harry, is here tonight and threatening to quit in the morning after just two days heading north. He's another experienced walker who's been to the Himalayas, yet has never experienced conditions like today. The look of fear is barely disguised as he shivers and explains he'd had to ford a freezing stream up to his waist. Di looks on horrified – that's our path tomorrow.

Before sleep whisks me off to calmer pastures, I think about the idea women have only received emancipation in the last 100 years. It seems farcical when I think about the couple of wonderful impressive women who walk with me. In creating this quest, I had no idea how brutal the conditions would be. Yet Debby has endured it all for weeks now, while Di has fought through fear and the raw elements into her third week. They've been resolute, uncomplaining and an inspiration.

Day 67 – to Torside

With trepidation I peer out of the window. The elements look subdued, some blue sky, but more importantly, no rain. We shoulder our packs at nine and with just two Pennine Way days left I choose to ignore all the body's minor aches and strains. Our first challenge is to negotiate a path around six reservoirs. With the weather in a rare kindly mood, we enjoy the peace and tranquillity following Blakeley Clough stream. On many days as we've battled through foul weather, cold, drenched and immersed in a forbidding environment, that hard edge of fear has lurked, close by but unspoken. What if I fall and break something, become physically exhausted, or get lost, what then? How different our thoughts today.

The degree of difficulty of a day's walk is determined largely by other things than the distance. The terrain underfoot plays a big part and today the ground conditions are our main concern. Every step goes either up or down, there's no level ground to be had. Worse still, most steps try to go up and down at the same time. We walk on rocky paths or in deep bogs, even on rough stone slabs that have half sunk or disappeared entirely under water. The foot's challenge is to not slip or snap under conflicting pressures, but to find balance and purchase to take the body's load. We often say we're taking this adventure one step at a time, and today I'm aware of every one.

The tortuous track grinds us down and the morning slowly wears away. Numerous river crossings require successive sharp descents and ascents. We head up to scale Black Hill (582m) and finally England's biggest county, Yorkshire, is behind us. One day I'll come back for more. My Mum was born in Leeds and would have been pleased to know I've come this close to her roots. Now Derbyshire is before us, home of the Peak District National Park. The change of man-made boundaries seems once again inconsequential. Our path continues with miserable, uneven ground, comprised largely of rich black peat bogs with some slabbing. A 25-minute lunch break is all I allow to eat the food that should have been yesterday's picnic. We just sit on a wet hillock by the side of our bog, but despite the crude situation, we're happy. The morning blue sky tempted me to wear shorts and as I eat, various insects enjoy lunching on my legs.

The afternoon meanderings lead us to a point where magnificent far-reaching views reward our exertions. The green and brown hues under cloudy skies are not remarkable in themselves, but the land below lies prettily folded into itself and at peace. We're high up, above Crowden Great Brook valley and I feel that now familiar sensation of spontaneous joy spreading through me. Ten weeks ago I would have been embarrassed to own up to it and I still don't understand what's happening. The difference is now I don't need to. I'm ready to just breathe into it and feel the unadulterated pleasure. I sense my body has instinctively found a way to connect me more deeply to my surroundings. Like the rush of emotions when I swim through sparkling water, my spirits are lifted on a natural high.

The view continues to be a welcome distraction from the challenges of the boggy, unforgiving terrain. A narrow track now directs us along the towering edge of Laddow Rocks. The grandeur of this vast valley rivals that of High Cup Nick we scaled on Di's first day. That was nearly three weeks ago but it's from another lifetime. Di has to face up to her vertigo again as the rough, narrow track precariously skirts a steep drop. We know she must tackle such inner turmoil alone, so as she bravely battles on we push ahead but never lose her from our sight.

It's five by the time we come out into a small forestry plantation, round Torside Reservoir, climb the last incline across a field, and reach tonight's stop. We've walked another 16 miles over eight hours and are done in. The rough terrain punished our bodies, but at least the weather was kinder than yesterday. James, our B&B host, greets us with the immediate uncalled for information that tomorrow's challenge is far tougher than we've faced today.

Day 68 – to Edale

The room's hot and we sleep poorly. It's early, but I give up on the night. A fuzzy headache and weary body can't block out the feeling of exhilaration of being alive today. The day has taken on a special aura, another day of challenge to my former settled orderly life. I turn on the kettle and pull back the curtains to see what nature will be doing to assist or obstruct us. Of course, this is the way it had to end. Behind the glass, torrential rain driven from low clouds by gusting winds obscures the horizon. It looks like a demoralised ski field, bereft of snow. In some bizarre way it seems so right for the Pennine Way to say goodbye in this fashion.

We go down for breakfast at eight sharp with bags packed ready to go. Everybody has told us today's leg to Edale is the most difficult. The guidebook confirms it as notoriously tough, not just physically, but also to navigate a path through the moor's stinking black peat bogs. Our host does his best to unnerve us:

'One walker got so lost he was a full seven miles off the track when he was found and brought out.'

He says walking is not advised in atrocious conditions like today. Even our hero, Wainwright, waited for four days in Edale for the rain to subside, and when it didn't he gave up and went home without walking. We don't have that luxury.

Before we leave our host tells us to avoid the first section along the busy B-road by walking across the field opposite. We take his advice and immediately struggle. There's no recognisable track and we're at risk of ankle injury with every footstep. The ground is rough, occasionally boggy and covered by thick grass clumps, hidden mounds and animal burrows. I feel a presentiment our quest could unravel right here in the first hour. We slog on with extreme caution and finally re-join the official track. We've used up far more energy and time than we should, but we're unharmed.

Now we have a sharp climb in strong winds and intermittent rain. From the top of Clough Edge (440m) a long walk along a tiny track follows the very edge of a sharp drop to Wildboar Grain. Di's vertigo slows her progress and I'm the first to reach the point where a wide panorama back to Torside opens up. I stop and stare and by the time the girls arrive the childish smile on my face is in sharp contrast to Di's where the trauma of the edge is still writ large. Now we drop down and into the depths of the black peat mire for which this area is famous. It's no comfort to know peat is a precious natural resource. It's 80 percent water and most of that seems to pass through my shoes! Almost immediately I take an awkward step and wrench an already weakened left calf muscle. My backpack grinds down and Debby hears me groan in the attempt to stand up. This is another worry to carry on a formidable day like today. Out here, I'll just have to get on with it, but I know Debby will carry her concern for me as an extra burden.

The route-finding challenge is steadily becoming more difficult in this wilderness area. Eventually it dawns on me we're hopelessly off track into a featureless black mire. It's totally unforgiving and there are no distinguishing features to help regain our path. The girls look worried and leave me to get focussed on the challenge in hand. I feel the perspiration creep across my body. It's not the sweat of effort but the fear of danger. I'm determined not to succumb to defeat and the indignity of being picked up off the moor. Yet somehow, I must turn off my combative ego's outrage and switch to a calm mind to get back in control.

This area takes peat bogs to a whole new level. I had no idea of such route-finding difficulty until today's immersion. Firstly, every step requires more exertion. As one foot sinks ever deeper in the mire seeking purchase, so the other has to be hauled out against the mighty suction of a creature from the deep. Here, high on the moor, the peat has formed large channels due to water runoff. The channels are eight to ten feet deep, going in no clear direction, and I'm at the bottom. With no visibility beyond the black greasy walls, I try to quell the feelings of intimidation and fear that the situation is hopeless. I tell myself I've used the compass successfully before and press on. After what seems an eternity I see the stone cairn with a wooden stake denoting Bleaklow Head (633m) – we're back on the Pennine Way.

I'm determined to hold things together now and follow the track more carefully. My muscle strain is playing up and the thought of extraneous energy-sapping challenges is the last thing any of us need.

Every mile or so old stone markers appear low down on the ground and I pay close attention. The going is tough in the wind and rain, but eventually we come out of the worst of the miserable wilderness to see the A57 Snake Road cutting across the landscape ahead.

Spontaneously we start singing songs to keep our spirits up. Once Featherbed Top is behind us an undulating path takes us up Mill Hill (544m) where we sit briefly for lunch. Digestion is not helped as 'Jacob's Ladder – The Reckoning' looks ominously back at us. Soon we're on its rocky ascent and I feel every step. My body hurts and wants to stop under the strain, but that's impossible. I simply try to manoeuvre myself at each step to relieve the pressure on my calf. I assumed reaching the top would make life easier, but it doesn't. The 600-metres-high Sandy Heys is not easy walking and the rocks alternate with more bog. This is nasty walking, but at least Kinder Downfall proves more attractive than its name. It's the point at which the Kinder River becomes a waterfall. We're tired, but there's still three hours to go and high up here the scenery is more uplifting. We draw raw energy from the pure air filling our lungs as we look out across the infamous Kinder Scout into sculptured valleys beyond.

The day's final ascent of Kinder Low (633m) brings us to the beginning of our descent from the moors. We cross the Edale Rocks to Edale Cross and then tackle a steep drop down the rocky staircase called Jacob's Ladder. We regroup at the little bridge over the stream with a growing sense of emotion. We're nearly there! A footpath leads us through the welcome simplicity of farmyards and open cultivated fields. Soon we're at Upper Booth and our ultimate destination, Edale, lays waiting. Rather than just today's end it feels more momentous. It feels like the end of an immersion in a different life.

It's five and we're here outside The Old Nag's Head pub. We've done it; our Pennine Way is complete. There is tiredness beyond measure, our bodies seem to ache all over, but also a deep well of satisfaction has been filled. During the past 26 days we've walked

331 miles to complete our Pennine Way. The distance is further than I'd imagined due to losing the way at times and all the logistical walking to reach accommodation and restock supplies. Right now one final challenge awaits, navigating our way to the obscure B&B we've chosen. A couple of abortive attempts frustrate us before we find the shambles that is to be our home this evening. As recompense, we steep weary bodies in the welcome bathtub.

As I soak my aches, I gain an insight of the typical clarity offered by hindsight. I'd come to the Pennine Way quite unprepared for what I was about to engage in. It had indeed proven very tough. Along the hundreds of miles we trekked down the Way, we were tested with all manner of terrains and conditions, including 'summer snow'. We'd been confronted by endless peaks needing to be scaled and for much of the time I'd found myself trying to locate and follow non-existent tracks through bogs. Our bodies bear the signs of the physical stress we've had to overcome and there were many times when we were taken out of our comfort zones. Sometimes we were scared at what we had taken on and we've now experienced our most frightening day ever, on Cross Fell, when our very lives were in the balance. Yet for all that I feel exhilarated beyond measure. I have lived life to the full and been present for every moment of the past four weeks. The Pennine Way has been a brutal taskmaster, but also a rewarding companion.

We get dressed under the familiar pressure to reach the pub before the kitchen closes. At the Old Nag's Head, Debby and I feel we've earned two large malt whiskies while Di celebrates with a lime soda. I suggest we begin the evening by simply sitting in silence to each remember what we've gone through to be here and to toast our own individual achievement. A quiet reflection on what this experience has entailed and means to each of us at a deeply personal level. An opportunity to embed the memories of all those met along the way, the treacherous conditions, and to be thankful we've been able to endure all the challenges encountered. I take out Wainwright's Companion book and read his words aloud with some greater sense of meaning:

> You have walked the Pennine Way, as you dreamed of doing. This will be a very satisfying moment in your life. You will be tired and hungry and travel stained. But you will feel great, just great. There is no brass band to greet you; there is nobody waiting to pin a medal on your breast. Nobody cares that you have walked and just this minute completed the Pennine Way… No, the satisfaction you feel is intensely personal and cannot be shared: the sense of achievement is yours alone, simply because you have earned it alone. Others cannot understand. Indeed it may well happen that, returned to 'civilisation' (so called) you will for a time feel lonelier than ever you did in the wilderness of mountain and moorland… You didn't do it to earn memories, but memories you will have and in abundance for the rest of your life.

Silence falls. It's hard to understand the feelings circulating through me. We eat our vegetable curries with a humble glow of satisfaction and yet are somewhat withdrawn emotionally. The laughter and celebration I expected are absent. We're somehow chastened and more serious than I imagined. Sheepishly, I say to Debby I have a sense of having grown up in some way and become a different man. At the risk of sounding overly profound, the impression is heavy on me that just possibly, life will not be quite the same again after all we have been through. Perhaps the words from our Trailblazer guidebook were prescient after all:

> For some the walk changes their lives. Certainly completing the Way proves there's nothing you can't do once you set your mind to it.

Emotions deep down have been stirred up by the physical experience endured and I have no idea what the result will be. For now, all we can do is bring this momentous evening to an end. We quietly stand up and leave the pub to walk and limp to our B&B down a pitch-black footpath. The irony is not lost on me that in the relative security of this village with the Pennine Way safely completed, I finally discover a need for the emergency torch I've been carrying all these weeks.

I'm tired and get straight into bed at the B&B but before I can sleep something inside me stirs. My mind turns to my two adult sons thousands of miles away in Australia. I love them dearly, and although we've been apart for longer periods, I've never felt a greater sense of separation than now. I feel I want to communicate with them at this very moment. Lost in emotions swirling like the dense clouds on Cross Fell, I feel an overwhelming need to send them a text message. My mind is brimful of memories of their mother. It may be ten years since Barbara passed away, but it is as if I have now been transported back to that late summer's day in Melbourne. Saying goodbyes at her bedside that afternoon and sitting with her through her final night, I remember just how hard she had fought. Through endless operations and treatments, she had courageously battled on to live for nine years, much longer than expected. Selflessly she had driven herself with the simple yet powerful belief that our boys should have a mother while growing up. Whatever struggle I've endured on this walk, it pales into insignificance compared to her courage and determination.

I feel embarrassed as my fingers tap out a text to the boys, dedicating my Pennine Way experience and hardship to them and their mother. It is as if the memories of the love and laughter we shared are bubbling up from a hidden well inside me. Coming together as naïve youngsters, Barbara and I had grown a mature appreciation of what it means to transcend an individual life. We became an essential and indivisible part of each other. James often said we had had a house full of love, and I feel compelled to tell my dear sons I now understand better the suffering and grief they endured as teenagers during their mum's illness. They had had to cope with the loss of this wonderful mother and face the challenge to find their life paths far too early.

Looking at the text I've written it seems too emotional. My male ego and British stiff upper lip urges me to leave it as a draft tonight and reconsider the wisdom of sending it in the cold light of morning. However, right here tonight it is as if some other less rational person is in control, someone compelled to act. I watch helplessly as a finger, over which I have no control, pushes the send button. With that, exhaustion finally carries me off to the oblivion I seek.

Day 69 – to Hope

Despite all my body's endured, the morning comes early. By five sleep has deserted me and I get up to the reassurance of daily ritual, tea leaves in hot water. The Pennine Way may be behind me, but my mind's full of it and I return to bed to write up the diary. I look at the bank pages, but my mind resists. I keep thinking of those texts I sent last night. What was it that compelled me to send the emotion-charged messages? What will the boys think? Perhaps a shower will clear my head. I swing my feet once more onto the chilly stone slabs. Before I can galvanise myself into action, I sense my body has other intentions. Sitting on the side of the bed something strange begins to happen. For some reason completely obscure to my thinking mind, I convulse in an emotional outpouring. Without prior warning, I start to sob. Not just shedding a tear of sadness, no, this is uncontrollable weeping, as if the elemental forces of nature have consumed me. As my body shakes and tears cover my face Debby tries to comfort me and asks what's happening. I have no idea. I cannot speak, and simply shake my head in mystified confusion.

Is this the work of the Pennine Way? Has something infiltrated my body as I trudged through that unrelenting black peat? My body become bog, the dark mire of pain and suffering hidden deep within, bubbling to the surface to be worked through? My mind is now full of the grief of Barbara's passing. Memories buried deep under so much vibrant new life have been unearthed. Her struggle and the pitiless demands all the family had had to endure to live with such a brutal illness. But why am I being called to account now in this torrid emotional outburst? Is this my own grief and sense of loss over my first love's death? Grief I had not fully embraced?

No, this outburst today seems more to do with my sons, and the anguish they endured. Not simply did they lose a mother but they were thrown far too quickly into the turbulence of my new relationship and a new home with three step-siblings. The Pennine Way has taken me to an edge of a well-hidden vulnerability. As each squelching thought takes hold, I'm at the mercy of different creatures rising from my depths to suck and hold me. I'm being made to confront another demanding experience. My tears flow unchecked and I can do nothing but relinquish all control to the greater forces released from within. This is unfamiliar territory, my bearings are all askew, no compass can guide me today. Somehow, I understand my head cannot find the direction I need, only my heart can find the way. I mumble to Debby to go down to breakfast without me. A full half an hour later with puffy red face, feeling quite confused, washed out and embarrassed, I join her for breakfast.

Today we have only about six miles to walk before two rest days in a hotel, chosen as a special treat after the rigours of the Pennine Way. I know I need these two days to come down from my exertions on the Way and get my mind back in shape. Completing the Way means we've registered 870 miles from John O'Groats. I never imagined the maelstrom of feelings this would bring forth. A deep-seated sense of fatigue was predictable, as was the inner satisfied glow. However, the waves of emotional turmoil unleashed were unexpected. I need to pull myself together quickly. In a couple of days we'll have to pick up the pieces and start over again. I'm conscious however much we've achieved to get here, we've only reached the halfway point. Right now the thought of ten more weeks of daily exertion with this heavy load on my back is impossible to contemplate. Right now my only focus is simply the hotel down the road.

A little after ten, we walk through what passes as a village at Edale. There's just a single tiny post office shop and down near the railway line, a small tearoom. That's all that's here. Quite why one of England's most famous walks begins and ends at two spectacularly insignificant dots on the map, is a mystery to me. Of course, there's something so very English about this. The eccentric spirit, combined with a phlegmatic, self-deprecating attitude almost demands the creation of the toughest walking challenge be set between two otherwise inconsequential places. Some would say that in completing the Pennine Way we have spent 24 days walking 331 miles from nowhere to nowhere, achieving nothing and bringing no change to the world or anyone. In one sense they would be right, but I now understand why that would be so misguided. In moving at Mother Nature's pace, I've learned the joy of being immersed in a magnificent web of life. It's as if I've harboured an unexplored need to do this at my very core. As if the essence of our existence and bliss can only be found through finding a way back to the harmony of our place in that web.

A simple 90-minute walk along a back road under a rare sunny sky and we're at the hotel where we hope to recover in the company of good friends. Immediately our world changes into one of white tablecloths, waiters and relaxation. The time races by and soon it's time to say goodbye to Di. She's walked for three weeks. A friend beforehand, we now share a bond of memories forged in hardship that will forever be part of our deeper story of connection. We'll never forget her fighting spirit and endurance, even as I tell tales of her bad lunch choices.

The afternoon passes lazily. Torrential rain returns to beat against the window. Tucked up warm and well-fed in a place of luxury like this it's an irrelevance. All is fine until I find there's no access to the internet so I cannot update the blog. My mind turns as black as the clouds outside; even in these pampered surrounds we humans can't create perfection. I get out the pen and start to write longhand.

Days 70 & 71 – in Hope

Close friends arrive to buoy our spirits and fill our world with jollity and merriment. Dinners are rich with grand storytelling and we are shepherded into a private dining room to spare other guests the worst of our uproarious laughter. Temporarily we forget the rigours of the trail. On Sunday morning I awake early as usual. I lie quietly in these plush surroundings and think back to the breakdown in Edale. What pain was I reacting to? Freed from the search for barely visible tracks in the physical landscape, my mind is now in search of other tracks, those mere threads woven through the cells of my body and mind. I want to try to make sense of that outburst.

It didn't seem to be my own sorrow I was reacting to on Friday morning. My pain had ebbed and flowed over nine years after my first selfish reaction of anger to the deathly sentence imposed on my life partner. And how could I ever really know what this sentence had meant to Barbara? It was her life that was to be taken. She had tried to come to terms with the awful knowledge she had unknowingly chosen a death sentence when the first lump had appeared. Rather than face the medical profession and all the fear it represented, she had suppressed her worry. How had those dark memories of loneliness when her own mother had become ill and been whisked away by medical people corrupted her own decision to deny diagnosis for a full year?

But instead of giving in to the disease, she had known her boys needed a mother and so drew the battleground on which to fight her fight. And in so many ways she had been the victor. Not only should the boys have a mother, but family life was to be lived! She winced over the potholes of outback travel but urged us on regardless. And together we endured bouts of resilience and resignation as frequent as the moons had waxed and waned. The floods of joy and determination to overcome were there in all the splendour of giant waves of emotion that we surfed together. Barbara became a natural at managing her health and her doctors. Through nine years of successive bouts of chemo, radiotherapy, and operations to remove disease and then later to insert metal supports as her body's bones crumbled, she flourished. Throughout it all she was an inspiration. In dying she found courage and earned the respect of which she could never quite believe she was worthy.

But of course, when I met Debby and new love, it had appeared to be all too soon. In some way, that chance meeting just six weeks after Barbara's funeral, however blessed in providing entrance to a wonderful new life path, had deprived the family of its time to find closure. Father Nigel had helped me understand I'd lived with Barbara through nine years of life before death and my grieving had been done with her. How many nights had I cupped her ravaged body in bed, talking with her through tears before rising to bring morning bowls of fresh yellow mango and cream to a sun-filled bedside when this was all she could swallow? Over the final weeks I'd sat on the end of the bed to comfort and enjoy her while the vice of that merciless illness had tightened around her fragile neck.

The final tide of acknowledgement had brought a simple act of compassion when I'd held my dear wife and through tears told her it was alright to let go and leave her pain with us. To embrace her destiny as we would have to embrace ours. And then, finally at peace, I said goodbye as I washed and dressed her brave depleted body for its last journey from my world. By the end, my emotions had been scoured leaving me hollowed out. No, Friday's outpouring could not be my pain. Mine was all gone.

No, my emotion was about her boys. Oh I may have donated the sperm, but then as I had raced around corporate life, so Barbara had nurtured and raised her boys. Somehow, this outpouring was about them. To have their mother gradually fade and pass was beyond my comprehension. What did it mean to lose the person who is your life support when you are still to fledge and find your way in a world filled with the frightening confusion of choice and calamity?

And then, at that moment just when their life looked as bleak as a midwinter landscape, I had left them. Not physically, but emotionally. As my joy of a new relationship had soared, so they had felt the remaining strands of support stretching thin. Stepbrothers and sister were thrust into their lives to sit before them at dinners in a house that was not their home because that had been sold. A step-mother could care for them but never be their mother at that time, so they'd had to negotiate a lonely, frightening passage through grief to find themselves as adults all too quickly. I knew my quick embrace of a new romance had condemned them to further traumatic ordeal.

I had told myself my decision was right, and still do. I knew I was building a replacement family to bring them the secure foundation and sustenance on which they would be able to chase their dreams. I wanted to re-establish family life and the presence of a loving female back into their lives. But, in those months as the new millennium unfolded, it had been all too early and would have appeared ghastly and callous. Forty-eight hours ago in some obscure bedroom this was the vision that had finally burst into my consciousness. The tears I had shed were the tears of guilt for her boys, the loves of my life. If only I could have made their path easier, but life just isn't meant to be easy.

Swallowing down that understanding of the heart, my mind reasserts itself. It's calling me to contemplate the journey ahead. I know there's never really time to completely relax and do nothing on an adventure like this. Physical and emotional recovery from the rigours of the trail must always be intermeshed with preparation for what awaits. Finishing the Pennine Way means we are now once again released to our own devices. A route must be found across England's heartland, home of much of its industry and human habitation, through to the northern tip of the border with Wales.

Our next appointment with an official walking track will be in the Welsh seaside town of Prestatyn where we'll join the Offa's Dyke Path. I reckon it should take about eight to ten days to get there, but if I'm honest, I've actually got very little idea what we'll encounter en route. At least now we've got more flexibility with no pre-booked accommodation. Apart from worry about bringing the blog up-to-date, I'm as relaxed as I have been these past 70 days. My greatest concern is to try to avoid too much human civilisation. We've come to understand we love the open countryside. Given we're about to walk through Britain's industrial heart, I know there's probably nowhere in this crowded island less conducive to finding the conditions we seek. It is not lost on me that when we set out tomorrow we will be leaving Hope behind.

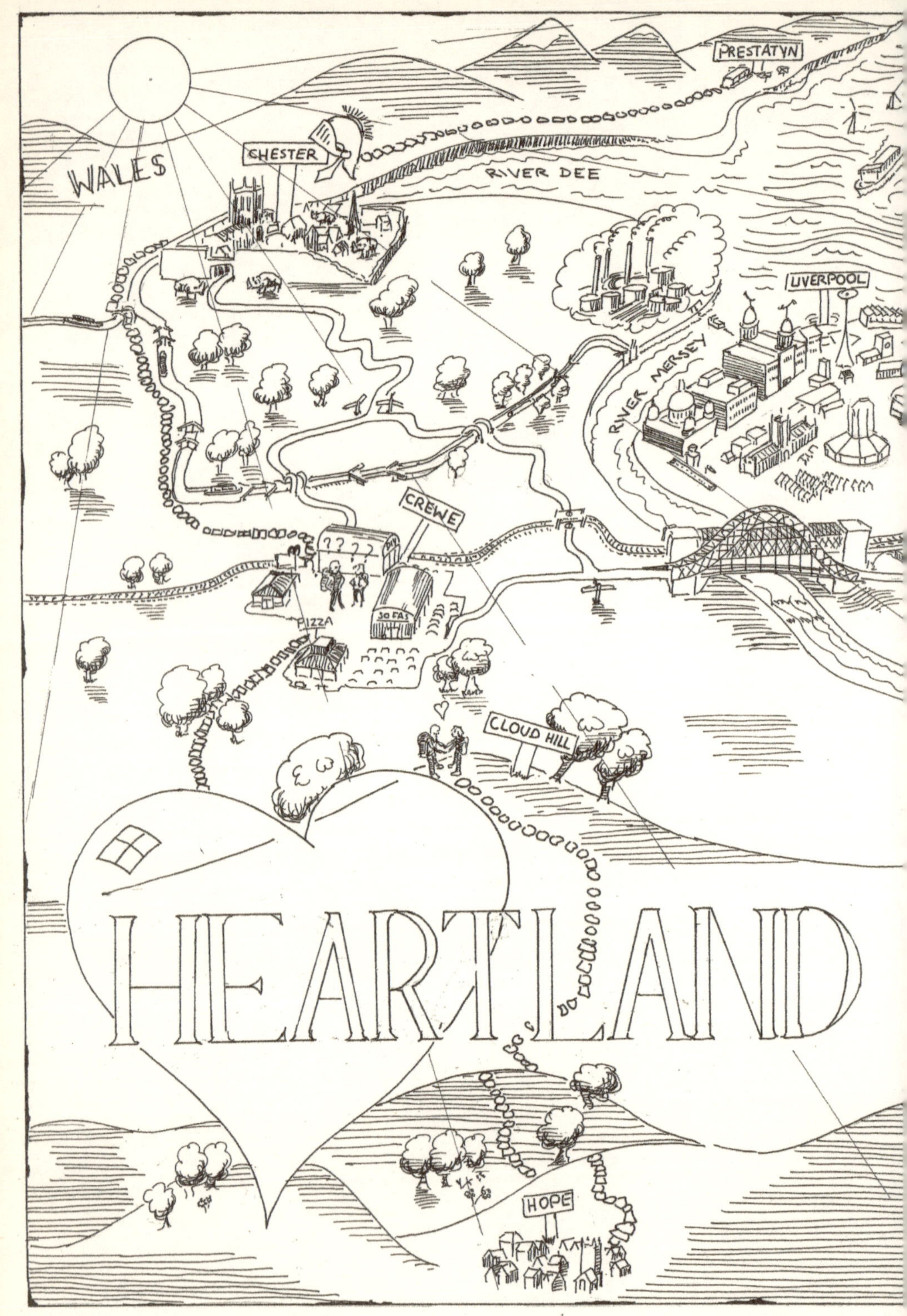
PRESTATYN
WALES
CHESTER
RIVER DEE
LIVERPOOL
RIVER MERSEY
CREWE
DIY
SOFAS
PIZZA
CLOUD HILL
HEARTLAND
HOPE

Chapter 8 – HEARTLAND

Day 72 – to Buxton

I'm grumpy after a poor night's sleep and breakfast doesn't make things better when I'm given the smallest portion of scrambled eggs in the room. Yet I'm the one who's just shouldered a big pack down the Pennine Way and walked 900 miles over the past ten weeks. *Surely if ever someone deserves a bigger portion, it's me!* I can feel the tantrum rising, but Debby adopts a mother's calm.

'Keith, you are special, but making a scene is not the best way to show it!'

I simply groan at life's injustice. I wasn't sure what physical or mental condition I'd be in after the Pennine Way and allowed for three possible rest days out of 12 on the way to Prestatyn. Based on my mood, I think I'll need them all.

We bid farewell to our friends and with sun overhead wander down a quiet country lane to Castleton where new companions await. When long-standing family friends were assigned to Formby on the Liverpool coast we visited and were introduced to their new neighbours, Chris and Wendy. Their names went on the Christmas card list and when they heard of our walk they committed to cross the country to walk with us today. They're experienced hikers and ready to lead us along a small footpath called the Limestone Way to Buxton. Chris is a confident navigator so I can relax and happily hand over the maps and reins of control for the day.

The track out of the village leads up by Peveril Castle, another impressive English ruin. Set high on a rock up a steep slope, it overlooks the village. Built soon after 1066, it was neither involved in epic power struggles, nor had to face down large armies under cannon fire. The wardens of the High Peak that resided here were more concerned with local administration rather than warfare, and the absence of a history of battle's gore and grizzle seems reflected in today's solitude.

Our path means a steep climb to crest Old Moor (471m) and then down again. As we come out of a field called The Cop, we take an adjacent footpath through a field with bulls. A mile and a half later Chris says we've incorporated the 'Derbyshire variation' into our route. He's lost the way and we have to backtrack. I can relax, someone else has made the mistake instead of me.

Under a blue sky, the air is tranquil and the path gently unfolds as a ribbon running through lightly wooded greenery. My mood has mellowed and we stroll along, bodies and minds relaxed, chatting, oblivious to the distance or undulations in the track. At Hay Dale it's well after two and we sit on the grass under a small natural limestone escarpment. Sheep come to drink quietly from an adjacent trough and in this simple setting the peace is exquisite.

After lunch we walk into Peter Dale where the woodland is a little thicker. This is all part of Monk's Dale, but the confusion over place names doesn't matter when our surroundings are so engaging. Chris is proving his worth, not just as a navigator, but as someone attuned to the natural environment. He draws our attention to a departing kestrel and silences us to listen to a sole woodpecker tapping for food somewhere deep in the woods. Next, we turn west through Wormhill on the Pennine Bridleway and then onto a tiny path set between two decrepit but serviceable drystone walls. No doubt an old farm access track, it's now congested with low shrub and gangly hawthorn trees, a reminder of farming byways of another era.

We know we have to skirt a limestone quarry before we can approach Buxton and from high up marvel at the size of the operation. A small little-used path leads us along the very edge of the quarry enclosure and gradually descends to the industrial railroad link. A formidable metal footbridge has been constructed here just for walkers. We're taken into a landscape completely at odds with our country walk. One minute spectacular Peak District scenery, the next a quarry moonscape. The contrast assaults us and we gaze in horrified fascination. The heavy industrial installation is an obvious blight on the vibrant living landscape, yet we hear the limestone here is considered to produce the best cement money can buy. Apparently, the Chinese are buying it with their ears pinned back as they transit towards a Western-style economy. However much this eyesore may offend me today, I know it's tiny compared to another pit favoured by the march of the Chinese middle class. We call it Australia.

The walk out of the pit is a long haul late in the day. Wendy displays tremendous stamina and confides not only is this the longest walk she's ever tackled, but it's her first since a hip replacement. The quarry falls not so gracefully behind and we try to reset our minds to the green slopes ahead. It only remains to press on along a small footpath through farmland before a gradual drop into the welcoming Victorian spa town of Buxton. Today's 21 miles has got the second half of our adventure well and truly underway.

Day 73 – in Buxton

Buxton appears to be a lovely place and it would be good to simply kick back. However, the absence of internet coverage in Hope means the blog is a week behind, so we knuckle down to a full day's computer session. By evening, our work's done and we head to dinner satisfied. This adventure is multi-layered – on the one hand the physical and emotional challenges, on the other the calm rational mind work of the writer. Individually they provide a sense of purpose and achievement, but together they combine to bring out a deeper meaning, something more lasting.

Day 74 – to Rushton Spencer

I wake early and immediately feel brimful of energy, ready to get to grips with some serious walking across central England. We may have spent yesterday's rest day at a computer, but there's the carrot of a double rest day at Chester in six days' time to urge us on. Our schedule calls for us to set out from Prestatyn in northern Wales along Offa's Dyke Path on 12th September. The route I've concocted to lead us there is something of a hotchpotch of smaller, less well-known and often little used footpaths. My intention was to avoid becoming embroiled with the large industrial centres dotted around this part of England, but the risk is these paths may not exist on the ground.

At first glance, there doesn't seem to be much in this fifth phase of about 150 miles that's of great appeal. However, the walk into Buxton has already delivered some terrific scenery. Today we'll still be in the Peak District National Park. Its 500 square miles are visited by two million people each year, close to the number that go to the most visited National Park in the world, Mount Fuji. Yet the Peak District still offers vast tracts of isolated empty moorlands to explore and for today I've selected the obscure Dane Valley Way.

Before leaving Buxton, I rush for a final flat white and take 20 minutes to exercise my passion at Scriveners, one of the UK's top ten second-hand bookshops. Here are 40,000 editions packed into five floors of tiny alcoves. I inhale the incomparable stale musty air before Debby drags me away.

The Dane Valley Way starts from a street in the centre of town, yet it's funny how finding it presents as great a challenge as those in wide open empty moorlands. Here I am walking past all manner of road signs on a busy thoroughfare with a big backpack and puzzling over a compass. It just feels so silly. From the paved streets we move into a confusion of tiny tracks through Buxton Country Park. Debby has a more instinctive sense of direction in these places of human invention and helps unravel the myriad intertwined paths. We leave past Solomon's Temple (440m), the highest point hereabouts. It was built in 1896 as a viewing tower and paid for by public subscription to provide work for the local unemployed. It seems we had a greater civic social conscience in those days. What a shame we can't support such public interest works today.

Now the path takes us uphill from Buxton towards open countryside. The sun is strong in a clear blue sky and the irony is not lost on us that it's 1st September. Summer is officially over and now the cantankerous British climate finally presents us with summer weather!

Our final destination today is south-west of Buxton, not much more than ten miles as the crow flies, although our track will take us much further as it winds along the valley of the River Dane. First though, we must get to the top of Axe Edge Moor (532m). We bend our backs and climb. After an hour and a half we're rewarded with wide panoramas and long horizons. The sun and dry weather lift our spirits, but we're still in the Peak District and that means peat bogs. We get wet and muddy shoes, but the challenge is laughable compared to the fearsome muscle-sapping mire we trudged through on the Pennine Way.

Now we're on top of the world and I let go of a nagging concern about our slow progress. The track takes us round the sides of several hills in what looks like an almost perfect wave formation on the map. We are following the contours around a set of hills and walking a long way out of our way. It's as if we're surfing up the inside of a wave of land before reaching a point where we can hop over the hill's crest and come back down its outside edge into the far side of the valley. It's mainly farmland, but we also negotiate waste spoil heaps from long-disused stone quarries. A few weeks ago I might have found this frustrating, but now I soak up the scenery and feel the relaxed sense of being alone and at peace with ourselves. Debby suddenly blurts out:

'I feel like a kid that's skipped school and I'm playing truant from life.'

We drop down to the beginnings of the River Dane at Three Shire Heads waterfall. I know we've still a long way to go, but half an hour for lunch here is too tempting and we cast off the packs. When we resume a narrow footpath leads us along a meandering valley and soon we rise well above the tiny tree-cloaked river. Drystone walls block our path and with no obvious marker to point the way, I lead Debby over a locked metal gate. This is always a dangerous manoeuvre as it's easy to become isolated on private land with no exit point. The going is tough and the land drops away into what's fast becoming a steep narrow ravine. We end up left perched high in rough sheep territory against a wall and I acknowledge my error. Turning to the only option left, I call on stubborn brute force and push through the thickets of snagging trees and undergrowth before climbing another gate. No damage done, but more delays and my confidence in this obscure route I've chosen is dented.

Gradbach car park sits off a quiet country lane and I begin to worry about the tiredness creeping over us. We sit on the grass for ten precious minutes to revive flagging spirits and then push on through a wooded landscape close to the riverbank. At a clearing we cross Dane Bridge and then continue beside the timeless shrouded waters of the Dane River. Any sense of time pressure and tiredness disappears, as if the very trees and wildflowers exude magic scents to lift us while waterfowl flap lazily to carry away our cares.

We emerge beside an old half-derelict house under renovation and talk to the two friendly fellows who've taken on what looks like a mammoth job. It's a mile down a rough overgrown track to the nearest road, their only access to the house. As we struggle on through the undergrowth, I wonder about some of the amazing projects people take on. Clearly, pig-headedness is behind all manner of follies being attempted, but some of these produce creations that make the world richer and more enchanting for us all. Not sure they'd say the same about our folly. One final cropped field to negotiate then we stagger out on to the A523. After a long day of rough walking our limbs are not as assured as they were this morning and we move tentatively along a road with no footpath, confronting fast traffic. Courtesy of our meandering path and various unplanned diversions we've walked 19 miles, nearly double the distance our lucky crow would have flown.

Our accommodation is also confronting. It's a run-down, cigarette-smelling shadow of the welcoming pub it might once have been. We learn without surprise we're the only guests. Two frozen salmon steaks microwaved into tasteless submission are dinner and then, tired and hungry, we head to bed.

Day 75 – to Alsager

Reality returns on sunbeams through a flimsy curtain. We both remember weird dreams with trucks careening noisily along busy roads. Now we realise the trucks are real and they're hurtling by about four metres from our pillows on the busy trunk road immediately outside our window. We have no expectations for breakfast and they are just about met. In defence of the publicans, we watch them prepare a special corn mixture for some ducks, creatures they clearly love.

At nine we walk off in full sun, negotiate the road and find the tiny path that leads to today's adventure. We set off across a field and immediately our feet are soaked cold by the heavy overnight dew. My mind begins to wander down other trails. The sparkling freshness of the day and tingle in my toes is reminiscent of another time and place. It's autumn nine years ago in Melbourne's Royal Botanic Gardens. At seven-thirty in the morning the sun has risen and Debby emerges radiant from between the trees on her father's arm. She glides through heavy dew, its tidemark rising inexorably from the hem of her soft-hued fuchsia silk gown. Gentle harp music plays while swans flap a noisy applause, uninvited guests arriving with a late flourish on the water. The official guests watch as Debby joins me on the lakeside, while female friends try not to think about their icy feet shod in flimsy shoes overwhelmed by the wet. If we inflicted this experience on our wedding guests on that happy day, then I can't complain about wet feet today.

It is still hard for me to believe such happiness could have sprung so quickly from the shadows of sadness that had enveloped my life. I'd sat with Barbara during the final hour of 1999 in the 25th year of our marriage to acknowledge the New Year would likely be her last. Wrapped in a blanket to protect her ravaged body from the evening chill, we had hugged, kissed and cried on the beach, a melancholy contrast to the city's distant firework festivities. By 19th January as the inevitable drew near, we avowed our never-ending love. It was the day of her birthday, she was just 46. Within days, she was in hospital with an infection from an innocent insect bite she no longer had the strength to fight.

On Monday 7th February the boys said their final goodbyes and I returned alone from home for that last vigil. To be with someone who is leaving our conscious world is an honour and, much as I had with my father six years earlier, I held hands, spoke soft words and looked searchingly for a final sign of recognition. I craved some special significance in the weak sigh of breath and dribble of saliva as the night unfolded, but to no avail. Her spirit had given up its grasp on mortal life. Dad had lasted 82 years, yet I wept on my mother's shoulder the morning after for her loss. Their marriage had spanned over half a century. In losing Barbara from my life, our partnership had been extinguished in half those years, and the tears I shed in that ward were for the tragedy of her spirit and our union snuffed out so early.

How could I have known what would happen next? The trite saying, *As one door closes another opens,* is meaningless in the sombre tunnels of grief. Each person is unique and must fiercely assert the right to forge their own path back into life. As I moved around with a mind empty of all but the necessary tasks of post-death detail, my body felt a hollow vessel for emotions to surge and abate at will. When a friend said someone had questioned whether I fancied a family friend who had helped deal with Barbara's clothes, I became angry. I had been re-categorised by my community as single and available, while I still considered myself married to a disembodied spirit.

However, on 31st March, just 45 days after the funeral, all that changed. Ed was rowing in the annual school regatta and I went down for the weekend with his big brother. At dinner I was sat next to someone called Debby, a mother previously unknown to me. We talked all evening and by the time I was back in the room with James, I could not tell him what had happened any more than I really understood it. There was a spring in my step, a sense of lightness and bubbling adolescent joy that had been missing for so long. I was smitten and spent more time watching the next day's race crowd for a sign of Debby's golden hair and blue eyes, than the rowers.

I overcame schoolboy nervousness a few days later to ask her out for a lunchtime coffee and sandwich. It wasn't a date I told myself, just taking the advice of close friends to spend less time sunk in a chair with my tears. We walked and talked for two hours around the Botanic Gardens and my heart swelled like the autumn blooms we passed. I was in love, but what to do about it? My rational mind tried to rein me in. There may have been a feeling of desire and a passion that had not been possible for the last couple of years of marriage, but for me I knew relationships must be built on more. As we shared our life stories, I could see all manner of connections that would underpin a meaningful life together. It was a week later on the second date in the more secluded St Kilda botanic gardens that the reins gave way. The passion that had welled up in me burst forth as I swept her up in an all-consuming hug and kiss inside those wrought iron gates.

We met the next day and every day from then on. The counsel I received from my mother's parish priest, Father Nigel, was not for religious guidance but for the sound advice of a man who had helped people deal with so much human drama. I encouraged him to be candid with me. Had I jettisoned my better judgement in the dash for pleasure? He reassured me my grief had largely run its course while Barbara had lived out her illness. I'd left corporate life to be by her side most days during that final year and now it was time to move on and find happiness afresh. I needed no further encouragement and, within a month, went away with Debby to a tiny cottage for the weekend. We hunkered down for two days and nights and found out how to live together. We bared our souls to reveal every secret that defined who we were, no matter how torrid or embarrassing. The words flowed and like limpets we clung more tightly to the coral wonderland we'd discovered. There was no need to embellish or try to be other than we were. We knew our love could endure anything but deception or fabrication.

On our return, I spoke to James and Ed about my love and intentions, and from their teenage perspective was told I had suddenly become 'interesting'. James, just 19, gave me the permission that I wasn't asking for but craved. With a depth of wisdom that stunned me, he explained we all had to move on and he was happy for me to have found a way forward even though he couldn't yet because he was still mired in grief.

Debby would say she 'created' me and there is no doubt I am no longer the man I was when we met. In delving the depths to understand herself, she had written visions of the life she would lead when she met her true love. In sharing these with me, it became obvious that this person she had conjured up over a year ago was me. Just as I had sought counsel from Father Nigel, so Debby had asked Barbara for a sign that she approved of our love. One morning as she walked alone by the beach holding her request in mind, a slip of paper blew out and settled by her foot. She picked it up and burst into tears. Its message: *Accepted by God.*

Almost five months to the day after Barbara's passing I sat in a friend's house in England. I'd taken the boys to a remembrance service for their mum at the small church in Limpsfield Chart where we had married. With Barbara laid to rest and the memory of the love we shared still strong, I took out pen and ink bottle to write a letter to ask Debby to marry me. Never was I more certain of a course of action and here today on this adventure in autumn's brilliance I couldn't be happier.

Once again the walk grounds me back in the here and now. The Gritstone Trail is another poorly-signed path and we've veered off, south-west rather than west. Falling out onto a country lane a splendid patch of shiny plump blackberries provides a tonic, a welcome supplement to our sad breakfast. We circle back to pick up the route to The Cloud (343m). This demands serious hill climbing but the reward is worth it. The early autumnal blush of pale browns and burnished red hues paints rich panoramic views out across a hazy distant landscape. The country rolls out quite smoothly to the west and very few hills stand before us. There's a stone marker with compass showing the direction and distance of places near and far. Even Land's End is marked, about 250 miles as the crow would fly. We can only dream of being borne up high on that bird's wings and whisked off to the destination that so fires our imagination.

This is a great spot and we only head down reluctantly. Halfway down a couple is picking very small blue berries in the woods. These we learn are bilberries and we sample their harvest, a more highly flavoured version of a blueberry. We add them to our list for future foraging potential and settle into what's become a lovely interlude. I'd no lofty expectations for these days, considering them a humdrum trek across the country. So, just when little is expected, life throws up a real gem.

Next we join the Cheshire Ring Canal Walk and tow-paths will be our guide for the rest of the day. It should be a pleasant break from more arduous trekking. We hop off the canal to visit a small parade of shops at Congleton Station to buy the ingredients for lunch. Before we can return to the towpath, a man who's chased us from the sandwich shop stops us. We chatted briefly as we bought food, but he's fascinated by our journey and wants to talk more. He's a farmer and a member of the Ramblers' Association, an unusual mix as farmers often seek to discourage walkers. He assures us there are good and bad farmers just as there are good and bad walkers. By the time we part, he thanks us for taking time out to share our experience and says, 'I think you're mad, but it's a wonderful adventure and I'd love to do it too.'

Canal walking is fine for a change, but as hours roll by it becomes a little mundane. The sun is out, the path is flat and everything seems quite peaceful. With no dramatic scenery to distract us we succumb to the barely hidden accumulation of aches, strains and weariness in our bodies. Our tiredness also highlights a rising concern that we've not yet organised tonight's accommodation. Canals pass silently, hidden below the surface of the landscape like a giant invisible spider's web. They're removed from the houses and roads that surround them and so in the absence of accommodation options, I decide we'll keep going to a larger town.

We press on to Alsager and arrive tired and badly in need of rest. Debby in particular looks exhausted. The early relief on entering town quickly dissipates as we realise this is a small residential town with no sign of accommodation for visitors. The bakery proves a godsend. Apart from tea and cake, the kindly women say they believe there's one place for accommodation somewhere in the far outskirts. A two-mile walk through drab streetscapes at day's end with a heavy pack, aching limbs and an uncertain bed is definitely something to be avoided. What's worse is to finally arrive at an attractive pub, approach reception and have our spirits crushed by a kindly landlord who explains apologetically he's just let the last room to a couple of cyclists on their way from Land's End to John O'Groats! He directs us further out of town to the only other accommodation, a dingy building where we mercifully find one last room available.

Day 76 – to Church Minshull

Debby is awake early but badly needs a lie-in. She not up until eight, but we're still on the pavement shortly after nine. Confronted by a busy B-road, my first task is to quickly get us as far away as possible from the deafening din of the nearby M6 motorway. We have to pass directly underneath it to find freedom. As we walk towards it, I feel my hackles rise. I seem to hear it more loudly than I used to, and to my new eyes its construction appears a crass waste. If only these drivers could step out from the metal shells which ensnare them in a surely futile world of frantic busyness, to experience the rich rewards of time spent in nature.

A small country lane leads onto the tiny footpath of the Crewe and

Nantwich Circular Walk. Two more hours and we're both tired. It's much too early in the day to be struggling with fatigue. We've had two consecutive 19-mile days, and with another in prospect today it seems deep-seated exhaustion has set in. Debby's haggard face speaks silently of the stress she's under. As she said, normal people walk the Pennine Way on the back of solid preparation and then have a good rest afterwards. I know she needs a break, but the map shows no attractive options for relief. There's nothing for it, I say, and make the decision to seek out early sustenance along a footpath to the northern outskirts of Crewe.

This is a place of major industry. Once famous for the production of Rolls Royce cars, it can now only muster Bentleys. I'm determined not to get caught up in such an industrial conurbation; however, despite a thorough check of the outskirts, it's clear there are no little cafés for weary travellers. We've no option but to walk on and within half an hour are in the bustling heartless retail town centre. We've now walked over three hours without a break and Debby is on her last legs. This feels a wretched place, but to be fair to Crewe, it could be almost any large town. Debby sees a chain coffee outlet, and while she drops into a seat I stand in the queue, yawning endlessly. I just want to put my head down and sleep. Faced with chronic tiredness my body's safety mechanism is trying to kick in. Slowly, under the influence of hot caffeinated drinks and soulless snacks, we feel some energy return. We need more time off our feet though and sit back to take in these different surroundings.

These chain outlets are expensive compared to the smaller cafés common to my working-class heritage. I still instinctively look for independent café operators, but they're often priced out by high rents in a property market bloated by insatiable debt. It all means higher prices and lunch here is £16, double that at yesterday's sandwich shop experience. At an adjacent table, I watch a woman of our age with her daughter, an impossibly young-looking mother with a tiny baby. The matriarch has shelled out nearly £20 as a lunch treat. I know the marketing allure of such places can be compelling, but can't help but think how much extra they would get sharing a sandwich in a local park surrounded by nature's inspiration. It's as if retail illusion locks them into a lifestyle where money is their jailer.

Perhaps I'm struggling with the stark contrast of being thrust into this congested anonymous concrete centre after spending so long immersed in the ever-changing moods of the countryside. I sit back and ponder the world I've helped construct. People appear to scurry around in the search for all manner of stuff, which I sense will be a quest never to be fulfilled. The marketing merry-go-round seems to confect endless promises of better lives while anchoring people to an unrewarding drudgery. I've lived my life in large towns and cities like this, artificial worlds constructed from concrete, bright lights and fake imagery. Yet, on this walk I've found the real world awaits on the doorstep, resplendent in a wealth of colour and vibrant life ready to invigorate our jaded senses for free.

A full two hours pass before we gird ourselves into action. To distract Debby from her body's aches, I hand over path-finding responsibility. Her first challenge is to get us out of the relentless grey suburban sprawl that taps our life force. Slowly, house by house, road by road, we extricate ourselves and slip unnoticed back into the welcome energy of nature's byways. Immediately we feel reinvigorated and walk more freely. The Middlewich branch of the Shropshire Union Canal will lead us to tonight's destination, Church Minshull, and to avoid disappointment, we've already booked a room so a certain bed awaits.

Also awaiting us is Dave. Friends since 11, our childhood bond led to mutual best man duties at marriages in former lives. Once again, our quest provides an opportunity to reconnect with an old friend, and in the perfect slow setting of a walk we can recount life's latest meanderings to become reacquainted. The conversation starts immediately over a cup of tea and carries on through an unexpected 40-minute twilight walk to the only place serving food. Stories are embellished, laughter shared and the evening melts away under a mantle of conviviality. The pub's new owner generously takes an hour out of his evening to run us home and by nightfall we squirm in a tiny bed adorned with unrelenting springs too numerous to count. Regardless, tonight we could sleep without a mattress.

Day 77 – to Tarporley

Despite the bed, we sleep until the alarm sounds and then get up to prepare ourselves for a walk along two canals to Bunbury. This farm is next to the Bridgewater canal so route-finding should be a breeze. We'll simply walk to the next 14 bridges over this canal, then turn on to the Shropshire Union Canal straight to tonight's destination. It sounds easy, although Dave quickly admits he's probably carrying a bit too much weight. We smile. This is the common problem of all new walkers.

We're now immersed in the world of longboats. The canal is popular and the boats come in all shapes and sizes. Most look decrepit, although some are marvellously spruce and colourful. Most sit quietly at peace, a simple unfulfilled repository of their owners' dreams. Occasionally one is occupied and even more rarely a boat moves. There's something peaceful, even serene, about a canal boat pootling along down this narrow ribbon of water. They move quite slowly and for the first time in 12 weeks, we are able to leave a form of motorised transport in our wake.

It's a languid sun-filled autumn day and I suggest an early morning tea break at the canal-side café. My initial optimism dries up promptly under the café owner's withering look. I ask nonchalantly for a strong cappuccino with the homemade scones and get the curt reply, 'There's only one coffee strength.' I should know better and am left trying to dissolve a lumpy powdered coffee sachet. I have no alternative but to drink the hideous liquid as the only way of swallowing a parched stale scone. It's a timely reminder of the advice I was given months ago: when in the presence of a 'homemade food' sign, always ask, 'Homemade by whom, where and when?'

We pass a couple of marinas packed with boats going nowhere and people actively enjoying the inactivity. This world appears to attract those more interested in the search for silly names, rather than speed. Canal boat owners seemingly delight in outdoing one another, the sillier the name the better. There is also something odd about the canal network. It has been constructed throughout large areas of often densely populated industrial landscape and yet remains largely unseen by those on the outside. It's as if by stepping down from a road onto a towpath we enter another world, a sub-culture of people hidden under the noses of society.

In due course, we reach the Bridgewater Canal's bridge number 1 and turn right on to the Shropshire Union Canal to join the Weaver Way. The busy A51 road runs alongside and we pass the back of ugly industrial buildings, their compressors churning out an incessant din, but are finally rewarded with pockets of countryside.

Our plan was to stay in Bunbury, but we find this quiet little village backwater has everything except accommodation. With help at the pub, we locate rooms in the nearest town of any size, Tarporley. Once again we have to lift tired bodies back onto country lanes to extend the day's walk. We pass Tilstone Hall along badly overgrown footpaths and grow frustrated. The going gets worse as we have to negotiate significant patches of nettles and thistles crossing mature cornfields.

We're not in a good mood when we reach Tarporley and the unappealing pub speaks of the pitfalls of booking ahead. We've covered another 16 miles and Debby is too tired to do anything but throw off her pack and lie down. Dave has had a day's walking to quieten his mind from the rigours of corporate life and over dinner we slowly travel back along the convoluted pathways our lives have taken since those early schooldays. We agree walking feels like a metaphor for life. As usual, before we uncover any great wisdom our bodies close down further ruminations.

Day 78 – to Chester

It's Sunday morning and by the time we're ready to go I've constructed a new route. We've covered 75 miles these past four days and are badly worn down. We could have a rest day today, with another two scheduled for Chester. However, because we've pushed ourselves so hard, we've a tempting opportunity. If we're strong enough to keep going, we could potentially get to Chester tonight and have a complete three day break. I've found a new string of little footpaths in roughly a direct line towards Chester. We would need to circle a large wood, Hoofield Covert, and then take a simple towpath from Hargrave into central Chester. I offer Debby the idea and despite her weary reservations, the three-day break is too enticing to ignore. We agree to set off and just see how our strength holds up.

The early footpaths are little-used and not encouraging. Most tracks bisect farmland and the farmers don't seem supportive. Electric fences run directly in front of stiles and gateways. These rights of way appear to have lain dormant for long years. We push on through thick knee-high nettles and thistles and then confront a more painful challenge. Unforgiving mature hawthorn trees have enveloped the stiles we must cross, their sturdy branches demanding a painful toll for passage. Still the demands grow and the path becomes more theoretical than practical. Now we must penetrate what can only be described as adolescent hedgerows. All manner of shrubs grow up from the ground to snare feet and legs, while at head and chest height the vicious thorns of more hawthorn trees seem to take evil delight in our misery.

We battle through but do not survive without cuts and raking marks that will stay with us for days. Major hawthorn puncture marks on arms and legs at least distract from the minor irritation of nettle rash. Next, a misplaced step on the bridleway brings Debby down into mud and mire. It seems none of us will escape this day's demands as future dinner tales are created. Now we confront a new form of track. Not a footpath, it's called a 'non-vehicle right of way'. This proves horrendous. Clearly, nobody has tried to pass this way for years and we find ourselves all at sea in a profusion of growth. Our rate of progress has now slowed to about one mile per hour while the energy we've dissipated has increased dramatically. Such are the pitfalls of attempting to follow these obscure rights of way. We finally emerge into Hargrave to be rewarded with an overhanging tree heavy with ripe damsons and gorge ourselves.

We re-join the canal now and drop onto a peaceful bench for a welcome lunchbreak. I pore over the maps and find Chester is still a very real possibility. We eat quickly and move on. The going by the canal is easier and at four we stop for a reviving cup of tea. When we ask how long it would take to reach Chester, the response brings tears to our eyes: 'The city's just a 45 minute walk up the canal.' No matter our poor condition, the goal is ours. Nothing could stop us completing this final stretch.

We arrive in sedate late afternoon sun, but we're disconcerted walking into the centre of this historic city. Chester has a Roman background and some fine old English Tudor architecture, but right now the city has a particular fascination with rhinoceroses. There are 62 very colourful rhinoceros artworks placed all around town.

We summon up the energy for a departure dinner with Dave. Tomorrow he will return to his normal world. He's walked over 30 miles and feels mentally relaxed while physically tired. As he says, 'Walking like this is just so different from everyday life. You can switch off, feel free and have a wonderful time. It's completely rejuvenating.' We smile and nod in agreement before bed calls.

Day 79 – in Chester

It's still dark as I turn over for the hundredth time. Overtiredness has seen off hopes of a good sleep. I'm alive to every ache and pain, sting and bite. Feet, ankles, calves, knees, thighs, hips, and back all want me to listen to their litany. My body cries, 'Back off'. I get up and leave Debby in bed. Already I have other issues to worry about. The box of replacement shoes and clothes we're relying on hasn't arrived. Logistical problems on top of physical exhaustion feel like the ultimate indignity. I go to the Post Office but when they can't find it, retreat meekly for fear of losing my temper and making matters worse.

The day slowly fills with the inevitable chores. Washing clothes, preparing for a blog session at the library, and downloading all 2,000 photos to disc. By dinnertime, we sit quietly over a simple meal, bemused as the rain falls steadily on a brightly coloured rhinoceros at the window.

Days 80 and 81 in Chester

Gradually we move into full rest mode over these days. The replacement shoes duly arrive and the blog is updated. Morning strolls with a bag of fruit are followed by the ultimate indulgence of idle time with coffee and newspaper. Our world is large, but our needs small. We're ready to go again.

Day 82 – to Dolphin

It's ten before we hit the road with Mike, our new walking companion. My early business mentor, he was always athletic, but immediately admits to being out of condition. His appearance gives more reason for concern. He appears dressed in attire more suitable for a night at the club, plush jacket and hush puppies, rather than a serious hiking expedition. However, we've no time to lose as we want to try to extend today's walk to carve out a rest day before launching onto Offa's Dyke.

We wend our way out of central Chester along the town wall and onto the River Dee Path. This early stretch of the Dee estuary reminds me of the varied life this watercourse leads, from Snowdonia's pristine mountains to Liverpool's harsh industrial heritage. A sign suddenly welcomes us to Wales. I had no idea Wales was this close and instinctively frown at the sky. I studied at the University of Wales an age ago and daily rain is a memory forever etched into my psyche. For now it's dry and mild, but I'm not ready to trust the Welsh weather just yet.

A gleeful man appears and tells us we're in for a treat. Within half an hour we'll witness a rare River Dee spectacle. A 35-foot spring tide on today's new moon means at the change of tide, a significant backwater wave will flow up the estuary. It sounds grand, but when a modest ten-inch wave of deep brown water gently passes we can only ruminate on the general level of excitement available to Chester's inhabitants for this to be considered special.

The track is long and straight and I begin to worry if it was a good idea for Mike to join us. Still, he asks no quarter and I've never known a more determined man, so on we go. Just before a power plant complex with steel and paper mills, we cross the river. Now we're trapped in a drab light industrial area, hemmed in by a rail line. We lose time and energy searching for an exit until we unearth an escape route under the track. Liberation only brings internment in a joyless residential area. We're weary travellers looking for lunch, but the area is barren. As leader, I take responsibility to identify a pub on the map at Northop Hall. I encourage the team,

'We'll be eating a good pub lunch within the hour.'

Fantasy images of thick soups, chicken and ham pies and roast beef baguettes are dashed on rocks of despair when we find the pub closed. It's a particularly cruel fate for Mike who looks completely done in. A small run-down convenience store with sparse shelves provides a lifesaver pork pie for me and a tasteless chicken salad sandwich for Debby. Mike wipes sweat from his brow but hasn't the energy to face food. He's now keeping going purely on the memory of his former physical capacity and keeps checking the phone for a call from his wife to say she's on her way to pick him up.

Now we're on tiny back lanes passing through a variety of smallholdings. Tiredness is building for us all and I wonder if extending today's walk was wise. The countryside is pleasant enough, but these quiet backwaters now undulate like a modest fairground diversion and the last thing we need is hills. Just when we least need it, Wales comes into its own and rain pelts down.

At 4.30pm we reach Halkyn and step into the Blue Bell Inn for a reviving cup of tea. We've unwittingly landed in a renowned walkers' pub that gets 150 walkers a week through its doors. The landlord is quite envious of our adventure and tells us of a great little walk to end our day. It means scaling the adjacent Halkyn Mountain for long-distance views. Warmed by the tea we surprise ourselves and cheerfully decide to give it a go. First though, we say goodbye to Mike. Dorothy has found her way here to take responsibility for her red-faced spouse who we've completely exhausted. Approaching 70, Mike has done an incredible job walking 19 miles with no preparation or kit. He's displayed all the features which have made him such a tough competitor throughout his life.

It's after six when we descend into our resting place for the night. With 23 miles under our belts, the pub offers good food to compensate for the deprivations of the day. I eat lightly and doze at the table, but Debby embraces a full Welsh culinary experience, Welsh lamb shanks and creamed leeks. Unfortunately when we retire the bed is in a shocking state. It's fully sprung and we feel every one of them while their loud squeaking infuses fitful dreams.

Day 83 – to Prestatyn

Dawn brings no respite and we awake aching and tired. In need of sustenance, we go down for a pre-arranged breakfast at eight only to set off the burglar alarm. We're all alone in a locked building with only frustration to feed on. It's 45 minutes later before someone arrives, and by the time we leave I'm grumpy and in a bad frame of mind to tackle the day's walk. I decide to shed ideas of obscure footpaths. We've heavy backpacks and are in no fit state to do more than the minimum. Also, I continue to worry about a swelling in the bottom of my left leg which has been with me for a week. No, I think, we'll play safe and walk a scenic bike path.

We head back up Halkyn Mountain, then down to Brynford on a path over the busy A55 and on into Gorsedd. It is clearly Wales, and just as the names are becoming more impenetrable, so the Welsh rain joins our walk. It's not cold and in some ways this makes things worse. We overheat in rain jackets and rue the pub owner's words:

'You can tell when it is summer in Wales because the rain's warm.'

In the midst of an already tiresome day, the pub calls to say I've left my diary in the room. This is very disturbing. The diary is 'my precious', more important than any wizard's ring. A veritable treasure chest of statistics and jottings, it has evolved into a priceless keepsake housing raw reminiscences as our adventure has unfolded. As such, it is more a memorial to this time in my life than any mere memento. There's no question of going on without it, so I ask the pub owner to put it in a cab as quickly as possible while we wait at the Druid Inn down the road. Somehow this 12th century staging post seems an appropriate place to wait. A full half hour passes as we stand outside the Inn. This place was once the most popular in this area, but now it's boarded-up exterior offers no comfort to a couple of weary travellers.

Once the trusty diary is back in my thankful grasp we wave goodbye to the taxi and move on from this sad place. It's interesting how things have changed. We'd welcomed the taxi's arrival as the carrier of my diary but did not think twice about letting the driver go from this lonely place without us. There was a time when we would have relished the prospect of a comfortable car to carry us and our backpacks, but not now. We're walkers and gird ourselves for the next effort. We must walk to Whitford, Berthengam and then Llanasa before we'll find any lunch.

We're very tired and so it's no idle dalliance to sit for an hour over a late Friday pub lunch. Feeling myself slide into a sleep-like state, we shake ourselves into some semblance of action and get back on the track. An hour and a half later we walk into Prestatyn. For some reason, our weariness feels as bad as anything we've experienced. Our only thought is to find a bed for the night. Hopes of any immediate respite from this gruelling day are thwarted. We assumed accommodation would be easy to find in a large seaside town, but no, it seems bereft of B&Bs and guest houses. We lumber around with backs bent and become more desperate by the minute. The few numbers we call prove fruitless; places are either closed or full. A 20-minute walk to the Information Centre provides no help. It's closed and our sense of misery deepens. Backpacks feel like bags of rapidly drying cement and our limbs quiver; our thoughts are heavier still. We take a long walk to another B&B without a phone. Our knock echoes, no response.

We feel like we've entered a nightmare of the first order. There's one last alternative to sleeping on the windswept beach. Prestatyn has a poor quality hotel we're told, a full half-hour walk out of town. Looking out over the muddy estuary that passes for a beach I shiver at the thought of laying my head there and call the hotel. Yes, they have one small double room, but with a wedding reception tonight the room is likely to be noisy. A final insult, but in our state of collapse beggars cannot be choosers. We're ready to agree to anything that's got a bed and we trudge to the hotel.

We check in at the sad foyer, go to the room, drop our bags and within minutes Debby is lying in the bath, sobbing in a state of physical meltdown. I unpack and lay on the bed. My whole body is shaking uncontrollably with exhaustion. I worry this might be some form of heart tremor, perhaps my body is breaking down under the strain. I try to still my mind to listen to my body's message.

Eventually Debby drags herself from the bath to collapse next to me on the bed. Here is my loved one, beaten down into a shocking state. Everything aches and the stress of overexertion has stripped away any semblance of self-control. I massage her trembling feet silently to assuage my guilt and she looks at me through tears. What on earth are we doing to ourselves? Are we doing long-term damage to our health? Even if I can go on, this hare-brained idea will potentially break the prostrate woman I hold most dear. I've been keen to push through any signs of weakness but now simply must recognise the accumulation of exhaustion. We need shorter daily itineraries and marathons like yesterday are out.

Debby is too exhausted to eat dinner and for the first time since John O'Groats 12 weeks ago, I leave her on the bed to find food alone. It feels almost surreal to sit in a second-rate hotel bar contemplating the effects of an extreme challenge. Although my body is still gently quivering from the day's physical demands, my mind has quietened. I silently observe the scene around me and experience myself as an outsider disconnected from the world of others. A flurry of specially-dressed people wander in and out of a wedding reception down the corridor, but I'm in a very different space. Like a rabbit caught in the headlights, frozen to my seat, I'm unable to move. In the absence of a malt whisky, I sip on a large blended Irish version and slowly eat a chicken sandwich. Sometime later my reverie recedes and I re-enter the world of the others around me. I look down in surprise and realise I've unconsciously completed a super fiendish Sudoku in record time. It's as if all distractions disappeared with my exhaustion and my subconscious mind was unleashed.

Day 84 – in Prestatyn

There is no peace for the wicked may be a trite phrase, but its truth today is self-evident. After all yesterday demanded of us, the night brought no peace. At one point, instinct got me out of bed to prepare for the day, but then the clock flashed three forty-five. I get up again to look out of the dawn window. The cacophony that had undermined our sleep is obvious; a veritable rainstorm has enveloped Prestatyn. Three days in Wales and three days of rain!

At breakfast Debby warns me I'm in danger of being considered a grumpy old man. Michael Bolton is belting out 'How am I supposed to live without you' and it doesn't help my digestion. I need calm to get through my bowl of sweetened straw posing as muesli.

We head out to blog and manage logistics and walk straight into a rainstorm. Sheathed in full wet weather gear we walk half an hour to the library, probably the toughest rest day conditions we've had. We hang out wet clothes and turn the library into a refugee camp as we blog for two hours until they close. Next I find new shorts and walking trousers in a hiking shop. With my waist now 34 inches, down from 37 inches a year ago, I'm thinking of taking out a patent on my sure-fire diet: *Walk long distances day in, day out with a 20kg backpack and eat whatever you like.* By mid-afternoon, we've formed the opinion Prestatyn is a place from the 1960's. The shops look like it, the people look like it, and the food tastes like it.

Following the heartache of arriving in Prestatyn with no obvious place to stay, Debby has been in H for Home mood calling B&Bs relentlessly, and we now have accommodation booked right through to the end of this week. Feeling more at ease we decide to bring the day to a close with a simple dinner in our room while watching 'Last Night of the Proms'. I may have lived in Australia for over 20 years, but I'm still suffused with national pride for the place of my birth as Jerusalem belts out.

It's time to turn the light out on phase six of our adventure yet we still haven't recovered. We understand the 19-mile daily average was too much, particularly since we've now walked 1,057 miles from John O'Groats. The last two days walking into Prestatyn were particularly dour and we've become disheartened. Debby drifts off to sleep, but I know Offa's Dyke awaits and pick up the guidebook.

The path was opened in 1971, the fourth of Britain's great walks to be established. Without the glamorous reputation of some other British walks, experienced hikers are said to appreciate its attractions. It transits through a magnificent diversity of terrain, worthy of comparison with any long-distance path in Britain. Its anchor is the earthwork created in the late eighth century by King Offa to keep the heathen Welsh out of his Mercia kingdom. He is considered the first great king England produced after the last Romans departed from Britain in 406 AD. The fact he ruled for 39 years until his death in 796 AD is obviously an achievement in itself for those days.

These were known as the 'Dark Ages', yet Offa developed good relations with the European ruler Charlemagne and coastal towns traded with their European counterparts. Medieval villages had well-established agricultural societies and with no individual land ownership, peasants cultivated strips in communal fields. By the time of Offa's death he had earned the title 'King of the English', having done much to expand his Mercia kingdom to be the largest of the seven kingdoms that comprised England. It is interesting to think that after all he achieved, he is today only really remembered for a somewhat dilapidated earthwork. By comparison his obscure predecessor King Arthur, about whom little is known, has become the subject of endless grand storytelling myths. History appears to have treated Offa poorly.

More to the point though, it seems the walk we'll set out on tomorrow will likely treat us poorly too. We'll have to hoist our backpacks over 650 stiles as we walk over 180 miles. From the northern coast of Wales, the trail moves like a wriggling earthworm south to Chepstow on the Severn Estuary, slithering between Wales and England repetitively and without concern for human boundaries. However, as our Trailblazer guidebook says,

> To journey through it on foot is the finest way to discover one of Britain's best-kept secrets.

It seems we'll have the spectacle of magnificent green countryside, scaling high ridges, following ancient drovers' roads, and descending to canal towpaths along meandering riverbanks. We'll experience firsthand the ancient majesty of King Offa's grand construction and have the opportunity to lose ourselves in the legends and myths surrounding those times. To get the most out of this next phase of our adventure, we'll need to let go of the physical focus and free our minds to inhabit the rich landscape and imaginary tales infused in it by our forebears.

Like the Pennine Way, Offa's Dyke was always going to be woven into this adventure. It is the mystery and myths of Arthur, Merlin, Excalibur and Sir Lancelot that have brought me to this spot tonight. There were more direct, easier routes and I know that after more than 1,200 years the earthen dyke is unlikely to be particularly dramatic looked at through 21st century eyes. No, the route we'll embark upon tomorrow was chosen for the glamour and romance of its legends. I'd imagined it would inspire and uplift our spirits, but I'd had no comprehension then of the weariness that would be etched deep into our bodies by now. The stark reality of further arduous walking weighs heavy. Somehow, we'll have to lift our spirits or the whole quest will collapse. As sleep wafts over me, I imagine knights of the round table riding to help us through adversity.

CHEPSTOW
ENGLAND
DYKE
WALES
OFFA'S DYKE
PRESTATYN

Chapter 9 – DYKE

Day 85 – to Bodfari

Sleep hasn't brought back my joie de vivre. It's a dismal day after heavy overnight rain. Before nine we check out and stand in the persistent downpour. My energy has gone missing and the backpack weighs heavy. On the first hill I feel chronically tired. And this is just Prestatyn's High Street. As usual it's Debby who comes to my rescue rather than any mythical knights:

'We need to create new energy for the Offa's Dyke Path. We're starting a new adventure today and must be ready to be stimulated and excited by what we find, not burdened by the past.'

I agree, but still feel mired in Ishmael's 'damp, drizzly November in my soul'. It led him to join the wretched whaler Captain Ahab in that maniacal chase of Moby Dick. Heaven knows where my desperation to get out of Prestatyn will lead.

It's said the darkest hour is just before the dawn and suddenly, as if by some magical wave of Merlin's wand, my dawn breaks. The hill climb out of town is steep and long, yet instead of buckling under the strain, the opposite is happening. I see the world through a different lens and my body feels different. Everything appears changed. Debby notices it too. The deep, disconsolate melancholy we felt in Prestatyn that dried up the sap of our adventure's spirit has evaporated. The weariness has fallen away. It's as if we've shed our packs and the higher we go the brighter our mood becomes. Rumi's advice comes to mind:

Start walking...
Your legs will grow heavy and tired...
Then comes the moment,
Of feeling the wings you've grown lifting.

What was it that brought on such a dramatic change to my world? In a single moment I saw black become white and now feel elated to be on a new path and away from towns and roads. On these high exposed footpaths, with distant views free of the press of people and encumbrances, we're immersed in a scene filled by vibrant heather, bracken and gorse. The clouds and rain still circle, but they are now mere support actors. It seems my energy had not disappeared, but was simply blocked. I must remember this lesson and not prepare for the day wearing the cloak of misery, but be open to my body's reaction to what the day serves up. I walk on dressed in the pure smile of a Hare Krishna devotee.

In Prestatyn we'd met a wiry man sitting exhausted by the Offa's Dyke finish line with his dogs. He had reinforced the guidebook warning that this is a tough walk across all manner of demanding hills. In particular the stiles, over three per mile, had really done him in. When we asked for any advice:

'Yes, don't take a pair of greyhounds that have to be lifted over the stiles!'

The stiles come thick and fast, but the route-finding is easy. Unlike the Pennine Way there are signposts. We're up high and distant views behind us reveal a sea dotted with wind farms and a northern skyline of Liverpool's industrial plants. Ahead lies a more inviting path; ill-defined by small stones set in mud, it leads us back into the green world of unkempt fields and raggle-taggle trees that are happy to leave us be. We move up and down the high undulating walk and with no roads or cars are happy to find a mid-morning snack of wild blackberries. Tiny Rhuallt reconnects us with village life and food for lunch, but then we head back into more hills. Moel Maenefa (290m) and the impressive Cefn Du (256m) are despatched as this new-found energy still surges through our limbs. It's as if the very atmosphere up here has infused our spirits like a heady liquor.

All too soon, our 16 miles winds to conclusion and we descend into the tiny hamlet of Sodom and on to Bodfari. The welcome we receive at the B&B threshold is warm and we know we've made a wise choice. Tea and cakes are placed before us, stories shared, a large bath offered and by the time we sit for another pub dinner, we're quite mellow.

Day 86 – to Clywd Gate (& Plas Efenechtyd)

It seems like the first time in an age we've both found complete restorative sleep. We feel rejuvenated and Debby is convinced there's magic at play in this B&B. Our host Dee talked yesterday about how the house is on an old pilgrimage route, and when they first inspected it she felt its healing energy and profound sense of calm. Just 24 hours ago, life seemed a grey dungeon, confining us to some Sisyphean labour. All that's disappeared now and we caper around a breakfast table overflowing with fresh ingredients. By the time we walk out onto the path we've been nurtured and replenished, the perfect balm for weary souls.

Today looks set to be challenging as we tackle the Clwydian Hills. A small bridge over the tiny River Wheeler leads us south-east up through bracken. We pass Moel y Parc (398m) with its nearby radio mast, before some steep climbs up to a hill fort at Penycloddiau (440m). Despite the work of our limbs, we're perfectly at peace up high in this countryside. The views speak in silence of a miscellany of labour over 100's of years as people have eked out their lives on small farms and settlements amidst nature's lush swathe of hills. We've stumbled into the Vale of Clwyd without expectations and this series of exposed whaleback ridges offers a kaleidoscope of scenes of our human attempts to harvest nature's abundance. Across the green valley floor the historic towns of Denbigh and Ruthin are neatly-packaged gems in an otherwise rural landscape. The solid grey overhead is an irrelevance; the stiles, as high as my waist at times, barely register; the heather overwhelms all, painting the land in a pale purple hue to soften the aged bracken and dark green and yellowed grasses of autumn.

From high up, the next path is inevitably down. And when the descent ends we're faced with a steep climb back up. The routine continues like a funfair big dipper without the carriages and we crest Moel Arthur (455m), Moel Llys-y-Coed, Moel Dywyll (472m), and higher still to a cairn where fierce winds force an aborted lunch stop. We do find shelter to eat, then gird ourselves for the routine to continue over Moel Famau (555m), Mother Mountain in English, the highest in the Clwyd hills.

Here we find the Jubilee Tower, built in 1810 to celebrate King George III. It's been rebuilt many times, but the tower's ruined state leaves little doubt that hereabouts a monarch's power is no match for the forces of nature. The wind today is frightening. If a glorious view makes the best walking companion, the wind is its evil twin. Always nagging and demanding, the wind relentlessly saps energy, chilling our bodies to the bone. My fingers are numb and my balance threatened. I'm fighting a losing battle with the wind and as its force increases decide subservience is the better option. I pay homage by bending double to drop onto all fours and move around for a while like a bloated cockroach. In this embarrassing position we suddenly meet the only other person about today. A Russian PhD Classics student from Leeds University, I hate to think what image he will be taking home of weird British behavioural traits.

One final climb, to skirt Foel Fenlli (511m), and then the day gradually descends to a conclusion through farmland where deep brown cows take no more interest in us than the dispassionate thorny old hawthorn trees. We arrive at Clwyd Gate, minds and bodies abuzz with the energy of the Vale of Clwyd's untamed world. We've had six exceptional and exhilarating hours' walking. The Welsh countryside is proving a wonderful surprise even if the weather isn't. Five days in Wales and five straight days of rain.

Our hosts whisk us off to their hideaway B&B in the tiny hamlet of Efenectyd. Sunk in deep countryside, we're greeted by a 25-year-old deaf and blind duck wandering under a magnificent holm oak tree. By bedtime we're feeling good. Our bodies have amazing recuperative powers as I was reminded yesterday. I'd had an infected swelling at the bottom of my left leg for a week, but as I sat in the bath last night, I watched a two-centimetre thorn slowly rise out of my calf as if by magic.

Day 87 – to Llangollen

Drowsy eyes take in the dank wisps of darkness beyond the curtain. It's five-thirty in the morning and there's still over an hour to sunrise – that's if Wales gets sun today. Rain, our unshakeable companion, arrives during breakfast, but we feel confident we can take on anything the Welsh weather can throw at us. The thick misty rain is still there, hung from a leaden sky as we set off. The higher we climb, the more the wind rages against our full wet weather gear. There's no way we can get cold this morning though: a warm inner fire smoulders. Whether it was Jones the butcher's hand-made sausages or the joy of Marilyn's homemade bread and preserves, external conditions cannot hope to disrupt my mellow demeanour.

There's a romance to these hills no matter the conditions. We're passing along narrow-cut, fern-laden paths dripping with abundant Welsh water, their beauty framed by distant misty landscapes. We'd no knowledge of the Clwydian Hills a few days ago, yet now we're about to say goodbye we're like children that don't want to let go. We absorb every last drop of energy from the heights, but then finally must descend.

The morning disappears into humdrum farmland. The ever-present stiles slow progress and we wonder what's made this farmer so grumpy. He's put up signs saying 'No Stopping' and 'No Picnicking' along the path. In the small village of Llandegla, we're disappointed. We'd planned to buy lunch, but it's one and the general store has another unwelcome sign, 'Closed from noon till 2.30 for lunch'. The pub is boarded up too, but we find some decrepit tables and chairs on a patch of green in the middle of the road. We sit, ease loaded backpacks from aching backs, and survey the meagre offerings within. A couple of old Welsh cakes, a mangled Snickers bar, one apple, and the Kendal Mint Cake given to Debby because it was nearly out of date. After lunch, I wonder what was George Mallory's greatest feat in 1924. Was it climbing Everest, or consuming Kendal Mint Cake?

We set off and soon disappear into farmland where nature offers a perfect antidote to our meagre lunch, a clump of sweet, deep-flavoured blackberries. The peace is meditative and at times we stop to breathe in our surroundings while sheep seem to stand and stare at us in awe. The path eventually changes and takes on a new aura. The gentle patchwork of a slowly-evolved farming landscape is left behind and we enter a dark mystical forest that speaks of time beyond measure. Everything is hushed. We gaze into thick forest gloom on all sides and a heavy carpet of fallen pine needles deadens our footsteps. The path is muddy but it doesn't worry us. Debby's eagle eye identifies a large patch of bilberries and soon we're enjoying our second fruit course.

This has turned into one of those days that just keeps giving. Taken to the edge of the forest at 480 metres above sea level, eyes blinking, we step out into a magnificent sunny day. Can this really be Wales? Slowly, the dark forest falls away, a mere black slash on the receding landscape. We're now in fine open moorland radiating out in all directions. Although the Pennine Way is a long way back, one thing this moor has in common with the Yorkshire variety is mud and mire. Our already soaked and dishevelled shoes now slosh through water and the dank blackness oozing from the marsh.

The moor path leads to a remote lane and we follow its interminable progress towards what appears to be the appropriately named World's End Farm. Before we reach this uncertain destiny, a track guides us into a new world. The landscape here is dramatic. The land rises steeply on the left, while to the right it falls precipitously away. The River Eglwyseg defines this area. The tiny river has etched a deep narrow valley and left the Eglwyseg Crags to tower some 200 metres or more above us. The track has narrowed and we're walking across steep scree slopes. To control my vertigo I avert my eyes from the magnetic draw of the valley's depths that seem to hang off the side of my right foot. The area is famous for buzzards and ravens and high above we can see these huge scavengers circle. I've an uneasy feeling these birds may be sizing us up as we tentatively make our way through such an exposed setting.

The rough shaley track threatens a landslide is only ever one small slip away and I'm determined not to create one this afternoon. The path eventually leads off the scree, down into the wooded valley and another complete change of environment to round out the day. Although we're tired and the day has already been much longer than expected, we still feel a sense of disappointment that it's coming to an end. Within half an hour, deserted country lanes bring us into the heart of Llangollen. Here the bustle of activity holds sway. Cars clutter the road and late tourists hurry along narrow pavements past shops craving attention to their tacky offerings. After a day of wonder in remote landscapes this has no appeal. However the town is built on the raging River Dee and despite all the trappings called civilisation, it appears the river has yet to be tamed.

In the evening we walk out to find food, but within two minutes the fierce cold wind drives us back into our bar. We've covered 17 miles today, enough is enough.

Day 88 – in Llangollen

Breakfast at nine is an enjoyable luxury. Slowly we tackle the various logistical chores and then settle in for the inevitable long blog session. The library's free internet service is welcome, and when we tune in to find we've had nearly 8,000 hits, it feels like we've sat down surrounded by friends. The rain arrives after lunch.

By evening, I tuck my second black journal under the arm as we head to the pub for dinner. Not the one with all the tiny spidery scribbles of our daily experiences, but the special one, reserved for more profound observations. We've been walking for three months and I feel I must have absorbed some great wisdom from the fields, fells and forests. Other species have entered my circle, while the weather has assailed my smug sense of human superiority. I want to capture any thoughts while they're fresh. After dinner I take up my pen.

An hour later the stark reality hits home. All that's flowed from my pen are twitterings about myself and my life. Simple personal reflections on my character and what makes me tick. Why have these tumbled out of me here tonight? Is this the effect of the landscape I've walked through? Perhaps the long exposure with the outer world has provided a new prism through which I can look into my inner world. I've been taken deep within, to marvel at what lies shielded from my customary view. This is not what I was hoping for. I tell Debby I don't feel satisfied. She's already drowsy and wants her bed:

'Keith, if it wasn't for you I would never have been able to keep going for the 1,100 miles we've walked. At the end of these days I'm tired and just want to eat and find a few hours' sleep for some relief from all my aches. Yet I love you and wait, yawning, as you draw the evening out by thinking deeply about things. Well remember, you once told me the only true wisdom is knowledge of self, so don't be disappointed with yourself tonight.'

Sheepishly I pack up my writing materials.

Back in our room Debby quickly passes into deep sleep. I look at the first thing I had written down this evening, and realise the truth of the words, 'I strive for strong loving relationships, nothing is more important.'

I turn out the light, but still can't quite let the evening go. Wales has some countryside that reminds me of that first week in the far north of Scotland. The plaque where Britain's last wolf was killed won't leave me in peace. It feels like a clear marker of the impact we humans are having on this planet's other species. When that last lonely creature was killed there were less than one billion humans on Earth. Now we're nearing seven billion, and the population has doubled in the last 50 years. Not only do we dominate the world with our numbers, but we consider ourselves superior to other creatures with an inalienable right to assert mastery over all.

Just as we decided it would be better for our way of life to get rid of all British wolves, so a casual indifference seems to fuel a voracious appetite for land development that could well clear most other creatures from the planet. And it's not only other creatures at risk. I can no longer ignore the fact we're dramatically changing the very fabric of this small planet on which all life's survival depends. On this walk I've felt something of the power of the elemental forces at play in our oceans, waterways, soils and climate. They're not to be treated lightly. Yet we're so confident of our power and knowledge, we continue to exploit the world for our needs and greed with barely a second thought. If we're to have any chance of understanding the full magnitude of our human impact and surviving the results, surely we'll need to rediscover our place in nature. I sense humility would be a good place to start.

I turn over, but sleep is elusive. I feel sad lying here. In converting the world into a purely human domain, we seem destined to eliminate not just creatures, but every last vestige of 'otherness'. Even to kill off the very idea of wildness itself. The yearning I felt to make this walk is an example of a human need to try to get away from civilisation and roam wild. I've chosen Britain because it's the country of my birth and where I've spent most of my life. Yet wildness has almost gone from here. Britain stands in the world's top dozen most densely populated larger countries. The trend is getting worse across the world and together with our pursuit of material pleasures, we seem set on eliminating something far more essential to our own wellbeing. What will be our destiny if wildness and freedom to roam can only be accessed as mental adventures, reading history books, watching movies or through virtual reality technology? At length tiredness carries me into an uneasy slumber.

Day 89 – to Selattyn

Despite my evening deliberations, I leap from bed at six after a great night's sleep. Before leaving town, I buy a cup of something called coffee. Without taste or colour, it resembles hot milk. Debby simply shrugs and shakes her head; she knows it's a lesson that eludes me. Straight up to Castell Dinas Bran (320m), a stiff half hour climb. The brooding ruins of the castle look down silently on Llangollen from their lofty perch as they have done for centuries. The climb has filled our lungs with fresh air, warmed muscles and fired our spirits. The scenery is powerful, the crags provide the framework for quintessential dour slate-rooved Welsh farmsteads. A small country lane takes us on down into a dark, mossy, damp, native woodland and we quickly feel we've gained admittance to a secret hideaway. We love to be alone in such places, it's an elixir of which we never tire.

Soon we come face to face with the world's highest navigable aqueduct. The Pontcysyllte Aqueduct stands on piles as high as 126 feet and the iron trough – 11 feet ten inches wide and five feet three inches deep – is carried across a 1007-foot-long span over the River Dee. This was Thomas Telford's brilliant idea to construct a 'stream in the sky' to bring the area's abundant coal, clay and limestone, to feed the Midlands' industrial boom, 100 miles away. Built between 1795 and 1805, the aqueduct not only required the construction of the 18 sandstone piers set in place with a lime, ox blood and water mortar, but also the building of the Horseshoe Falls weir on the River Dee to supply the 12 million gallons of water which still pass daily over the aqueduct. There's a majestic beauty in Telford's achievement still evident 200 years later, and it seems fitting it's been recognised as one of the great civil engineering feats of all time with a World Heritage listing. We cross the aqueduct with some trepidation given the confronting sheer drop on either side.

It's past two now, so halfway across the next large grassy field we throw ourselves down. A dog walker stops to pass the time of day. She's never seen anyone picnicking here before and we agree people can be too confined by perceptions of what is normal. What is normal though is the inevitable arrival of Welsh rain. Soon we're introduced to the highlight of this path. In this field is a mound, but not just a nameless mound – it's King Offa's Dyke. Varying between eight feet and 12 feet in height, it's not the most impressive human achievement we've seen on our travels. Indeed, if it we hadn't been alerted to it by the guidebook, we wouldn't have noticed it. However, as the great King Offa constructed it over 1,200 years ago, we display due reverence.

At this juncture, the Dyke is the current border between England and Wales. We walk along the crest, which looks like a long low hillock. Trees have grown up along its line safe from clearance for crops. A greater threat to the trees comes from the large holes bored around their roots, the yawning openings of badger setts. From up here we can see Chirk Castle to the north-east, an impressive building continuously inhabited by the Middleton family since 1595. It stands in sharp contrast to a hideous belching factory where humans attempt to better nature, or perhaps batter would be more accurate. Here wood is broken down and recompressed to make wood flooring. It sounds farcical until Debby reminds me we have a reconstituted stone kitchen bench in our Melbourne kitchen.

After a stiff uphill walk we emerge onto the little-used B4579 at Craignant, where a stone bridge displays an insignia of the bloody Battle of Crogen in 1165, when Henry II was defeated by Owain Gwynedd's Welsh forces. I'm fascinated by the presence of places of historical significance in Britain, but now realise the countryside is packed with such places. When a local birdwatcher points out the deep lustre of a blue kingfisher below the bridge, we happily exchange human history for natural history.

We arrive at our remote farmhouse B&B and Mrs Jones, a 76-year-old who has been widowed for more than 25 years, greets us at the doorstep. She's lived here nearly 50 years, the only bed and breakfast accommodation in this hamlet. More than that, she includes a simple three-course dinner in her B&B tariff. She's a marvel and tells us she's determined not to stop, even though her sons would rather she did:

'I've told them, it's how I meet people, it's my life.'

Day 90 – to Llanymynech

Over scrambled eggs, our eyes drift upwards to the sight of buzzards circling high in the sky. It's been raining hard for a good part of the night, but we walk off into sharp, bright daylight. Sunshine slants between branches of luminous trees, while the breeze brings down a light shower of overnight rain from quivering branches. Within ten minutes of departure we're climbing a hill through a woodland and have to tackle a run of stiles that could have been set for an athletics steeplechase.

The Dyke soon appears and we walk along the top, continuing uphill to the radio mast on Baker's Hill (351m) before Racecourse Common. Here are the remnants of Oswestry Racecourse. Established around 1800, it became quite an important part of the local social calendar. Race weeks were lively affairs with balls and festivities as the lords and gentlemen rode their horses. I imagine *My Fair Lady* with Rex Harrison introducing Eliza at these posh races. By 1804, the guidebook says, 'outsiders and horse owners from the lower classes' were winning the races and rowdy behaviour had begun to disrupt the meetings, bringing lower attendances. Racing was abandoned in 1848 and all that remains are a little ruined stone-built grandstand and this meditative lush green common land. I feel I would be very happy to live here.

I become disorientated in Racecourse Wood and lose the way before the path leads us to the River Morda. A shiver runs through me. Was this place Tolkein's inspiration for Middle Earth's centre of evil? We press on to little Trefonen, more Hobbiton than Mordor and a good spot for an early lunch. We sit peacefully in sunshine on a stone wall before rising to scale the summit of Moelydd (285m) for views out to Snowdonia. These climbs aren't high but we're feeling the effects more. Late wild raspberries, blackberries, Victoria plums and a damson tree provide a bountiful energy boost. The damsons are so prolific, I eat a good pound.

We descend from this peak through yew and hazel trees into Jones' Rough Nature Reserve. All goes well until I hear Debby cry out and turn to see her on the ground. She's twisted her ankle on a rock. No lasting damage, but a reminder of our tenuous grip on this quest. Tired bodies are most at risk in the afternoon. Only yesterday I fell off some wet wooden steps late in the day. We need to be more careful. The final ascent is steep but brief and through a bluebell wood which I imagine a purple extravaganza in spring. Once we're over Llanymynech Hill (226m), it remains to simply wander down across a number of stiles into our small village for the night.

Today was 15 miles, but it feels longer and we're both ready for bed early.

Day 91 – to Forden

Pulling back the curtains I notice for the first time that autumn has really arrived. It's six, still pitch black, and cold. How things have changed since those days of almost perpetual daylight in the Orkneys. I feel lethargic, but when we step outside the autumn morning has a lightness to lift us. The sun has risen confidently in a clear sky, its mastery absolute. For now though its power lacks heat and the atmosphere is astringent. My skin shrinks back to avoid its frosty touch and fingers blanch white, yet despite the chill, I can feel joy insistently breaking out.

The disused Montgomery canal sets our day off. We duck under the first bridge striding out confidently, but by the second we stop and stare. The still, cold waters present a perfectly framed reflection of the far bank's dense foliage. The real bank and its radiant identical twin image merge into one dazzling scene. Human beings may have created this canal with an industrial purpose in mind, but once attention is switched to newer inventions, nature quietly resumes its authority. A profusion of green has overrun the canal and threatens to engulf it completely. The air is alive with small flying insects and swallows, martins, redstarts and flycatchers swoop down, just touching the canal surface to feast on their harvest. There's even a pair of kingfishers nearby.

Our path diverts at the tiny village of Four Crosses and our escapade in nature comes to an abrupt stop. We've entered a milk-processing depot and stand amidst tanker trucks being loaded with their cargo. Yellow lines are painted through the facility to indicate the walkers' right of passage. In this concrete complex something fundamental is at play. I've lived overseas for many years and traditions like this right of way delight me. Nothing speaks more clearly of the importance of recognising our heritage. Right here society acknowledges the might of industry is only worthwhile ultimately if it observes the rights and wellbeing of the individuals and communities that live within their sphere of influence. The pendulum of power has swung significantly in many countries, including my own home, Australia. Money-making ambitions of business often now transcend people's needs. Britain is not immune to these influences, but here today, these yellow lines speak of the individual's importance, and it's with a skip in my step we move through.

The path is dull now and follows the River Severn meander. This river will ultimately make a grand exit into the sea. However, here it's a mere muddy grey confused channel and we go quiet in the bland surroundings, as if our words have sunk into the mud.

The Breidden Hills loom large in the east. There's a monument sitting up there to recognise the exploits of Admiral Rodney in 1782 at the Battle of Dominica. Apparently these hills also have a connection with Caractacus who held out against the Romans in 43 AD. My only knowledge of King Caractacus was gleaned half a century ago listening to the Sunday morning Family Favourites radio show. Spontaneously the song springs from my lips:

'And the fascinating witches who put the scintillating stitches in the britches of the boys who put the powder on the noses of the faces of the ladies of the harem of the court of King Caractacus, were just passing by!'

Debby's look of horror brings back the silence. It's well past one when we walk into Buttington. Mary and Lance, the next friends to join our adventure, will meet us here and take our backpacks to the cottage they've hired. It will be good to climb this afternoon's high hills without backpacks. We wait at the Green Dragon, a tired pub being managed by a young man trying to do his best against all odds. Despite the dispiriting food and the rain that starts to fall, we content ourselves that support is on its way.

Inevitably, the arrangement falls through. The Pope has come to visit the UK and the roads from London are blocked. Now we're late and have no option but to wearily hoist packs and step out to tackle the hills and rain. The farm track rises steeply up a small snaking path to an Iron Age hill fort, Beacon Ring peak (400m).

Within an hour we're walking around the crown of trees planted at the top in 1953 to commemorate the Queen's coronation. We walk on feeling elated and descend through the Leighton Hall Estate to the mysterious Offa's Pool. This body of black water is hidden in an obscure spot, and we feel a strange atmosphere descend as we approach. We're relieved to move on and soon we've the company of hundreds of pheasants to distract us, running hither and thither across our path.

It's five-thirty as we walk out of the woods into Kingswood. Our friends still haven't arrived. It seems travelling by car takes even longer and is more unreliable than moving around the country-side on foot. When they do we're whisked us off to a comfortable cottage, and over a convivial dinner the powerful bonds that have brought us together resurface. Mary and I shared the oil industry excitement in London 40 years ago and I was responsible for her introduction to Lance. I hired him and then fired him and somehow we've all stayed friends throughout.

Day 92 – at Forden

Although today is a rest day, Lance has a Welsh mother's genes and wants to show us the Wales he loves. He drives us into Snowdonia and in true Welsh tradition, while he waxes lyrical of the mountain scenery, Wales does what it is most famous for: it rains. To be more explicit, rain teems down shielding all landscape behind a light grey opaque curtain. Venturing from the car briefly, we're quickly soaked. My contention that it rains every day in Wales is proving true. We've been within its borders ten days and it's rained on us every day.

Day 93 – to Newcastle-on-Clun

It's just past six and I bound out of bed, ready to embrace the morning. I look out into darkness; the only thing discernible is the rain. In the self-catering luxury of this cottage, I slip downstairs to enjoy my home breakfast ritual: fruit, muesli and yoghurt. Eggs are so B&B! By the time we set off it's with another simple luxury. We don't need to repack all our stuff and can leave the big backpack and its contents scattered all over the bedroom floor, rediscovering the joys of teenage life. For three months, our end of day routine has been to unpack all our worldly belongings in tight rooms and find places to secrete them, particularly where they can air or dry. Early the next morning, often under time pressure, we've had to gather them up and, akin to an IKEA purchase in reverse, arrange them in a tight pack in the right order to suit the day's logistics. Today therefore is a treat, and when Mary and Lance drop us back in Kingswood at the precise place we were picked up, I happily ignore comments they share with Debby about how I was always a stickler for precision in the office. As we take our first footsteps the rain comes down.

From relatively flat farmland we're soon on the Dyke itself and the heavy misty rain gradually abates. We cover six miles in two hours and feel good. Signs keep popping up, welcoming us to Shropshire, the English county border with this part of Wales. The Council's PR signs pronounce Shropshire an 'Area of Outstanding Natural Beauty'. I can only think of A.E. Housman's 1896 collection of poems, *A Shropshire Lad*. He caught the spirit of the place with 'those blue remembered hills', but with a tone too pessimistic for me. The young men who inhabited his verse were invariably doomed to die prematurely.

We descend into a dank woodland dell as morning passes. A thick mud-lined secluded lane leads towards the impressive Mellington Hall where I imagine hot strong coffee and a fruit scone await. When we get there, the house and gardens are impressive, typical of the grand constructions that British gentry have built over the centuries. Gazing in the windows, starched white tablecloths, fine cutlery and stemmed glassware are all arrayed, but I sense something is not quite right. The door is locked.

The whole setting has the air of a ghost ship, a land-bound Mary Celeste drifting absent-mindedly through deserted countryside. There's no information so we sit at wooden tables left out on the immaculate lawns to scavenge our backpacks for some sad offering. My slim volume about the teachings of the great Stoic, Epictetus, have told me how to avoid such disappointment. Once again, I've conjured up a wonderful expectation, only to discover the reality is but a pale shadow. When will I learn the Stoic philosophy that we cannot control life, only our responses to it? This whole journey is a lesson in Stoicism.

Our afternoon is challenging. We confront a series of steep hills known as the 'Switchbacks'. Often we're on the Dyke, then off on country lanes and along the Kerry Ridgeway. Up and down we go, our quads and calf muscles working overtime. This is the way to appreciate the Dyke. Striding along this grand old earthwork is the only way to understand the manual effort required 1,200 years ago to construct this dyke, 60 miles long, up hill and down dale.

With one final descent through a forestry plantation we gingerly negotiate a precarious, steep, slippery ribbon to emerge into sunlight on the valley floor. Here we find the peaceful churchyard of the tiny St John the Baptist Church where we can rest. We relax on a bench as steam rises off our hot bodies and shield our eyes from the unfamiliar glare of the sun while we eat our picnic lunch. The strain of our day's effort falls away. It's as if the peaceful surroundings are being absorbed by our bodies and minds. Some magic is being woven around us here and it would be easy to pass the afternoon curled up with a book on this bench in other circumstances.

A small tributary to the River Unk has to be crossed and then we're back in woodland on a steeply rising track. We forge up to Knuck Bank (404m) before dropping down then climbing back up to Hergen Hill. The pattern repeats, a tiny stream crossed and another hill crested. We're back on the Dyke now, the path overgrown in many places. By the top of Graig Hil (369m) we're exhausted, but loving every moment of the challenges. The day comes to an end when we drop down to the River Clun and out onto the B4368 ready to meet our support team. We passed George Herbert's birthplace in Montgomery this morning and the words from his 1593 poem 'Virtue' capture our sentiments exactly:

> Sweet day, so cool, so calm, so bright!
> The bridle of the earth and sky –
> the dew shall weep thy fall tonight;
> for thou must die.

On the hour's drive back to our cottage we're eager to regale our friends with stories of the things we've seen. The cackling skein of geese that flew by in the morning mist; the sheep that walked up to Debby to eat from her hand and be stroked; sheep decorated with black eyes, ears, noses, knees and feet; and the raven that swooped over us, apparently one of only 7,000 pairs said to exist in the UK. We tried to describe the switchback wonderland we'd walked through; how we'd lived life to the full today, and that nothing could compare with these green fields, rolling hills and valleys – but gradually we fell silent. The richness of the world we'd inhabited could not be imparted by mere words.

Day 94 – to Dolly Green

Sleep was deep but we both feel weary and need more. Evenings spent socialising with old friends are not ideal given our daily challenges. Mist has enveloped the cottage at breakfast and I hope it will burn off for clear views to energise our progress. An hour later we set off up the morning's first hill, the mist still thick. Slowly I sense my body react to its surroundings. My nerves seem to tingle under the chilly fresh cloud. Nothing is asked of me as I absorb my morning tonic. Gradually the mists become a translucent curtain through which the early sun shines. Yesterday's switchback walking is continuing and this early peak, Llanfair Hill (430m), is the Dyke's highest point. The guidebook quells any sense of false optimism though as the official path reaches twice this height before it's finished.

We plunge down to a small stream then go steeply back up through bracken and on to the grassy hill of Cwm-sanaham (406m). The views compel a stop for an apple. We sit on the grass summit and inhabit a floating kingdom in the clouds. In the peace and solitude we can now appreciate sights and sounds normally obscure to our cultured city minds. The distinctive soulful cry of the curlew precedes the captivating sight of a raven flying close by. Its deep-throated croak calls for attention while the reverberating beat of its wings carry it out into the landscape. With nothing to distract us the sounds mesmerise, and we think we'll never lose track of its distinctive soft wingbeat. No doubt it's totally absorbed in its own business, yet today its connection to us feels palpable.

Our life has become simple out here. Pleasure is rich and arises unannounced from the abundance in our surroundings. The land is simply magnificent and the creatures and flora which inhabit it appear to understand true wisdom is found in the simple enjoyment of the fruits nature has lain at their feet. Perhaps one day we'll see through the folly of trying to dominate and control nature and embrace the Francis of Assisi maxim that the whole of creation is our companion.

Soon the hillwalking brings us down into the prosperous little town of Knighton. It's here we'll confront a tragic part of our family's life. When Matt's girlfriend Kathy passed away over two months ago we were in Scotland. Debby's immediate reaction had been to return home to be with her son. Matt urged her not to and the fact we kept walking was perhaps the greatest challenge we overcame. Since that day, we've realised that in the absence of his mother, Matt was able to grow as an adult. We've learned the best way to help our children is often to get on with our own lives and leave them the space to make their own.

Our grief has still to be properly engaged though and when we heard that today, in this obscure spot, Kathy's mother Sue will be reconnecting with their strong family ties to the Welsh borders, we realised it was an opportunity not to be missed. We arranged to meet the family. So, for two hours over lunch we hear the details of Kathy's final weeks, her funeral and how her family are coming to grips with her passing. By the time we part, we've established a bond and promise to contact Kathy's grandmother, Megan, when we walk through her Cornish home town of Bude next month.

After such a long lunch break, it's heads down and back to the job of walking. We go straight up into the heights and enjoy walking on top of the Dyke, a magnificent 15-feet-high bank crowned here by mature trees. Scaling a succession of hills and hurdling a procession of stiles, we descend to our destination through Furrow Hill three hours later. It may sound like some kind of confectionery, but today Dolly Green is the place we stop.

By bed I'm tired, but my mind turns over the day. We've followed the border, walking from one side in Wales to the other in England and back again. This is Marches country, now a peaceable middle ground, partly Welsh, partly English, and characterised by soft rounded hills and wooded river valleys. For centuries people have contested and fought over this land. However, criss-crossing from one side to the other today, the specific country label seemed irrelevant. Our attempts to conquer and name a particular piece of land seemed such small affairs in this landscape, a futile yearning destined to lead to endless strife. A few nights back we dined in a Ruthin pub while melodic Gaelic conversation arose from an adjacent table of young Welsh people. I'm not sure they felt our Australian twang as tuneful, but these are the distinctions of different traditions and cultures that enrich all our lives.

Day 95 – to Gladestry

It's 5.30am and I get up to prepare for the day. I plod downstairs to make the early morning cup of tea and feel the autumn tingle. A strange sensation passes through my body and I feel compelled to go out the back door to stand barefoot in the cold, early morning gloom. It's a feeling I haven't experienced for a long time. I'm being called to swim! Something elemental is surging through my body calling me to walk out into Melbourne's Port Phillip Bay to swim with Rocket, The Oracle and The Commissioner, my fond companions in the Icebergers' B-Team. After walking for over three months the swimming urge has flooded back into me, but it's going to have to wait a little longer yet.

By the time our bulging backpacks are packed and we're dropped off ready to walk it's 11 o'clock. We say goodbyes with profuse thanks to Mary and Lance. The packs grind into our backs, and after the queasy long drive we walk off like zombies into misty cloud. We have energy for nothing beyond moving along the path. No thoughts arise and we don't talk, we simply walk. A loud quarry siren grates on for five minutes, but neither it nor the small explosion it heralds, disturb us.

Even nature cannot not stir our minds. Acorns pop from grand oak trees to sprinkle on our heads, but all to no avail. Some dim awareness of our silence hovers, but not a word passes our lips. It's a full two hours before we stop for homemade sandwiches on an anonymous hilltop and we discuss our morning experience. We agree the absence of communication had not felt odd. The silence was not bad and the deep peace which had descended on us this morning had taken us to a place where our minds were completely at rest, while our bodies were in motion. We'd felt entirely open and connected to our surroundings. Somehow we heard our world. Our senses were enlivened and the effect was restorative. I recall my favourite Tomas Tranströmer poem:

> Tired of all who come with words, words but no language
> I went to the snow-covered island.
> The wild does not have words.
> The unwritten pages spread themselves out in all directions!
> I come across the marks of roe-deer's hooves in the snow.
> Language, but no words.

A long descent brings us to the village of Kington and we stop at a café while rain spots appear on the window. Tea sets us up to tackle the final hills of the day. From the village, our small lane gradually deteriorates into a farm track, which dwindles to a wisp discernible only to goats. We're on open moorland and after a sharp ascent to the top of Hergest Ridge (425m), find open common land. It's like Devon's Dartmoor and small wild ponies graze with the sheep. Birds of prey circle, scouring the moorland, but suddenly their place is taken by three more fearsome raptors. They're part of the Fleet Air Arm practicing dog-fights. They dart from side to side of our path, sometimes just above our heads, and then they drop below us off the side of this high moor. Despite the noisy interruption to our solitude, we're captivated by their energy, sound and aerobatics. Such is the power of technology's call.

Day 96 – to Hay-on-Wye

I look out at pouring rain, another normal day in Wales. At breakfast we remember the downside of staying in pubs. No matter how welcoming the hosts, or the charm of dinner amidst a bar's quiet conviviality, in the morning there's no more soulless place. The prospect of today's destination though, does inject some excitement. We're going to Hay-on-Wye, the second-hand book capital of the world. With one second-hand bookshop for every 30 permanent inhabitants, today I'm walking to 'book heaven'.

Out on the road everything is sodden and dripping. Our feet are soaked, but with an easier walk in prospect we're soon well into it. We rise up through farmland, progress onto open common and enjoy ourselves. Our footfall brings alarm to animals along the path, chickens scurry haughtily away into their farmyard, then from sumptuous dense green wetness frogs leap, and even a distracted rabbit only just survives my footfall into thick grass. Once we're back out on tarmac lanes we feel cheated as high hedgerows block longer views. We know there's another universe teeming with life inside the hedgerow, but our inquisitive eyes don't know how to tune in to appreciate it.

Our route takes a steep drop into thick woodland, the path a treacherous combination of slithering mud and roots. The day's final chapter requires us to cross three large tracts of farmland. To make matters worse, the second field has been deep-ploughed for potato growing and is a brown muddy expanse. As we look across the rain becomes serious, and by the time we extract ourselves the trail shoes have added a few inches of mud to our height.

We return to the banks of the Wye and the rain gives way to a fragrant perfume that wafts from a dense bank of wildflowers. Soon we're in Hay-on-Wye, in time for a late lunch and an afternoon blog at the library. While I struggle with the pronunciation of certain Welsh names a helpful library assistant produces a fact sheet on the Welsh language. She asserts that not only are there vowels in the Welsh language, but that Welsh is easier to pronounce than English. I'm not convinced.

Day 97 – in Hay-on-Wye

Over breakfast our host tells a delightful story about the 'Welsh Dragon' sausages nestled alongside my poached eggs. He says an official standards officer working to European guidelines informed the esteemed local butcher he would have to change the name because it implied the sausages contained dragon meat. I almost choke as the dragon meat goes down the wrong way. Could we really reach such a tragic state of civilisation that common sense would be completely suspended in favour of tick-box standards manuals?!

We finish the blog update before Angela and Alan become the latest friends to join us. It was late in 1971 when I met them. I was there the day they met, the day I started my first proper job. Winter had set in and when I walked into the Metropolitan Water Board, Angela was there to launch into a new junior clerical assistant role like me and was allocated to Alan's team. Not only did Alan's training work wonders, but a romance blossomed and marriage followed. Although my career took me to far flung places and a life on the opposite side of the world, we will always share a memory of that important day where our life paths first crossed. Also, Alan and I share a love of National Hunt steeplechasing and today the races are on in nearby Worcester.

Well today certainly wasn't a roaring success. My inner Stoic wasn't surprised the day unfolded differently to my rosy-hued vision. The weather was shocking: fierce cold winds were more suited to a ski-field than a racecourse. The fact none of us picked a winner was not a surprise and nor was the shocking takeaway food. But when one horse tragically broke a leg and ran the final three furlongs on three legs before being stopped directly in front of our grandstand to be crudely despatched behind flimsy canvas screens, any shine went off the day. Debby raised uncomfortable questions about why we need to organise such events when there's so much more beauty and wonder in nature. For once, I was at a loss to answer.

Day 98 – in Hay-on-Wye

Today is cold again. The guidebook says the next three days are the longest and three of the toughest. Tomorrow we go to the highest point up in the Black Mountains. Of course, reading of what lies ahead can be dangerous and demoralising. The saving grace of distance walking is that the whole track is never revealed all at once. The curves, obstructions and undulations in the track save our minds being troubled by the sight of challenges up ahead. I put the guidebook down and head out to peruse more archaic tomes. By evening I've loitered the day away in a dozen shops and, conscious of the backpack weight, have restrained myself to buy just one slim volume. It's a diary from the mid-1800's by a local curate, Francis Kilvert. And this took my eye:

> of all the noxious animals too, the most noxious is a tourist. And of all tourists the most vulgar, ill-bred, offensive, and loathsome is the British tourist.

Day 99 – to Pandy

Angela has left with our backpacks and Alan is ready to walk with us on what promises to be a gem of a day. As we step out the ruddy coldness immediately pinches our fingers. Frost has settled from a clear overnight sky and frozen the heavy dewfall. The sun is ascendant and shines down brightly from the deepest clear blue sky to make the track glisten. It's a classic walking day if ever there was one. We start down through the dingle to reconnect with the Dyke path and the chill immediately settles over our bodies. A strange snorting sound in the woods brings a further shiver before we realise the fearsome creatures are simply three large porkers in a free-range pig farm. By the time we climb up beyond the shadows of the trees, I can feel the light touch of morning warmth on my shoulders.

It's ten and Hay is far below as we look up at the top of Hay Bluff (667m). We feel invincible. The woodlands and farm enclosures have fallen away and we're up onto open moorland. The sun's heat is gaining power but moderated by the cooler breezes. We press on straight up the side of Hay Bluff to reach the crest in just two hours. We wait for Alan to catch up and he says he's noticed how we seem to walk straight uphill without pausing or puffing. When we're fresh, it's clear we're a force to be reckoned with.

Here on the ridge we can enjoy the fruits of our labour. Bright sun illuminates a diverse panorama. To the east the handiwork of generations of the West Midlands farming community is on display, a patchwork of agricultural soils and crops delineated by walls and hedges at a size that can be grasped. To the west, the contrast is stark as wild, untamed mountain ridges and valleys roll out to a distant horizon. This is a unique geographical landscape. Beside us the land falls down into the typical 'U' shape of a glacial valley formed in the last ice age. Yet as we peer over the next ridge, we see the beginnings of a sharper 'V' valley, not one formed by glaciation. We've learned this is one of few places in the country where two such valleys can be seen side by side. Of greater importance to us though, is the faintly glittering grey strip that sits directly ahead on the southern horizon. This is our first view of the Bristol Channel, the piece of water that defines the start of the West Country. Once we cross that watery strip, we'll turn to face our ultimate destination for the first time. Another quiet shiver runs through me as I try to imagine what that ending will bring.

We're walking along the Hatterall Ridge, at 703 metres, the highest point on the Offa's Dyke Path. There's about three hours walking up here and although the path is a little stony, to breathe the clear fresh air is a delight. At one, we sit beside the path to share a simple lunch and then move along to look for the small track where Alan will leave us. When the time comes to say goodbye, Alan says he's walked further than ever before. His final words suggest we may have infected him with the walking bug:

'I get it. Now, I understand the pleasure you get from doing this.'

The afternoon wears on as we follow the simple grey flint track. We feel good under a big sky where clouds offer gauzy white shapes to fire the imagination, rather than the usual dark downpour. It's a rare treat to see the landscape under bright sun. The animals are sparse up here like the groundcover. Wild ponies run in a herd and then stop to graze nonchalantly, while the sheep we pass include some of the finest examples we've seen of our namesake badger sheep. Eventually the undulating path brings us to the trig point that heralds a gradual descent into the hamlet of Pandy.

There aren't many places to stay here, and our B&B is a mile off the path. After a long arduous day any extra distance is unwelcome.

However, when our host Keith welcomes us into his eccentric rundown but palatial 16th century manor, I know this will be another special experience to add to the annals of our adventure. We've walked 19 miles and feel weary, so when we're offered a lift to the local pub for dinner, we jump at it.

Dinner is as uninspiring as the local butcher's sausage and mash are large, and with full stomachs we gird ourselves for the walk back. It's over a mile and with little human habitation the pitch black night offers no useful landmarks. My emergency German-engineered torch comes to the fore and in time, we remember our way back to the driveway entrance. In the dense black away from the torchlight we catch glimpses of bats flitting just above our heads and wonder if we might find Uncle Fester at the door welcoming us to the Addams family home.

Back in the room I write up the journal and log. Day 99 is at an end and we've now walked 1,243 miles. However, a second quick calculation shows that while we dodged bats on the driveway we were crossing another memorable barrier: 2,000 kilometres from that Scottish outpost at John O'Groats. This adventure now feels like a true odyssey. I try to share this exciting news with Debby, but she's tired and quickly reminds me she only committed to this journey on the basis we stick to 12 miles a day, not today's 20. I try to assure her I'll do better with the route planning in future. She shakes her head:

'I'll believe it when I see it!' she replies.

After a day of such walking pleasure, I'm tempted to share the Queen's response to Alice's similar assertion in Lewis Carroll's *Through the Looking Glass*:

> 'I dare say you haven't had much practice,' said the Queen. 'When I was your age, ... Why, sometimes I've believed as many as six impossible things before breakfast.'

Day 100 – to Monmouth

I awake with a bad headache and prepare slowly for the day. Outside the weather has obviously reminded itself this is still Wales and the sky has a grey heavy blanket tucked over it. However, today is important. It's our adventure's 100th straight day and we've avoided any inkling of a cold or illness, despite exposure to the daily elements. By the time I've licked the last trace of marmalade from my fingers, we set off watched by the scatter-brained hens that provided our eggs and I'm in a contented frame of mind.

We pass through rolling farmland until being enticed into the old church at Llangattock Lingoed. Given the Welsh climate, I know I'll never spend long enough here to even go close to learning how to pronounce these names. The church originates from pre-Norman days and a 500-year-old painting of St. George and the Dragon has been discovered on one of its walls. We take some time out to admire it, but then move on.

We reach White Castle, another fortification marking William the Conqueror's determination not to lose land to the Welsh princes. A light misty rain is falling and we decide to spend a little time here to let the history add depth to our sandwiches. The place is deserted which adds to its evocative setting, but the cold gradually seeps into our tired wet bodies. We remember Angela's parting gift, a small bottle of homemade sloe gin, and each take a swig for some inner fire.

Our afternoon landscape offers nothing dramatic and all is very quiet. We walk through the Bulmer cider apple orchard. Heavy-laden, the fruit is beginning to drop onto a carpet of wood chippings, but the endless trees planted in strict rows give the impression of walking through an open-air factory. It's a reminder we're now entering the traditional cider apple country. More fields follow, then the River Trothy takes us on into King's Wood and finally Monmouth.

So, Day 100 was just another day on the track, mostly farmland with no particular highlights. We've again walked over 20 miles and so I'm still not inclined to share with Debby the Queen's advice to Alice.

Day 101 – to Chepstow

Our 'Mum and Dad' support team have come down to check on progress. We share stories and large coffees to counter the effects of a poor night's sleep and then make a spritely start at nine. Today will be another long day and as it's our last day on Offa's Dyke we're keen to make the most of it. The weather provides a dramatic backcloth with low cloud and heavy swirling mists. To leave the town our cold muscles have to confront the daunting prospect of an immediate climb up to The Kymin (250m). Four double arrows in the guidebook means it doesn't get any steeper, but we warm to the task and by the top are awake to the day.

The wooded hillside exudes an atmosphere dense with the possibility of meaning and magic. My mind conjures up scenes of what may be lurking. In the stillness of chilled mists, I feel the eerie presence of something not far off in the woods. It feels like the 'hubble bubble, toil and trouble' of a witches' coven that so haunted Macbeth farther north. We move further up and stumble out into a modest clearing to discover The Kymin's treasure. It's unclear to me why the people of Monmouth decided to dedicate this spot to the British Navy's heyday, but it still stands as testament to the admirals who created Britain's 18th century dominance of the oceans. Britannia sits defiant on top of this now dank moss-covered peeling monument with the names of the men who inspired a nation. Needless to say Nelson ranks a panel at the top. Having read all Patrick O'Brian's great seafaring novels of the period, my imagination is all at sea in the swirling mists, transported to the smoke of gunpowder spewing out below decks as cannonballs rip into sailing ships of the French and Spanish fleets. Today, this evokes a timely reminder of the horrors that accompanied Britannia's determination to rules the waves.

There's no time to dally so reluctantly we move on. A descent precedes the next inevitable rise and now the woods have a different hue. They're dense, a rich dark autumn green, redolent of mysterious ancient places. Will it be Gandalf that walks out of the mist or a horde of orcs? Or perhaps somewhere deep inside are the ghosts of Merlin and the young Arthur. Will we suddenly come across a stone with the sword still held? Again we move along, but within these surroundings time flows fast and it's suddenly nearly noon. We stop to sit on a log with our apples.

Offa's Dyke has been the most clearly marked footpath, but now the signage disappears and I'm forced to explore different options. I lead Debby across a field before we find the track, but we've lost time. We had a lunch date with 'Mum and Dad' at Tintern Abbey, but there's not much walkers can do to meet deadlines. The feet can't move much faster. As the track leads uphill I forget temporal affairs and absorb the calm of the grand trees overhead while ferns brush our legs below. The oak leaves and acorns that coat the woodland tracks have already turned brown, a reminder that autumn is now well into its stride.

I know I've lost the track again when we emerge onto the hidden gardens of grand houses festooned with elaborately carved seats and croquet lawns. The grandeur here is highlighted by the sunlight that penetrates the mists to coat all with a golden aura. We may be lost and running late, but it's impossible to be downhearted. I try to recover the situation but go further awry. In this woody wonderland, dotted with private homes, there are few choices but for me to explore some rough driveways. One fruitless effort after another results, before I feel confident of a particular track. However, it simply transports us down onto the back lawn of a strange building.

It looks like some sort of youth hostel but is deserted. It's as if we've wandered through a time warp. When we find a driveway out I read the sign. We've trespassed onto private land and are on the site of a small Polish church with a monument commemorating the Polish soldiers who died at the Battle of Monte Casino. Quite why this monument and church are here, hidden away from the public, is another of today's mysteries.

At last, our descent gives way to the banks of the River Wye with its footpath to lunch at Tintern Abbey. Unfortunately the path is long and we're tired so it's nearly three when we eat. 'Mum & Dad' are typical parents and not amused. But by the time I've then spent half an hour after lunch in the little gem of a second-hand bookshop, neither is Debby. We've already walked 16 miles and she's not in the best frame of mind. It's already after four as we walk away from Tintern and there's still a fair tramp into Chepstow ahead of us. I recognise the moods of autumn are no longer those restricted to the weather; perhaps the bookshop was not my smartest idea.

Just when I need the path to support me, it turns the knife. I'm lulled into a false sense of confidence as we set off along an ex-rail trail. The walking is easy and the gentle lap of the River Wye waters soporific. The trail gradually wanders into the woods and before I realise my mistake, it disappears. A few unmarked tracks, mean I have to explore again and I feel the sharp edge of frustration. When I stumble onto an old gravel road I tell Debby to follow me. After half a mile we arrive at a dead-end. The sheer wall of an old quarry towers above the trees on our left and the administration building is locked up. While we're considering our options, a siren begins to wail and some disembodied voice sternly announces we've entered a secure area. If we do not leave immediately, the authorities will be called. Tempted though I am to wait for some authorities to be called to give us some route guidance, we turn on our heels and retreat from whence we came.

At length I find a way to bring us back on the official path. It's very late in the afternoon and we're nearing some outlying houses. I can smell the wood smoke of an open fire and on a day of rich emotional journeys follow that unique scent down one more diversion to days long gone. I'm back in the early 1970's courting Barbara and we're on a late afternoon walk around Limpsfield Chart woods before dinner and a chance to warm chilled hands by the pub's fire. The path now brings me back to the here and now and the street lights of Chepstow's outskirts. We're both tired and plod down the small pathways and alleys that take us to our destination. It's been a wonderful day, but it's gone on too long.

By the time we walk across the bridge into the town centre it's seven and quite dark. All Debby wants is a bath and bed. However, we have two couples of old friends who have journeyed to have dinner with us downstairs. Somehow, we wash, change and are ready for the engagement within forty-five minutes of arrival. It's a lovely meal with good friends who are bright and full of fun, but after a couple of hours we're both shattered and speechless. We give our apologies and head to bed. Debby has walked 23 miles today, her equal longest, and for me the extra distance exploring dead ends has made it my longest day, some 45,531 steps, or nearly a marathon. The walk was demanding, but carrying off this social evening was arguably a bigger achievement.

Day 102 – in Chepstow

Sleep has eased our bodies' aches and the painful memories entwined in yesterday's adventure have dissipated. It's a rest day, but time to tell stories of the blessings Wales has bestowed on our adventure on the blog. The glory and magic of Offa's Dyke are too good to let slip, so as the rain arrives to offer its farewell we head to Newport, the nearest place with internet coverage.

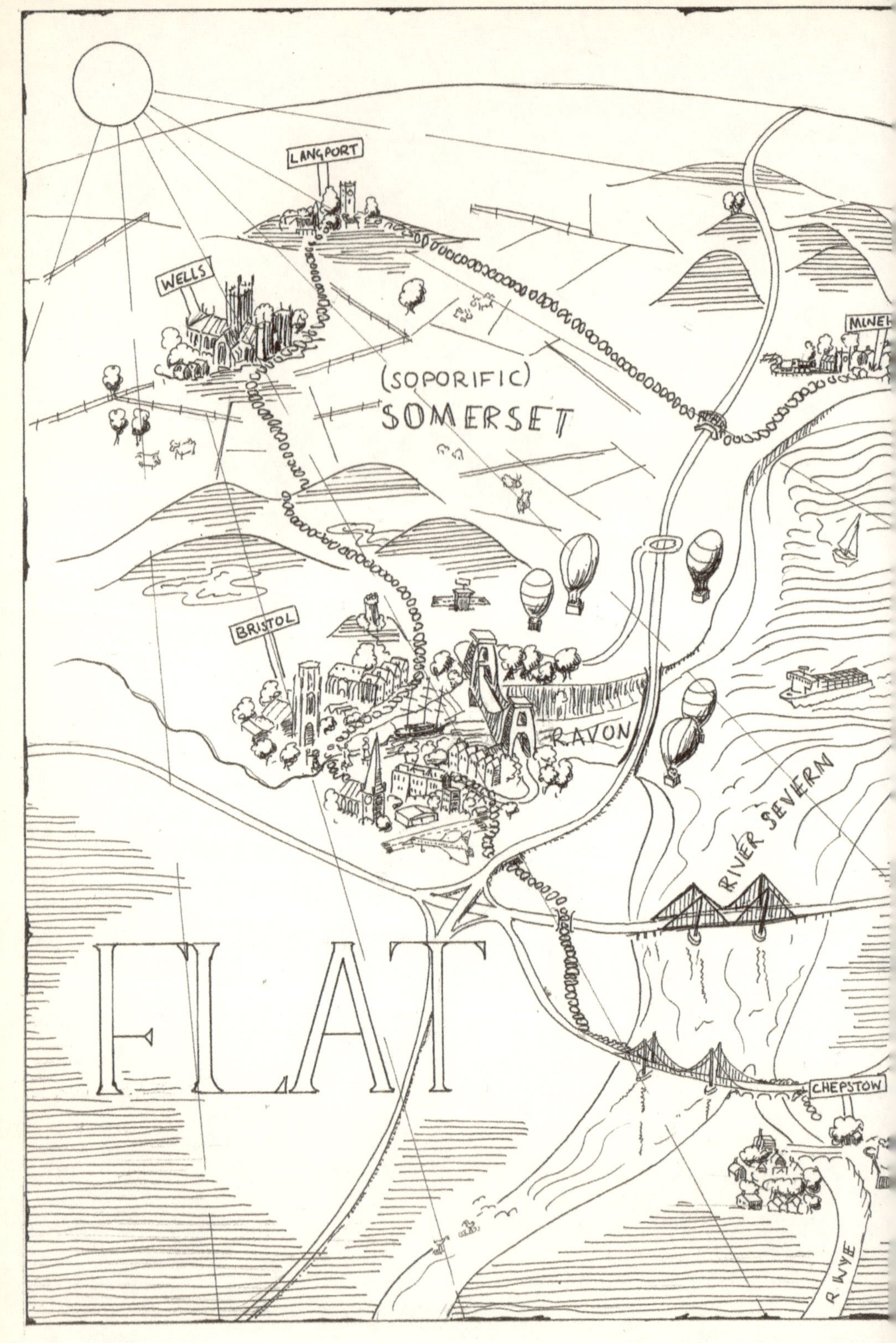
LANGPORT
WELLS
(SOPORIFIC)
SOMERSET
BRISTOL
R AVON
RIVER SEVERN
CHEPSTOW
R WYE
FLAT

Chapter 10 – FLAT

Day 103 – to Bristol

I'm awake at five. It's perverse – my body craves rest but I'm too tired to sleep. I know it will take more than another couple of hours' shut-eye to ease the stresses my body carries, but a bit more sleep before we start a new phase would help. I sprinkle tea leaves in the cup from our inexhaustible stash and begin the solemn process of packing up and preparing myself for the next challenge. Another chapter concluded with Offa's Dyke. Wales is ticked off and now we stand on the doorstep of the eighth and penultimate phase of this quest.

Several weeks of long-distance walking still remain, but at first sight, this next section looks unassuming. I've put this route together seeking some simple West Country pleasure rather than the drear greyness of the Bristol Channel coast. I like to think Pythagoras might also have seen beauty in its triangular construction. We'll walk about 140 miles, heading due south at first, and then at some obscure hamlet we'll lurch 90 degrees to the right and head due west to the coast at Minehead. The countryside is renowned for flat, low-lying geography, so it should be an easier section before tackling the dramatic coastal cliffs.

Walking today is a new experience for us. We're on a major A road heading directly to the Severn Bridge across the Bristol Channel. The bridge opened in 1966, is a mile long and carries a four-lane motorway for a mile. As we reach it the views out across the surging waters below are stunning, and in the distance we can see the newer bridge built in 1995, six lanes and three miles long. Is this a metaphor for human endeavour? Once we master a new idea, are we destined to keep repeating it at ever bigger sizes, rather than reflecting on whether there just might be a better systemic solution?

Being here on this bridge feels almost surreal. Two small humans, we're moving imperceptibly over a massive construction built of thousands of tons of concrete. We're invisible to our fellow earthlings here. They're encased in weighty metal shells, focussed on some existential need for speed, streaming by oblivious to us and the vibrant world we inhabit. While we think of the joy they'd get if only they could escape from behind the screen of their windshields to have our nature experience, even if they could see us, they'd probably just think: nutters!

Estuary life is a little different from the countryside we've traversed these past few weeks. It's full of life but calls for a different eye. At first, we notice the cows are munching on seaweed off the flat wide muddy banks, rather than grass. But looking beyond the farm animals, there's much more happening in this dark grey, muddy ooze. The estuary is described as an international filling station. Some 240 different birds from all over the world have been identified here. Migratory birds find this the ideal stop-off point to replenish their energy stores while en route to far destinations. As a transition zone between river and maritime environments, estuaries have the high levels of nutrients in both the water and sediment, to put them among the most productive natural habitats in the world. Of course, to us it just looks like sludge.

Once we're off the bridge, nature's power to overwhelm our human attempts to conquer and concrete is immediately evident. Scrub and small trees have combined to recolonise a man-made wasteland at the base of the tons of concrete which form the support pillars towering overhead. Throughout it all, as ivy tendrils weave an ever-tighter straightjacket onto human might, the speckle of wildflower blooms redefine the whole into a cloak of unexpected beauty. Freed from our reliance on metal straightjackets and moving at a more human walking pace, we appreciate nature's handiwork and can sample tasty hidden blackberries as we go.

The Severn Way footpath follows a green dyke by the side of estuary mud flats. Apart from the odd fisherman, we're alone. Gradually we're steered away from the waterside through an industrial area with power station, aluminium plant and all the associated spirit-sapping decay that accompanies it. I scour the surroundings and find an obscure footpath along a rank-smelling drainage ditch that steers us from the apparent dead end of another industrial park. We then duck under a railway line and turn to face the Bristol metropolis teeming with over 400,000 people.

Our challenge now is to cross two motorways to penetrate the city's bounds. Railways and motorways are two of the toughest barriers for walkers to negotiate. Planners assume the highest-priority travellers use these industrialised transit systems and proceed to ring-fence cities with them. Travellers on foot beware. I find an old footpath on the map that should get us in if it's still functioning. At the first motorway, we're presented with a tunnel looking like something from a dark, suburban-crime TV film set. Vague images of violence are conjured up to mix with the stench. We're ill at ease and move through quickly. On the second path we feel smug passing a sign, 'Road Closed – Pedestrians Only'. The feeling of superiority soon evaporates however, when we reach the very edge of the motorway. The bridge has been removed. There's a temporary concrete barrier standing on the rough-hewed road edge with the rush of motorway mayhem madness directly below.

I seethe and swear before finally accepting the futility of attempting to run across a busy six-lane motorway with backpacks. I pull out the maps. The quickest alternative route entails all the frustration of backtracking. We retrace our steps hurriedly through the previous unsavoury tunnel and then find a little-used path to the south under electricity pylons. The map shows a tiny path and I'm determined to try our luck again. Now we're taken to the very brink of the Bristol sewage works and become engulfed in a putrid smell. This city's waste is clearly no better than that of the Lagos slums I left behind 30 years ago. It seems for all our more civilised ways, the smell of our shit, no matter where it originates, has not improved.

Now we confront one of our stiffest challenges. An apparently impenetrable mass of brambles has grown over the old derelict footpath. Debby is reluctant, but my determination, fired in a cauldron of stubborn only-child frustration will not be deterred. We don wet weather trousers for protection and set off to thrash our way through. I soon feel like I could be in the Amazon jungle, the spiders crawling up my chest are so big. Visions of Indiana Jones brushing away tarantulas come to mind, but in my bloody-minded obsession I cast off my arachnophobia tendencies and simply fight to keep them down from my throat.

We do finally emerge into daylight and onto a road leading straight into Bristol. It's after three now and the drab Spar supermarket is the only option for equally drab sandwiches. We sit outside and eat to regain our composure. Debby struggles to resume walking after the challenging 16 miles we've covered, but we do manage the last mile or so into Stoke Bishop. My old mentor Mike comes back to whisk us off to another of his relatives. More people blissfully unaware of our existence until tonight have offered us food and a bed.

Once again, tiredness cannot excuse us from the social life. At dinner, we even try briefly to fix the problems of the world before words fail us at 11pm. I go to bed after expressing profuse gratitude to these former strangers for their kindness and hospitality. Briefly I grapple with the conundrum of why such generosity is so readily given when we tend to be wary of people we don't know and talk of humans as intrinsically selfish. Oblivion quickly whisks me off to the equally complex challenges of my subconscious.

Day 104 – in Bath

The sound of pouring rain brings us back to reality and the delightful prospect of a rest day with old friends. A train ride to Bath, a joyful reunion and then, as good friends do, they understand our simple needs. We're given a computer and left to blog until dinner.

Day 105 – to Winford

Our level of tiredness seems to defy deep restorative sleep. My shrivelled 79kg frame wobbles as I heft the 18kg backpack into the hall. Debby is more concerned with a nasty bruised lump on her forehead, a souvenir from a tree in a dark forest, standing up from a not-so-comfortable comfort stop. However, we can't lose any time as we've just agreed a new finish date with our London support team. We need to be at Land's End by Friday November 5th, exactly five weeks from today.

A spirited family breakfast with Sue, Derek, Yolanda and Phil and their children is the perfect preparation before hugs and kisses are exchanged and we're on the train back to Bristol. In the blink of an eye we're back at Stoke Bishop. Inevitably the walk takes us straight uphill. The green expanse of Durdham Down is followed by Ashton Court Estate and then we leave Bristol over the Clifton Suspension Bridge. Next comes Long Ashton, a hotchpotch village created from combining several small outposts strung along the road. Calling it a linear village seems a little bland.

At the small library I enquire about the Monarch's Way footpath. The librarians' intense focus on the internal world on their shelves appears to have precluded any knowledge of their outer surroundings. I believe this particular footpath runs directly past their front door and for 610 miles follows the route taken by the 21-year-old King Charles II after he was defeated at the Battle of Worcester in 1651. For six weeks he was pursued by Oliver Cromwell's parliamentary forces, heading north to hide in an oak tree at Boscobel, before turning south through Bristol and on to the south coast and a boat to France. I've unearthed the Monarch's Way path because the literature suggests it's a major British long-distance path. The fact the librarians haven't heard of it and there are no obvious path markers is immediately a concern.

I choose to ignore the librarians' forebodings that there is no such track, and lead Debby straight into a housing estate. By now we know housing estates are to be avoided by walkers as they're often constructed with no pedestrian exits. Regardless, I'm convinced of the path's route. In time we negotiate the jumble of small houses to find our first Monarch's Way sign. I enjoy my brief moment of achievement, and then the day moves into fast forward. Across a railway, under a main road, up and over Barrow Common to Dundry, past the radio masts at the crest and before we know it we're descending down through farmland to finally duck under a large eyesore of a rusting pipe into the back of a churchyard. We've arrived at a tiny hamlet called Winford. It's five-fifteen and we've completed what feels like a very short Saturday afternoon stroll, just 12 miles.

Although today wasn't too bad, we're on notice that following this route will be harder than I'd imagined. There were times when the markings disappeared and the track became a shared bridleway. This is never good as horses' hooves have a particular gift for concocting a shocking putrid confusion of mud and dung. Also, the farmers hereabouts seem to not encourage walkers. We've found gates tied up with barbed wire and deep-ploughed fields without any recognisable footpath. But worse than all have been nature's defences. Brambles reach out or hang down from trees as a painful entwining ambush while nettles seek to electrify unsuspecting legs. In the shower, I can see nature's bite on my sensitive inner thigh. The bloody trails snaking between my legs are a souvenir of brambles that raked the skin. Never mind, it's all part of the adventure we signed on for. Of course, one benefit of tackling such challenges is the grand stories it gives us to share with friends over dinner.

Day 106 – to Wells

Heavy overnight rain has left the sky dry but the ground underfoot is a quagmire. With all the vigour of fresh growth, dripping wet vegetation welcomes us back to the track with an ardent soaking embrace. As we acclimatise, the sky plumbs hidden depths to summon up more water. Heavy rain and strong winds mean this is clearly not going to be an easy day. To make matters worse, the track continues to be elusive. Each field or woodland we enter now offers very little evidence of an exit point and often there's no sign that feet have ever left an imprint. I have to waste time and energy searching for clues about exits. It's not just the farmers' dislike of walkers that turns their crop fields into featureless mud heaps but their cattle also leave a disgusting slurry to deter us. Electric fences are more problematic around here as well and at one point I unhitch power leads rather than risk stepping over a flimsily covered live power line. And then there's the poor state of the stiles. Often rickety old constructions in a bad state of disrepair, sometimes they are treacherously slippery with mossy growths on the broken wooden remains. And all the time we have to contend with heavily overgrown tracks and an onslaught of stings and scratches from nettles, brambles and thistles. Yes, not an easy day at all.

I forget one of the cardinal rules of walking on waterlogged farmland. Debby had managed to negotiate this reasonably well but I decide to do better. With the gloop of mud sucking at each of my footfalls, I try to avoid the mire by stepping out to the side of what I thought was the worst of it. First my walking pole and then my foot and leg descend into a bottomless morass. I strain my calf, yanking my leg out quickly to avoid disappearing altogether. Debby overcomes her weariness to burst into laughter. It seems her H for Humour commitment is to know no bounds today.

We pass Nempnett Thrubwell and I'm reminded that however improbable the spellings of many Welsh place names, England's south-west has plenty of its own oddities. Our bodies are tired, sore and muddy as we enter Compton Martin, so outside the Ring O Bells pub, I assert my M for Meals authority: 'Debby, we've worked hard; for a change we're going to have a roast meal with a pint and a G&T.' When a classic carvery plate arrives with six accompanying vegetables, I give thanks to have stumbled upon a fine example of perhaps the greatest English institution, the Sunday pub roast lunch.

On a full stomach we walk off with contentment evident in our smiles. Within 15 minutes we're lost and back down to earth. In time the day's modest high point is crossed, East Harptree Wood comes and goes, and then we turn off into Stockhill Woods. Here we're in dog walking territory and I become distracted by a particularly fine Dalmatian. He has a bright red collar and runs and jumps around me in exuberant playfulness. It's a marvel that such a magnificent animal could have such a spotlessly white coat in these wet muddy conditions. By comparison, I just look a mess.

The day wears on, a storm passes through, and trudging down these last back roads we're both done in. The thought of limestone caverns below us at Wookey Hole do not register. I'm on auto-pilot, legs moving independently of consciousness, while Debby is struggling, her cheeks wet with tears. We've had to extend our day to Wells' outskirts to find a B&B, and although nobody answers the door we go straight in anyway and sit down to remove our sodden shoes. After a while, we call the phone number thinking it might be on redirect. It's answered straight away by the people next door. We're in the wrong house. By the time we reach our room Debby tells me she can't face going out to find dinner. It's well after six and we've walked 19 miles, but it's been a far tougher assignment because of the conditions.

I ferret around in the backpack to find any food. A couple of boiled eggs from a few days ago, a single dented Cornish pasty and a chocolate bar. After a large lunch it's all the dinner we need, and in our depleted state it's the last of Angela's sloe gin that really hits the spot. We sit disconsolately on the bed and again I ponder how much more of this quest we've got in us. Debby is terribly beat-up. She's in constant pain through her hips and feet and I worry about what lasting effects this may leave. My left Achilles tendon continues to play up and I've a permanent limp. The more recent rash wounds from yesterday are temporary but painful and were compounded today by long bramble strands which hung down to ensnare me like Tarzan's vines. Our kit is also in a shocking state. Shoes lie sodden down in the porch, caked in mud and stinking, probably the worst they've been on the entire trip. There's nothing for it but to slide under the bedclothes and get away from the day.

Day 107 – to Barton St David

Sleep is long, deep and rejuvenating. The body really is a remarkable thing. In the midst of excruciating exhaustion, it's difficult to see through to moments like this. A few hours ago we were in no state to do anything but lie down, yet this morning we feel we've got the energy for a sightseeing trip to Wells to see Vicar's Close, the only fully preserved medieval street in Europe. We can't dally though and soon re-join our Monarch's Way path as it rises gently up through farmland. The sun's up, the ground's dry underfoot and our spirits are buoyant.

Of course, the reality of our quest gradually infiltrates the day. The overgrown paths and route-finding difficulties never seem far away. Stung by nettles and scratched by brambles, our legs continually tingle as if the hairs are picking up tiny electric currents from the breeze. I've always considered the UK is a particularly good place to walk because there's nothing here that does any harm. There are no deadly spiders, snakes or the miscellany of nasties that confront walkers in Australia. Britain is benign, I've always told Debby. Well, Debby is now ready to argue this contention. Southern England's rampant plague of nettles and brambles are getting her down.

Always alert to distractions from the rigours of the track, once we've passed through Wellesley Farm and between Twinhills Woods and Meadows, we're captivated by the creativity of the spiders. Walking between high hedgerows the spiders unfurl hopeful threads of the finest web to drift in the air above us. A little later, we find ourselves in remote dense woodland. Suddenly we hear casual guitar strumming and perceive some rough infrastructure through the trees. A small community seems to be living in seclusion here. A hollow in the landscape has been incorporated with two makeshift sleeping facilities connected by old pieces of plastic drainpipe. We can't see anyone, but don't disturb the peace and simply slip and slither quietly away down a steep muddy track. We'll never know whether this was a group of travellers, some obscure cult or just a group of old hippies mesmerised by the lure of nearby Glastonbury.

We zigzag across farmland, descend down hidden paths Charles II no doubt cherished and head past Sticklinch up Pennard Hill (125m). It's a token rise, but our highest point for the day. On the ridge the landscape flows softly out in pastel greens and yellows in all directions. It's time for lunch and, without fanfare, fortune smiles on us. We stumble upon an idyllic setting: a small unkempt organic vineyard growing grapes and raspberries in higgledy-piggledy fashion. It's a peaceful hideaway, the sort of place to soothe away all life's hardships.

There's nothing too organised here, just the gentle interplay of the vine plantings surrounded and interspersed with flora that nature appears to have selected at random. The scene is one that would defy orderly human planning, yet speaks of casual beauty beyond measure. Full trees line the vineyard's borders, the unkempt grass underfoot shines bright green in a strong sun, while birdsong and butterfly flutterings induce a sublime sense of ease. We throw down our gear, laze back in the warm sunshine and gaze up through dappled light into the broad canopy of mature trees fanned out high above us. No setting could be better for our needs, and as we lay out our simple food we soak up a feast of the senses. I've heard people talk of rapture, but today I feel I've experienced its spell. Now I understand John Burroughs' words from a century ago:

> I go to nature to be soothed and healed, and to have my senses put in order.

It's hard to move on. We agree this is one of the journey's real highlights, a place and time we'll never forget. It's one thing to enjoy an experience, but we've learned on this trip to pay more attention – to be fully present and understand how special an experience is, in the living of it. This lunch is etched into our memory and we know it will live on to reproduce joy for years to come. Reluctantly we leave the enchantment and acknowledge that, after all the challenges of the Monarch's Way, it's another reminder to never lose faith in the potential for a surprise delight in nature.

We take a footpath to a back road beside Baltonsborough, then down along the River Brue, and take the Tootle Bridge crossing to our B&B. In the evening we stroll to the local pub for dinner and the owner suggests we visit Glastonbury:

'I went there in the 1970's and a guy playing his guitar in the High Street told anyone who'd listen the town would become a great centre for spiritual healing. Everybody thought he was just a deadbeat, stoned hippy, but the amazing thing is, everyone else was wrong and this bloke knew best.'

We walk the mile back along pitch-black lanes with smiles on our faces; the pub owner has offered another reminder to be open to new ideas.

Day 108 – to Langport

We set out along a deserted lane into faint, misty rain under a grey sky. Gradually the day awakens, gently shaking off the early mist while a lazy sun burns off the remaining cloud. Once again we're walking through sleepy Somerset, a countryside that just makes us yawn. Not that it's boring, just so relaxing with this gentle sleep-inducing, sculpted patchwork landscape. Despite our languor, we cover the ground into Keinton Mandeville surprisingly quickly and locate a new footpath to follow for the next five days. Called the MacMillan Way West, it has been created to raise money for the cancer charity. I only hope the signage and track conditions will be better than those on the Monarch's Way.

One thing that hasn't changed are the place names. Barton St David last night wasn't too odd. Even Baltonsborough and Hornblotton, in close proximity, didn't unduly disturb me. But as we move on following footpath signs to Butt's Pieces, I begin to think someone is perhaps playing a game with us. Now the situation becomes ridiculous and a swathe of silly names are unleashed – Martock;

Badger Cross; Somerton Randle; Charlton Mackrell – as well as the neighbouring Charlton Adam; Little Load and its companion, Long Load, and Huish Episcopi. Sport gets a mention at Cricket St Thomas and its alternate Cricket Malherbie, North Curry is just about acceptable if we were looking for something spicy, but what of the fierce competition at Curry Rivel; and Creech Heathfield, really?! One place is even so confused it's called 'Northmoor Green or Moorland'. The hamlets roll by: Middlezoy, Goatshurst, Combe Florey, Thornfalcon, Orchard Portman, Fishpond Bottom, even a Holy City. However, despite all these, the day's most amusing sign is not even a place name. At Long Sutton, a poster has been put up inviting people to the week's big event: Mouse Racing.

Unfortunately, time is against us and we have to move on. With no real sense of surprise our new path seems to show all the same problems we hoped were behind us. A lack of signage and decayed stiles slows our progress. However, the slower pace seems to suit the temperament of this place. The vista offers up no real excitement, just what appears to be an unnatural flatness. We have come to expect nature to comprise rugged hilly terrains cut through by deep valleys and, despite our tiredness, we're missing that. It's often while traipsing up and down hills we find inspiration. We take a late lunch in the peaceful graveyard of Long Sutton's Holy Trinity Church and soon after reach a significant turning point. Our southerly march stops and we turn to the west to head to Minehead on the coast. This is where we'll rendezvous with our final new beginning.

For over 90 minutes we follow the River Yeo and wade through thick grasses before finally, we're done. We stop at Langport and wait to be picked up by friends for the evening. Can it really be 40 years since I first met Richard and Dot? I haven't seen them for at least 20, and of course, they've never met Debby. Regular Christmas letters have preserved the threads of relationship. No matter, by the time they've whisked us back to their home, the conversation is flowing as if it had only ever been on hold. Once again, this adventure is weaving in people, new and old, like a gift that keeps giving.

With limited supplies and no ready home for the night, we've exposed our vulnerability and sparked a spontaneous reaction of hospitality from others. Until we are prepared to step out from behind the impermeable shield of capability and control we work so hard to preserve, others are denied the pleasure of being helpful. Whether it's old friends or new acquaintances, we're being showered with great kindness.

Day 109 – resting in Langport

Over a lazy breakfast we enjoy the slow uncharted chatter of old friends catching up on the circuitous wanderings of family lives. Slowing down the clock to allay the busyness of lives led on the run, these stories, tiny flecks shared in a daunting universe, feel this morning like they are taking us to the very essence of what it is to be human. I've long felt there's nothing more important than the relationships we forge with people circling in and out of our lives, and walking has slowed us to a pace at which we can do justice to them. We have the time to connect in a way that brings meaning as we discover the happiness that draws us together as companions and collaborators in life's mystery. This is a time to cherish and I already sense that with the impending completion of our adventure, we'll return to the hurly-burly of hectic lives, and lose something very special.

Day 110 – to North Petherton

Another good night's sleep and after reluctant goodbyes we're whisked back to the very mark of our last footstep. Before Richard leaves, he tells us stories of his little home town, Chard. Their old butter factory used to be the biggest in the world, they elected Britain's first female MP and a former resident, Mr. Stringfellow, invented the first powered flight, even before the American Wright brothers.

It's just after ten as we start the relatively short walk to North Petherton. With the companionship of a lovely autumn day and no fearsome challenges, I feel myself relaxing into peaceful solitude, cosseted by the bucolic surroundings. Our walk will range between zero and five metres above sea level all day. This is the Somerset Levels. Once flooded wetlands for much of the year, numerous pumping stations and a system of canals and ditches are testament to the unceasing human attempts to put nature in order. The water now flows neatly in a muddy channel and this is the glistening brown serpent we'll follow for much of the day. Walking across this landscape, though easy on the body, is unremarkable. I'm yearning for the hills and valleys and the surge of energy they bring.

The day clearly needs an injection of something to focus our minds and around noon I make a serious mistake to create it. We stop for morning tea and like a mouse attracted to mouldy cheese, I spy a bargain too good to be overlooked. A £1 kilo bag of damson plums from a farmhouse honesty table. Finding their taste as compelling as their value, I gorge myself on half the bag. Debby more cautiously samples a couple, questioning their quality. Within half an hour, I have my focus. The Somerset Levels have disappeared from view as my entire attention is channelled within. All my mental and muscular strength struggles to control my basic bodily functions. I must find the nearest public convenience, and quickly. This is a very different challenge to anything I've yet encountered. With a reduced stride and buttocks clenched, I carry on. The only possible relief could come at a distant pub. I manage to keep going to the Thatcher's Arms at Fordgate. When I find the pub closed, I want to scream. However, courtesy of old British building traditions, there's an outside toilet and it's unlocked!

Now I can relax and we take out lunch. After a Cornish pasty, sandwich and heritage apple picked from Richard's tree, I sit back and reflect proudly on just how quickly I can bounce back from a digestive disorder. With lunch behind us, we resume in the uneventful manner the Levels engenders. Little-used roads meander besides the river leading to a tiny back road over the M5 motorway and on into North Petherton.

It's early and we drop our bags outside a fine old church and pass inside through a time warp back into history. Christianity came to England with the Romans, brought to this distant outpost of their empire in 250 AD. When the Romans left, the religion waned under new conquerors but remained strongest in this area of south-west England. This impressive old Minster church was built before 1400 when Geoffrey Chaucer, of the Canterbury Tales, was Warden of the local Petherton Park. The pulpit dates from the early 15th century when the English and French were having one of their regular run-ins at the Battle of Agincourt. Although I'm not a churchgoer, such places are part of my heritage and I can sense peace here, a reminder of those who have come to sit at these pews holding their joys and sorrows over the centuries.

Back outside, Mike's sister Sheila and husband Andrew arrive to collect us. Once again, we've been presented with the opportunity to meet new people and enjoy sharing a home-cooked meal. And again we're humbled as we're taken into the warmth of the home of strangers and treated as guests. The social evening ends when we're shown to the computer room to blog away to our hearts' content. Like a powerful animal compelling attention, the blog demands completion. The beast finally sated, I lay weary head on pillow, my last sight for the day a clock face signifying the midnight hour has come and gone.

Day 111 – to West Bagborough

The prospect of a relatively short 12-mile stroll in the Quantock Hills is appealing after the humdrum flat lands of previous days. Once we've done justice to a gargantuan breakfast spread and collected a generous packed lunch, I know hunger will not be our undoing today. The day is warm and humid, different to almost any weather we've experienced so far on the walk. This is the true Indian summer of my rose-tinted memories of England.

Today's walking is much more enjoyable. The greater variety of woodlands and hills sparks interest in contrast to the dispiriting, languorous flatlands of yesterday. The Levels might be a wetland haven for birds, but we need hills to march up and a landscape of trees imparting their magic restorative energy. Dappled woodland paths take us up through Kings Cliff Wood, Stream Farm and past a classic lake setting, all willows and swans.

A classic 'holloway' path awaits us in the afternoon. Deep marks show how wooden carts wore ruts into the earth which eventually broke down to lower the track bottom. This is a classic specimen, completely sunk in the landscape and enclosed by gnarled trees and thick vegetation on all sides. Earthen banks rise up four metres high walling us in. It feels like a magical setting, as if we've walked through a portal and time has stopped. Fleeting glints of sunshine occasionally penetrate to light our way as we're welcomed down a giant rabbit hole. The track winds on and on reducing to a narrow single file passage, where pheasants run frantically ahead.

We are delivered into open fields and the pheasants disperse running hither and thither. I marvel at their number until Debby pulls me up to stop just inches short of an electrified tripwire and mesh fence. Another piece of paraphernalia to protect the pheasant until they're worthy of being shot. We retreat and force our way through a small hedgerow into a ploughed field to once again muddy our boots. Mud has been a feature of today. Many of the paths in this charming landscape have been shared bridleways and not even hippos could have done a better job of creating the quagmire we've traversed. Spontaneously my childhood subconscious takes over and I sing out, 'Mud, mud, glorious mud, nothing quite like it for cooling the blood.' Debby is unimpressed, reminding me H for Humour is her domain.

Now we're out on Cothelstone Hill (330m) and I can appreciate why it's said one can see 14 counties from here with a telescope. On this sunny rump of a late autumn afternoon though, we simply stride out joyfully towards the outline of Minehead, a watery mirage floating on the horizon above the day's last vestiges of mist. The end of phase eight looms, still just beyond our grasp for the moment. As with all good things, the magic ends and we take the path down through Twenty Acre Plantation to the pretty hamlet of West Bagborough.

Day 112 – to Williton

It's six in the morning and I'm raring to go. We've been told we'll have to wait for breakfast as it starts later on Saturdays. Giving particular names or importance to specific days of the week seems irrelevant. Every day moves to the same beat for us. Today is a bit shorter though, only around five hours' walking awaits.

Our host explains that to reach the high ridge track we need, there's a steep uphill track at the side of the inn, an alternative to the more gentle official path. This hill is a vertical 200 metre ascent of mud, rocks and roots. Apparently the local challenge, we're told, is to get up it in 15 minutes. Immediately I say, 'We'll take the steep track.' Debby smiles and blinks, but is not fazed. She understands my peculiar sense of fun.

Despite the swirling mist and frigid air, I strip down to t-shirt, hoist the backpack in place and set off up the hill at a fast pace.

My t-shirt soaked in sweat and with a feeling of elation, I step into thick mist out on the ridge 13 minutes Later. As the glow of success spreads through me, Debby arrives bang on the 15-minute mark. I congratulate her, but she explains she only fell back to take a long mobile phone call on my behalf. My sense of male ego is dented, and I wonder if I may be competitive after all.

The atmosphere is denser now. We're walking along the wooded spine of the Quantock Hills and, despite the mist, a strong wind is blowing the trees into a frenzy of autumn confusion. On a track that was used as the main thoroughfare in the Middle Ages, the swirling conditions today conjure up scenes more likely to confront Sherlock Holmes in his search for Dartmoor's 'Hound of the Baskervilles'.

Joining the MacMillan Way, we leave Aisholt Common and gradually the trees fall away. We push out onto open moorland with Hurley Beacon, Thorncombe Hill, and Black Ball Hill our route markers. It's majestic walking. The mist hides long vistas, but breathing in the fire of sharp, fresh air feeds our spirit. We're on the inside of nature's shroud. A ten-minute break to crunch through an apple is only disturbed when Debby suddenly announces, 'Wednesday is a great walking day.' I politely remind her it's still Saturday and, mildly disconcerted at my partner's state of mind, we finish the morning tea break in silence.

The Macmillan Way turns off but we stay up high for longer on the ridge track. A steep path eventually leads down to a wooded valley and our world changes. This one is inhabited by pheasants and a cheerful bubbling stream to keep us entertained. The track is now quite isolated and a huge fallen oak limb appears to have completely blocked the path. Debby sees my dismay and with her usual combination of poise and endeavour finds a way through. Meanwhile, I struggle with rogue tree branches and undergrowth intent on bringing me and the large pack into even closer relationship with nature.

Tumbling out of the woodland into farmland and deserted country lanes we find a new landscape. The ancient-looking village of Woolston comes and goes, followed by more country lanes with a few smallholdings. Just as Debby's hot feet need a rest, I find an opening into a field with a small wall to hide behind. It's a charming picnic spot and the resident bugs scurry for cover before my bottom lands on their home.

The afternoon exertion is mercifully brief and we soon walk into Williton, our haven for the night. Immediately we're disappointed. This looks a drab, uninviting little town. Things go downhill when we attempt to buy afternoon tea at the only teashop in town. It's well before three, yet we're told they closed ten minutes earlier. Everything appears bleak and a local sees our dismay. He says Williton is a shocking place to live and sympathetically offers to drive us up the road to a café on the coast. It's kind of him, but hardly a welcome to warm the cockles of our hearts. We decline the offer and trudge to tonight's B&B.

Just when I've written a place off, again I'm proven wrong. Sue and Tony welcome us with real warmth and fete us with homemade chocolate beetroot cake and a pot of tea. By the time I lie down, the familiar waves of weariness flood over my body. I start to read and imagine myself lying in the ripples of a sun-washed sea. Despite my best efforts to read, I just keep nodding off. Thankfully, neither Debby nor I are suffering any particular physical problems, but accumulated exhaustion is now our constant travelling companion.

Inevitably the pub dinner proves disappointing and we embrace the opportunity of an early night. Before sleep comes to fetch me for a different adventure, I find my mind filled with trees. Nothing has been more important in bolstering my spirits on this adventure. Friends who've followed the blog have observed that despite my saying the sea is my natural element, it's the trees which appear to resonate in my writing. They're right and I know the close bond I feel is deep-rooted.

Spending such a prolonged time in nature is having an effect on me I can only guess at for now, but being in daily communion with the trees has become my greatest joy. I've come to understand their importance as the lungs of the earth, but so much more. Their beauty is captivating, whether gazing up into delicate transparent leaves while standing on staunch roots in the shade of a regal field oak, or peering through driving rain at an unyielding ash, perched on a clifftop, windswept, contorted, but resolute in its destiny. Each one epitomises an elegant resilience and evidence of the stamina and patience needed to live a full life, sometimes for thousands of years. However, it's more than that. They demonstrate a grace in their recognition of an annual life cycle in harmony with the ebb and flow of the seasons. Yet, beyond their own wellbeing they offer food, home and so much more to other life, a lesson in generosity that's not lost on me. As surely as they mark the landscape, they're leaving their mark in my heart.

As sleep comes to claim me I try to contemplate tomorrow. We'll be walking to the coast to start the last phase of our adventure. I feel confused. Quiet elation is mixed with another emotion, a sense of disappointment. This quest will all too soon be part of my past, just another story that defined a particular life path to my destiny.

Day 113 – to Minehead

We both awake from a dead sleep at five-thirty. Debby is at her impressive best moving straight into a yoga practice. I envy her ability after all these months to bring yoga back into her morning routine. As she delights in the immediately beneficial effect on her body, I feel leaden-footed with tiredness. Our meagre belongings infused with the sweat and dirt of too much effort are scattered across the room. I know I must pack the bag but I crave a rest day, or better still a rest week. Debby tells me to sit and gives my feet a rub. By the time I trudge to the bathroom I feel the world heavy on my shoulders.

And then just as my mind is implacably closed to the idea of walking, blogging or even picking up the soap, everything changes. A new dawn rises to herald the excitement of a new day. Is it the crisp air at the window inviting me out? Or the plaintive cry of a seagull, lost over Williton's drear scenery? Or is it the knowledge that today we'll reach the sea? I know I'll want to feel its embrace and the stark, chill needles of the water penetrating my skin. The sea is indifferent to who it encounters, but it will demand I bring the best of myself and so again come to know who I truly am. Something has happened walking along the corridor to the bathroom this morning and, at an elemental level, I've awakened. There's juice to be had today and it can flow through my veins to stoke a fire of memories. I return to Debby revitalised.

Out on the pavement a grey dawn has settled over Williton and it's with no regret we make an early departure. We leave town via a footpath past the Bakelite Museum. It seems sad but appropriate that this town features a Bakelite Museum as its claim to fame. We move quickly past the plastic three-wheeler car and caravan, heading back out to contemplate Mother Nature, a true colossus, leaving the pallid plastic imitations in our wake.

Soon there are little pigs scurrying around in a field with chickens and a ram with impressive horns. Not the most stimulating environment, but well ahead of Bakelite. We carry on uneventfully into Stream. The name suggests a lack of creativity, but surely the locals could have done better than Higher Stream up the road and Lower Stream down below? On grey days like today, we revert to the one sure way to spark things up. We kick acorns and conkers. I demonstrate my school third eleven soccer prowess to Debby by kicking them further while keeping them on the track. Undulating muddy paths develop and lead to bigger inclines. We stop for morning tea at noon on old steps at the back of a farm at Golsoncott. After well over two hours of walking our ten minutes break is as hungrily consumed as our apples.

An hour later the track has led us to Withycombe with its imposing hill. We're up high and gazing out across the Quantocks when a bench seat materialises. It's part of the local village's centenary celebrations which included planting a ring of 20 beech trees. They're still mere saplings, but the bench is in fine condition and we shed our backpacks for lunch. The atmosphere high up here on this misty day is a better accompaniment than any fine wine. After lunch we climb higher through a wood before descending into the little ancient town of Dunster, with teashops and aging customers, drawn like moths to candlelight. In the rosy glow of an autumnal afternoon, we too are duly caught in the flame and stop for that English staple, afternoon tea and cake.

More hills await now, Grabbist Hill comes first then we're onto Knowle Hill (250m) and can finally look across Aldersmead to the sea at Minehead. The sun has penetrated the cloud cover and burnt off the mist to present us with an autumn scene to relish. Walking along a path lined with gorse and ferns, our eyes flit from vibrant sun-draped greenery to mellow browns and yellows. An ancient stonewall looks at peace with its fate. Its identity was lost long ago as powerful trees entwined their thick roots throughout its length. Coated in lichens and moss it has gained a strength, beauty and permanence beyond the imagination of any stonemason.

In lighter contrast, a profusion of tiny webs paints silken strands on the gorse bushes at our side. This is autumn in all its flawed beauty. We amuse ourselves by speculating where in the world we might spend the four seasons if money and circumstances were no barrier. I'm not sure about summer and winter, but plump without second thought for two autumns. The perfect, still swimming days of Melbourne in the southern hemisphere autumn are too good to miss, but so too these days dyed gold in England's summer decay.

Does it say something of my age that I would rather swop the effervescence of spring in favour of a double dose of this season's near death experience?

A fairly steep, slippery, stone-filled descent and then we're out onto the roads of Minehead, our largest town since Bristol. As usual the first challenge is to find tonight's B&B. Fate proves a cruel taskmaster – it's on the other side of town, up a very steep hill. Immediately we drop our packs inside the door, I realise we've entered a Fawlty Towers Institution. Alex, the owner, has the same attitude of superiority over his guests as Basil and is not shy about 'calling a spade a spade', as he puts it, while belittling guests. I like the faded grandeur of the place and smile at 'Basil's' antics, but we press on to attack a huge tub of washing before more unmemorable pub grub.

In bed I bring the log up to date. Phase eight of our adventure has ended and we've now walked 1,429 miles in 113 days. Of course, 26 of those have been 'rest' days. Well, strictly speaking, washing, blogging, logistics planning, mapping, reorganising and repairing days, rather than any true days of rest.

Day 114 – in Minehead

Breakfast is memorable only for Alex's amusing performance. He berates a couple of guests for not knowing the difference between a 'cafetiere' and a coffee 'plunger'. A war-time spirit prevails and as soon as Alex leaves the room we share much laughter with the brow-beaten couple. In these days where service standards are meant to be improving, Alex seems to operate a well-supported establishment without service. What does this say about British attitudes to service? Perhaps we really are more comfortable with criticism. It's doesn't surprise me that this town also boasts a large Butlins Holiday camp which in my childhood seemed to organise holiday fun with such fierce, structured efficiency they were more like POW compounds.

Once the blog is done we emerge into a sunny mid-afternoon. This is a British-style late season holiday resort town. The holiday-makers in t-shirts and shorts that traipse past the jaded shopfronts and cafés do not seem to feel the tentacles of autumn chill now creeping over the country. Morning light only appeared about quarter past seven today and soon the clocks will go back to drive out the last vestiges of afternoon daylight by five.

The gathering twilight softens the dirt and grime built up over the holiday season and my mind turns to tomorrow. The momentous barrier will lift and the last phase of our journey will begin. From the first, it had seemed obvious to finish along the South West Coast Path. I realised its demanding succession of cliff climbs would come when we're at our weakest, yet some strange attraction had seemed to bubble up from within. We'll be heading into Cornwall, reputed to have over 5,000 years of known history and where legends abound. While forging lives in tough conditions remote from the din and press of large urban communities, the Cornish have developed a deep spiritual heritage. Whatever else we find, there's no more evocative place to wander a coastline than here.

Perhaps embedded in the physical challenge of a dramatic elemental landscape, I'll find the conditions ripe to stimulate my inner consciousness. I've already had some experience on this walk where under physical challenge my mind has become distracted and the unconscious set free. These last few weeks may be an opportunity to journey inside myself to consider life's deeper meaning. As we approach the final piece of country on the very tip of England, I'm looking for answers to questions which circle but resist clear definition. I wonder what state I'll be in when these walking shoes are taken off for the last time? Something stirring inside tells me this walk may have effects which will endure beyond the final blog entry. Despite uneasiness over our physical condition, I relish tomorrow and our final date with a new beginning.

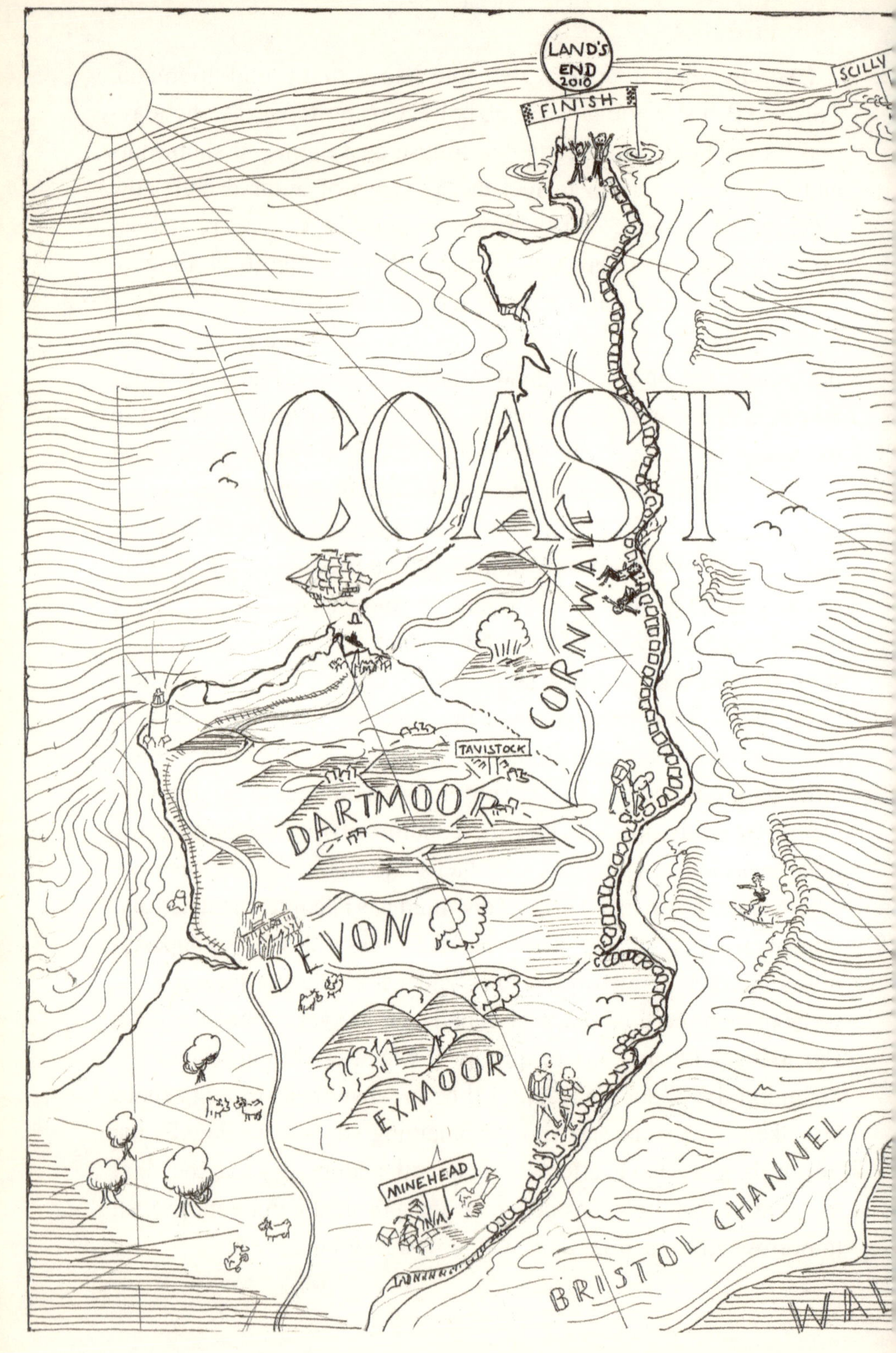
LAND'S END 2010
FINISH
SCILLY
COAST
CORNWALL
TAVISTOCK
DARTMOOR
DEVON
EXMOOR
MINEHEAD
BRISTOL CHANNEL
WAL

Chapter 11 – COAST

Day 115 – to Porlock Weir

The South West Coast Path may only have officially opened in 1978, but the coast-hugging track's origins date from HM Coastguard's attempts in 1822 to counteract smuggling. We start here in Somerset but within 20 miles will cross the Devon border and then on to Cornwall. Devon has a softer feel than its close cousin Cornwall, yet the coastline can be just as harsh. While Devon has a history caught up in smuggling, pirates and brooding moorlands, it's now better known for twee thatched cottage B&Bs and tourists risking their arteries with clotted cream teas. Cornwall though has forged a wilder reputation for untamed myth and magic.

Coastal paths typically offer the walker a great variety of landscapes and weather, everything from sun-bleached sand to savage turbulent seas and skies. Sea salt will be an ever-present taste on our lips. The air will be alive with the smells of rotting seaweed, wet earth mould and smoke from smouldering logs in isolated farmhouse grates. Seagulls will cry out above us as they soar effortlessly in wind that will gust and moan to threaten our passage. And the clamour of the sea will reverberate to the crash of breakers that throw up spume and swirling sea fret. And then an occasional heart-stopping silence will descend when clouds and wind disappear to leave the sparkle of an aquamarine sea. This journey has brought us into direct contact with the elements, but this reunion with the coast should be a dramatic finale.

Of course, there will also be hills. This last phase means we'll tread a cliff path that constantly rises and falls along a ragged-edged piece of storm-beaten geography. Muscles, joints, every sinew will be challenged. Whatever reserves of energy we have will be dearly tested. Yet as an ocean swimmer nothing could be more fitting than to have the sea as companion for the final 250 miles or so.

A year ago I set our schedule to keep the walks to no more than 15 miles a day to allow for tiredness, but I worry I've only allowed three rest days in the last 25. Hopefully the history and scenery will lift us to our destination.

We step out onto the steep hill into Minehead and immediately the morning chill envelops us. We'll need to get used to colder days from here on, particularly with the biting sea breezes high up on the headlands. But first, ritual must be observed. We head to the official South West Coast Path starting line on the foreshore where two giant metal hands hold up a half-unfolded map. It's the most impressive hiking statue we've seen. We turn to face our first steep track to the summit of North Hill, I hoist my 20kg pack and then, one foot at a time, we set off.

We've been walking for 17 weeks, but both notice a new lightness in our bodies reminiscent of the climb from Prestatyn. It's the joy of another new beginning. No sense of tiredness. All the walking that's gone before is forgotten, any aches shed like autumn leaves. We revel in the climb. Wooded tracks fall away and out on the ridge expansive views open up over the channel to Wales. The grey sea looks morose, brooding with intent, so I turn my attention inland to Exmoor's kinder bracken and gorse moorland.

At the summit, the safe 'official' coast path vies with an 'alternative rugged' coast path. Our bodies may be travel-worn, but today is not a day for restrictions. We plump for the alternative track, despite an hour longer walk. No sooner is the choice made than we're thrown onto a rollercoaster. The path is no more than a goat track – a narrow thread that skirts high up around the headland. Then we plunge down to a tiny stream which, belying its size, has created a huge chasm. Then we climb up back into the rich oxygen of the high moorland edge. Then we do it all again, and again, and again.

Up high we sit behind a sheltered bank with plums and pears for a short break. Protected from the wind we barely speak. Across the sea stands the grey, indistinct landscape of southern Wales, where I know it will be raining. We move on, the Eastern and Western Brockholes fall away and we re-join the official path at Bossington Hill. Next comes Hurlstone Point and then the descent along an ankle and knee-wrenching steep rocky path.

We've been told to seek out the tearooms at Bossington. During the morning a German couple have haunted our walk. The track hasn't been busy and as we've taken a breather this couple have passed us and vice versa. Polite nods have been exchanged but now we arrive together at the tearoom and agree to sit together. Formal introductions provide names to the faces. Over cream teas we share stories of our families' lives and find we have much in common. It feels quite natural that here in this tiny spot we're sitting with Germans and the cook is their kinswoman from Bavaria. In a world where animosity against foreign nationals can be wilfully trumped up to incite fear, I show solidarity and choose the chef's special, Lebkuchen, the German Christmas cake of life. We share photographs and although we may never see them again, Manfred and Rosie have just become two more collectors' items woven into the lucky-charm bracelet of this adventure.

The day peters out across flat fields and dry marshland dotted with dead trees. The last stretch on a wide pebble and rock beach with heavy backpacks is hard on tired feet. By five it's over. We're in a small hotel, right on the Porlock Weir seafront in a little secluded harbour. It's an eccentric haven filled with antiques. Paintings, stuffed animal heads and other curios fight for space on the walls.

We seem to be the only out-of-season guests and a sense of peace hangs over an honesty bar in the comfortable lounge. Bing Crosby gently croons in the background to stroke tired travellers' spirits. What a setting this would be to hunker down around an open fire for a Christmas house party.

Day 116 – to Lynmouth

It's six and I write my journal while waiting for the sun to come up. It's seven-thirty before I'm sure we've nothing more enlivening than a solid grey smudge for sky today. Will I swim? Outside neither sea nor beach look inviting. It's a typical dreary English setting and the memory of yesterday evening's pebbles is fresh. I've carried my bathers, goggles and towel for months, yet presented with a swimming opportunity, I can't summon up the enthusiasm.

Breakfast is served with great good humour by a Russian waitress with a big smile. I decide to have sausages with my egg, which turn out to be enormous. When I comment, the waitress grins and says, 'You, big man, have big sausage!' Debby stifles a laugh while I supress an uneasy feeling of inadequacy.

With backpacks in place we set ourselves for the initial steep climb back to the top of the headland. The path is supposed to be clearly marked and I relax for an enjoyable day. A striking toll house sits on an arch astride the road. The owners are still allowed to demand £2 from each car that passes along the road underneath. We exact a different penalty on the severe road climb to 300 metres above sea level. I check the map and curse out loud. The path left the road at the toll house and we've climbed much higher than necessary. Debby is phlegmatic and suggests we go back. That's inconceivable! I remind her I never go back and stubbornly work out a new circuitous route woven from an assortment of obscure country lanes. We move off in silence.

When we do reconnect with the path, we're presented with a dilemma. We've passed Culbone, the home of St Beuno's Church. Although we've visited many old churches this is one I'm loathe to miss, though it will mean a steep descent on a rough woodland track. Debby reluctantly agrees and we descend the track back into history. The church was mentioned in the Doomsday Book of 1086 and even without all our advanced building techniques these walls made of rubble, rendered and lime-washed, still stand 900 years later. And the stonemason can be proud. His mark remains visible in the north chancel 'two-light' window that he carved from a single sandstone block a thousand years ago. And there's an 800-year-old font and a 700-year-old bell that still rings true.

Inside the church is a record of the human history. I look down the list of all the Rectors since Ralph Lucy in 1329, just 49 of them. The list delicately omits Thomas the Chaplin who in 1280 was shown in Assizes as having struck Albert Ash, one of the parishioners, on the head with an axe and killed him. Hardly a spiritual act. The real defining characteristic of St Beuno's today though, has gained it a listing in the Guinness Book of Records. At 35 feet long, it's the smallest church in England with a parish in operation and is said to seat 33, 'in some discomfort'.

This church has witnessed much human misery. Three of the rectors between 1348 to 1353 died suddenly, probably from the Black Death which killed one third of Britain's entire population. The Culbone population is small today but in past years was boosted by the inclusion of vagrants and a leper settlement which by 1544 numbered 45. To think Culbone warranted a church of its own is remarkable. Its peak population, achieved in 1831, was just 62 people living in 11 houses.

For a few minutes I stand alone outside surrounded by dense woodland. It's taken great effort and dedication to create this edifice in such a remote place and I wonder why. I can only marvel at the trials people would have endured over centuries to get here. There are fortnightly services nowadays and attending would be no less of an achievement given there's no access for cars. It was something of a nightmare for us to descend the tortuous path; awash with rains or covered in snow it could be lethal. The religious ardour of this community is not in question. Perhaps the search for meaning compels us to create these challenges? And perhaps that's why I've made the trek back to see it. I'm pretty certain by now my search is not for a revealed religion and an all-knowing God. My eyes have been opened on the walk, away from the city's concrete framework. The teeming flourish of life in sky and landscape has awakened my spirit to the unfathomable mystery of my part in a rich web of life.

It's an hour before we're back out on our path, but the diversion was worth every minute and ounce of energy expelled. A tiny isolated road, populated by two or three stone built houses, leads us on an undulating journey – indecisively, one minute up, the next down, never flat. At first far-reaching views are a reward for our exertions, but then a path takes us off between dense hedgerows and moorland farms. We pause briefly after Broomstreet Farm for an apple and nuts and feel the now familiar sense of peace settle on us. We'd love to while away hours here, but the walk won't allow it.

We scale Sugarloaf Hill and then a steep drop follows into woodland to cross another small stream. Rhododendrons are everywhere, but despite their beauty they overrun the track, poisoning the soil so nothing else can grow. It's a reminder we can have too much of a good thing. In a deep valley on a cliff walk there's only one way to go, up! It's a very steep climb on a rough track and as the A39 nears I become uneasy. Once again I've navigated like a midnight drunk in a maze and lost the path completely. I endeavour to control my anger and frustration. In finding a way forward, never backwards, we pass the 'Welcome to Devon' sign. So, it's official, we've entered the penultimate county of England.

I begin to think of Tim, a work colleague over 30 years ago in those days of African oil exploration. He'd sent me a text message a few weeks ago to say he would join us somewhere along today's walk. That was it. No more details, no where or when. After two unplanned deviations, if he's just going to pop up along the way, the odds are not good we'll find one another. I redouble my determination to do better with navigation. We've climbed too high again and eventually drop down to find the right path. And what a path it is. Lined with massive trees gnarled with great age, they stand like powerful sentinels that could have auditioned as Ents for *Lord of the Rings*. Within minutes of re-joining the official track, around a deserted woodland bend comes Tim. It's a real 'Dr. Livingstone, I presume' moment.

We push on along a path that snakes over a cliff face through an area labelled as 'desolate' on the map. The machinations of the path seem designed to test our limits. Steep falls to cross streams followed by extended climbs back up to precipitous clifftops, and then the formula repeats. Our energy drains into the track, until I call a halt at Sister's Fountain, where Jesus is supposed to have stopped to drink with Joseph of Arimathea on his way to Glastonbury. The fountain eludes us, but the excuse for a break is welcome.

A final long narrow descent along the cliff face brings our day to an end at Lynmouth. The chipper atmosphere of this traditional English seaside resort is infectious and our faces light up with smiles. It's a nice feeling to welcome weary travellers. The town has been devastated by water torrents pouring out of the hills on several occasions, but today the River Lyn flows quietly along the valley reinforcing the town's 'Little Switzerland' moniker. It's after five when we find our basic B&B and wash off the sweat of a 16-mile day. We go out for dinner only to sit shivering in an authentic alpine atmosphere. It was cold up on the cliffs and my fingers went white more than once, but the last thing I need is for it to happen over dinner. Well before nine our bodies are closing down and Tim understands it's time for our bed.

Day 117 – to Combe Martin

It's six and the world is solid black beyond the window pane. The tea kettle feels heavy and I suspect a cold is settling on me. Apart from fatigue we've stayed healthy, but now it appears we're not immune to life's everyday setbacks. At breakfast the owner doesn't lift our spirits as he tells stories of 'the Beast of Exmoor'. He says he saw it when he was a taxi driver. Funny how such stories seem idle fiction in a newspaper, but take on a new chilling edge when recounted by an eye-witness. We set off in subdued mood and walk slowly through the cold streets and closed shops of this small off-season seaside village. In the chill drab early morning light only the tiny newspaper shop offers a weakly-lit welcome. There's nothing more edifying here though than a chocolate muesli bar, all card-board and chemicals by the look of it.

The small bitumen footpath has a one-in-four uphill incline from Lynmouth to Lynton. We criss-cross under the funicular railway and at slow pace can appreciate this example of Victorian ingenuity and engineering. For over 100 years the carriage has covered the 862-feet-long track using a water counterbalance system. It's the ultimate 'green' travel mechanism, with zero emissions and only water flow working the lift. Once we leave the town, we move out along steep headlands, high up with views across the Valley of Rocks and beyond to the dramatic Castle Rock outcrop.

Next, we come back from the cliff side onto a quiet back road. The day becomes tranquil and all is at peace. There's a weak sun overhead and it feels as if nothing dares move in the green open landscape for fear of breaking the spell. We pass Lee Abbey, a Christian Retreat centre where people circulate through the gardens in contemplation. One man sits cross-legged on an old stone wall besides our path. He's engrossed in his Bible but looks up briefly to smile as we pass. Either the person who created this spiritual retreat was in tune with the serene countryside hereabouts, or perhaps it's the aura of these gentle folk that envelopes the landscape.

Tim asked last night if there are mornings when we just don't want to walk. It's the regular fascination of someone looking at our adventure from the outside. From the inside, I know it's the sheer variety of scenery that keeps us stimulated and coming back for more. Even today as my cold develops I'm filled with wonder. We leave behind the cosy contemplative scene and walk out into breathtaking beauty. We're high up on cliff edges, our eyes drawn into a gauzy green blue sea which belies its reputation for Atlantic fury. Barely a ripple disturbs the surface which I imagine stretches to Newfoundland. We stand and marvel as our eyesight seems to trigger the release of some unknown chemical. Debby simply calls it, 'zing'!

We drop down on a small footpath, pass Crock Pits, Slattenslade, and circle Woody Bay on to the beacon near Highveer Point. Now a dramatic descent throws us into Heddon's Mouth Cleave. We keep walking around the headlands until after one, when we stop to sit in rough grasses back from the cliff edge. It's cold at this height so we can't rest for long. The sun still lacks warmth and the heat quickly drains from our bodies. A basic pasty provides some sustenance, but after 15 minutes we move on again.

Now we descend a steep drop to the bottom of Sherrycombe. A tiny river flows here, an insignificant thread that over thousands of years has worn its way through solid rock to cleave a passage. This feature is repeated time and again along these cliffs in a pattern that's recurred regularly throughout our journey: the movement of water, small runnels that appear weak and not worthy of attention, but ultimately create deep fissures in the landscape.

This path has become my teacher. Just as I've tried to build strong defences to shelter from life's tragedies, there are streams of sorrow that have etched their way through into my psyche. I've discovered the marks they've created cannot be ignored. They are riven deep into the geography of my personal landscape. They're a part of me and their existence must be recognised and acknowledged. I've come to terms with this on the walk and in finding my way through the physical geography I've come to better understand my own emotional terrain is every bit as varied.

No sooner are we down than we again strain our bodies to rise up a sharp incline to the top of the foreboding Great Hangman, the highest point on the track at 318m. Afterwards, Little Hangman awaits and then we follow Lester Cliff and drop down into Combe Martin. What a walk this has been! Another 16 miles and one of the finest coastal paths yet.

Day 118 – to Woolacombe

We blogged until after eleven last night and paid the penalty of a disturbed night. How many times have we lectured the kids about the perils of sitting at a computer screen for long hours before bedtime? What's worse though, it's still not six and here in bed surrounded by dark, chill air, my cold has taken hold. Each swallow feels like sandpaper on my throat. In the tiny bathroom a shower emits lukewarm misty condensation rather than water spray. It's impossible to get fully wet and I can't even turnaround in the tiny cubicle. Disconsolate, we pack up and step outside. Immediately I make a beeline for the bakery. I need thick black coffee to lift my spirits.

Soon the merry-go-round resumes. Valerie and Paul arrive to spark new energy into our adventure. It's over 20 years since this larger-than-life couple walked into my life. They were just another English couple on a temporary work assignment in Melbourne back then. Originally friends of Barbara from the early years of our sons schooling in Australia, our families bonded and as my wheel of life revolved, so they transitioned with me to the new life path I'd chosen. The result of navigating such tough times together means our friendship has a depth impossible to forge in more benign times and their joy now lifts my spirits.

After ten we walk up a dramatic coastal path, one that follows the very edge of the land's submission to the sea. As we rise up over one cliff – usually 50 to 80 metres high – we then descend back to a tiny cove, harbour or beach. It makes for superlative walking and nothing too strenuous for our walk- hardened bodies. The morning gradually runs out when we descend into a typical off-season English seaside town, Ilfracombe. It's certainly nothing to write a postcard home about, but these places are in my blood. The sight of jaded seaside cafés still conjures up childish excitement. The fact blue skies and sunny beaches were never part of my childhood experience is irrelevant. I dug tunnels in the sand with chilled fingers and chapped cheeks and created a trove of joyful memories as rich as the old Italian's handmade ice-cream.

It's less than three hours since the bakery indulgence, but I suggest lunch. Sandwiches in hand we sit overlooking what passes for a beach. The harbour would be more attractive but for the fearsome smell of old diesel and rotting seaweed. Ilfracombe appears unconcerned by such foibles though and seems to be challenging visitors to take the town as it is or just piss off! I admire its candour and unlikely self-confidence.

Even my rose-tinted image of Ilfracombe as an unaffected fishing village crumbles as we walk off past two large upside-down concrete funnels that look more like a thermo-nuclear power plant than a town theatre and civic buildings. I shake my head, grab a quick tasteless takeaway coffee and we turn our backs on the town once and for all.

The afternoon starts with an uphill stretch and soon we crest the day's highest point shortly after Torrs Park at Brandy Cove Point. Here we contend with something incongruously called Flat Point, which seems anything but. And so the afternoon unravels, our footsteps pointing up then down in endless repetition. Shag Point, Lee Bay, Bull Point with the lighthouse, North Morte – all pass by before we step out to Morte Point. Seals swim by the rocky shore here, while Lundy Island is perfectly framed on a gentle horizon. We sweep around the headland and drop into tonight's destination, Woolacombe, another rather sad-looking off-season resort.

At first the B&B seems fine. However, Valerie and Paul are soon driven from their room: a massive seething black swarm of flies has covered the bedroom wall. Like a macabre Hitchcock horror movie set, the flies won't be denied, so it's the humans that have to make way, more stories woven into the fabric of our friendship.

Day 119 – to Braunton

After a good sleep we descend to a dining room fresher than a supermarket freezer isle. Our host is an old surfer who likes the outdoor life and by opening all the windows and doors tries his best to bring it indoors. We eat breakfast in bright sunshine at about eight degrees. Shortly after nine we're back on our feet, backpacks in place. We walk across the road to a wide expanse of sand reminiscent of Australian beaches. It's a treat in England to see the rocks and pebbles replaced by something easier on the feet and I realise I've come to take the benefits of Australia for granted.

Although it's cold, I know we're likely to have a good day. The weather is on its best behaviour with the sun set proud in a blue cloudless sky. The only shadows today lie within. Debby tells me of her sense of extreme fatigue. I'd like to show more concern, but I'm worried my cold is becoming worse and I feel the rucksack grind into my back. I'd love to swim, but right now don't feel I've the energy to cross several hundred metres of sand to the water's edge. Maybe later. We leave the beach to mount a low headland around to Baggy Point, press on to Morte Bay and follow the coast into the sands of Croyde Bay. To my surprise over a hundred surfers are trying in vain to ride a one foot swell. I can't resist the opportunity to show them what to do with this type of water and strip down to my 'budgies'.

As I walk in, the familiar embrace of icy needle pricks welcomes me, a reminder I've been away too long. I dive under the surface forcing my mouth closed as the frigid hit passes through me. Quickly my body changes and now I'm part of the water. I can frolic in the 12 or 13-degrees temperature and imagine it carrying off my cold symptoms. After ten minutes a sore shoulder speaks of my lack of swimming condition and I beach myself. I dry slowly savouring the moment, a fresh body newly minted with a smile to match. I re-join the team in a café and the poor coffee is irrelevant.

We lunch in the comforting knowledge that today's final destination is only about a mile away by road. I'm adamant though we'll follow the much longer costal path. We head south down a long expanse of beach and on through a dangerous military training ground in the dunes. The track slowly takes us all the way around the bulbous head of the River Taw estuary before we turn back along a grassy dyke by the banks of the River Caen. The unusually strong sun reflected off bronzed sands saps our energy. Three hours have passed since lunch, yet we're only back near our starting point and we're still not finished. Frustration has set in and Debby in particular is in trouble. We're strung out and she's well behind.

At last we reach Broughton, but it does nothing to lift our spirits. Valerie and Paul's friend arrives to pick them up and we still have no idea where our B&B is. Debby is completely done in and leaps at the offer of a lift. Despite my preference for searching on foot, I acquiesce. During the car ride Debby summons up hidden reserves of energy to provide a lengthy explanation of why she considers me completely obtuse to her needs.

This village is the largest in England and our B&B is at the extreme edge. Worse still it turns out to be just a dingy room in a house strewn with the owners' belongings. We gingerly pick our way around the cold, messy room and the absence of heating is particularly hard for Debby in her exhausted state. Still, we rally ourselves and get ready to be whisked off to the pub for dinner. Valerie and Paul's friends add vibrancy to the meal with sparkling snippets from their lives. It's a good job we've been introduced as friends otherwise I might just be thought another uncouth Australian. While I've talked, unbeknown to me my nose has streamed into my lap like a tap. Debby somehow rallied despite her desperate tiredness, but when we finally fall into bed near midnight I know we're likely to regret such socialising.

Day 120 – to Instow

We overcame the misery of our surroundings and extreme exhaustion to find deep sleep. I'm still worried about Debby though. Her stamina reserves are depleted and today won't be easy for her. Once again, a social dinner could bring our downfall rather than the walk. Breakfast at eight and the atmosphere is as cold as the messy house in which we're stranded. There's nothing here to nurture our spirits and by nine we're happy to be back out on the road.

As usual, I insist we traipse back into Braunton to pick up our quest at just the point where we were whisked away by car last night. We feel disconsolate to start with, but it's a stunning day and my mood can't resist the weather's prompts. The air is biting cold but the sun has already asserted its authority in a clear blue sky.

There's a promise of heat to come, just the fillip we need. This is the classic England that stirs my dreams and on such autumn days I would swap it for nowhere else. Everything I yearn for in a climate is encapsulated in this moment: a fierce bright glare that brings life to the early morning streetscape; searing frigid air to fill my lungs; breath exhaled in a mist as white as my icy fingers; hairs that stand alert on my forearms along goose-pimpled skin. Once again, the weather has taken control to switch on our senses to the simple joy of being alive in this moment.

An hour into the day and we've left the village behind. My third day with a cold, but I feel I'm in control. As I suck in great drafts of fizzing air I sense the bacteria leaving with the white plume of breath exhaled. Life may be retreating from my dead white fingers, but the rest of my body is alive and charged. It's as if a healing magic is at play today. For all my joy though, the wand has not been waved over Debby. She's struggling and just wants her bed:

'Everything aches, my feet, legs, hips. My energy's gone and I've got nothing left to give.'

It's only mid-morning and already she's facing her wall. In the still chilly morning light, tears begin to roll down her face. I try to talk to her, words of calm and common sense, but I know her day will be long and one full of demons only she can confront. Today is particularly tough as we can see our destination from the start. Directly across the river, it's not much more than a mile away as the crow flies. Without that bird's big black wings we'll have to walk all the way down the inlet to the bridge at Barnstaple and back up the other side. The four or five hours it'll likely take is a depressing prospect. To add insult, the path has been tarmacked to provide a better surface for cyclists. For the beaten bruised feet of long-distance walkers nothing beats grass.

The scenery is dreary. We walk along the side of Chivenor's highly fortified Marine airbase. All high fences and razor wire, the

CCTV cameras are brooding silent sentinels, watching our labour as we pass. Even in these conditions, however, we can still take inspiration from nature's handiwork. In the still chill atmosphere spiders have laced adjacent hedgerows with delicate silver filigree webs. These adornments flicker and reflect back the strong sunshine like fairy lights on an early Christmas tree. I quickly suppress the thought that December's next festive explosion of over-indulgence is just 10 weeks away.

Once we're past the military base, our vista broadens out. The River Taw estuary is a muddy mess, with boats lying on their sides like flotsam and jetsam left behind by the receding tide. It seems inanimate and lifeless apart from the odd bird. It's hard to reconcile that such muddy slime houses the greatest biomass of any habitat in the world. That's more living stuff per square metre here than anywhere. It may all be hidden from our view, but the birds and fish are working hard to eat as many of the worms, shrimp, snails and smaller organisms as they can. I try to distract Debby with this knowledge, but she's beyond inspiration. She's retreated from the external to seek refuge in the iPod, her technological crutch. I walk at her side in silence while she floods her head to block out a sense of despair welling up within.

In less than three hours we enter Barnstaple. It has a warmth and buzz to invite exploration, but we go straight to a chain coffee shop. Debby slumps at an out-of-the-way table while I go to fetch yet another coffee to complain about. I offer Debby a scone that she says qualifies as a rock cake. We sit for two hours and do some serious soul searching. Debby is confronted by what appears an enormous mental barrier and is stoically trying to clamber over it one brick at a time. She's very near the end of her tether and knows the wall is hers and hers alone. There's not much I can do right now.

Once we get up and hoist backpacks I know we need to keep moving, so quickly grab snacks to eat lunch on the go. We leave town across the 13th century bridge and are now finally on the same side of the estuary as our destination. We head for home, our pace a gentle stroll on this sleepy mid-October afternoon. Debby is coping better and can once again appreciate the splendour of walking rather than the pain. The sun has real warmth and the lazy muddy meander of the estuary with its slow ebbs and flows creates tiny rivulets of water that appear and disappear. The grey-black slime oozes quietly, continuing to belie the teeming diversity below and, for now, our minds float peacefully on the surface as we settle into a torpid Sunday. Sheep graze on the salt marshes as they did on North Ronaldsay back in the Orkneys. Can we really have walked from that distant outpost so long ago? There's so much we've experienced, but perhaps that's what R. S. Thomas meant:

> The point of travelling is not
> To arrive but to return home
> Laden with pollen you shall work up
> Into honey the mind feeds upon

Instow is a sleepy little village. Left behind by modern development, it's all the better for it. We check in at the pub and Debby goes straight to bed. By dinnertime and with the sea close by, we order fish and chips with a double side serving of 'vegetables of the day'. We need the nourishment of good fresh vegetables to boost our health. The substantial platter of this day's 'fresh' vegetables are no more fresh than our walking shoes, just two big piles of frozen peas and corn. No wonder British pubs are closing in their hundreds.

Day 121 – to Westward Ho!

Five thirty, too early, but sleep has departed after a disturbed night. The cold weighs heavy like a lead blanket. I tell myself I can beat this infection and must will myself to walk through it. Debby's needs are of far greater concern and she needs my support. Determined to be on the road by nine, we finish a nondescript breakfast and when the waitress can't work out the credit card machine, I gruffly take over in frustration and do it myself.

We're walking inland along a river again, this time the Torridge. Across the river, Appledore looks like a charming seaside village, but for now it's a torment. Despite its close proximity, we won't get there until late afternoon. We've got to walk all the way into Bideford to cross the bridge and walk back. There's no sun and the wind blows under a leaden sky leaving us cold and demoralised. At least it's not raining, I tell Debby, but she looks as grey as the day. She's grappling once more with her wall. Already the balls of her feet, toes, leg muscles and hips all ache. Progress is slow and I look for distractions:

'Debby, there's the old Instow railway signal box, dating from 1861. It's the only one in the South West of England.'

'I couldn't care less!' comes the curt reply.

Today's walk is short, just over 12 miles, and will bring to an end the laborious circling of slimy grey estuary mud which so bogs down our spirits. I put off our rest day until tomorrow thinking a rest day by the sea would better serve Debby's needs. My mistake and typical of me to overthink an issue. Right now Debby just needs a bed, any view is irrelevant.

The river scene is a little more interesting than yesterday. Snowy white swans flap gracefully across the turbid water while waders busy themselves ferreting for sustenance below. The walk passes more quickly than I'd thought and we arrive in Bideford after not much more than an hour. It's a bustling town with an attractive 'Long Bridge'. Built in medieval times, it's 677 feet long and crosses the river on 24 arches of all different sizes. The engineers of the past seem to have regularly displayed great flair. Today's designs are so often soulless and drab by comparison. Our engineers appear caught up in efficiency and building regulations over which a financial straightjacket attempts to squeeze the highest possible monetary returns. It's as if we cannot find a way to value the joy found gazing at buildings of beauty. I suddenly feel sheepish. How many times have I pored over the financial spreadsheets of a project proposal and rejected it because the financial returns were inadequate? Is this the great achievement I've built my career around?

One look at Debby and I realise now is not the time to open up a deeper discussion. I remember yesterday's lesson and guide her straight into a café. Meanwhile, I reconnoitre the town's facilities and find a terrific library where we can catch up on the blog. It's now a full week in arrears and we need a long session. I suggest to Debby that if we spend a few hours at the library we could take a shortcut via Northam that would cut the day down to just ten miles. This bargain is just what Debby needs and we pass the remainder of the morning in the library. When we finally pack up and get back out on the path Debby is brighter. For the first time in three days she's walking without pain. The bricks in her wall are being removed as if she can almost sense Land's End is just over two weeks away. The afternoon disappears, each footstep like another grain of sand falling through the hourglass of this adventure.

We soon stroll into Westward Ho! It's the only place name in the world ending in an exclamation mark and this seems the only characteristic worthy of note in what today is a grey and lifeless little town. In the mid-19th century Charles Kingsley wrote a novel of this name, claiming sailors cried out 'Westward Ho!' as their boats passed this place, the last land they would see before America.

The drear drabness of the place lifts as we arrive at the B&B to find Mary and Jack, our new walking companions. The last time we walked with them teeming rain had drenched us on an uphill trudge through mud in the Otways rainforest a few hours from Melbourne.

They were part of our preparation and are now here to walk with us for a week near the end of our quest. We've looked forward to this reunion and hope the arrival of good companions combined with inspiring cliff scenery will be the formula we need to break the back of what remains. My biggest concern is that after tomorrow's rest day we'll have to average 16 miles a day, with only two more days off in the next 17.

Day 122 – in Westward Ho!

Dawn breaks and Debby decides to spend the day in bed. As fellow Icebergers, Jack and I walk off to the beach with our togs. A meagre light infuses the early morning pallid seascape and little else moves. It's a disheartening place; even the grey sea appears reluctant to come to Westward Ho! The tide is far out and the prospect of a long walk over a bleak low-tide beach is not enticing. The swim loses its appeal and we retire for a shower and breakfast. Later, I blog alone back at Bideford library, but my progress without Debby's keyboard skills is much slower.

Day 123 – to Clovelly

It's shortly after five and weariness circles like a bird of prey. Eventually it disappears into the pre-dawn ether, but my concern for Debby won't go away. I don't doubt she'll get to Land's End now we're so close, but what state will she be in? Yesterday's rest helped, but she's close to the edge of her endurance and I continue to worry about the longer-term impact of this trek on her health. We get up slowly and follow the well-rehearsed routine – shower, repack backpacks, fill water bottles and descend to breakfast – silent zombies that won't be denied.

By nine, we're on our way to the bakery for lunch supplies and twenty minutes later walk along a typical cold, blustery, off-season

British seafront. It's hard to conceive that Westward Ho! with its harsh pebble and rock beach was, until a couple of months ago, a holiday destination. The pouring rain and fierce winds of yesterday evening have left a washed-out murky grey daylight in their wake. Jack and Mary comment on just how different our spirits would be back home. Early autumn mornings in Melbourne tend to be clothed in stillness with a sharp sun to lift hearts and face-paint smiles on even the most uncompromising. The climate does so much for people's *joie de vivre* and its effect on the dour, browbeaten faces of my British kinfolk is plain to see.

Our path leads south on a high rocky headland. I tell Debby I'm still distracted by the poor quality of my poached eggs, but she has little sympathy. She shoulders far weightier challenges and suggests I'm becoming a tad irascible. The cliff track is L-shaped and will in time turn west where today's destination, Clovelly, is already visible as a distant whitewash slash in the rocks. Behind us, Saunton Sands Hotel still stands leering at us despite our attempts to cast it off. We walked past it five days ago.

We settle into the customary routine demanded by cliff paths. We're either climbing or going down, but can never develop a steady rhythm on even ground. Also, the weather plays petulant games – one minute blustery showers, the next watery sun. Our bodies swing between feeling chill to overheating as rain clothes go on and come off in turns, each change the usual tedious and frustrating interruption to our routine.

From Babbacombe Cliff the track becomes more woody, and by the time we leave Peppercombe we cross the small stream into a more gentle, undulating track through woodland. Sunlight emerges weakly from the crowns of the ragged old trees sheathed in deep green moss. Broken light flecks the dead leaves that soften our footfall. This doesn't feel like a coastal setting and the change is welcome, but soon we round the curve of the coast, turn west and drop down to the remains of an old quay and the large grey pebble beach at Buck Mills.

The beach is deserted and we take half an hour for lunch perched on a stonewall. The quay here was built by Richard Cole of Woolfardisworthy in 1598. Not a name I thought I had ever heard of, but he was none other than the 'merry old soul' who gave his name to the nursery rhyme, Old King Cole. Another feature of this little cove is the impossibly small 'cabin' in which two English artists of the early 20th century, Mary Stella Edwards, a poet, and Judith Ackland, spent most summers until the 1970's. The tiny home seems to stand as a mockery of the modern need for ever-bigger accommodation. Filled by our lunch rolls and inspired by our encounter with the past we head off and tackle the straight climb to our day's highest point.

A little over two hours later we're on the hard flint track of Hobby Drive descending into Clovelly. The history of this place is hard to comprehend in a time where redevelopment and changes of land ownership are so commonplace. We've entered a village which is under one single ownership and over the last 800 years has been owned by only three families. It has always had a fishing fleet and the quay is still in good order despite having been built 600 years ago by the Cary family. Sailors from here have often done battle with tempestuous Atlantic weather, although the tragedy that occurred 189 years ago this month took a shocking toll. No fewer than 40 boats and 35 men were lost in a storm.

Right now though the water in the small harbour looks calm, and despite walking 14 miles, including some stiff cliff climbs, there's only one thought in our minds. Dispensing with backpacks, Jack, Mary and I don our flimsy Iceberger bathers and stroll nonchalantly down the cobbled street. Car transport is banned in the village and few people bear witness to our progress. Just before daylight fades, we jump off the harbour steps into chill water we estimate to be about 13 degrees. This is my favourite temperature but now it feels cold given my new skinnier physique. Looking back from the water through the dank atmosphere of a late autumn day, the whitewashed wattle-and-daub cottages with low roofs of weathered dark-grey slates seem hunkered down. In 1804 Clovelly was described as 'a place notorious for smuggling' and today everything looks to be in lock-down.

Later, we return to the harbour for dinner at the pub. Perhaps lulled into false optimism by stiff drinks and a roaring fire, Mary and Jack make meal choices I consider brave, to say the least. When the food is placed before them they try to conceal their confusion and remain in good humour. Mary's plate of unidentifiable deep-fried pieces bears no resemblance to anything called a seafood platter in Australia, but she says the green salad is good. As for Jack, he has no idea what to make of his order of breaded scampi, or as I know it, the 'dreaded scampi'. He picks at the plate of deep-fried frozen nuggets and calls for another drink to bring the day to an end.

Day 124 – to Hartland Quay

We sleep surprisingly well in this tiny B&B's small bed, but once the tea leaves are stirred into boiling water I have to buckle down to the discipline of writing up yesterday's blog notes. At breakfast, any hopes of a fulsome meal are quickly quashed. Debby's foolhardy choice of poached eggs arrive hard as seashore pebbles, while my 'safe' option of fried eggs are as tough as scallop shells.

Out on the steep cobbled stones I wait for the others. My gaze lingers for one last time down through the village carved valiantly into the cliffs. I look in vain for the ghost of my 23-year-old youth, newly wed and walking hand-in-hand on these cobbles with Barbara. The youth has disappeared just as surely as his bride, but somewhere here our footsteps have etched their marks. For a moment, the memory of a passionate embrace at the harbour's mouth surfaces to remind me the history of my life's journey is etched into the fabric of who I've now become. Time runs only one way though, and I can no more go back to those days and hold that young woman than I can stop the clock of life. The day marches on and so must we.

Time ticks by as the sun moves into its ascendancy and our footsteps negotiate a path alternating between cliff edge and woodland settings. There are a few human adornments from another era. A large covered wooden seat known as 'Angels' Wings' and a well-preserved lime kiln are a distraction, but they play second fiddle to the grander spectacles of land and sea. At Windbury Point, wide ocean views open out to a raw beauty. Below the bracken and gorse of the clifftop lies a power beyond my comprehension. From up here, the vast ocean appears deceptively blue and inviting. Yet the rocky crags bear the scars of its fierce mood swings. I wonder why I so often choose to stare into a computer or TV screen. These cliffs and the seascape beyond are particularly spectacular, but I've learned on this walk all life offers a form of majesty for those with eyes open to it.

It's nearly two as we reach Hartland Point and its tiny wooden hut. We left Clovelly before any food shops were open and had pinned all our lunch hopes on this kiosk. The hut is deserted and so we rummage in our four backpacks for food. All we find is one tomato pulled from the depths of Debby's bag. I cut it reverently into four quarters. As expedition leader I know it's my duty to self-sacrifice and leave my quarter for the others. With no particular reason to dally, we're soon back walking, our goal the pub at Hartland Quay.

Along Exmansworthy Cliff we're presented with the ever-changing face of nature. This morning a docile calm blue sea greeted us and lobster pots bobbed gently in the water. Lundy

Island was clear and inviting. Now there's rain far out over the ocean, but the weather lords seem more focussed on lashing Lundy Island than the mainland. The island gradually disappears behind a dark grey curtain. The sea is now a fierce frenzy of black, white and grey. Everything is still going well for us until Jack utters the fateful words:

'We've been lucky, it's missed us.'

I remind him to never take anything for granted, particularly second-guessing the weather. Needless to say, within minutes it starts to rain. At first light showers fall and I press on without wet weather trousers. Gradually the tempo increases and before long my naked battle-scarred legs are too wet to cover. The rain is heavy now and the strong wind drives it with the force of buckshot. Silently I endure the indignity and stifle any thought of blaming Jack for his words.

Mary distracts us by producing a new item of kit, a large bright blue poncho which goes right over her entire body and backpack like a nun's habit. The theory is sound – however, in the gusting wind the poncho rarely covers her body but more often acts as a billowing blindfold around her neck and head. With heads down we trudge on through the deluge. The rain does eventually dry up, but not before the chill has driven all feeling out of my hands. There is an upside though: when I fall into a gorse bush I'm able to pluck the five needles out without feeling any pain. As with every other day, the walk does eventually come to an end. Today's end is a rugged coastal pub set down in the rocks where waves explode over the entire building in rough weather. Now, the white foam-capped waves surge over the rocks below us. It's just a 'normal' rough day.

Inside we drop our bags and order four cream teas with whisky chasers, another first for this adventure. The rigours of the day slowly fall away: bodies feel the embrace of warm water and clean towels, clothing and shoes are hung over radiators. By dinner, we're adrift in the comfort of relaxed conversation. The day's memories soften, airbrushed to the point where by bedtime we all agree today was one none of us would want to have missed. Debby seems to be stronger. Once she got sufficient metaphorical bricks out of her wall, it completely disappeared. The 12 miles we walked today seemed further because of the conditions, but with 1,554 miles under our belts, we're nearly there.

Day 125 – to Bude

The ceiling is black, a dark deep ocean that offers no solace. I wish the illuminated dial said something later than five thirty, but I'm awake and my head is choked. The cold has taken hold. There's no prospect of more sleep, so wearily I place one foot after the other on the floor. Despite the looming challenges of the day, I still get pleasure sprinkling the fragrant Earl Grey leaves into this 125th anonymous cup. Somehow, today this small bag of tea leaves carried from the other side of the world reminds me of where I now call home.

I love Britain and wouldn't swap my heritage and sense of connection with these shores for all the tea in China or India, but I don't live here anymore. I've poured my energy and life force into traversing this land for months now and soon it will be time to return down under, to a different world where spring is afoot and the promise of rejuvenation awaits. I smile and as the tea leaves swirl, a kaleidoscope of images from this journey fills my head to drive out the feeling of sloth. The thought of just how much life has been squeezed in between these 125 daily cuppas brings a joy that I instinctively turn to share with Debby.

'Why can't you be quiet? I've listened to you snore half the night and when I finally get to sleep, YOU WAKE ME UP!!!'

The dawn brings solid grey skies, the type England serves up when it can't think of anything more exciting. Soulless bacon and tired eggs maintain the mood at breakfast, but things pick up when Jill arrives to collect our bags. Since meeting Kathy's grandma Megan on the Welsh border last month, she's adopted our walk enthusiastically. Tonight we'll stay at her home in Bude and she's dispatched her friend Jill here to lighten our load.

We set out uphill. Hearts beat, breath billows, muscles burn, but we're rewarded by views across a blue-grey sea that laps lackadaisically at the rocky headland below. The grey ceiling overhead is cracked now and blue veins have opened to reveal occasional glimpses of watery sun. To our left an inland vista competes with the ocean for attention. Patches of downy green lead off to harsher grasses and shrubs and into the bright brown bracken that lines a glacial valley that‘s long forgotten the power which created its beauty. A waterfall gushes from a cliff face down to a frothing demise on the rocks far below. We move higher and the wind nags insistently with a force to rake the landscape. We zip up jackets and pull down hats, but agree we're blessed to be walking through this setting.

Gradually we tick off various names on the map that bear little significance to our venture. At Knap Head we pause for an apple, then press on to descend into Welcombe Mouth and down to Marsland Mouth. Here, at exactly twelve-thirty, a small wooden sign bleached pale grey by the weather speaks of something more momentous. It's the county boundary of Cornwall. We've traversed 33 counties throughout Scotland, Wales and England taking little notice of the markers that have indicated human boundaries. They've seemed irrelevant to the non-human landscape underfoot. Yet now, as we enter Cornwall, the 34th, or 'the final frontier' as Star Trek's Captain Kirk might say, I'm aware of its importance to our adventure. This is the county that reaches so far out into the Atlantic it's been able to capture an idea called Land's End. An idea that's inspired our walk. Yet in the true understated British manner, the border is announced by nothing more than a piece of rotten wood.

It may be a new county, but nothing else has changed. We scale Marsland Cliff and then almost immediately descend into Litter Mouth, then rise up and descend again. Next it's up Henna Cliff and down into the Morwenstow church valley. Here in a sheltered alcove at the base of Vicarage Cliff we find a thick blanket of soft downy grass, the perfect place to rest weary limbs. We sprawl on the ground and give ourselves twenty minutes to eat lunch. We may have tackled six major climbs and descents this morning, but there are another eight ahead before we reach Bude. Cornwall is announcing itself with one of the coast's most strenuous days.

Lunch over, we start the endless climb up Vicarage Cliff. The cliff scenery distracts our minds from the effort of the climb and so we resume the morning's well-established pattern to rise up and drop down successive severe undulations. Our movement feels in tune with the ebb and flow of the sea's tides. This is classic cliff walking with razor-edged grey rocks that have endured the ocean's might over eons, soaring up only to fall away dramatically from the edge of the sometimes tenuous path we follow. I notice my vertigo has disappeared, forced into submission perhaps by the splendour I've witnessed following such paths.

Just when the day's routine seems set, drama arrives at Hippa Rock. Debby has lost our English mobile phone. Convinced it fell from her trousers at lunch, I tell the others to press on while I go back to look for it. Now my day becomes a race, a chance to pit myself against the elements. I set off and at first find I can run up and down the cliffs. The sun shines down and before long, rosy visions flit through my mind of my induction into the wizened clan of fell runners. The exhilaration of lithe movement across hillsides gradually subsides as the reality sets in. Parched lips and a forehead salty from dry sweat alert me to the folly of setting off without water. In the end I find no sign of the phone and turn around meekly to resume the path. One hour after leaving Debby, I'm back at the spot where we parted. Now to catch up.

After Stanbury Mouth, I run up to an enormous radar station with one of the best views along this coast. The ground turns boggy and I temporarily lose my way amongst fearsome-looking large-horned cattle. I walk out onto Steeple Point Cliff to follow the track as it turns down the cliff face before running precariously back inland just above the mighty waves. My vertigo announces its return and I steel myself to tackle this challenge alone. I focus intently to get through without calamity and give thanks for the mercy of mild weather. The late autumn sun has mellowed the ocean's temper and fresh breezes have moderated the heat. I push on, before each descent looking across to the far clifftop for any sign of Debby, Jack and Mary. As the descents come and go, I'm repeatedly disappointed.

It's well after five, nearly three hours after we parted, when we're reunited on the path into Bude. Immediately we're swept up by a new support team. Jill is here to guide us to Megan's, where copious cups of tea are dispensed with reviving fruit cake. It's a social event and other locals have turned out to meet us. Everyone is very kind and the chatter animated, but there's no rest and soon we have to duck in the shower to be ready for a dinner gathering. With pride of place at a large table at the local hotel, we eat and drink to the accompaniment of tall stories and much laughter. It's just the convivial evening we love, but I can see the effort writ large on Debby's face. Her tired red eyes are mere slits in puffy wind-rouged cheeks. By ten o'clock we call a halt to festivities and head home.

After a few jottings in the journal, it's eleven as my head hits the pillow. Before sleep draws down the blinds, I sense there may be a price to pay for today. Debby has walked 14 significant ups and downs, a very tiring 16-mile day. Courtesy of the abortive search for the lost phone, I repeated a few of the cliff climbs and covered about 20 miles. Whereas I feel I'm coping well at this stage, Debby has low energy reserves. Also, to be the centre of attention from the moment we arrived meant our 20-minute lunch was the only rest in a 16-hour day. Debby needs all the rest she can get and laying here cosseted in the warmth of Megan's guest room she has immediately blacked out. I only hope deep restorative sleep brings her fresh energy to tackle the final 14 days.

Day 126 – to Widemouth Bay

It's six, earlier than necessary, but blocked nasal passages have finally defeated sleep. I feel shocking and disturb Debby as I go in search of tea. She tells me she's had a wretched night too. Despite every comfort, the room was hot and filled with my chainsaw snoring. She dozed, but saw each hour pass. She's only just found sleep and tells me to leave her alone for a couple of hours. I slope quietly away to clear my head with a shower.

We idle over a late breakfast and chat about the challenges ahead. Debby says her awful night was the worst preparation for another physically demanding day:

'Every muscle in my body needs rest.'

I hear her words but assume once we're out on the track she'll rise to the day's challenge as she has for the past four months. When we do step outside it's obvious the weather is in no mood to help us. It has the makings of a wild day. Strong winds gust and as the dark storm clouds circle, they show their displeasure by dumping rain in heavy showers. We reunite with Mary and Jack and head into Bude to tackle a couple of errands. Once we're ready to go I suggest a cup of coffee to cheer us on such a dismal day. The hot drinks bring no relief and all the time I feel Debby's sense of frustration and unease grow.

The walk leads up the grassy headland of Compass Point and although the path underfoot is easy, the wind is shocking. Mary is in a clear plastic poncho and while the girls attempt to restrain an urgent flapping that threatens to blow it over her head, Jack and I march on ahead. By the time we reach Higher Longbreak and look down at Widemouth Bay, I realise some drama is unfolding. Debby has raised her crossed sticks, the signal we've agreed to be one of ultimate distress. I stop and wait and by the time the girls catch up it's clear Debby is in great trouble. She's crying and tells us to go on without her while she finds a bus or taxi.

This is the moment I've feared but never really imagined would come to pass. Suddenly my world is as bleak as the scene that holds us. With ragged grassy sand underfoot, we're at the back of the beach and have followed a rough stony path between low scabby dunes. It's easy walking if we were out taking the dog for a stroll, but nothing to lift flagging spirits. The long flat beach looks a forlorn companion staring back as we stand under a grey damp sky. Coated in melancholy, the weather offers no respite and the wind howls at us. I try to find some hope of breaking the scene of despair but looking along the coast road nearby nothing presents itself. An out-of-season hotel and a couple of tiny shops are all closed up to add to the sense of desolation.

A beachside kiosk optimistically advertises coffee and ice creams a few hundred metres ahead. It offers no prospect of relief from the elements, but at least it's open. We head there and I order hot tea while trying to create a windbreak to protect Debby. Jack and Mary express their support but none of us really know what to do. Debby has completely cracked, pushing me away as she howls through her tears. I'm staggered things seem to have got so bad so quickly. I try in vain to calm and reassure her she'll be OK after a rest, but all that appears to do is heap another layer of frustration on her already weary body. I try to remain calm:

'Let's stop for today and come back tomorrow. This is not the time to be talking about major decisions to give up on our grand quest.'

Of course, the thing about rational discussion is that both parties need to be up for it if it's to make any sense at all. Debby has now moved beyond her edge and is somewhere far beyond engaging with common sense, whatever that may be. She confronts me with fierce anger, shouting through her tears:

'Why can't you hear me?! You're not listening, it's over for me! I don't want to stop you. In fact, I really want you to keep going and leave me alone to get a lift. I can't handle the pressure you bring trying to help me!'

Slowly it sinks in that my attempts to help are doing exactly the wrong thing and making matters worse. Debby's meagre energy stores are all used up and all my concern does is inflict more pain. If this is a critical moment for Debby, it's no less a watershed for me. I begin to see there's something deeply flawed in how I deal with such situations. I always attempt to pour oil on troubled waters and quickly resolve conflicts. Now I'm being told in no uncertain terms that that is not only not helping, it's doing the reverse. Here in this moment, the woman I love is screaming at me to simply be heard. *Don't try to fix this issue Keith, just let the pain of her wretched condition be expressed and heard. Recognise the brave battering her body and mind has soaked up over 125 demanding days to get here. Until we've honoured that pain, attempts to calm and settle matters are futile.*

After more heated exchanges I realise it's hopeless for me to try to communicate with Debby. While Jack comforts her, I look around for some way forward. The kiosk owner provides the number of the only taxi in the area, but when I call, the driver says he's booked on an all-day job. Circumstances seem stacked against us. I walk up to the road and find a country bus stop. I have to think about what day of the week it is to make sense of the timetable. Pretty sure it's Saturday, so there should be a bus in about an hour. Back with Jack and Mary we agree, despite Debby's protestations, that we won't desert her and will all abort the walk for the day.

The bus duly arrives and our luck finally breaks on the strength of human compassion. Although not scheduled to go all the way to Crackington Haven on weekends, the driver takes one look at Debby's distress and dismisses all bureaucratic scheduling niceties. Despite the other passengers' expectations, he drives well off his route to drop us outside the pub we're staying at. While Debby is helped off the bus, I offer profuse thanks. It's as if this cheery soul has been sent by some greater universal power, one where timetables are less important than human suffering. Inside the pub, Debby goes straight to bed and tells me in no uncertain terms to stay out of the room. If I wake her it will be at my peril. Chastised and confused, I head for the bar and with a large whisky in hand, draft a quick depressing blog update:

> Today, Debby hit the wall again, but this time there was no moving it. After 90 minutes of battling fierce clifftop winds and rain, it was clear she could go no further. In tears she was led from the track... It is with heavy hearts that we inform you as of today our adventure is in limbo… Debby is asleep in bed, and Jack, Mary and I are in the bar drinking heavily wondering what will happen next...

I sip the whisky and ponder what will happen next. Jack and Mary tell me they're happy to go along with us whatever we decide. With Debby beyond caring right now, the maps and itinerary lie before me and I know our grand adventure rests in my hands. It's still beyond my imagination that we're finished, but even with a new plan my biggest challenge will be to rebuild Debby's enthusiasm and re-establish productive communications. Thoughts circle but keep bringing me back to a central point: I'm determined to give Debby every chance to reach Land's End and complete this adventure despite her assertion that she's finished. Land's End is not much more than 65 miles away as the blasted crow would fly. With a bit over three weeks left before we have to return to Australia, surely we can't be beaten now?

I order another drink and at four Jill and Megan arrive with my stepson, Matt. He's come to walk with us for a week and looks in pretty good shape for someone who's just completed the long trip from Melbourne on planes, trains and cars. We settle down in the bar and I brief him on his mum's plight. At length Debby comes down to be reunited with Matt and we sit for a surreal dinner. The status of the walk and today's events are off-limits, the elephant in the room that must be circled but ignored. Finally it's bedtime and we agree to see what tomorrow morning brings.

Even with the light turned off my troubled mind won't be stilled. It circles through endless possibilities for completing what we've started. Today was the first day of our penultimate week after nearly 18 weeks on foot. I know now the prospect of completion has such a hold on me I can't contemplate any alternative. In the bar this afternoon I understood that my passion for bringing this grand adventure to conclusion is not about my finishing. Debby has already given me permission to go it alone. No, this is about my stubborn determination to achieve a dream. I want to reach that finishing line with Debby by my side. My burning ambition was the burden Debby felt today when her strength departed and I tried to help her. Looking at her brave exhausted body asleep beside me now does not make sleep easy.

Day 127 – to Crackington Haven

It seemed unfair with all the emotion and exhaustion in our room that we should have to share it with disco music from the bar. However, I still slept the sleep of the innocent; I gingerly look across at Debby. She smiles gently back and assures me she also found some restorative sleep. I leave her and join Jack for a swim. Pebbles and rocks submerged below the surging water bruise our feet, but finally we reach the breaking surf and dive under. It's almost a full tide and the conditions are perfect. It's a raw cold morning and a stiff frost looks down on us from the grass-covered cliff banks in sharp contrast to the vivid blue sky above. The sun hasn't yet penetrated this tiny valley but as cold water swimming tragics, we frolic in the frothing waters. Our bodies come to life and yesterday's cares are left for the fish to feed on.

Back in the room a hot shower drives out cold. Debby has prepared herself for the day and is keen to go down to breakfast with Matt. Tentatively I mention the walk and what's to be done. With the elephant named, there's no avoiding the inevitable discussion. I reassure her that whatever she chooses to do the group will support. Whereas yesterday I tried in vain to keep her focussed on the possibility of continuing, today I feel reverse psychology may be better. I stress she can simply bring the adventure to an end right now. After all, we've walked well over 1,500 miles and there's no shame in stopping at this point. Indeed, our greater goal than reaching Land's End must be to protect our bodies from serious long term damage. Debby looks at me with clear eyes and calmly explains:

'Yesterday the weather was horrendous. The wind was howling, the rain sheeting down and I felt chilled to the bone. Your insistence on shopping and a coffee stop at the start used up what little energy I had. As Mary and I were battling the fierce clifftop winds and rain I just knew I didn't have the energy in my tank to walk in this weather. I felt wretched and completely spent and had to stop. You wrote in the blog: "Debby cracks and we abort the walk to get the bus." The outpouring of support from our blog readers overnight has been amazing.

'I'm not comfortable feeling vulnerable and even now thinking back on it makes me want to cry. The fact the bus driver took one look at me and drove off his normal route says how bad I was. I desperately needed to rest and catch up on my sleep. And of course, all this happened on the same day Matt arrived. It was wonderful to see him and even more so because it was the first time since he lost Kathy. I realised last night just how much I'd missed him, especially as he's endured one of life's toughest traumas in my absence.

'His presence and encouragement has lifted my spirits and I feel I can get back on the trail. After all, Matt has come to walk and as a mother all my instincts are to share this experience with him. I know today was meant to be a rest day but I know you'll want to get us walking so we can catch up on the bit we missed yesterday. That way we'll be back on schedule and still able to say we've walked every step of the way. I guess you'll even want us to get that bus back to where we stopped. Well, I'm even ready for that. After all, I wouldn't want to muck up the spreadsheet!'

I hug her and sheepishly acknowledge she knows me better than I do myself. By the time we assemble for breakfast at nine and share Debby's decision we're ready to start all over again. Outside the day has taken on a sparkling quality. One could even say it is a cracking day in Crackington Haven! The sun is bright and the frigid early morning air prickles my freshly-shaved head. There's a lightness in my stride knowing we are going back out on the track. It's impossible to be unhappy in weather like this. Even a terrible double espresso while waiting for the bus can't dampen my enthusiasm. The bus arrives, and twenty minutes later we're back on track.

It feels like the universe is smiling on Debby. I watch her walk confidently with Matt at the front of the group; she looks strong again. Matt has arrived like the cavalry, riding in to rescue his mum from doubts and flagging spirits. We briefly trudge through the disconsolate sand dunes of yesterday's drama. Weekend surfers are displaying British Bulldog hardiness, but soon we're up onto a headland with the joy of far off views and crystal clean air.

The scenery comes and goes, one minute up high, then down through woodland to cross Dizzard Brook, on up past Dizzard itself and Long Cliff. The guidebook warns of double-arrow descents and a deadly, very steep triple-double-arrow ascent back up, but after all we've tackled these past months nothing holds any fear for us. Instead, I soak up the sunshine and let my thoughts loose to join the hawk circling and crying plaintively below us, as we circuit a high cliff valley. All too soon, we descend back into Crackington Haven. This time yesterday we were demoralised, Debby had been broken and our mood was austere. Now we're resurgent!

Day 128 – to Tintagel

Sleep eludes us both and after a rotten night we wearily eye hard-poached eggs without the strength to complain. Back in the room to pack, I focus on today's walk. It looks like at least six hours and I'll need to keep a close eye on Debby now I know she's vulnerable. We get underway and leave this little cove imbued with so much of our journey's drama. The sky's clear and the atmosphere laced with an icy edge that nips at our noses and fingers. When the sun comes up it should be a great day. The sea is oblivious to us and our quest. Its ever restless rise and fall, set within this modest amphitheatre of rocks and grass spiked white by the frost, is our morning meditation. Up high we're back in the world of long views, cliffs, rocky headlands and tiny islands, jewels scattered in a twinkling sea. Coves far below occasionally have a sandy patch, but mostly are strewn with dark grey jagged stone. The north Atlantic has left its brutal mark on the fearsome coastline for which North Cornwall is famous.

As we climb Cambeak, we gain distant views south to The Strangles, Lower Strangles and Voter Run before Rusey Beach. After demonstrating such flair with their place names, it seems odd that Cornwall's highest cliff, which sets our hearts pounding and muscles quivering, is simply called High Cliff. Over the top, we're on a roller coaster of steep ascents and descents. We pass the Beeny Sisters rocks and then go up and around Hillsborough, a name that will forever be a byword for tragedy. It seems inconceivable that just 20 years ago 96 people could head off to Sheffield's football stadium and see a mere five and a half minutes of the game before losing their lives. Another 766 people were injured in the crush that day and still the memory of incompetence and ill-fortune jars.

Boscastle is a thriving tourist village today. In August 2004 vast quantities of water swept down through the village reaching above ceiling height of the houses along the High Street. Houses and cars were carried away into the sea. Blinking in the bright sun above tourists scurrying for lunch, the only reminders of that onslaught are small plaques positioned on first floor walls at the floodwater's limit. More visitors come here now to gawp at where the torrents flowed than to visit the 12th century Bottreaux Castle, from which the tiny village got its name.

An hour later we're fed and back on our feet. As we walk, low-flying helicopters skim the waves while goats eke out precarious lives on sheer cliffs above an ocean that awaits any loose footfall. A series of energy-sapping switchbacks confronts us and we look for distraction overhead. Ospreys swoop by us making the noise of mini jet planes. We rest weary limbs briefly at the attractive Rocky Valley and a passer-by stops to chat. He's interested in our quest and tells us of his good fortune. He's landed one of the great jobs. He's paid to live at a lonely cliffside caravan site during the six months it's closed over winter. Another human forging yet another version of life.

We find zest from eating oranges as we move out of Rocky Valley to look down on the grey swollen bodies of seals lazing on rocks far below. The languid turquoise of the sea under bright sun is reminiscent of Caribbean tourist brochures. Out around Barras Nose though we find ourselves confronted with the land of myth made real. This is Tintagel, the old castle ruins strung out as if scattered by wizards across a remote set of rugged headland cliffs. It's certainly a grand, evocative setting and easy to imagine King Arthur and Merlin behind any number of rough-hewn rocks. I can almost sense the ghosts of those brave Knights circling Bossiney Mound where the Round Table is said to be buried. Our challenge today, although not as glamorous as those faced in legends, is nonetheless demanding. We must climb up the steep paths to Tintagel, our resting place for this evening.

Once again, the day has taken its toll. The 15 miles of solid hill-walking have taken six and a half hours. Debby is done in by the time we reach our room and drops onto the bed. The pub dinner is a struggle and she succumbs to sleep immediately her head hits the pillow. A last thought circles before sleep takes over: the breakdown means we lost a precious rest day and are now involved in a marathon haul. Today was day six of the final 17-day stint. Only one more rest day is scheduled and that's still five days away. It would be a big ask at the best of times, let alone on 26th October when you've been walking since mid-June.

Day 129 – to Port Isaac

A poky bed under a low-angled ceiling wasn't promising, but we've slept until six and feel somewhat refreshed. I know this doesn't necessarily mean much. Any sense of strength can be illusory and disappear without warning on the track, just as the owl took that mouse at Dunrobbin Castle. There's a thought. That was four months ago and we're still walking! And blogging! Our B&B hosts welcome me into the family kitchen to use their internet to update the blog while they make breakfast.

The weather is doing its best to demoralise us. Pouring rain, black sky and gusting winds are today's recipe. When we do set off it's straight into Tintagel's most famous pasty baker. Inside, the indomitable British spirit is alive and well. It takes more than foul weather to dampen spirits around here. With a selection of the largest pasties Cornwall can muster stowed in our packs, we go back out into the pouring rain. Within minutes we're out of town on rain-sodden paths, slipping and sliding in the mud. Straight away the sheer force of the driving rain penetrates patches of our wet weather gear. Feeling wet cold skin underneath drenched outer garments is unsettling, but however bad it is for us, I can see misery etched on Matt's face. His basic army surplus gear is soaked.

Signs of old tin quarries are all around. It's hard to believe a county that now relies on agriculture and tourism for its economic success received a World Heritage listing on the back of its mining endeavours. A particularly imposing huge rock stack stands proud on the beach. It's reminiscent of the Old Man of Hoy in the Orkneys, but is a human creation from the quarry years. On days like today when nature has drawn up her damp cloak of secrecy, Gull Rock looks back defiantly from the ocean as if to taunt those with the temerity to risk these precarious cliff edges. The track is perilous and we risk injury every time our eyes stray to look at the intricate rock formations. Tiredness also comes quickly on these uneven paths in such conditions. I hope Merlin's spirit of benevolence will grace our passage. We trudge onwards and I hear Debby mutter, 'I'm sodden and ploddin.'

The next descent brings Trebarwith Strand into focus and an establishment that bedraggled walkers dream of. The Strand Cafe is not a mirage though and we dive straight in for respite. We don't care what the food or drinks are like in this lonely outpost, we simply seek somewhere warm and dry for our outer selves and something hot and wet for our insides. As we stand dripping on her floor, the young mother who owns it tells us she's come all the way from Hawkes Bay, New Zealand. The café is as warm as her welcome and while rain streams down the window outside, steam rises from the clothes we hang up to form droplets on the inside.

Over the next half an hour we're served some of the finest double shot lattes and chocolate brownies we've found in the UK. Perhaps Merlin did cast a spell for us, after all? As Debby cups cold hands around her steaming drink, she reminds me we've been here before. Five years ago I looked at Gull Rock and vowed to return to swim around it. Clearly, on this storm-lashed piece of coastline, today will not be that day. Today our challenge is different. A total of nine cliff descents and ascents await and several of them will be steep and slippery. Although it's not the longest, this section of coastline is considered one of the toughest on the coastal path.

We set off and start to climb. As usual we look for distractions to ease our passage. Jack offers a fascinating tutorial on the more esoteric building measurements he learned as a junior surveyor. I was introduced to horse racing at Plumpton as a three-month-old, so was well aware there are eight furlongs in a mile. However, I was not aware there were one hundred 7.92-inch links to a 22-yard chain and ten chains to a furlong. It seems there are no bounds to the useless trivia this walk bestows even if it does explain why the metric system was adopted. At two, it's lunchtime and the prospect of a monster pasty makes my mouth water. Yet again, my expectation far exceeds the reality and I'm left with shocking heartburn. I tell Debby I'm foreswearing any future pasty consumption.

By mid-afternoon we're at our destination and it's a delight to see Debby smile as she says,

'Thank you Keith for bringing me on this adventure!'

She's made a remarkable recovery and her wall has quite disappeared. At dinner we toast Mary and Jack's accomplishments and thank them for their support and enthusiasm. Their friendship has helped us through challenges we could never have imagined. Tomorrow we'll go our separate ways.

Day 130 – to Rock

In the early morning black I take stock. My cold seems to be returning with a vigour my body has lost. I'm groggy, my throat a rasp and my nose a tap with a faulty washer. All night I tossed, turned and snored. Night-time wakefulness provided no sense of peace and plenty of time to worry my way through the remaining ten days: what direction to take, visions of horrific geography ahead, timing constraints to negotiate, Debby's energy levels and my deteriorating health. Also, 'Mum & Dad' have booked a cottage near Land's End to be with us for our final week and we'll need to live up to the dates I gave them. My mental fortitude seems to be disintegrating along with my weak body. All manner of distractions loom to further congest my head and I seem resigned to chase after them, intent on worrying them into existence. It's as if the prospect of finishing is receding faster than we can walk. I'm not sure what's more daunting, the physical effort the track will demand or some warped fear of completion.

The Padstow ferry is another conundrum. I like to think of myself as a purist when it comes to doing the right thing by a challenge. When I swim our Iceberger two-kilometre 'Big Course', every post must be circled. Hence, to walk from John O'Groats to Land's End, every mile must be walked. When I mention this, Debby is not amused:

'We're now following the South West Coast Footpath, a much more arduous and longer track than taking the most direct route.

This official footpath crosses the Camel River on the Padstow ferry, so it's OK to take the ferry. Also, by the time we've finished this adventure we'll have walked about 1,750 miles, almost exactly double the most direct route from John O'Groats to Land's End. In other words, we'll have effectively walked there and back! So, don't be so silly, we are taking the ferry!'

I know better than to upset her after all she's been through. Meekly I acquiesce, although with some discomfort that I may be selling the adventure short.

At eight my mind turns to a more familiar conundrum. Why it is so hard to get a soft poached egg? And do four quarters of one mushroom really constitute a portion? Our host lacks some confidence and Matt refers to him as being like a character out of *Lord of the Rings*. Given that Matt has never read *Lord of the Rings* or seen the films, it is unclear which character he had in mind.

Out on the track I can see Debby is in better shape and walking quite strongly. Our roles have reversed. My cold will not be denied and energy seems to stream out as my nose runs. At least the weather is fine and the few puffs of cloud can't disturb the cobalt blue swathe overhead. It's cold out of the sun and a temperamental wind still comes and goes around the headlands, but it's a day to raise spirits. The views are spectacular, rocky cliff formations everywhere towering over sandy beaches burnished golden in the strong sun. Can this really be England? Even the sea is blue again.

In this weather, we spurn possible shortcuts and follow the path on longer deviations. The track follows a path wound around precipitous headlands and at times we really do appear to be living life on the edge. Conscious of our limited reserves though, I make sure we break the day up more often. We stop briefly at noon, then press on until two for a 20-minute lunch stop in the rocks at Pentire Point. All morning we've enjoyed a serenity built simply on bird cries, wind moan and the sea lapping at cliffs. Now tourists appear, apparently come to look at features with such alluring names as Seven Souls Rock, The Mouls, King Phillip and Newland. I wonder where they've suddenly come from, but around the corner of the peninsula, Polzeath's golden sands lie before us, full of people.

As walkers, there's no reason to tarry here. Rock is our destination and despite the soft sand, I insist on going down to the very edge of the estuary which is now at low tide. It looks to be only 200 or 300 metres across to Padstow and I'm sorely tempted to get in and try to swim across – far more honourable than taking the morning ferry. I finally accept my fate though; I haven't swum seriously for several months and have no knowledge of the strong currents in these waters. Common sense prevails and I let Debby lead me up off the beach. I casually mention I'm really feeling a bit depleted and she stops in her tracks to look me in the eye,

'Wow, so you finally understand that? It's so obvious to me, yet it's the first time I've heard you own up to it since we set out.'

Today's walk was not much more than 12 miles, but we're all limping and suffering: Debby's feet and hips are sore, a painful hip has added to my cold and Matt has knee problems. Of course Matt's in his mid-20's and has the energy and strength of youth, but long-distance cliff walking in all weathers after flying halfway around the world is still no mean feat. He has two more days to walk and whatever mark the walk leaves on him, he's been a lifesaver for his mother.

Day 131 – to Porthcothan

The night provided no respite. My nasal passages struggled to function while my brain worked overtime. It's still pitch black and I feel shocking. In contrast, Debby is quite chirpy. At breakfast she's intent on rebuilding her energy with a large plate of cooked food. I envy her, but don't have the strength to eat more than a modest bowl of muesli. We set off in time to catch the ferry and while it moves across this small channel, I ease my disquiet by walking on the spot.

Once we step onto the far jetty, I go straight to the information spot and before ten log in to a computer to address the blog's demands. Matt provides support in the form of strong coffees, vitamin C bombs and Echinacea. Today is a pseudo-rest day or as Australians call it, a Clayton's rest day. That's to say the rest day you have when you're not resting.

After three hours at the computer, it's lunchtime. Padstow is reportedly a food mecca with its own resident celebrity chef. There are many signs of fine dining experiences, but after a futile search we accept there are no simple takeaway bakeries or delis. Despite swearing off pasties two days ago, we walk out of Padstow eating hot pasties from the bag. We've booked accommodation in Porthcothan. It's only about five miles as the much-envied crow would fly. Of course, we'll have to walk much further, so there's no time to waste. We decide to circumvent the coastal path for some rural scenery and head down the River Camel along the Saints Way.

Back into the thick of the countryside progress is slow. The ground is sodden with plenty of mud through farmland along the side of the Little Petherick Creek. I've been worried for some time about the state of my shoes, but here they're a liability. The punishment they've endured means they've been used well beyond their recommended life. They look shocking, but it's the badly worn tread that makes walking in mud treacherous. We've walked for 90 minutes to reach Little Petherick and still have a fair way to go. Now we're road walking, which is rarely a joy, and the afternoon takes on the dull lustre of an extended plod.

By the time we arrive at Old MacDonald's Farm, it's taken close to four hours. We've walked 12 miles, typical of my organisation of a rest day. Our B&B host is welcoming and drives us to the pub for dinner. Over drinks we're subdued. Today's walk has emptied

Debby's tank and I've struggled under the weight of the cold. I badly need to just stop for some rest. However, before dinner concludes we feel a faint sense of pride when Matt announces:

'I don't know how you do it, walking every day like this. I certainly couldn't do it!'

Day 132 – to Newquay

Another day beckons through the blackness. I stagger from bed, dress and boil the kettle before my eyes clear sufficiently to see it's just four in the morning. Not the best start to the day. I return to bed grumpy and wake Debby. She's frustrated and has had to grapple all night with her recurrent problem: she's overheated and thirsty, smothered in yet another thick duvet.

When morning finally arrives, I find my pedometer has run out of battery. Purchased in Inverness four months ago it was meant to last a year. Perhaps it's trying to tell me it's been overused. My body feels the same, just wrung out of all energy. I finally admit to Debby I'm not sure I'll be able to keep going. Listlessly I try to gather my pack contents, but look at the bed and know I should be spending the day there. Outside the weather once again promises no relief for mere mortals. The wind blows hard with intermittent rain driving in from solid grey skies. The prospect of stepping outside is daunting. I feel the cumulative weight of all these months of exertion in my body even before I pick up the backpack.

At the doorstep, our kindly host shares part of her life story and unknowingly helps to raise my morale. She talks about the need to take advantage of time slots that occur in our lives, typically between children or grandchildren and when parents are healthy or don't need support. She still holds herself to blame for disagreeing with her husband when he wanted to have a year off before they started this new farm venture. Perhaps the opportunity is now lost for good as grandchildren have arrived. She loves the idea of doing something like we've done.

Of course, she can't comprehend what such an expedition like this demands, but this is a timely reminder of why we came on this quest. We're blessed to have been able to take it on and the joy of these past four months has been beyond my wildest imaginings. The only nagging concern is whether the physical effort we've made will have lasting, debilitating consequences. It's a dark shadow, a permanent conspirator that's lodged in my psyche these past couple of weeks.

Stepping outside we're immediately assailed by another world, one no human could create. The power unleashed is wild and unforgiving. High winds gust dangerously and the sea is an angry lather of white foam. Small fragments of cliff rock are whipped off and hurled abrasively at our cheeks in a mist of sand and grit. To experience the coastal path in these conditions is exhilarating, but our bodies seem so puny by contrast, mere matchwood to be played with by elements indifferent to human concerns. We walk in awe, engulfed by raw nature in all its intimidating magnificence. Control of body movements under the wind's strength is a lottery. Feet placement go awry and we bow heads in a reverence the conditions demand. At once it's terrible and wonderful and we struggle along slowly.

Every rock and cliff here appears to have been labelled: Mackerel Cove, Diggory's Island, Queen Bess Rock, Samaritan Island, Bedruthen Steps, Pendaves Island, Whitestone Cove, Carnewas Island, and all before Mawgan Porth where we plan to take a break. In the presence of such formidable geological creations the names seem mere flickers of human meaning, momentary shadows on the might and mystery of a planet billions of years in the making. This landscape was here before humans arrived and will be here when we're no more than a thin line of sedimentary remains. Once the names will have represented useful markers for earlier inhabitants, but now they're no more than quaint map descriptions to drive past or fly over. Yet even if their origins are forgotten and the words meaningless, their very presence feels comforting. The names attempt to bring nature down to human size, to tame it and quiet our fear that such wildness may be a threat to our imagined supremacy.

In this place, the split between my ordered lifestyle and nature's volatile moods has never been more evident. As the tempest rages and tumultuous seas fracture land to sweep away any flimsy human adornments, we can see ourselves in stark relief. The battle of the cliffs and the sea will rage on for eons until the eternal dominance of the sea will inevitably assert itself. But the human folly of smug superiority and control seems exposed here as no more than the cloak of an emperor with no clothes. I close the guidebook and let go of the map names to experience my smallness and frailty set in sharp contrast against this raw, rugged landscape. To be here in the midst of power without measure, formidable forces beholden to no one, I feel more alive than I can remember. I stand in wonder to play my part in this dizzying vortex and give thanks for my life. For being filled with life on this quest, a walk joining two ends which has now become so much more.

Despite the wind's rage, birds rise above our plight to ride thermals with ease. They appear to be offering a lesson on how to be in the flow of nature rather than fighting it. Before I can grasp any meaning, the sky opens. Torrential rain falls and we struggle like ducks out of water to come to terms with it. It feels like we're fighting a losing battle. Muscles resist the effort of walking up steep slopes in the downpour. Energy levels sink once again and I look around for inspiration. The surly gaze of a cruel bleak landscape looks back. All is dark now, surging seas, foreboding cliffs and steel grey brooding skies full of water. The sheer physicality of this experience and the wretchedness of our condition seems too much.

The battle to reach Mawgan Porth lasts over two hours. I buy some food and eat. 'Feed a cold, starve a fever' was the adage Nan drummed into me. She probably wouldn't have understood the concept of a ciabatta roll while striving to improve the nutrition of my infant father close to 100 years ago as he battled rickets. Today it's sufficient to bolster my energy level. Half an hour later we press on to tackle the length of the great sandy Watergate Bay. By the time we stagger into the outskirts of Newquay the 14 miles we've completed in gruelling conditions feels like double.

We head to a café and, as my chilled fingers wrap around the warm cup, a sense of achievement infuses my body. It dawns on me that after walking 1,665 miles over 132 days, we've arrived in Newquay on exactly the date I'd predicted. To think my trusty spreadsheet has held up despite all manner of obstacles. When I drew it up I had no idea Matt would be walking with us, or why. I'd had no conception of just how tired our bodies would be. Yet the discipline of following the spreadsheet has got us here. I sip the tea with quiet satisfaction, but the silent quiver running through my body reminds me how desperately I need rest and the closure that awaits at Land's End.

Day 133 – to Holywell

In the murky pre-dawn light we exchange hugs and wave goodbye to Matt before his taxi pulls away. This week we've learned first-hand something of his grief. Another thread of meaning has been woven into our adventure and more stories have been created to strengthen our family bonds.

While Matt sets off to return to Melbourne via taxi, bus and planes, the contrast with our situation is stark. He will complete a trip of over 10,000 miles by tomorrow, while we'll take a week to cover the remaining 75 miles of our adventure. While he'll travel faster, his body will land in Melbourne to all the confusion of a different time zone, climate and culture. In moving one footstep at a time, we will continue to travel at a more natural speed. Our bodies can tune into the world we're embedded in at walking pace and appreciate the nuances in our ever-changing habitat. Someone suggested our minds work at about three miles per hour and now, I understand why.

Later, we venture out for breakfast. To move through the pallor of Newquay's quiet early morning streets is an unedifying experience. Off-season, Britain's surfing capital drums up little excitement with its drab bricks and concrete. Despite the glorious natural advantages it possesses, human development has not done it proud. The few sad people moving about the dingy streets look washed out and resigned to their fate. Back home under Australia's generous sun, this setting is impossible. There can be grime and shoddy building works, but nothing to make the bronzed surfers and their clan downhearted. By ten, an internet café opens and we take up residency. We stay five hours until the blog is up to date and set off for what should be a very short day.

I quickly become aware the blog may have tempted us to cut our daylight window too short. Winter is beginning to settle in around us and we've eight miles to cover. The clocks go back tonight, so it will be dark by six. It's unsettling to think of walking in the dark through dunes, particularly now we're trying to complete our 11th straight walking day without a rest. This is the longest stretch of continuous daily walking of the entire journey. Also, the day was dry, grey and cool, but it's now rapidly deteriorating and the sky looks ominous.

Our first challenge is to get across the River Gannel flowing into the sea just south of Newquay. I've checked and it's close to low tide, which will make the crossing a little easier. Stepping down into the estuary mud, we walk across the sludge and onto the Penpol footbridge. This small construction spends much of its time under water, but now we're able to cross it without difficulty. Rather than climb the bank to find the official path, we decide to chance our luck and follow the channel bed's slippery edge out towards the sea. When we do clamber up over the unctuous weed-covered rocks we emerge into a surfers' car park.

The rain now starts to fall steadily and the wind picks up. Silently, I curse the blog addiction that's devoured the best of the weather. We work a way out of dunes onto a grassy track to Pentire Point West, down onto the Porth Joke beach then climbing back up out to Kelsey Head. The light begins to fail and we've become a sad bedraggled couple. What's worse, although we're near Holywell where our lift is waiting, we're confronted by a series of high sand dunes. A spaghetti-junction of tracks criss-cross one another going in all directions. The confusion seems to only add to our wretched state. With no idea of the exact whereabouts of the inn we have to reach, and knowing there's a river running through the dunes, we plod on more in hope than confidence.

By the time we emerge, the world has turned black and our wet, tired bodies sparkle in the golden illumination of the pub's signage. Here are our London support team waiting to welcome us as any loving 'Mum and Dad' would. There could be no happier sight and they whisk us into the inn. Despite our rain-sodden, mud-and-sand-splattered condition, it seems we're the most normal people in the bar. The setting feels surreal until someone explains it's 31st October tomorrow and we've stumbled into a Saturday night bar decked out with Halloween paraphernalia and people in full costume. Such dates and events now pass us by. We've plenty else to occupy our days.

Over pints we share long stories and tall tales. Later we're driven to dinner at the cottage our support team have hired as home base for this last week. Even though I'm ravenously hungry, my body starts to close down before dinner finishes. The chill of a wet late-autumn afternoon seems to have driven all the energy from my body. The cold I've grappled with these past two weeks has now become infected and settled on my chest. For the first time in 133 days I know there is no way I'll be able to walk tomorrow. It will have to be a rest day.

Day 134 – in Holywell

I feel wretched and have no energy to even get out of bed. My lungs take in shallow breaths that return as involuntary groans. My body is saying stop. Coughs and sneezes bring up a gruesome palette of colourful fluids that wouldn't have looked out of place at last night's Halloween celebration. I won't be able to get over this infection quickly and have been told it could turn to pneumonia if I keep exposing myself to the cold and wet. My very life force seems to have drained away and I fear my body is simply collapsing as I keep pushing it. I just can't see how I'll be able to go back out tomorrow. The situation is made worse by looking out from our cottage nestled in this large attractive cove. It's the ultimate indignity, to face a sandy beach without the energy to swim.

Debby looks at me and insists on offering advice that does little to ease my woe. She feels much better after a good night's sleep and proceeds to regale me about my core British trait:

'My feet are sore and I'm looking forward to this day off, but I expect to be ready to go tomorrow. As for you, a week or so back you told me great challenges like ours should bring pain and take us to the very limits of our endurance. You even went so far as to say you'd feel somehow disappointed to reach Land's End with energy to spare.'

I tell her to stop, but she's now in full flight recounting her theory that the British are famous for a deep-seated belief that nothing good can be achieved without first experiencing suffering. This is the last thing I need to hear this morning, but she won't stop:

'Now you've woken up feeling so bad, perhaps you've created the conditions you need to be able to go on and finish this quest?!'

She closes the door to leave me with my misery. All this intellectual theorising is cold comfort and the day slowly passes. For the first time in 134 days, I don't go outside.

Day 135 – to Porthtowan

It's five, and with the luxury of the first living room in four months, I get up to quietly read without disturbing Debby. It's 1st November, another month starts and I'm feeling a little better. My cold is still heavy, but it feels like something has broken overnight. Perhaps all Debby's theorising was correct and I've been able to let go of the need for more anguish and pain. At breakfast, I tuck in to an enormous fresh-fruit salad with muesli. I feel full, but cook up a bacon and egg roll to stoke the energy reserves, just in case. Debby follows my lead, but with some reluctance:

'I may never eat another egg once this adventure is finished.'

We are driven back to last night's grim scene to resume. Immediately I'm in a different mood, even the weather's on our side. There's little wind, the sky is relatively clear and the sun is up. In the light of day it's easy to find our track, and where the huge sand dunes were a depressing barrier in the dark, now they're a joy. We confidently stride off towards the next dot on the map, the military firing range. With no reason to stop we push on around Ligger Point to Perran Beach, its two miles of golden sands our entry to Perranporth. Again, the long sandy beaches remind me I'll soon be going home to an Australian summer.

That thought of Australia as home feels a little odd today. I've become so immersed in the capricious, variegated nature of the

British countryside on this walk, I can feel my roots. I left here 23 years ago to transplant a young family to Australian soil, but before that there were 35 years where this environment was my own. I was passionately British and remember with embarrassment that when Margaret Thatcher set out to regain The Falklands when I was 30, I would have gone to war for her. Since then I've changed sides and cheer on all Australia's sporting teams with gusto, loving nothing better than a victory over the Poms. But these things float on the surface.

Somewhere deep inside I sense I'm still British. Whether it's the call of a cuckoo, the urgent 'keows' of English seagulls, the horse chestnut's glossy conkers waiting to be kicked, the oak tree's offer of an incomparable embrace, or the woodsmoke filtering through dank woods on a late autumn afternoon, these things bypass my brain to connect directly with my body's cells. I love my life in Australia. It's where I choose to live and I've established the early first-generation roots that my sons may build on. There's nowhere I would rather call home, but the British countryside will always have first call on my heart.

At Perranporth we buy lunch to tuck into the rucksack and head off up past Shag Rock and out to the far headland of Cligga Head. We've now stepped back into Cornwall's grand mining era and the reason for its World Heritage status. Tin, copper and lead have been extracted from this remote peninsula for over 2,000 years. It's astounding to think they achieved so much with so little modern technology. Romans sailed their ships up the Hayle Estuary and for several centuries Cornwall was the largest producer of tin and copper, underpinning the industrialisation of the world. Such facts seem bizarre in this setting, yet in the early 19th century shafts were constructed over 300 metres deep that extended out below the sea bed. This gave miners the eerie opportunity to hear the rumble of boulders rolling across the seabed during bad storms. Their life in these mines was tough; the constant dampness and intense heat meant the average miner's life expectancy was under 40 years. My efforts on this walk seem trifling by comparison.

Ruined remnants of this past are strewn everywhere: ancient chimneys projecting from cliffs, spoil heaps, mine shafts with conical covers, engine house ruins, old quarries in impossibly inaccessible spots in the cliffs and sometimes right down at the water's edge. They stand as edifices to another time and are now no more than photo opportunities. Seagulls provide the din of activity while silently these monuments are surreptitiously reabsorbed back into the landscape. For all that hard human labour and ingenuity over centuries, now only tiny flecks in the fabric of nature remain.

As is usually the case when confronted with stunning scenery, grand history and reasonable weather, life is good. This is the best tonic available and we're walking along feeling somewhat renewed. Debby looks to have some rhythm back after the challenges of the past weeks. Her feet are permanently sore, but as long as she gets a reasonable sleep, she reckons she can still manage 14 miles a day. It's two when we pull out lunch on a bench seat overlooking Trevaunance Cove. We can't delay, and 25 minutes later walk down into the cove and out around St Agnes Head. A dangerous crumbling path takes us slowly down into Chapel Porth before it's back up Mulgram Hill and then we call it a day. Another 14 miles ticked off and a good Monday's work. Yesterday everything seemed bleak and now it seems nothing can stop us reaching Land's End on Friday.

Before going back to our cottage, it's early enough to put some work into the blog. We marvel that it's now had over 13,000 hits and wonder at the mystery of who all these disembodied hits represent. With the blog sated, we even have time to visit 'The Bucket of Blood' pub. The origin of its gruesome name dates back to when the landlord brought up a pail filled with blood. The broken body of an unknown man was found down the well, and although several attempts were made to sanitise the name – including a stint when it was renamed The New Inn – the name of local legend stuck. In keeping with its gory image, ghosts are said to frequently come and go through the stone walls.

After a couple of drinks I know we've overdone it. Debby is utterly exhausted and in pain by the time we reach the cottage. Once again, we've used our depleted resources to their limits out on the track, then run chores and attempted to socialise. At this stage, our weakened bodies can't cope with any activity beyond the demands of these coastal paths. It's ten-thirty as we get into bed and while Debby passes out immediately, I spend another hour writing up the day's diary. I'm conscious the discipline of documenting this journey is demanding a dangerous trade-off of precious sleep, but the blog has a life of its own.

Day 136 – to Hayle

Not a great night, but Debby tells me she's discovered the ultimate cure for insomnia. Plug in the iPod and listen to the 59-hour audio book version of *War and Peace*. Apparently, France has just won, but she has no idea what else is happening! Just as she's getting her sleep quota, I'm envious. My health is now a day-to-day proposition and I feel washed out again this morning. This is our longest remaining day and I feel too weak to take it on.

We get dropped back at last night's finishing spot. The idea that by day's end we'll be able to walk back and up the garden path to our cottage without assistance has some appeal. However, the thought it's just taken 30 minutes in a speeding car to get here, and we'll have to cover the entire return on two very tired pairs of feet, is hard to imagine. The prospect feels depressing and becomes an even weightier spectral companion when we walk up the first hill out of this small settlement, past a straggle of isolated clifftop homes. My limited energy reserves immediately evaporate. A fierce headwind buffets us under a sour sky and Debby becomes counsellor:

'Keith, one step at a time. Don't think further ahead than the next footstep.'

Now we've climbed up high we at least have the inspiration of classic clifftop scenery. A grey day can't dampen the stimulation of this setting. We walk where the land falls directly down from our feet into the frenzy of white spume-crested waves. Now the day's roller-coaster cranks into action. One minute we're staring out across the ocean and then we have to tackle a steep descent only to climb back up. Inland a high wire fence protects yet another Ministry of Defence landholding. This is the Nancekuke Common airfield. Thought to be a radar station, its purpose is not broadcast and it looks deserted. Yet another bureaucratic establishment occupying prime coastal land with spectacular views going to waste. Another steep drop leads to its incumbent climb back up from the valley past Sheep Rock. The going is slow and by the time we follow the road into Poltreath it's taken 90 minutes, 15 minutes longer than the maximum time suggested by our guide. And this is first thing in the morning when we're fresh.

We fill our packs at the bakery and leave the town. Poltreath has an attractive triple harbour but seems to suffer from poor town planning. Back out on the clifftop the roller-coaster recommences. The sharp drop down is followed by a climb back up steep steps, and that's just a taster to get the lungs going after morning tea. Down again before Porthcadjack Cove and then a major ascent. Once the struggle back up from sea level to the next clifftop is complete, we're then asked for a repeat performance. From Carvannel Downs by Samphire Island we head back out of the valley. My body moves by memory now. I'm completely stuffed yet we've still got a long way to go. *Just focus on one step at a time, Keith.*

The rain is holding off, but the wind nags relentlessly as if coveting every last ounce of our life force. The track has moved back from the edge of the cliff. The danger of being blown off in these high winds is reduced, but we're deprived of an inspiring coastline. We settle into just slogging it out. Every step the wind denies part of our progress. The views, where we get them, are shrouded in faint mist. It's as if nature has thrown dust sheets over these headlands that she has no purpose for today. We're left with nothing but indistinct greyed-out images and my spirit slowly ebbs away.

Past Dead Man's Cove, I see a solitary vehicle in a rough car park below. Inside a couple sit eating their fish and chips. Cosseted in the warmth of their car, their windshield has become a steamy TV screen through which they watch the elements as the wind whips up the sea's fury. We turn our heads back down. No such luxury for us – these elements are our direct companions for the day.

Hell's Mouth comes and goes and momentarily we enjoy the distraction of birds flying high, circling nesting holes that cover the cliff face. How is it in such a wild, seemingly inhospitable place, sheer cliffs above foaming seas, that these birds find succour to raise their young? And down in the water seals glide through the ocean's mighty power with ease. The contrast between humans and the other-than-human lives that share this Earth seems stark here. While other species appear perfectly happy to live in harmony with the world on its terms, we humans try to construct ever greater physical and mental structures to separate and protect us from nature. But there's something else at play. We do seem to have a hunger for something more visceral. It's as if there's a spark embedded deep in our psyche that calls us out to experience raw nature. We may today be in pursuit of a more extreme connection with Mother Nature, but it's perhaps no different to the urge that brought out that couple to gaze in awe over their fish and chips?

We push on, out on the Knavocks, to Nathaga Rocks and Godrevy Point. The spectacular white lighthouse stands 300 metres beyond the Point as it has for over 150 years. I may be in a sorely depleted condition, fingers white and numb, but still discount the idea of cutting the corner across the promontory. We're following this track and that's all there is to it. Walking back in from the lighthouse view, it's two o'clock and we head down behind the tiny closed Surf Lifesaving hut to shelter as best we can from the wind. Like feeding time at the zoo, we devour lunch. Just as badly as we need food, we need some time to rest. In the cold wind though we must preserve our body heat and so take just 25 minutes. Six of my eight fingers are white and lifeless and I feel the cold seeping deep into my core. I need to walk now to build up body heat and get the circulation going. Debby says I should have a possum fur beanie like her. She says it's the best piece of kit she has and it keeps her whole body warm.

The afternoon leads us away from the rocks to Gwithian, a completely different environment. Here we're in sand dunes and wending our way through them never provides the reassurance that we're making any great progress or even keeping to the right track. There is a constant temptation to find an early track down onto the long hard sandy beach of St Ives Bay where our cottage awaits. However, when we finally can resist it no longer, the tide rises menacingly and we're forced to retreat back up into a last patch of dunes to bring the day to a close. After six hours and 16 miles in our depleted state, to have to push aching limbs through soft sand feels an insult.

The day has taken its toll. At the house Debby has to use the keys to enter, my frozen fingers just aren't functioning. Once inside, tired and cold, the kettle goes on and the bath is run. Gradually, life begins to return to our veins. By six-thirty we're ready for dinner, but within two hours our bodies are failing and we drop into bed.

I can barely summon up the strength to turn the lights out. Before sleep comes, I return to the vision I had today of looking forward to St Ives on the far headland. If we can round that tomorrow, we'll have our destination in sight with the scent of Land's End and completion in our nostrils.

Day 137 – to Zennor

It's four-forty-five, the battle for more sleep lost. A headache has roosted on my brow and I'm back in the pits of despair. My chest is heavy and ill-coloured coughing fits are a sign of the infection that's taken hold. Someone wrote on the blog to be careful to watch for pneumonia. In the dark, I weigh up the pros and cons of continuing to walk through this. Might I be doing serious damage? If I can manage three more days I'll be able to rest and bask in the satisfaction of a quest accomplished. Once Debby is awake, we sit lethargically on the bed in the half-light of a grey, uninspiring morning and I attempt to dictate a blog draft. I know we can't stop the walk. It might break us, but we must simply try to push on to Land's End. The peace of mind that will bring would be the greatest salve possible.

I try to take on a large breakfast, but after a bowl of fruit, muesli and yoghurt, neither Debby nor I have the strength for eggs. At nine-thirty walking is the last thing we feel like, but we rise, step out the back door and into day 137. Immediately I appreciate it's warmer and less windy than yesterday. We appear to be walking through sand dunes into a sad-looking holiday village followed by an industrial area. Another one of the days we dread, having to traverse uninspiring scenery down the Hayle Estuary, while looking for a bridge to lead us back out the other side of St Ives Bay. Once we reach the centre of this strung out little town of Hayle, I'm brought to an abrupt stop. A sign confronts us that surely can't be right. It reads, 'Hayle, the birthplace of the Industrial Revolution'.

We read that an engineer, Richard Trevithick, designed and built not only the world's first car, but also the first steam engine. The car was the Puffing Devil, dating from 1801, and the first steam engine came three years later. From the illustration, the Puffing Devil more resembles a small train. However, the sign recounts all the contributions Hayle has bestowed on a world in search of industrialisation. It produced the fastest paddle steamers in the world: in the 1850's, for instance, the SS Cornubia did 20 knots while supplying both sides in the American Civil War. Brunel also used the local foundry to produce thousands of suspension bridge chains. And so it goes on until the spell of all this industrial ingenuity breaks and we drag ourselves away.

Now we're confronted with a more dramatic memorial. It's dedicated to Cyril Richard 'Rick' Rescorla, born in Hayle in 1939. He gave his life in 2001 saving 2,700 lives while directing the evacuation of the World Trade Centre. So, Hayle reminds us of our tremendous human potential, both to cause great harm as well as offer selfless sacrifice. We walk on in silence as a dirty day develops. Here on the banks of another dreary estuary we have just a selection of tiny fishing boats for company, beached in the mud as if a careless parent hasn't cleared up after pulling the plug from the kids bath.

A curtain of fine rain falls from the grey sky and we go through the tiresome routine of removing backpacks and applying wet weather gear for the umpteenth time. Next a soaking sea mist envelops us and the wind blows directly into our faces. With spirits at low ebb we slowly make our way along to Lelant and the Badger Inn. I smile for the obligatory photo outside, it's about the limit of my physical capacity. From St Uny's churchyard we go through into sand dunes and across two fairways of a links course, unmoved by golf balls being driven directly over our heads. More remote dunes lead into Carbis Bay and, directly behind, the cottage we left ninety minutes ago is still evident. Depressing to think it's less than a mile away as our friend the long-envied crow would have flown.

I feel the last of my energy disappear and have no appetite to go on. We're coming out of the back dunes into St Ives and I tell Debby I'm going to have to stop. Demonstrating the depth of understanding we've developed over these months, she suppresses her own tiredness and immediately takes control:

'You need warmth and some hot food, wait here while I find a café.'

It's the off-season and most cafés are closed, but she finds the Yellow Canary. I'm ushered inside with words of encouragement. Bowls of pea and ham soup are soon produced, followed by chocolate tiffin and a coffee. Now it's time for a serious discussion. I just want to call off the rest of the day's walk, it feels like the only option given how bad I feel. I've set too demanding a schedule to try to finish on Friday, that's only the day after tomorrow:

'Debby, we've both hit walls in the last couple of weeks, we're just not listening to our bodies. By the looks of what's coming out of my chest I may have pneumonia, for heaven's sake! Let's just accept that to try and walk 13 miles a day along these cliffs on the back of the last four months with only one rest day in the last 17 is plain crazy!'

With this admission now out on the table amongst the empty soup bowls and coffee cups I feel wretched. Is this the way to end? I know part of me wants to go on, but a larger part just wants to throw a temper tantrum and say why the hell do you expect me to do any more? The challenge of walking 70 miles over the last five days has just beaten us.

In our moment of crisis the support team arrive. I tell them my thoughts and after some reflection Colin, our wise 'Dad', reminds us the weather is expected to deteriorate after today. If we can just get through the next three-hour walk, we'll be so much better placed. Somehow, through the screen of exhaustion I can perceive the wisdom. Today is Wednesday, the week's halfway point, the 'hump' day. To get through this would break the back of it. Then again, who am I to be having this tantrum? Debby has battled through so much to be this close to the end. I wouldn't let her give in at Crackington Haven, so how can I let her down now? My stubborn temper demands a break, but my frustration is really directed at myself for feeling so lousy. With no sense of confidence, I drag myself out into the dismal St Ives streets and try to turn the challenge back on Debby:

'Are you really up for this? We only have about three and a half hours of light remaining. Our guidebook says we'll need most of them. We're both weak, but I can't have you lagging and holding us back. There won't be any room for errors. Being out on cliff edges in the dark in our condition could spell disaster.'

On this note we pay homage to the Universe at large, bend our backs and bow our heads in the form of religious devotion the weather gods demand from penitent walkers. We set off up the steep streets out of town.

As soon as we reach the cliffs something peculiar suddenly happens. It's wonderful, yet beyond my comprehension. Stung into an instinctive reaction to my challenge, Debby has immediately lifted her pace. She's now walking the way she had been in the early days of our journey, her face wreathed in smiles. To witness this change lifts my spirits. I feel energy flowing back through my body as if plugged into a power pack. A hawk on the edge of some high rocks suddenly comes into clear focus. I realise we haven't been paying as much attention to the wildlife around us. I'd become completely internally focussed and my aches and pains have taken control of my mind.

Something has shifted. I feel a different man. Even the wearying headache I've been carrying has flown off into the landscape. Dark has become light as we both stride out, and where there was no way forward, now there is no way back. Everything is positive and a smile has recaptured my face as I'm once again aware of the landscape coming into clear focus. I can observe the change permeating my whole self as energy and joy supplant weary thoughts and a new self emerges from the disconsolate depths of indecision. The wind has picked up, but is no longer our enemy. Now it has the opposite effect, becoming the ultimate healing remedy, a rich elixir full of sea spray and just the cleansing tonic my lungs need to finally drive out doubt.

Debby is now leading the way, capering in the true goaty way of a Capricorn woman in her prime. In the sheer joy of the moment we start laughing and imagine we're flying. Inspired by the hawk, we've re-joined the landscape of coastal drama and sensory delights. We're embedded back in our adventure, alive to the sea's rush onto a remote beach, the drag of reluctant pebbles back into its clutches, the mist of broken waves, and the salt air fresh on our faces. We're alive right here in this moment and nothing could be better. The guidebook says these rock climbs are supposed to be the toughest on the South West Coast Path, but not for us, not today. We've the memories of much tougher times on the Pennine Way etched into our muscles and our minds. This section is supposed to be muddy and rocky. Well yes, but hell we've been up to our shoulders in mud in the Pennines. And rocky, well what about Pen Y Ghent, Cauldron's Snout, or the Devil's Staircase!?

This is pure enjoyment, and so unexpected. The real joy of suddenly having our minds liberated from fears and negative thoughts brings a lightness to every step. It was clearly my mind playing games. We're in the last week of a 20-week marathon and I've been struggling with the concept of completion and saying goodbye to such daily adventure. I know now I'm ready to finish. But we're going to bring it to an end in style and enjoy every moment. Even the scenery now begins to resemble the North Scottish coastline, as if we've come full circle.

The afternoon now becomes a wonderful string of improbable geographical names: Clodgy Point, Pen Enys Point, Carn Naun Point, Mussel Point and Treger, Porthzennor Cove and around Zennor Head. The climbing is as exhilarating and challenging as the names are to say out loud. Well before daylight departs, we walk off the path up towards the little settlement of Zennor. We've walked for two and a half hours straight, at a speed that belies our physical state. 'Mum and Dad' are waiting to assist us at the little rough car park, and immediately notice we're changed people. I try to explain that once we changed our minds, we changed who we were, but they're just bemused. With energy to spare, I insist we go straight to the library to blog. We need to capture some of these events while they're fresh.

Before going home for dinner we even have energy to visit the local pub, and with pint in hand reflect on today's incomprehensible mental contortions. At ten, I lay my head on the pillow completely at peace. With a grin on my face and happy sense of contentment, I stretch out my arm to the light switch to extinguish a day of extraordinary contrast.

Day 138 – to Cape Cornwall

It's five thirty and I feel great. I've slept solidly all night and energy is surging through me. I spring out of bed, it's time to take the day by the horns. Debby is dozing, so I shower and dress, but by six I'm ready to go. As I place the tea mug at her bedside she stirs and looks furious at the disturbance. I'm incredulous, how can Debby be so grumpy on a morning like this?

'The wind blew hard all night and there were all kinds of bumps and noises. I got up and tried to make things quiet. I took that picture off the wall. I folded postcards and wedged them into the banging cupboard door and windows. And you just slept through it all! I made everything quiet except the one noise that cannot be quelled. The steam train that was coming from the other side of the bed. I know you badly need your sleep, but so do I. *War and Peace* couldn't block out the noise you were making. Instead of counting sheep I recited every one of the 137 place names we've stayed in since leaving John O'Groats, but nothing seemed to work. I've had about two hours sleep all night so please, BE QUIET!'

I creep away to leave her in peace, but the way I feel nothing can bring me down today. Tigger is back!

Breakfast is a different affair and I attack everything before me, finishing with a big plate of scrambled eggs and bacon. At St Ives library we upload another day into the blog. It's just one day behind now and I've a great sense of being in control of this adventure, rather than at its mercy. Debby got a little more sleep and by the time we're dropped back at the Zennor settlement, we're both ready to embrace our penultimate day with gusto. Over the past couple of weeks we've been depleted shadows of the people who took to the path in John O'Groats, but not today. We're walkers and here to walk, simply out on the track continuing with our quest. This is what we do.

Debby shows she's as strong as she's ever been and I can't get the smile off my face. Today will not be about us and our drama, we'll just let the scenery sweep us into its embrace. And what a day the weather lords have laid on. Already sunny and warm, there's a light haze shielding what promises to be a rich blue sky. The sea reflects back the sense of calm certainty we feel. Strong headwinds are blowing, but today we accept them as simply part of this dramatic coast. The wind may be wild and cold, but it no longer chills to the bone. It may play with our limbs, like a pussycat toying with a mouse, but it's not an adversary.

The coastal path is said to be at its 'fearsome worst' on the first stretch to Pendeen Watch. We negotiate the mud and rock fields that follow but we're enjoying the challenge. When deep mud forces me into a fierce gorse bush gouging my leg badly, I acknowledge the pussycat is capable of more than toying with us. The swipe of her claws will be with me for days, but she can't dampen my spirit. There's precious little of this adventure left, but like at the end of a Christmas feast, I'm determined to suck every piece of meat from the turkey bones. We briefly encounter three experienced walkers and their reaction on hearing of our adventure is a surprise. Suddenly, these strangers are taking their hats off to us, shaking us by the hand and asking to take our photograph. They say they're just so impressed, and all we can do is shake our heads in disbelief.

Our hearts race and I realise we're rushing through this day too fast. I call a halt at the top of Trevean Cliff and we stop for ten minutes to eat the last piece of apple cake and soak up the splendour laid before us. The raw air races across our bodies seeking out every nook and crevice. Pockmarked rocks covered in the fine threads of lichen provide seats and our eyes are carried out through the sparse shrubs and bracken into the ocean's timeless ebb and flow. Far beyond, a misty horizon shimmers milky grey from where the sky rises with the deepest sapphire-blue radiance to melt our hearts. We look at one another and acknowledge the rapture of this time, and the sad thought dawns that just twenty-four hours from now such experiences will be over. Where will we get this kind of buzz after tomorrow?

The track plays its usual games taking us up and down endlessly, but nothing today is a problem. We can virtually run up the inclines. If there is one thing I've learned on this journey, it is the importance of the ups and the downs in life. They are the yin and the yang, simply different sides or perspectives of the same mountain, issues seen in daylight or by the dark of night.

We're near the lighthouse at Pendeen Watch, which means we've broken the back of today's walk. Next we descend into Portheras Cove, a sandy trinket amongst so much harsh battled-scarred rock. We reach the lighthouse at two and are back in a mining wonderland from another age. Old mine chimneys and ruined remains dot the landscape. We're hungry, so we drop down to the old Geevor Tin Mine site to perch on a crumbling wall to eat sandwiches. It's sad to think this will be our final picnic out on the track. Lunch won't taste as appetising after today. We take time to enjoy the scenery and both sit silent in personal contemplation. Happy and at peace with one another, words are unnecessary. This adventure has meant different things to each of us but we both realise this is a special moment.

And then we're up to tackle the last stretch down to Cape Cornwall. Around Botallack Head there's a final descent at Zawn Buzz and Gen before we find ourselves all too quickly walking into the National Trust car park at Cape Cornwall. It's four o'clock, earlier than we'd expected, and with time to spare I read the history of this place. It was owned 100 years ago by Captain Francis Oats, a Cornishman who started his career down a local tin mine at the age of 12 and went on to become Chairman of De Beers mining conglomerate.

The geology is almost unique for the UK. It's a cape, one of only two in Britain. The other, Cape Wrath sits at the extreme tip of north-west Scotland. Apparently to be a cape, two oceans or channels must come to meet at the one point. Cape Cornwall was once thought to be England's effective land's end. If the cartographers hadn't changed their mind I guess our great adventure would now be over. Thankfully we've one more day to cherish, number 139. There in the distance, dimly visible, is the promontory that has been our focus for the last 138 days. Barring some unforeseen event we'll walk out onto that headland called Land's End tomorrow and draw a veil over our journey. I can't imagine what that will mean.

Day 139 – to Land's End

We both sleep well, which is a real bonus before our last day. 'Last day' – it has such a ring to it. To have been completely submerged in an adventure like this for so long means I've lost track of life without a 'track' to pursue every day. My emotions are all stirred up and will take some time to unravel. To reach the end has obvious appeal. We'll be able to say 'we did it' and prove the doubters wrong. Yet there's something else gnawing away below the surface. Today's walk might not be the last word. I feel certain after all we've done to get here we're going to complete the final gentle eight-mile stretch into Land's End. But I suspect this adventure has its claws in us and won't let go that easily.

Whatever happens next, I know that even at this late stage discipline is vital. We write up the blog onto a memory stick while still in bed and have the comfort of knowing we can upload it at the library before setting foot on today's path. We must keep our supporters up to date; after all so many have cheered us on, or challenged us in the Iceberger tradition. We may have done the physical side of the walk, but it wouldn't have been possible without the help of so many others, whether in spirit or through tangible support along the way.

In particular we've had massive support from 'Mum and Dad'. 'Mum' especially, has been our Number One supporter. Phyllis, as she used to be known, is my cousin and has managed our bulging suitcase in London to keep us supplied all along the track. She's received parcels of fetid mud-stained clothes that may well have walked from the letterbox to the washing machine by themselves. And when the going was tough, Phyllis was always the one to send us text messages to check how we were going and wish us well. It's fitting she will be by our side today as we walk the last mile into Land's End.

We get in the car and 'Mum' drives us to upload our blog at the library. I try to still my mind, but it's abuzz after all the trials and tribulations we've overcome for this day. I'm like a kid on the way to the circus, excited at the thought of Mother Nature's showtime up on the cliffs. I just want to be walking. Of course, with that comes the adult sense of uneasiness. The walk today will return us into an unknown. I've no idea what tonight's completion will bring.

We both feel healthy and have thrown off all the sloth and questioning of the past few weeks. With only a two or three hour track remaining, we'll soon be saying, 'We're here, we've done it!'. What does the Tour de France leader feel on his last morning, knowing that no one will challenge him as he rides into Paris and certain victory? Bit different for him of course. He's competing against the world's best in one of the most fiercely-fought competitions. We've just been wandering around the country in what Debby used to call a glorified long pub crawl. But still, this has been a marathon adventure for us and one we had no idea we could complete. Along the track I've also learned that although reaching Land's End was a goal, it was somehow just a small part of it. There's no way we're not going to cross that line, but in some ways it feels anti-climactic.

From the car window the weather looks so similar to what we walked away from at John O'Groats on 20th June, 139 mornings ago. The sky is grey and the wind strong. A heavy misty rain is drenching the landscape and every living thing mad enough to be outside. Looking back at the diary, I see we enjoyed day one nonetheless and I'm determined we'll do the same today. Also, it hasn't escaped my attention that we're finishing our wonderful, eccentric adventure on 5th November in a country I've come to think leads the world in eccentrics and lauds their peculiar achievements. Where else would the population continue, every year on this day, to remember and celebrate Guy Fawkes' 1605 attempt to blow up Parliament? That's just another part of the rich complexity of one of the most endearing national psyches. Today I feel I'm doing it justice.

Just when I thought nothing could possibly go wrong, the Penzance library computer system crashes before we can upload the blog. I freely acknowledge my stubborn streak lies like a reef, only ever barely submerged when the weather in my life is set fair. Now it is revealed in spectacular fashion. Debby tries common sense:

'Keith, don't be so silly. Let's get the walk over with and worry about the blog tomorrow.'

I'm having none of it. *Find me an internet café!* Not quite the desperation of 'My kingdom for a horse', but it had a similar ominous ring. We march off some distance to a major computer support establishment and start again. The tension mounts rapidly, but halfway through, the unthinkable occurs and the entire system suddenly crashes. Is there some dark hand behind the scenes pulling the plug on my best efforts? If the weather gods have failed to stop us, is there now some other gremlin, human or ethereal committed to thwarting us? Is it my addiction to the blog that will finally bring us undone? I fold my arms and like a five-year-old that won't leave a birthday party, insist we wait. Debby and 'Mum and Dad' look on with a resignation formed from years of knowing me. The clock ticks, the tension grows, meaningless small talk is muttered before finally, the machines crank back into life. The blog is uploaded. Now for our destiny.

It's noon as we take to the path. We march straight off up the hill to leave Cape Cornwall in our wake. There's no great height in these cliffs today and surveying the Atlantic Ocean the water is greyer with fewer whitecaps to demand our attention. This is our last day, surely it should be more special? Yet, it's not. It's somehow just normal, just like any other day. Why doesn't it feel more profound? At what point today will I discover the secret of life? Surely that's what this must have been all about, wasn't it? And so the stream of consciousness rolls on looking for a depth of meaning I've read about in books.

Gradually my mind tires into peaceful acceptance. We just keep walking like the 138 days that have come before. The sight of Dr. Syntax's Head, the most westerly landmass of England, provides a focal point. It looked a long way away, almost lost in the mist when we started, but all too soon I can see we're closing in on it. The path turns rocky for a while and we have to scramble over a couple of short sections. Now we're in dunes at the back of White Sand Bay. The scenery's picking up with the wind and we tarry briefly to watch perfect sets of white horses rolling in.

Back out on the headland a silky grass carpet is laid before us. How can something so soft and delicate live this close to the harsh reality of rocks and salty sea spray? Its downy surface cushions our footsteps and, as birds of prey circle above, the setting has a majestic touch, a red carpet turned green. The joy I feel to be at one with this scene is already tinged with sadness. Soon such beauty will be gone from our daily life. For now though, we're going to embrace it for all it's worth. Any melancholy evaporates when Debby suddenly breaks into a run down the green slope and flaps her arms trying to join the birds. I can't resist following her lead. We are clearly in a dangerous condition right now and probably need some solitude to calm down before attempting to re-enter civilisation. Not only are we mimicking birds, but we're responding to their calls, crying out:

'Wake up humans, get out here and feel alive!'

There's no doubt we're dangerous right now and so-called 'Civilisation' will not be amused!

By the time we reach Sennen Cove it's been a comfortable two-hour walk. This small hamlet is the last community before the end. It seems a lifetime since we visited here in the early flush of our romance, but was probably just six or seven years ago. Timelines in our memory have been played with since we stepped off the world's merry-go-round so long ago.

And here is the support team waiting. This really is it. The final leg, a mere 30-minute walk around to the point where so many tourist destinations end. I know it will pass in the blink of an eye and do my best to be conscious and aware of each step to make it last. But all too suddenly the finish line is in sight, just 50 metres to go! A small group of friends have come to celebrate with us. They're holding a tape across the path, our finishing line. I try to emulate the slow motion sequence in the opening credits of *Chariots of Fire*, but to no avail. In a moment the last vestige of the adventure slips through our fingers. Without any great sense of significance we simply break the tape.

And so it's done. Champagne is produced and it's all hugs, congratulations, back-slapping and loud laughter. We make a hardy group, impervious to the windy onslaught that's begun to ravage the headland. In time the rituals of completion must be attended to. The professional photographer who stands by his mock signpost ready to immortalise the moment sets the distance measured by our Australian pedometers: 2,801kms.

Next, there's the issue of the pebbles. We've carried these three stones with us for 139 days just so we could hurl them into the raging waves at this moment. I look at mine as I have every night with such a variety of emotions. However, I'm a man of tradition and dutifully summon up what strength I can to throw the pebble far out beyond the rocks into the heavy surf. By contrast, Debby has become so attached to her heart-shaped stone she decides to keep it. And then there's the pebble 'Mum' entrusted to me to carry. I return it to her and with a tear in her eye she also decides it must be preserved. In our endless search for meaning, these two small stones plucked from a vast ocean of anonymity on an isolated

Scottish beach have now become imbued with human emotions too precious to release.

Past the first rush of emotion it's time to be practical. We need food and drink. It's a great shame the John O'Groats to Land's End walk has to start and finish at such tacky, touristy places. We set aside our pride and wince at the pub bar as we celebrate with a late lunch of the only hot food available, 'Cheesy Chips' – just the sort of junk food we've tried to avoid for 138 days.

Gradually the afternoon wears away and our group splits up to head to their homes. We retreat to Sennen Cove for a celebration dinner with 'Mum and Dad' and friends Derek and Sue. It's a joyful noisy affair in the company of old friends, but somehow nothing can do justice to the sense of an ending I'd imagined. Slowly the familiar feeling of tiredness seeps through our bodies and we all head off to Derek and Sue's home in the quiet of Dartmoor's Tavistock.

Finally we're in bed with the light out, but I can't sleep. My mind is alive and I'm looking for profound conclusions. Well, certainly we lived a simpler, more satisfying life. And we got a great sense of the effect of extreme physical exertion on our bodies. We proved to ourselves that we had the determination and strength to see this quest through. Although I've lost 12kg, neither of us had any major injuries, although Debby's feet are very sore. We may have a level of deep weariness in our bodies, but I know we could continue if the path did. In fact, we're going to miss our daily appointment with a walking track. Perhaps more than any of this though, in a world of electronic technology and virtual experience, we proved our resourcefulness in the physical world and found our way successfully from one end of the country to the other.

This adventure has certainly been the most fantastic, life-affirming experience. For months we've communed with nature on a daily basis and our life has been stripped of so much trivia and wastefulness, simplified down to the basics nature taught us. And as our daily routine unfolded, we experienced a profound sense of contentment, feeling we did no damage to anyone or anything. It was the length of the journey that was so important. Not the distance, but the days it took. Each day other than sleeping, eating and arranging a bed for the night, we simply focussed on our walk. We were either walking or remembering the walk on our blog. The hardest daily decision was which of our two sets of walking clothes to wear. In the evening there was no such decision required, as we only had one relaxing, or 'best', set. Remarkably, although we stayed at hostels and B&Bs for most of the 139 nights, I've worked out we spent less than if we'd been at home.

All kinds of individual daily memories swirl through my mind. Day 6 was special, when I swam with seals off Brora and we were entertained by Dunrobbin Castle's birds of prey. And then Day 13 offered an out of this world experience in the wild Scottish highlands at Rory's Café. All far removed from the retail café society we're soon to re-enter. But these are fleeting images from a kaleidoscope of thousands that it will take time to reflect upon. Perhaps the most warming memory we carry though, is of the wonderful people we've met, who have shared their lives and sometimes their homes with us. It's also clear the blog became a much more important part of the journey than we ever could have imagined. Despite my early reservations, it became almost an addiction, a lifeline to friends and supporters across the world. Far more though, it will be a rich source for us to relive what has been such a big event in our lives.

Now all that remains is to return home and indulge in long relaxed storytelling over hearty meals with as many family and friends as will listen. Lying here though, I'm worried about what now lies ahead. This end was not what I had imagined. I don't feel ready to move on or return to my life in Melbourne. In some ways I don't feel like the journey is over at all.

LOST
LAND'S END
?
?

Chapter 12 – LOST

<u>Under the backyard Peppercorn</u>

You drop your fruit on an effortless breeze
And I know there's wisdom here for me

No quick reactions just quiet reflection
On all you've witnessed and seen disappear
What does it all mean and what can I learn

My mind's full of frames that no longer fit
What my eyes discern and my teachers thought
My challenge now, to make sense of this world

To understand my place and set a new course
To see through the veils I've carefully woven
And gaze into the great web of life on this Earth

What's my role in this infinite beauty
Peppercorn, please sprinkle your wisdom on me

12 days later – In-flight

This is a day completely disconnected from land, the substance with which we've formed such an attachment these past months. We boarded the plane last night and will arrive tomorrow morning in Melbourne. It's a last opportunity for quiet reflection about what we've done before the barrage of questions friends will ask when we arrive. We've quickly come to terms with the fact our adventure seems to be the most interesting thing about us now. Everyone, from the waiter who overhears mention in a café to our close supporters, wants to glean something from the experience we've had. Of course, it's still front and centre of our life and we don't think of much else. When we meet strangers we simply look for the first opportunity to tell them about it. After confused looks, the questions flow around why we did it, what was the hardest part and the best bit.

Ever the sensible one, Debby suggests we use this time in the stratosphere to collect our thoughts to prepare for our homecoming. The blog may have stopped at Land's End, but I pick up my pen, there's still space in the journal:

> People immediately assume difficulty relates directly to the number of miles we had to cover each day. We've learned that's not the case.
>
> Firstly, there's the weather. A four-hour walk into brutal driving wind and rain was much worse than tackling an eight-hour stint in fair weather. Bodies exposed to the very tough conditions we regularly encountered lost energy more quickly and limbs ceased to work as effectively. Feet became leaden and more care had to be taken negotiating the path, so progress slowed. My hands and fingers often became numb, making any manoeuvre using maps or equipment harder. We learned the weather reigns supreme and to respect it. To try

to fight against it is usually counter-productive and it's no good getting angry. Whatever the weather gods serve up, just accept it.

Next, there's the path underfoot. Not where the path leads, but literally, the state of the piece of ground directly under the foot. It was a very different prospect walking on lush grass without rocks or hindrances compared to walking on soft sand, or hard jagged flints which beat up badly on the soles of feet. A deep muddy quagmire would sap the energy and spirits, while even just treading on uneven stony ground presented the threat of every footfall twisting an ankle. The track conditions largely determined how quickly we covered the ground.

Then comes the number and steepness of the climbs and the terrain in general. Obviously it takes longer to go up and down hills than walking along flat landscapes. However, often walking up hills would bring wide vistas to lift flagging spirits and inspire greater energy. We learned that as in so many physical pursuits, the mind plays a key role in determining the body's experience. A solid two-hour climb into a bright, dripping, early autumn morning from Hay-on-Wye rewarded us with such a spectacular view that all the effort expended melted away as if by magic.

Then there's route-finding. Walking in a straightforward manner along a clear track meant progress was relatively quick. However, once the track became indistinct or overgrown, or worse still, disappeared altogether, progress stopped. The search for a path would waste time, particularly when we had to return from a dead end or wrong turning, and these events would soak up disproportionate energy and sap our mental fortitude.

Finally, after all these other measures, the difficulty becomes the length of the day's walk. We knew before we set off walking that 12 or 13 miles a day would be ideal. Unexpected events can always crop up to disrupt best intentions, so we tried to have something in reserve. We knew we could manage a walk of about double our ideal in fair conditions. In the end our daily walks averaged about 15 miles and given the weather, terrain and track-finding conditions, that was manageable.

Debby looks over my shoulder, 'It was more than enough for me!'

When people ask 'what was the best bit?', we know they expect to hear of a particular segment, perhaps somewhere they can go for a day's walk without taking months out of their lives. Unfortunately, we can't break our experience down like that. Any one of the 139 days wouldn't be the same unpacked from the whole adventure. It wasn't so much the physical act of walking but certain other features which were key:

Firstly, it was the people we spent time with. We'd imagined some of our friends might join us for a day's walk or perhaps just a convivial meal at day's end. As it turned out, we were blessed to have so many people join us, even a few who flew in from Australia.

Debby reminds me,

'You never let go of people, Keith, no matter how obscure or distant the connection. I keep meeting more of your old friends in the UK and from all around the world and it's a lovely part of our lives.'

I hadn't really thought of it that way up front, but there's no doubt people were an important aspect of our walk. We clearly fired the imagination of friends, their families and others met along the way. When we stayed with strangers, they were usually fascinated by what we were doing – even though some thought we were completely mad. Others were quite envious and would have loved to be walking too. Quite quickly we found we were not only extending ourselves physically, but also building our circle of friends. It would be easy to fill the journal with stories of people we met. Like the man who chased us down the street after we bought lunch one day, just to hear more of what we were doing. He thought our trip was amazing. Perhaps the woman in her 80's whose farm we stayed at on Offa's Dyke best understood the principle:

'My sons say I shouldn't have people to stay any longer. Well, I say the people who stay here are my lifeline.'

And not only was it the people, but all the animals and other life. Our walk was filled with a rich abundance of creatures and flora that share this planet.

Debby's smiling now:

'One of the things I loved most was the opportunity to see so many different varieties of farm animals, and sometimes I could even pat them. England has an amazing collection of designer sheep breeds. And don't forget there was even a badger sheep! Mind you, it was sad seeing our namesake badgers lying dead by the side of the road. We never knew whether they'd been dumped there by farmers or really were roadkill.'

With hindsight, perhaps the most poignant moment came early in northern Scotland. We passed the stone memorial where the last British wolf was hunted to extinction in 1700. At the time I hadn't understood its significance. It worried me more as we walked and I became aware of the pressure of human development on all wildlife. Now I've seen statistics that show 97% of all vertebrate animals on the planet are humans or the creatures we domesticate for either companionship or food.

We seem to enjoy looking at wildlife, but can't let them live their lives on their own terms in the wild.

Other than the people and animals, simply the physical impact and experience of each day was the highlight. Debby said before we started that her philosophy for the whole walk was 'one day at a time, one step at a time'. And that's what happened. If you just keep going, sooner or later you get there. We'd both been reasonably healthy and done a fair amount of preparation, but as one specialist had warned us, 'The only thing that will get you fit for this walk, is walking.' Once we were out on the track, we became stronger and fitter. In my case, the heavy backpack stripped some fat and I've lost 12 kilos, a weight I haven't known for 30 years. It's not surprising when I think of how far we walked. We both wore pedometers and recorded our steps and distance covered. By the end Debby had registered 3,696,000 steps.

Debby sighs:

'That's why my feet hurt and I still can't walk barefoot on the floor!'

Every day we experienced physical tiredness and were often taken to our limit and beyond what we'd ever thought possible. But the wonderful thing about the human body is its ability to recover. Every night we would fall into bed exhausted. Then in the morning before getting up we would check in with each other: 'How are your feet? OK. Knees? OK. Legs? All good. Right then, let's get going!'

It's hard to describe how great we feel and how much we've enjoyed every day. There were a few really difficult moments and it often seemed the end of a section brought exhaustion while starting a new path created energy with the new sense of beginning. It proved impossible to forecast just what effect each day would have on us at daybreak. Until our emotions and minds engaged with the walk, we had no idea where the day would lead.

And then there were the food stops and in particular the lunches. I persisted in the search for good coffee most days, but it was usually a forlorn hope. But if that was the low spot, a high point every day was lunch. There were 139 of them and there was a story with every one. We found some spots had a magical quality and came to realise we were eating in the finest restaurant settings in the world. Under a natural canopy of branches, gazing out over rippling waters or a woven landscape filled with life, we could feel the soft brush of grass on warm tired feet and the breeze on our cheeks and nothing could beat it. And often along the way, in almost all seasons, we found nature a wonderful provider. There were bountiful harvests on offer of wild raspberries, plums, bilberries, strawberries and blackberries. Our hands were often stained with their juices as we gorged ourselves silly.

13 days later – in Melbourne

We're back on Australian soil and the immediate priority seems obvious. Instead of heading home, we go straight to our favourite café for the flat white coffee and toasted sandwich I have fantasised over for five months. Somehow the actual experience is not as good as I'd remembered. It's enjoyable and the food and drink can't be faulted, but it just seems so very normal.

Once we set foot back in our house there's a similar sensation. We love our home, but now I feel odd here. It's as if I've become detached. Like an old favourite piece of clothing unworn for so long, I've forgotten quite why it was a favourite. It's unsettling, but I put it down to holiday blues. In the meantime, I just get on with unpacking and trying to make myself feel purposeful, even though there doesn't appear to be a particular purpose any longer.

In the evening an old friend joins us with my son Ed for a simple fish and chips dinner. Inevitably, they ask about the walk. It seems this escapade has now come to define us. As a Buddhist nun and counsellor, Ree is interested in the emotional impact on our lives.

Now, that's a deep subject and not an easy one to explain. As the evening unwinds we try to relate some incidents that seem important. The day we put our lives in peril crossing Cross Fell in thick fog, that was pretty emotional, but then not all days were as extreme. Probably as the walk unfolded we became more receptive to our surroundings and more deeply affected by them than would normally have been the case. After a while, there was at least one moment each day where we stood still and said, 'Oh my God, look at this.' It might have been something huge like a cliff face, waterfall or rainbow, or something small like a spider's web.

And then there were the legends and history which had preceded us along the route. Our imaginations were fired up by the stories of human beings who had left indelible marks on the landscape, whether physical or psychological. As our minds were opened up to a wider range of emotions, so we became receptive to the ancient stories that had become part of local folklore. They came to be no more strange to us than the everyday explanations we use to frame modern reality.

And then there was the quiet power in the landscape of the trees. The more we walked the more we became aware of the trees. We seemed to feel their strength, their great age, and their importance as reassuring guardians of the land. They seemed to watch over us whilst energising us with their beauty. We came to realise trees are markers of place and providers of habitat and shelter for so much life. It wasn't uncommon as the journey wore on for me to simply stop and gaze at a tree, feeling some elemental connection. The trees became our friends and we gradually fell in love with them.

Days were filled with a miscellany of different sights and sounds to stir our emotions. The coastal paths were always changing: a rocky beach, energy-sapping sand dunes, steep cliff paths and scary tracks through loose scree. Scrambling over wet rocks beside a raging waterfall in pouring rain was challenging too. We walked by canal paths, along overgrown lanes, along paths that drew you forward and bent double through tiny tunnels under train lines or roads. Often the paths we followed dated back thousands of years. At times we passed straight through the middle of cornfields, ploughed fields or right inside farmyards to look at cows in their cowshed. Most farmers were friendly but occasionally there were those indignant souls who didn't want walkers on their land and left no room for passage or erected electric defences.

However much we had physical challenges, we also had the rewards of overcoming them. Steep rocky paths initially challenged Debby's knees, but gradually her legs strengthened. Although a much slower walker than me in the arduous hills of Scotland, by the end she kept up confidently. At times we walked soaking wet through bogs, our faces wreathed in smiles, and then sometimes were downcast as we saw our destination disappearing as evening twilight descended. Through it all we experienced a wide span of emotions, but were never bored, simply thankful we'd given ourselves this opportunity.

There were days when we were at low ebb with little energy even for talking. On these occasions we realised that silence was not something bad to be avoided. We understood that we could be perfectly relaxed and in tune with one another during these times and experienced a sense of prolonged deep peace between us. It was as if we'd been taken to a place where our minds were completely at rest and our senses fully alive.

More important than any other aspect of this adventure was the insight it gave us into our relationship. We knew we got on well before we set out, but by the end we understood the depth of our connection. We had tackled all kinds of paths and were often done in by the end of the day, but throughout all that our love held firm and we remained good friends. I guess we can consider ourselves lucky.

Ree looks at us with an amazed stare:

'You were together 24/7 for 20 weeks? Lucky?! I think it's a bloody miracle!'

I'd never thought about it in quite this way. We certainly understood the powerful bond of love and friendship that we'd forged beforehand and knew how to support one another. If it was her love of me that inspired Debby when she hit the wall to get back up and carry on, it was my admiration for what she was doing that deepened my respect and love for her. No matter what came our way we knew nothing could get between us, and that made for a certain feeling of invincibility and strength well beyond our own individual capacity. In our case we knew one plus one made more than two.

The evening has disappeared in storytelling and we head to the bedroom. The first night back in our own bed for five months and I'm pleased to be here. Not in the way I expected though. Not the joy of home, but simply the prospect of a welcome retreat away from a strange new reality that exists here. I feel stirred up and can't imagine what tomorrow will bring, but for now just want to hide from it.

We've done well to reach ten o'clock, but Debby has already blacked out beside me. The conversation about our relationship reminds me of the writing I did on that night in Llangollen. I reach for the battered old journal and read the first entry I'd written of what the walk had taught me:

Being in a strong loving relationship is important above all else... Debby is a wonderful partner. She's as caring and loving as she is strong and reliable, but above all else she is my ever-present supporter, a true soul partner. She tells me if it weren't for the love we share, she wouldn't have been able to keep going for the 1,100 miles we've walked. By finding Debby, I've better understood my deep desire to share my life with a loving partner. With Barbara it was a natural youthful instinct, but finding Debby as a mature man has helped me appreciate the great gift I received when she sat down next to me at that rowing dinner. It's hard to comprehend we've already been together for ten years and that two such different decades could sit next to one another in my life.

I consider myself blessed to have had two wonderful women choose to walk through life with me. I came into the world of women as a late developer. Fiercely independent, I was a very shy, introverted only child. Yet somehow I understood the potential of giving up some of my independence to create a greater whole. In the sacrifice of some part of my single-man freedom I was not losing something, but liberating myself for a richer more fulfilling existence. My life would be unrecognisable and much diminished without the unity of relationship I've experienced with Debby and Barbara.

14 days later – at home

It's a bright spring morning and I decide to embrace the day before yesterday's uneasiness can resurface. I step to the wardrobe, open the doors and look in. Layer upon layer of shirts, jumpers, shorts and trousers sit above shoes and sandals, while suits and jackets hang silently by their side. I stand and stare in disbelief. A feeling of utter confusion overwhelms me before dizziness sends me reeling backwards to slump on the end of the bed. I shake my head and try to understand what's going on. Whatever warning signals I'd felt yesterday, nothing had prepared me for the shock.

These clothes just don't make any sense. All this choice is a nightmare of confusion. How could I possibly need them all? For nearly five months I've carried what seemed a heavy backpack with just one change of clothing for the day's walk and a spare 'best set' for the evening. Each day the choice had been easy. Would it be this set that I'd worn yesterday? Were the clothes badly soiled, did they smell, or could I wear them again? Walking for that length of time with just two sets of clothes had convinced me that was all I needed. Now as I gaze at this wardrobe, it's as if it's become my new backpack, but a far heavier one than I'd ever carried on the walk.

I sit and stare at these belongings and see them in a different light. These clothes I've spent years and a good deal of money acquiring, all the accessories of a successful and civilised life, are a burden. In this instant the world feels topsy-turvy, yet I know this new insight is somehow fundamental. It's as if a deep change has happened within me and I'm not the same man that flew to John O'Groats. When we walked into Land's End I thought there was nothing else to do but head for home and resume life as it had been. Yet in this moment I know my life has changed. I sense today, 19th November, heralds the beginning of a new appreciation of life, the ramifications of which I can only guess at. The walk may have finished, but I haven't reached the end of the journey yet.

We've returned from an adventure that has consumed more than a year of our lives. After finding my way for 139 days along all manner of obscure and sometimes non-existent tracks, overcoming numerous challenges, I've returned home to find I'm lost. And it feels well and truly lost, all bearings seemingly gone awry. I can recognise the mourning for the loss of our great adventure, however that's just at the surface level, the normal reaction to returning from an extended holiday. This is something very different. It seems reaching the end of the walk is not to be the end, but only a portal to the next beginning. Now, I desperately need to understand the new life I inhabit. A new quest awaits, but not a tough physical challenge like the one we've just completed. I suspect though it will be every bit as difficult to navigate.

I didn't sign up for this journey. Without knowing, the die was cast in that pub at the end of the Coast to Coast walk in 2009. By bringing to life that crazy idea to walk from one end of Britain to the other, I've set in motion an inevitable second journey: a journey from the person I've been, to the person I appear destined to become. If our great walk had been an outdoor experience embedding me daily in the wider external environment, this will be a journey within. I'll need to take stock of my world of understanding, to delve the inner depths of how I've framed my human presence on this planet. My body has had its experience and intuitively knows things now that my brain doesn't. I'm being called upon to question how my intellect functions. My body, unlike on Cross Fell, has asserted its authority and I sense my heart must take the lead to drive a better understanding of what is going on around me and which path to take. If the physical walk stirred me up, sitting here today the journey ahead feels every bit as scary and uncertain.

I can't yet understand the nature of the terrain I'll have to negotiate, but I realise it's a new path for me. I feel like I've had an out-of-world experience, but in fact I simply stepped into the actual physical world and for 20 weeks lived in closer communion with it. I experienced the reality of this planet I call home, rather than being distracted by the human imagery in which it's submerged. While walking in nature I stepped through the curtain of marketing fantasy that hides the world and connected with the life from which

I've been isolated. In reconnecting with the natural world and all the myriad life it nurtures, I've been enriched and fulfilled beyond any man-made contrivance. I've had an experience no amount of money can buy and become somehow more than I had been. Instinctively I know I have to try to share this with my fellow humans. Staring at the open wardrobe door it's a daunting prospect. I realise most people won't be interested in my thoughts, and the fact I've no idea how to explain it in terms they'll be able to understand will not make life easy.

16 days later – Melbourne

I'm awake early, but my mind doesn't feel refreshed. These days are so difficult. No longer faced with a weighty backpack and arduous walking, my mind has descended into a convoluted labyrinth. I want to talk about what I've experienced on the walk. But when I describe my reaction to so much nature and its effect on me, people just turn away. They want to hear about the walk, but to them that means the best bits of the geography we encountered, maybe laced with snippets of history and trivia. I'm left to simply sit quietly, not daring to mention the emotional turmoil I'm trying to come to grips with.

I get up, sprinkle familiar tea leaves in my cup and pour on the hot water. Barefoot, I step out into the early dawn light of our garden. The quiet of a windless Sunday lies around my shoulders and I instinctively know this is where I now belong. Here no questions are necessary. I sip the hot tea and feel a sense of communion with the pair of trees we planted a decade ago. The thought of communing with a tree once seemed odd, yet now it comes naturally. Each tree has a distinct character. It's too early for Debby's favourite crepe myrtle to put on its show of pink bloom, but my silver princess eucalypt leans regally above me dangling clumps of red-collared gumnuts. I stroke the smooth young caramel-coloured boughs of the crepe myrtle and offer my praise for all it brings to our home. I confide softly of the challenge I face to return to my life here. I have no idea why, but it feels in this moment like I'm connected to all the life around me. I breathe deeply and finish my tea.

I'm aware I move more slowly nowadays than those around me. It's the speed I've become accustomed to and while I'm feeling lost, displaced from the sense of home Melbourne should provide, this is fast enough. I try to step back into my old routine, but can't really find peace as I grapple with the emotions that surge within me. The sheer noise of life is an acute struggle. In the mornings, as soon as I turn on the radio news while shaving as I have done every day for most of my adult life, I can't cope with the clamour. The jabbering seems so pointless. Bemused, I watch as my hand involuntarily turns it off.

The morning swim beckons, so I pack some togs and walk down to join the swimmers. I still don't feel at ease behind the wheel of a car. The Sunday swim is one of the important rituals in my life. For many years it's been a mainstay, and while trudging through the mud and mire of Britain's countryside I missed it. In the changing room today with a group of people I know well, my body's reaction is once again a surprise. The din of chatter, banter and laughter, of people babbling about everything and nothing, is too much. It feels physically painful. I cannot engage and quickly pull on bathers to run outside in search of peace. Of course, they can't appreciate my mind was quietened on the walk and I'm struggling to cope with coming back out of it.

In the steam room after the swim I sit with a few close friends and fall into deeper discussion about the walk. I explain that it brought Debby and me a deeper awareness of the natural world and at times took us to the edge of our ability to cope in a way we rarely encounter. We faced the very real prospect of physical calamity. Once again, I find myself calling the walk my greatest achievement and most important life experience. Somehow, any success in the business world pales into insignificance by comparison. Marcus, another swimmer speaks up:

'You were truly living in the moment, Keith!'

Of course, he's right, but more than that I was experiencing life in all its forms without the technological buzz that used to haunt my footsteps. The materialistic life of consumption fell away and I was able to appreciate a simpler way of seeing the world. I could tune into the ebb and flow of nature, the shortening of the daylight hours and the movement of so much life which had previously been hidden from me. Just talking over the adventure brings back the memories and the deep contentment I'd felt. I look at their faces though and realise that for now I don't have the words to communicate my joy and this sense of wellbeing. After an uncomfortable silence the conversation moves on to lighter subject matter and I slink away to shower.

18 days later – Melbourne

After the swim this morning I spend time with a couple of business friends. One is very focussed on recent developments in Australian politics, while the other pontificates on the state of the global business world. It's as if they have a seemingly unquenchable thirst to prove their knowledge. I used to engage with this and join the battle of the egos. But now I'm detached from it. I've shed my fascination with politics and big business. Here today I can recognise we are all searching for meaning and trying to make sense of a human world, but our exchanges somehow feel aggressive and vexatious. These people are my friends, but their frame of what's important in the world means they're blind to what I've experienced. Of course, from their perspective they consider I've been out in the sun too long and lost track of reality. I need to steer clear of such discussions until I've learned better ways of communicating about my thoughts.

I visit the office to catch up with Michael, my business partner, and by the time we part we've agreed I can limit my involvement to occasional non-executive director's duties.

21 days later – Melbourne

I have to run chores and for the first time feel comfortable driving the car. The radio is still a step too far. The drone of the news channel spewing out relentless disasters, death and destruction is impossible to bear. Even the music channels and their mind-numbing succession of hits seem simply a distraction, a drug to keep reality out. By the afternoon all I want to do is sit in the armchair quietly thumbing new editions in Clifford's Grumpy Swimmer bookshop. I know the time is fast approaching when I must make more sense of how to get on with my life, but not today. Today there's no better goal than to stay peaceful and nurture the calm and contentment that came home with my backpack.

22 days later – Melbourne

It's a Saturday, yet after the early swim a friend immediately wants to regale me with proud stories about his heavy work schedule. I normally enjoy his company, but now his words seem ridiculous. I'm fortunate to have retired early, but more than that, not only have I lost interest in stories of work, I have begun to question them. Friends older than me with lovely homes and money that my dad would have been embarrassed to own, seem rusted into a behaviour pattern to chase money. It frames their very existence. When I try to suggest that pursuing greater monetary resources in their circumstances is irrelevant, they stop talking, look at me through wide open eyes and suggest I just don't understand. And they're right, I don't. I now regularly find myself retreating within to question what is the reality of our life on this planet.

I walk back from the café conscious I'm moving at the right speed. The trees lining the back roads are virile in the strong green leaves of late spring and I run my hand down the trunks of my favourite ones to feel their joy. In these moments I can sense the state of calm that accompanied me on so many of those British paths. Bliss is back while I walk. Although I'm now swimming each day, I've come to understand I'm more naturally a walker than a swimmer. I've never been fast in the water, but back among the flotilla of Icebergers I feel uncomfortable with the competition that underpins the relationship many of them have with the water. What's more, the hubbub of noise and activity in the changing room is still too confronting. I excuse myself to seek solace away from the crowd and swim by myself. When I move to my own slow rhythm and feel the water flowing across my body, my mind is at peace. Perhaps it doesn't matter so much whether I'm in water or the countryside, it's simply the way I bring myself to it.

If slow movement brings bliss, why are work, travel, communication, and indeed most social activities, increasingly fast? Why is it that we've become so swept up in the need for speed? In nature I became rooted to a more natural pace, the pace which underpins the living world. Yet now my eyes have been opened, all around seems to be in conflict with this living truth. Even at the meal table, the changing seasons have been jettisoned as foods are flown at speed around the globe to offer an uninterrupted flow of every choice imaginable. In all this choice we've lost the greater sense of place, taste and time. To remain calm within this maelstrom of human striving is now a daily challenge.

50 days later – Melbourne

Christmas Day, and before getting up to start the early morning preparations for our family feast, I pick up the annual letter I sent to friends and relatives last week. What must they must think of me? To speak of my mental state with such candour is not the British way and I cringe on re-reading:

> I'm suffering a melancholy of the mind which is worse than any underlying weariness that may rest deep in my body. I'd not appreciated the profound sense of calm and contentment which had settled upon me while communing with nature for such a prolonged period. We passed through some of the most beautiful and diverse countryside at a pace that enabled us to breathe it in and become as one with it. Instead of cars and a house stuffed with belongings, we survived, nay, thrived with just a backpack. Instead of the fruitless thinking about so much which we cannot influence, we actually became aware of and thought about the small realities of our existence… Now I am home, I'm struggling with the frantic level of activity and noise that I have returned to, and which more than one dear friend has observed, is the normal frenetic pace of Badger life.

To publically acknowledge my mental state is one thing, but it's the damage we humans are doing to Earth and other life that haunts me. I've been trying to cling on to the comfort of my former settled secure life as insulation from this greater reality. I know I've got to let that go though and feel the discomfort of a new consciousness that seems embodied within me. I'm being forced to pass through a frightening and confusing passage away from everything I've known, into a world where much appears the opposite of what I had believed. Intellectually I know I'll have to better understand what's happened to me. My brain, for so long used to being in charge of my body and my life, is now all at sea and will have to hand over to other forms of knowing.

At lunch we're seated around the large table replete with turkey and all the trimmings and radiant laughing faces. A clan gathering for the traditional feast and celebration. At the ritual interlude between the main course and pudding each person offers up their annual reflections on what they're thankful for this year. For me it's the walk, 'my greatest life event', and the fact I've been blessed with Debby as a partner. The walk has changed my life forever I say, but they all know it by now.

54 days later – Melbourne

The New Year looms and I feel like the man who asks an Irishman how to get somewhere and he tells you: 'Well you wouldn't want to start from here!' Where do I go to set out on the journey to a destination called 'Understanding'? Starting from a place called 'Lost' is probably not a good idea, but that is where I am. I know it won't be possible to plan and prepare for this journey. There are no maps to show these bearings. To add to this challenge, my mind and body seem to be on different paths. My mind needs to try to understand the experience my body had. For someone who's lived life mostly inside his head with little depth of connection to his own body, let alone the practical side of life, this challenge feels daunting. I may have been considered a successful finance director and chief executive, using my head to deal with the complexities of the business world, but now I have to find other ways of relating and understanding the world and my place in it.

As someone who has always sought to understand life through reading and conversation, I've already started leafing through books and talking to anyone who'll give me the time of day to listen. I'm open to opinions and information as never before, but my head quickly fills with questions. My problem is that the books I'm searching at random are not the ones I'm familiar with. I'm looking to string it all together quickly in a well-structured way, as if constructing a new business strategy. I need to develop a new frame for my intellect to engage with the world, but one that's aligned with my body's experience.

I normally enjoy conversing with people, but I've noticed something has changed. People are generally kind, but recognise something is amiss with me and behave differently. I begin to feel how a demobbed, battle-scarred war veteran must when being visited at the sanatorium during convalescence. People appreciate something is wrong and either seek to shake me out of it, or politely excuse themselves to get far away.

It's lunchtime and I'm meeting Greg, a friend who I've barely seen for ten years. He'd received my Christmas letter and called to suggest we catch up for lunch. I'm not getting much help or inspiration from my closer friends, so I know I've got to reach out to a wider group. Greg is one of the first corporate consultants I worked with in Australia and was always reliable. It's a pleasure to meet him, but with his psychology background, I figure he may be able to help me shed light on my situation. He kindly listens to my story and the searching questions I have about my condition:

'Keith, it sounds like you need to read *No Destination* by Satish Kumar. He's an ex-Jain monk who did a long walk from his home in India.'

The suggestion sounds as intriguing as the title. Hopefully this isn't an omen for the journey I've embarked upon. I wouldn't normally read a book like this, but perhaps the serendipity of this connection has reason. I've learned to trust my gut reaction as I've got older. I know whatever wisdom I may have accumulated from life experiences is often embedded deep within and can bubble to the surface unannounced. After lunch we walk to the Grumpy Swimmer bookshop and I place an order for Satish's book. Perhaps another piece of the jigsaw of meaning I'm trying to complete.

As I walk home I think of Dad and how good it would be to be able to talk my situation over with him. I may be 58 years old, but today would be his 99th birthday and he's on my mind. He's been gone nearly 15 years, but I feel I now understand him and his values better than ever. He was always focussed on other people and developing strong enduring relationships. He lived and worked in Streatham in South London when it was still a village community. An ex-merchant seaman, he would have been able to provide the anchor to hold me fast as I drift in search of answers.

227 days later – Melbourne

It's June and the year is flying past. My head is brimful of ideas and contradictions. I'm voraciously consuming information like a shipwreck survivor gorging at a cruise liner buffet, but it's hard to make sense of it. The clarity I seek won't come. Reading Satish Kumar's book has opened up a whole new area in my investigation and caused me some real discomfort. On the one hand I can immediately relate to the experience he describes:

> I enjoyed every moment in complete peace and solitude.
> Walking became a meditation and every step was teaching me to be mindful... I was breathing the universe into myself. ......
> I was one with the world.

However, other comments seem to jar with the life I've built. The very idea that he set off with a colleague to walk for two years with no money and relied on the hospitality of others was too big a mental leap. He says the 'differences between rich and poor, educated and illiterate, all vanished; and beneath all these divisions, a common humanity emerged.' I want to believe it, but then why is society set on building divisions?

I've been stirred by this writing and feel there's some wisdom that's permeated my core. Instead of moving on to another subject, I want to know more about Satish and his life works. He became editor of Resurgence over 30 years ago at the behest of E. F. Schumacher and a dozen years ago founded the Schumacher College in Devon. I have followed up these leads by subscribing to the magazine and ordering a copy of *Small is Beautiful*, Schumacher's most influential book. I need to understand why a world-renowned economist, who the US President invited to the White House, inspired the creation of a college now famous for its Holistic Science Masters education.

Throughout all the reading and research, we're also planning a long trip later this year to explore a new travel destination. Debby and I have harboured an ambition to visit South America, the only continent other than Antarctica that I've never set foot on. Patagonia seems to offer somewhere I might be able to lose myself as Bruce Chatwin had and perhaps go on another long walk.

268 days later – Melbourne

It's my birthday and we've just made quite a strange decision. Today we notified the travel agent our South American holiday is off. This trip should have had all the makings of something special. But it never quite felt like that. There was something insipid about it. The prospect of visiting one of the most visually and culturally colourful and dynamic parts of the globe was not resonating with me. We seemed to be going through the motions of doing what's expected to become a tourist for the sake of it. I sat down and drew up a list of every country I've set foot in. It's exactly one for every year of my life as I turn 59 today. I've led a blessed life in so many ways and have seen cultures and geographical wonders in great measure. I've witnessed more than my fair share. I've come to realise I really don't need to do more tourism. In cancelling this trip, I realise I've possibly just consigned South America to be forever beyond my horizon.

After four months of planning, I've also realised that world travel is likely to just offer more of the same. Apart from a town sign or airport arrivals board to distinguish places, I can now be lost anywhere in a world of dreary sameness. It's as if global retail chains have emasculated the very essence of shopkeepers' cultures and passionate creative individuality. The world seems wrapped in a bland unedifying frieze, whose only goal seems to be to keep people spending while cosseted from waking to life's vibrant reality. At a time of flaunted individuality, we are more likely now to wander like zombies through a dull 'one-world' experience that's lost all meaning.

I've spent this year reaching out and adapting my lifestyle, while learning much about the state of the world. What I feel I need is a stronger, more rigorous grounding in some of the science that underpins the way Earth functions and some more ideas about how to contribute to bringing change in the way we live on this wonderful planet. Instead of pushing out through new boundaries, I've asked Debby to humour me with a special birthday present. I want to go to college.

Over breakfast one day, I'd read in Resurgence an advert for the Schumacher College and their range of short courses. At the same time we were talking of flying to remote Argentina on holiday, I spotted a one-week course in Social Activism run by Bill McKibben. Suddenly here was something that grabbed my attention. I'd read a couple of McKibben's books and knew him to be one of the world's leading climate change activists as well as a good writer. It took very little time to decide this was something far more appealing and relevant to my present state of mind. I feel I want to 'save the world', so if I'm to have any chance of success, surely a Social Activism course could come in useful.

Debby is immediately supportive and so we reframe our holiday around a UK study trip. I'll sign up for the course in Social Activism and then we're both going to attend a second course called 'Cultivating an Ecoliterate Worldview'. A two-week intensive, followed by a six-month on-line program, I'm hopeful it could bring the answers I seek.

My reading and research are having a profound effect. I've delved deep into business and economics books, including those in particular that tried to unpick what had occurred during 2008's global financial crisis, or the infamous GFC as it's become known. The evidence that the economic system is broken seems so stark and yet we continue to believe in it. The more the system struggles and produces unhealthy outcomes, the more people vested into the system want to drive it with all the relish of a mad jockey thrashing a broken-down nag, like the one I witnessed at Worcester races.

Fritz Schumacher's writings have made me sit back and reflect. His book's subtitle, *Economics As If People Mattered,* and the chapter comparing our western economic approach to Buddhist economics, are certainly thought provoking. In reading *Small is Beautiful*, I can begin to understand the compelling common sense of his writing. As a Rhodes Scholar and economist, he wrote in a way my business mind can absorb, yet his interpretations are quite different. Now I'm beginning to understand that it's impossible to consider the economics of business and financial matters without a consideration of our natural world.

I knew economics consisted of the three elements, labour, land and capital, but the more I've reflected on this, the more I feel uncomfortable. It appears business has ramped up the search for ever-higher returns on capital over the last 40 years. At the same time, every effort to reduce the labour component has been applauded despite any resulting social breakdown. And the destructive effect on land, or the natural environment, has mostly been ignored. Both economics and ecology have the same Greek root 'oikos', meaning 'earth household'.

So, if economics is meant to be about managing the Earth's household, I can appreciate how far we've strayed from that path and feel I need to better understand the whole subject of ecology.

336 days later – Schumacher College, Dartington, Devon

Wow, the Social Activism course finished today! Attending Schumacher College has been a remarkable experience and one that's lived up to all I'd hoped for. The more I'd investigated the quality of the institution and the outstanding range of teachers brought in from around the world, the more I'd looked forward to being here. The community life is vibrant, friendly and energy-charged. The participants come from all walks of life and all different backgrounds and countries, while the magnificent old building and extensive grounds are perfect for wandering and refreshing the mind.

It seems so natural here to interact with others of diverse cultures and debate ideas at any time of the day or night. I can lose myself in the old library. Knowledge seems to glint from every mote of dust playing on the sun's rays above my head while I lean back on the window seat and absorb the atmosphere of engagement. Resident and visiting lecturers are available to discuss concepts and contribute to a deeper understanding of the way life has developed and the workings of planet Earth. We're allocated to teams to work together on daily communal tasks, like food preparation, cooking, cleaning or gardening. It's a refreshing antidote to modern society's focus on individualism and isolation. In developing bonds of relationship with fellow participants we also have great fun. Community life is so much more rewarding than I'd expected. Life here is certainly different to what I'm used to, but it's very quickly become so very natural and enhances the learning experience.

Debby went off to a Green Cuisine health course in Wales, while I'd settled in with a group of 20 activists from countries as varied as

Brazil, Columbia, UK, Estonia, Ireland, France, Italy, USA, Nepal and the Maldives. Bill McKibben was good, but apart from learning some key skills and hearing some activism 'war stories', I learned something vital about myself and my calling. Whereas Bill is a natural activist, never happier than standing up to fight the next fossil fuel industry excess, that's not my strength. Whatever natural facility I may have is more aligned with encouraging and supporting people to carry out good work. It's not that I wouldn't be prepared to endure the unearned suffering for my beliefs that's often part of an activist's life, but I now understand how best to bring myself to the challenge.

352 days later – Schumacher College

It's Sunday afternoon and we've checked back in to the Schumacher for the start of our main course, 'Cultivating an Ecoliterate Worldview'. This is the one we've both been looking forward to and it's the one I hope will deliver broad answers to resolve my dilemma. It feels an auspicious day and I'm lazing on the bed working through some of the excerpts from the recommended reading list. Suddenly, in the middle of David Abram's *Becoming Animal*, I find a passage which explains what has been happening back home for me to be drawn outside barefoot with my early morning cups of tea:

> On some mornings I step outside before pulling on any socks or sliding my feet into their shoes... My feet receive directives from the ground… My legs inadvertently slow their pace as the sensitive presence of the land seems to gather beneath my feet, the ground no longer a passive support but now the surface of a living depth; and so my feet abruptly feel themselves being touched, being felt by the ground. My steps slow down further... each patch of ground requests a different kind of step, which my legs discover only in the doing. My

> feet are like ears listening downwards, and a dark rhythm rises up into me from this contact – a pulse that slows down and deepens the private beat within my chest.

I've heard a Japanese scientist has developed a way to count the microbes present in soil. He believes there are one trillion in every gram of natural, untreated soil. That density is beyond comprehension, but what it suggests is that the soil under our feet is a living organism. My conscious brain may have been unaware of this, but intuitively my body had understood it. Even though all this has been hidden in the churning of my conscious brain, somehow I've sensed it. There's a web of life of which I'm just one more piece. But if I switch my brain off and tune in through my senses I can feel my connection, just as my bare feet can sense life feeling me.

I realise this instinct has always been within me. I'd long turned to the ocean for comfort and nurture when the aching pain and sadness of life had enveloped me. I would take myself off to gaze out over the sea when my first wife Barbara had lain dying, and would then throw myself into the water to soak up the vibrancy of its ancient molecules. My subconscious understood they rewove me back into life's web and provided succour to lift my spirits as nothing else could. The refracted light shining down into the depths below my goggles would reflect back from all manner of darting fish and spawning new life and somehow reassure me of our world's endless cycle of life and rebirth. Death will always be an inevitable part of life and this was a reminder to flourish while I have the gift of conscious life. The water and all it contained would comfort me with the same unqualified love mothers offer their children.

365 days later – on the train to London

And that's it. The Schumacher experience has ended today and we're on the train back to London. Exactly one year ago we walked into

Land's End and the start of a new journey. Today the journey within has concluded. It's taken me a full 12 months to reach this point where I've come back from a wilderness of confusion that has challenged the fundamentals of my world. The course has been compelling and more than any other single experience has brought me the foundation of holistic or integrated understanding I've sought.

Just as we're part of an interconnected community or web of life, so I now understand we can also each choose decisions to live our lives to a different beat. I can now see getting 'lost' was a gift. Without reaching that point, there could not have been this journey to 'found'. I've spent my life sleepwalking to the drumbeat of the system. Until now I've slavishly followed its false allure like a rat in thrall to the Pied Piper. On the walk my eyes were opened and I've been inspired to live life differently. On this course I've learned how to weave my experiences into an intellectual understanding of why this is important and just how rich life can be.

It's clear to me that during our long walk my body, with all the intrinsic intelligence of the trillions of sensing cells with which it's comprised, had intuited the connection we humans have with nature. To put it in simple terms I reconnected with the natural world. My body had plugged back into the true external environment, our natural home. As a result, I'm now on a different path. My body made the decision based upon all the information it sensed when let loose beyond the framework of meaning my mind had accepted and which is entrenched by society.

The nub of understanding my situation came early on in the course. The vital information which unlocked the conundrum of what had happened to me came from studying the works of a Norwegian, Arne Naess. As long-time chair of philosophy at the University of Oslo, he had been synonymous with Norwegian philosophy for 50 years. In 1972, he was the first to coin the term 'Deep Ecology'. He differentiated this from more shallow, human, technocratic environmentalism, which he said concerned itself with pollution, resource depletion and the health and affluence of people in developed countries. In contrast, Naess had identified Deep Ecology as something which stems from a deep personal experience, which then leads to deep questioning and finally to a deep commitment, or the wisdom to live with the facts of how the world works. Here was the understanding I'd been seeking. The Deep Ecology description dovetailed with my own experience and now I could point to what had set off such a major change in my life.

So, the walk had transformed me and given me a sense of commitment to the ecology of the planet. But also during this time at Schumacher I've been exposed to the work of the great British scientist, James Lovelock. In demonstrating that Earth is a self-regulating entity and effectively alive, he has provided a more holistic understanding of the planet that holds us. Originally Lovelock called his theory 'Biocybernetic Universal System Tendency'. Bit of a mouthful, though I couldn't help feeling that name would have been much more acceptable to the scientific fraternity. However, sharing a walk with the writer William Golding, he was persuaded to give it the name Gaia.

When I'd come across the term Gaia before, it had felt fanciful, something more akin to magical folklore. Yet, now I understand the science, it seems so logical. During my childhood, I'd found it common to refer to 'Mother Nature' without so much as the blink of an eye. Somehow it felt obvious that the world of nature should be revered. Lovelock had chosen the name Gaia in honour of the Greek primordial deity. Colloquially known as the Mother Goddess, she was believed to be the personification of the Earth, the Great Mother of all, the creator who had given birth to the Earth and the entire Universe. So for me, an avowed atheist who has long felt my spirituality flowed from the natural environment, I realise there is no difference between my Mother Nature and Gaia. Now I have a name I can use which not only has a scientific theory to go with it, but also is aligned with my own spiritual sense of things.

Someone on the course suggested that by taking ourselves into nature for such a long time, we could say Gaia had touched us on the shoulder. To think Gaia would be aware of Debby and I sounds self-important, but when I reflect on what happened, it becomes more likely. My experience of the walk came from my body reconnecting with the natural world. My body discovered its true nature, as if Gaia had pulled back the veils and I'd found the real world, a planet buzzing with life where humans are just one part.

I've finally reached a point where my brain now comprehends what happened to me during that walk. I'd gone down a different path, one that meant going back to the life I'd known before would be impossible. I don't yet know what to do with this knowledge, but it does mean I'm now comfortable with my new path. I can already begin to appreciate that it's because of our human disconnection from nature that our world is so out of kilter. I feel an overwhelming need to do something to change the situation and this will be the core purpose which now drives my life.

I've heard people say that in any person's life there are two very important dates. The first is the date we are born. On this date our life is turned upside down and we have to overcome the enormous trauma and challenge of being born. In childbirth we have to leave the safe cocoon of the womb and the fundamental union with mother. Contractions force us to confront the claustrophobia of an initially blocked passage and the extreme physical challenge for survival under intense pressure, before squeezing out into a new world and having to take a first breath as the security of the umbilical cord is severed.

That is the natural struggle a baby goes through to exit from the womb and become a person in their own right. Clearly the day we are born is the most important day of our life. It brings us into the world and presents us with all the potential of a life filled with learning and development. It's said the second most important date is when we work out the reason we came into the world. Why was it we pushed and struggled to come screaming into the world? What are we here for? What is our role to be? What is our purpose for being alive?

I now know that for me the 14th November 2010, at the age of 58, was that second pivotal date. Fourteen days after finishing the walk I opened that wardrobe door back home in Melbourne and finally discovered my purpose. I didn't have the intellectual understanding at that point, but intuitively I knew I had to try to help the world and the rich diversity of life it harbours.

Now it's time to return home and change some things. I know determination and optimism are my strong traits, and if being born is a difficult process, then it's perhaps a suitable metaphor for the trauma I may have to go through to better understand how to pursue my purpose.

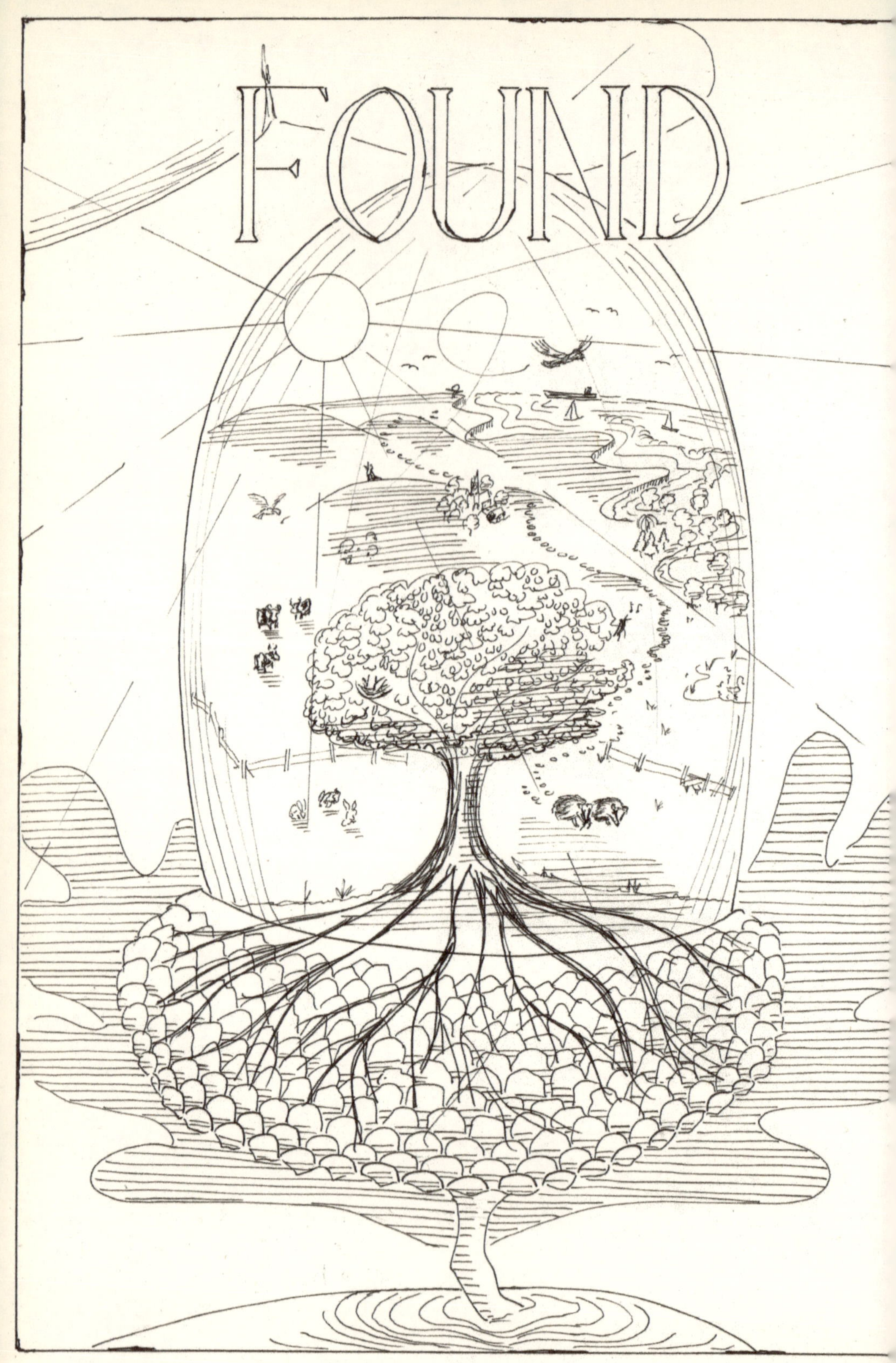
FOUND

Chapter 13 – FOUND

The highest education is that which does not merely give us information, but makes our life in harmony with all existence.
– Rabindranath Tagore, Nobel Laureate

400 days later – understanding a life purpose

One month back in Melbourne and it's nice to have a Sunday to sit down for some quiet reflection and time to write the Christmas letter. Last year I arrived home from the walk in confusion. This time I've returned enthused and ready to act. One of the first big decisions has already been taken. Before we left Melbourne we put our large family home on the market. We thought we would move away from the bustle of suburbia to a more remote coastal community, with greater alignment to the new way we want to live. However, I remembered Gandhi had said it's no good to leave the world and live in caves or monasteries, thinking that the world is a trap and the only way to be liberated is to escape from it. No, if we want to make a difference to the world we need to stay in our suburban community, the one we have called home for more than 20 years, and make our changes here.

A year ago I used to say 'I want to save the world.' Now I understand it's not the world that needs to be saved, it's life on Earth that's under threat. When we set off for Land's End on Day 139 I'd hoped the meaning of life would be revealed, perhaps delivered in a thunderbolt from an all-powerful weather god. When that didn't happen my brief disappointment disappeared in the glory of another day embedded in the raw of life. It's taken over a year for my head to catch up with what the rest of my body had quickly taken to heart. The secret of life's meaning had been revealed. Not once in a final-day lightning flash, but every day, minute by minute. Life itself is the meaning.

Life is a mystery and like every member of the human race, I'm part of its rich mix on this one planet in a Universe of billions. Every moment of every day I experience that mystery. Each day may be a repetition of seemingly featureless tasks, yet each is unique. From the moment I throw water on my face to shave, caress my mug of hot water and tea leaves in the predawn garden, or walk out on the pier for my morning swim, if I am conscious I experience the wonder of life. The sensation of water molecules that arrived on icy asteroids billions of years ago running across the stubble on my cheeks, the quiver of leaves on my favourite tree in a gentle breeze, or the flare of a dawn sunburst illuminating distant city buildings across Melbourne's bay as I walk along the pier to swim, such are the wonders of life. To experience the act of being alive in the moment and in relationship with so much other life, face to face, life with life, this is the meaning life holds if I'm awake to it.

My passion has come from the profound feeling of being touched by Mother Nature, or Gaia. And I want to help others to wake up to it. Out on the track, my body sensed life in all its exhilarating complexity and felt what it was like to be at peace. I learned the pleasure of a simple life. The pain, struggle and challenge of physical exertion, combined with awe in the presence of the planet's might and power, had left me at day's end exhausted, yet brimful of joy. Unconsciously, as I'd overcome the daily obstacles, I'd slipped into the web of life to feel community and connection at a grander level than before. I felt a joy that I wanted to shout from the rooftops for everyone to share. This was the 'Why' that had infused my subconscious and spurred me to take on our long walk.

The seed of the idea that sprouted in that Robin Hood's Bay pub had been sown during the Coast to Coast walk. Already my body had sensed a new life path awaited. Since returning, I've learned the 50 trillion cells in my body are more complex receivers and processors than silicon chips. And it's the environmental signals from life in all its diverse and multifaceted forms that determine the chemical makeup of my cells, including how I feel and the spirit I bring to life. Throughout the walk I was aware of life as never before, and in the process of moving at a slower pace and exchanging stories, I developed a deeper rapport with my fellow humans. Whether it was the woman on the Black Isle on Day 10 with whom we revealed the raw extent of our life stories, or the man on Day 75 who chased us down to the canal because of an irrepressible desire to simply talk more, we uncovered a mutual yearning to let go of facades and simply be present with the lives of fellow humans.

On Day 32 we walked into the Scottish borderlands and I sensed our human limitations to quantify the universe we inhabit. As I marvelled at the splendour of this world and its mystery, I suspected then it was this very ability to wonder that was the unique gift we bring to a fathomless cosmos. Now I feel more certain than ever. In all my reading and investigation it seems life has probably evolved as a fluke of the Universe. And because of the incomprehensible set of random events that had to occur to bring life into being here, it could be unique. As Marcelo Gleiser, the Brazilian physicist and astronomer says in *A Tear at the Edge of Creation*,

> Life is awesome precisely because it is rare and fragile… If we don't care for it, chances are the Universe won't either.

A multitude of non-human lives rely on this planet for their well-being. The dazzling proliferation of life has helped me understand the smallness and insignificance of so much of what I'd devoted my life to. Just as each person has unique special talents, so does every other living creature. Some say we cannot truly appreciate our humanity until we see ourselves reflected in the eyes of an other-than-human creature. Certainly we are inextricably linked in a web of life, and the way we work in relationship with other life is what matters. Buddhists have developed an inspiring image called Indra's net to capture this point. It depicts every form of life in the Universe as multi-faceted jewels hung in a web of connection, reflecting on one another.

Despite my relative insignificance, I realise I can use my time to either enrich and contribute to other life on the planet, or be destructive and destroy it. I've had time to distil what my body learnt and now my brain's caught up. With the intellectual framework in place, I've come to understand my life purpose. Put simply I want to help life flourish on Earth. That's all life, in every wonderful, fascinating and often surprising embodiment.

The good news is that as a human being I'm well adapted to this task. It's perhaps the defining trait of our species that we enjoy helping others and working in collaboration. People sometimes say we're selfish with an in-built drive to compete and beat others. However, life hasn't developed from its beginnings as bacteria over three billion years ago and spread across the planet in such amazing diversity by combat and selfishness. Competition can play a supporting role in organising people to band together, but it's the networking and development of a web of positive relationships that ultimately lead to productive outcomes and determine how happy and satisfying the life we lead. And humans are naturals at it. As the Dalai Lama once succinctly explained at a Melbourne seminar, it's only when we help others that we find true happiness. It really is that simple.

634 days later – turning sixty

My birthday and I still marvel at how much my life has changed since the walk. For the first 58 years I'd been a product of my background, a South London working-class boy pursuing the narrow goal of financial success. Whatever I'd achieved was underpinned by my fortune to grow up at a time when there were far more public support services than now. Not only could my parents live in a decent secure council flat at an affordable rent, but I was able to attend a good state-run grammar school at no cost. If that wasn't enough, I was able to go to university without fees and even receive some allowance for student digs. After university I'd had to work hard to achieve a professional qualification while working full time in a demanding job. However, I'd had a lot of help from the society in which I grew up and been able to buy a home at a mere fraction of today's prices, even after allowing for inflation.

However exciting and rewarding my career was, I recognise I never had any real passion for the underlying business of the companies in which I worked for over 35 years. My interest was in people. When asked to give advice to my sons and other young people, I used to describe my career as simply a 'life on the buses'. I joined companies which took me on life journeys that helped create the person I am today. Each time I joined a new company or took on a new role, I never thought about where this would lead. It was like getting on a bus, but without ever looking at the destination board at the front. Instead I focused on who was on the bus, the people with whom I'd be sharing the working days. I knew this would be the group that would become a large part of my life.

So for me the human relationships were paramount, but what the company was actually doing never greatly interested me. Certainly I applied myself diligently to the challenge of making companies successful and enjoyed myself, but there was nothing there to really get the juices of my passion flowing. That has now all changed. I have a purpose that fills my life with passion. The impact of the change has been felt within the web of people close to me. It was best summed up at last night's birthday celebration organised by my Iceberger friends. As the speeches flowed, it was my youngest son, Ed, who announced to all that his dad, for so long a respected businessman and father, had suddenly become a 60-year-old hippy! The group of swimmers resoundingly agreed and have bestowed a new moniker. I'm now simply known as 'The Reverend'.

788 days later – a timely reminder

Another New Year dawns and I wonder if 2013 will be the year when some sanity breaks out. I believe I can now see the biggest threat to life on Earth. Consumerism has focused society on money-making and accumulating stuff and the world is breaking down under the strain. The tragedy is, we've lost track of our most precious element. Everyone is born with a much more valuable bank account: the one lodged at the 'Time Bank'. I've learned the meaning of life is life itself, and so the most important thing we have is the time we get to be alive in the world. Unlike the money bank which can dominate the daily routine as we work to earn money to convert into all manner of consumer temptations, each person's Time Bank account is as full as it will ever get. Every minute of each day we spend it, often with little thought. Regardless of what we do, time flows out of our account relentlessly like grains of sand through an egg timer.

There are no bank statements for our Time Bank and we never know how much is left in it. It could turn out to be empty by tonight, and yet we don't think of our time as particularly valuable or concern ourselves greatly with how we use each day's priceless ration. When I lost my first wife to illness over 12 years ago I got a reminder of the true worth of the contents of the Time Bank. On the walk I got reminders, like on consecutive days in Scotland when Kathy died and then we contemplated the heinous massacre at Glen Coe. I came to fully appreciate my time connected to life, both human and other-than-human and understood it made for a richer experience than anything money could buy. It was a timely reminder, but also a gift, to understand we're living a lie to organise ourselves as fundamentally materialistic consumers.

The system seems all-pervasive, but once we see it's not geared to help us, it is possible to live differently. From the moment I got home and opened my wardrobe I knew I would simply buy far less. What I then came to understand was the positive cycle I'd set in motion. Once I buy less stuff I don't create so much waste or need so much money. Potentially that can lead to working fewer hours, having more free time and a less frazzled life, spending more time doing things I enjoy or simply being in community with family and friends. This positive cycle from spending less on stuff to having more time for ourselves makes me optimistic more people will see through the empty consumer promises and change lives for the better while helping all life flourish. With more time we can help people we love, put time into our local community, and suddenly we don't need the latest gadget to distract us. As I know now, no human technology can ever be more complex and stimulating than bringing ourselves fully to life with love and laughter.

1,079 days later – engaging others

It's a lovely spring day and the most impactful project we've collaborated on has finished today. Just like a Schumacher short course, it ran for seven days and nights from our home. When we made the decision to keep our big family home it was with the idea we could host such initiatives, and so it proved. The idea came to joyful fruition when a group of participants from all over the world arrived for an intensive residential course called the Tao of Sustainability. Nine people lived at the house throughout and various experts passed through to give courses in both the theory and practical application of everything from power generation and usage, to transport, food systems, waste management, cleaning, product lifecycle analysis, business and the economy. Participants spoke of it as the most powerful education they had experienced. One particularly pleasing practical outcome was the demonstration of how waste can be minimised. At the end of seven full days and nights a thoughtful approach to purchasing, composting and recycling meant we sent just 35 grams of waste per person to landfill.

The idea of opening our home to a group of strangers seems very natural now. We learned on the walk it's instinctive human behaviour. Then, we were often the beneficiaries, but since arriving home we've regularly welcomed people here as we reach into the community in a variety of ways to widen discussion and consideration of sustainability issues. This year we began hosting a monthly 'Schumacher dinner' where we gather a dozen people around our family dinner table to discuss a question. These have become wonderful evenings. The question is drafted and circulated to invitees with a connection to the issue. We've considered questions as diverse as: 'What role can adult education play in creating a more sustainable world?' and 'How can art and artists help create a more sustainable world?'

Some of the people who've come we knew, some were referred to us, and some were simply people who we'd heard about. The only rules we set for the evening were that once seated with dinner, everyone was part of one discussion about the topic. When somebody spoke everybody else listened. In another fledgling initiative we've launched a Resurgence readers' group. We welcome up to twenty people a month for a convivial evening of discussion and sometimes run film nights. To have people from all walks of life, some strangers, come together in our home has been a joy. The act of bringing people together to explore ideas to challenge the status quo is liberating and opens up a wider consideration of alternative stories of how to live.

The more we interact with new people, the more snails' trails of connections have left their meandering threads in our lives. Through Resurgence I met Jacques Boulet, a gentle, generous academic, and joined the board of a graduate school offering Australia's first fully accredited Master's Degree in Sustainability and Social Change. Through another link I've become Treasurer of our local EcoCentre. This organisation has a strong reputation for its role in bringing sustainability awareness into schools, and implementing diverse projects that range from reducing sea water plastics pollution and land-based litter, to harnessing rainwater and developing organic gardens.

Another pair of threads which came to our door for a Resurgence readers' group one chilly winter's evening were Professor Frank Fisher and Anthony James. Frank looked haggard and worn out, yet apologised for not coming on his bike. He softly explained he had terminal brain cancer and had had a busy day of meetings and chemotherapy. Frank had been Australia's first Environmental Educator of the Year in 2007, but was a humble man. I had no idea just what a doyen of the field he was at first, and to say he stood astride Australian environmental science like a colossus would embarrass him but not be unwarranted. If they say the measure of a great teacher is the mark he leaves on his students, then Frank was truly in a special league. Once I got to know him, I kept tripping over the enormous trail of life-changing experiences he'd created in students from all walks of life.

Our lives are filled with people who come and go. Usually they pass through like nothing more than a light breeze, barely raising a goosebump. Then there are others who have a more profound and lasting impact. Taking up a life of activism typically leads to new circles of friends, often pretty stimulating ones. And so it was for Debby and me. During the last months of Frank's life I became better acquainted with his colleague Anthony James, another man with a deep understanding of the issues underlying sustainability from a systems viewpoint. Not only does he have a wonderful grasp of the onion-like layers that exist in trying to unpick sustainability issues, but he's a sensitive person with a love of life.

Anthony and I decided we wanted to work together and we've hosted major public events with people from across the world, including Satish Kumar. We've also created The Rescope Project, an organisation dedicated to our shared passion to help life on Earth flourish. It was only through Anthony's inspiration and know-how that the Tao of Sustainability was such a success this week, and it's only due to his prompting that I'm now writing this book.

1140 days later – the consumption addiction

It's now over three years since we walked into Land's End and my understanding of life changed. People say I had an epiphany and I guess that's true. The walk reminded me of this great web of life, how precious it is and the joy and good fortune I have to be part of it. By absorbing nature's stillness I'd been freed of the way I saw life. It was as if Mother Nature had taken the duster to the blackboard of my mind and wiped it clean. I'd been able to see things differently. By Day 66 I could walk out of moorland wilderness to gaze at the M62 motorway and write 'we stand staring at the greatest blight on the landscape'. Without the usual clutter of reasons I'd learned to defend and rationalise such things, I saw the M62 with great clarity. It is a blight on the landscape. Surely if we started with no such concept as a car and all its attendant inefficient and damaging infrastructure, anyone who suggested we create one would now qualify for a mental institution.

These few months in nature gave me a gift. The preconceptions I'd lived by had been pulled back as morning curtains to reveal sunlight over a rich landscape beyond. While walking I'd experienced the simple life of less and found a life where to have more money was irrelevant. On Day 76 we wandered into Crewe's central shopping plaza to be confronted by an example of what's held up as the normal way we should live. It felt like a trap, like I was looking directly at the hamster wheel of drudgery. I felt sad as the people around me seemed to be cogs in a frightening machine, unknowingly enlisted to work harder and harder to keep the wheel turning. Their goal to earn more, to buy more and more stuff that gives less and less satisfaction and is mostly stuff they don't need, bought with money they don't have, to impress people they don't really care about. Unfortunately everybody thinks of themselves as smarter than a rodent and so they keep doing what they're doing. Of course that scene was no different to most shopping centres throughout the world. I'd never before really questioned the system whereby people are brainwashed to buy so much more than the food, shelter and clothing they need for a happy life.

It's only a few days before another Christmas brings 2013 to an end and it's a joy to have turned off the festive consumption imperative. Last year we 'came out' to our friends and family and told them about our new sense of a life mission. Several hundred got the letter and some were embarrassed for us. They thought we'd perhaps lost our minds. However, we've already found that by talking openly we've given people permission to raise these issues with us. It's remarkable how many harbour similar unspoken concerns. There appears to be a deep rift in society between the promise of our present system and the reality we experience. In a group, people often feel intimidated to express opinions which may conflict with those shouted by vested interests. However, when we talk openly about such issues, it's as if we open up a large umbrella people can step under for a discussion while sheltering from the storm of critics.

Some argue the system has served us well, but whatever its benefits may have been, it's evident it is no longer fit for purpose. Large numbers of people feel in their bones our system based upon gross over-consumption needs to change. They feel it's dangerously out of control, but feel ensnared and helpless. The system may roll on, but increasingly the damage it creates cannot be ignored. I keep checking the latest facts about what's happening to our planetary home, hoping our ingenuity is improving things, but the evidence suggests they're getting worse. The lifestyle of more and more consumption has accelerated so fast that by 2050 the demand for stuff will be 75 times what it was when I was born. We're already exceeding our planet's capacity, but we'll likely need half a dozen planet Earths to satisfy our demands by then. The fact all our purchasing is not helping people live happier lives and is creating a debilitating and destructive fear of our fellow humans is the final indictment.

The increase in our human population may make it harder to create a sustainable world; however, it's the impact of higher personal consumption levels in the developed world I inhabit which causes most damage. Yet our leaders are obsessed with wanting higher consumption to grow GDP. Of course, when I try to communicate the impossibility of continuing an economic system that requires endless growth on a finite planet, the defenders of the status quo paint me as a lunatic. Someone who's mind became unhinged on a long walk. In some ways they're right. By stepping out of the system, I did detach myself and was able to see it in a new light. I feel like the boy watching the royal parade go by. Where most see consumption-fuelled economic growth as weaving the Emperor's gleaming new robes, I see they're fake and the Emperor is naked.

There are any number of indicators to affirm the damage we're doing. We become upset about the extinction threat to popular creatures like gorillas and elephants, yet the evidence suggests we're eliminating creatures 1,000 times more rapidly than normal. We've started the sixth mass extinction of life on the planet, the first since an asteroid wiped out the dinosaurs 65 million years ago. This is the first mass extinction event caused by one species, us humans, and we'll probably wipe out 50% of life on Earth.

And the outlook for human life is grim too. Climate change is simply one symptom of a planet that's become dramatically disturbed by the economic system we've constructed. Overconsumption means oceans are becoming massive rubbish dumps and getting warmer in a way that creates acidification and kills the coral reefs we love. Meanwhile, land clearing to rear ever more livestock or produce intensive crops at industrial scale is depleting soil nutrients and straining fresh water sources. The rabid exploitation of many mineral resources just adds to the litany of symptoms now evident across the world.

The system we feed is now reducing resilience and creating such imbalances, it threatens to wipe out much life and the only planetary home in the Universe that we know can provide a cradle for it. All the evidence suggests our future is not rosy and we could well become extinct ourselves. Like the fall of the Roman Empire, we look to have already commenced a gradual slide into more violent competition for scarce resources, greater climate calamities and increased social inequality.

The way we configure our thinking about life and make decisions in relation to it seems full of anomalies. It's predicted there'll soon be four billion vehicles on the road, which means our rush for personalised convenience could see cars become mere jigsaw pieces in a global gridlock, redundant as a means of transport. The food conundrum is even more bizarre. How can we produce so much food that while about a billion people go to bed hungry, we throw away between a third and a half of our food in developed societies and have made obesity-related illnesses the biggest cause of death? We'll even keep overeating and rely on having stomach bands fitted to make us stop, or have fat surgically cut off. We've turned food into an industrial, processed product which is no longer about human nourishment and bears less and less resemblance to the real food and nutrition which literally grows on trees.

There's no doubt this system, that's doing so much damage for so little gain, cannot continue. Unfortunately our politicians seem unable to lead any meaningful change. At the last election I heard a young political candidate questioned about whether the level of inaction by all parties on climate change showed a lack of ethics. His response came with gusto: of course it wasn't an ethical issue, but an economic one. After all, he asserted, we live in an economy. So, no recognition we live on a planet or as part of an ecosystem, we're simply part of a human financial system.

No, politics appears to have become simply a coliseum for adversarial battles to be fought, a place where opinions are polarised as the main game. All politicians are stuck with short electoral cycles and can't begin to tackle the scale and complexity of the problems we face. Prime Ministers and presidents know the situations they face are highly complex yet they want to be seen as decisive to be re-elected. The same is true of business leaders; in short, everyone needs to perpetuate the system to achieve short-term goals.

It seems efforts to improve the world will need to be led from outside the conventional political arena. Of course we're also our own worst enemy. We're instinctively drawn to the forthright voices of political and business leaders who explain issues in simplistic black and white terms, removing all the messy greys that frustrate us when dealing with the highly complex problems we face. It seems we've become conditioned to overlook any ethical concerns about what we're letting happen to the world future generations will have to exist in. Perhaps we need to reflect on the Indian philosopher Swami Vivekananda's advice from a century ago:

> If it is selfish it is immoral. If it is unselfish it is moral.

Earth is a pretty special planet, but it is little more than a blue dot surrounded by a fine layer of atmosphere in a vast cosmos. We think we can control nature, but our knowledge is not capable of controlling the climate any more than tectonic plates or planetary cycles. Yet, we have the power to change this future. Before leaving

Schumacher, change-agent Anne Miller encouraged us not to get demoralised, but to simply get smart. Don't try to shout louder, she'd said, just try to show how the status quo cannot work, make connections to things people care about and provide alternatives for their psychological safety.

Well, the alternatives are sprouting up around us all. People are beginning to change the way the system works by making conscious decisions to simply step away from it to live happier, more rewarding lives. On the walk I learned why buying more stuff was a distraction to experiencing the joy of life. In fact it is the opposite. Sharing life in simple community with other people while marvelling at nature's handiwork brought us a joy that's enriched human life for thousands of years. This was the gift I received and it's why I'm optimistic we can gradually deflate this gross consumption machine. Others less fortunate will need help to overcome their challenges and make choices more in harmony with personal and planetary wellbeing. However, that's what being in a community is all about.

1,153 days later – a new way of life

It may be New Year's Day 2014, but one thing is unlikely to change in my world. I've got used to people defending the status quo being only too quick to accuse me of hypocrisy. If I don't personally live up to the impeccable standards of abstention which they contrive for me, I'm a fraud, and any concern I raise can be easily dismissed. To be truly sustainable, many feel, would require me to live a dour bleak existence in a cave. Of course this is all a distraction from the fact human unsustainable practices are real and need to change. Whether I personally have all the answers, or have mastered the art of living blamelessly, which I certainly have not, some people can justify their inaction by my faults. Of course, in our developed society it is well-nigh impossible to live in an entirely sustainable way. Change is happening though. It may seem like the overarching system is as impervious as a hippopotamus to fleas on its hide, but it's early days and people are beginning to call for change.

At home, we've made some significant changes to align our lifestyle to our beliefs. We'd come home from Schumacher with the clear conviction to be the change we wanted to see. It's all taken time though and we know we've still got a long way to go. I've realised it's impossible to remove ourselves entirely from the system that frames western culture and recover a sustainable lifestyle. However, we've had fun trying and I like to think we're more mindful in how we live.

With the advice of a permaculture specialist we set about making our home productive. We built raised garden beds with our son Tom, saving money, but also enjoying the sweat and sense of achievement. And as the vegetables began to grow and the first bean shoots popped into the light, so we felt the joy of a bond with our food supply. The garden has developed into a wonderful receptacle for much of our organic waste and we've reduced our landfill to one small parcel wrapped in newspaper each week. We operate a comprehensive six-stage recycling system. Chickens and worms are part of it.

The real estate agent said our home would be worth more if we put in a pool, but instead we built a chicken run and the arrival of six chickens was a particular delight. The eggs are great. Although not vegetarian, we're very conscious of the environmental damage done by the industrial systems of livestock production and so have substantially reduced our consumption of meat and unsustainably caught fish. None of this at all interferes with our enjoyment of food as we've accumulated an extensive repertoire of yummy vegetarian recipes. We still enjoy a glass or two of wine and with outstanding vineyards on Melbourne's fringes really have no need to chase wines from across the world.

Once again this Christmas there were no gaudy knickknacks or presents. We enjoyed a traditional meal at home that we hope nurtured body and spirit of the family and friends that joined us. In our world there's no longer a place for presents for the sake of a date in the calendar, be it Christmas or a birthday. We now simply look to help friends and family with meaningful gifts when a genuine need arises.

Two years ago I returned from Schumacher with the intention not to buy any clothes for 12 months. That led to an enjoyable year so I extended the commitment for another year. Every time I open the wardrobe door I see I still have plenty of well-loved clothes to choose from. More than just not buying clothes though, we've simply stopped all discretionary consumption. No more clothes, home paraphernalia or convenience appliances bought because of a marketers whim. Repair or reuse have become our watchwords. When we do feel we need to replace something that's worn out we try to buy quality products of local provenance. One thing that won't be curtailed though is my research. I'm a reader and source much of my information from books. I expect the Badger bookshelves will continue to grow.

By now we've almost entirely stopped shopping at large supermarkets. Our needs have become quite simple. The walk taught us that we didn't need the clutter of shampoo, shaving creams, body gels or deodorants, just one block of soap was plenty. Also, paper towels, tissues and cling wrap were unnecessary. We mostly shop for food now and try to buy local produce from independent shops. We've always enjoyed farmers' markets but now also go out of our way to support Bruce, our long-established organic grocer, and the other local community shops. We try to centre our cooking around seasonal produce and enjoy the variety of eating different foods at different times of year. I still consider my flat white coffee essential, but with a KeepCup can avoid disposable cup waste. This seemed a logical step once we moved away from plastic bags to cloth ones. In fact, despite the relative small size of these initiatives, in some way they feel more powerful. Each time I say no to a plastic bag or cup, I hear myself saying I care and know I'm being seen in a public place confronting the system.

The wonderful by-product of our decision to reduce our consumption has been less time spent shopping and more free time. It's the perfect cycle of positives! By unmasking and rejecting marketing fantasies we haven't made life difficult or dour, in fact, quite the reverse. In abstinence we've found amusement and another form of Arcadia. We've stepped off the endless escalator of envy which can often lead to homes full of stuff, crammed offsite storage units and even holiday homes packed with yet more. We've found as we spend less, we have more time to spend in the real world to engage with life.

In addition to curtailing our engagement with retail we've also reduced our travel. We've largely lost the desire to be tourists. The artificial nature of so much of the fabric which surrounds global tourism increasingly leaves the experience unfulfilling. And air travel is one of the most destructive forms of carbon emissions, yet its use is ubiquitous and growing madly. We're not prepared to completely stop flying, but know we want to travel thoughtfully. Whether for education, advocacy, or simply to strengthen our personal wellbeing and the foundations of our friendships, we're looking for our travel to have meaning.

Another immediate change we implemented was to dramatically cut down our car usage. We now take trains around town and have dusted off our bikes for most local travel. Being in the world on a bike, rather than looking at it through the frame of a car window, brings a felt connection with the elements and our community. When I do drive, I've found I can channel my competitive spirit from beating other drivers to beating the fuel gauge by keeping the rev-counter down. Our second car has become redundant and we're going to sell it. None of the changes we've made have been a hardship. They're life-enriching, and have brought the unexpected result of saving money.

We've also enhanced our home's resilience. We quickly reduced water usage by showering at half pressure and flushing the toilet less often: 'If it's yellow let it mellow, if it's brown flush it down,' is our mantra. We've also installed a comprehensive water catchment system with tanks to ensure rainwater is harvested for times of drought. We installed solar panels to tap the sun's free energy and have changed to low energy light bulbs. With our central heating turned down to keep it off for longer and an outdoor fridge moved inside to reduce its power usage, we now produce more electricity than we consume. The tumble dryer has become redundant as ceiling pulley hangers dry our clothes.

I've learned that the best way to confound the system that's holding so much of humanity to ransom is to take meaning away from money. What's been surprising for me as an accountant though, is the dawning awareness of a second meaning for the term conservation. One of the changes we've made has been to weather-proof our old house. However as we conserve our power usage we conserve money as well as the planet's resources. It seems the more I let go of focusing on money and simply try to behave more sustainably, I find my life has more meaning, I enjoy it more, yet I'm saving money and my bank balance is growing. The journey to sustainability seems to be a bit like that, full of conundrums. It's as if the more I focus on filling my time with love and laughter, the more joy fills my life and money simply becomes the support tool it was originally designed to be.

By spending less, we've found we've more money to plough into more productive avenues. It's easier now for instance to support the organisations we donate to. This is of itself very rewarding and I consider flouts the dominant principle of consumerism. By recognising the sophisticated advertising messages as mind-altering propaganda, we simply ignore them and have more money to give away. I can only marvel at the change I've experienced. A few years back at the conclusion of a personal development course, I was asked to draw a picture of my personal vision for a successful future. I drew a large dollar sign. As a friend reflected afterwards, I was the only person in the class focused on money-making, yet I probably already had more than everyone else. How things have changed; now my focus is on how to give it to charity.

I research the organisations we support more carefully now than those we invest our pension in. Our focus is to try to change underlying destructive systems, rather than simply help offset the problems they cause. Debby's Dad tells me the Bible says we should donate a tithe, or ten percent of our earnings to charity. Perhaps in turning my atheist back on the Bible I may have thrown the baby out with the bathwater. Like many of the bible stories I learned as a child, most offered simple wisdom about how to live a good life. Never mind, it's never too late to put things right. We've doubled our gifts to exceed a tithe and look set to double again.

I'm also trying to realign our retirement investments to support sustainable companies, although I have to admit it's still a work in progress. It's an altogether more challenging process than I'd first thought. I'm not sure there are any companies, certainly not big stock exchange listed ones, that can honestly state they're sustainable in terms of not being a detriment to human and other life. When companies talk about sustainability, they do so in a way that stems from a lack of understanding embedded in a system outside their control. As John Ehrenfeld describes in *Flourishing*:

> Sustainability is the possibility that humans and other life will flourish on Earth forever. Reducing unsustainability, although critical, will not create sustainability.

We lead active lives and Debby inspires me with her attitudes to caring for people and the rare gift she brings to her yoga and Vedic chant classes. The other thing on which Debby took a lead was the creation of a Deep Time walk to emulate the experience we'd had at Schumacher. Every month come rain or shine she leads a group with me as support crew, walking people 4.6 km (just under three miles) on a guided representation of the 4.6 billion years the Earth has existed. It is always so powerful when people understand that after 4.6kms it is only as they take the final 30cm (one foot) step that they enter the era when humans have appeared on the scene. We are truly an infant species and it's no wonder we have so much to learn.

My friends tell me I'm lucky to be able to afford these views. Many can't understand why I chose to stop work early given they often keep working regardless of whether they need the money. Although I don't come from a background of moneyed privilege, I'm considered well off. I don't hide from the fact I did well in my professional life and managed my financial affairs sufficiently carefully to be able to retire early. However, the overarching reason I've been able to do well is more a product of much broader societal changes and the countries in which I have been fortunate enough to live. Anyway, just because I've benefited from the system, I don't consider I have any less right to make comment about its failings and indeed feel a duty to do so.

Another year awaits and I seem to have plenty to keep me busy. Whether helping out the not-for-profits, networking or mentoring others, it provides all the reward I could ask for. As friends have pointed out, this offers plenty of opportunity for my favourite way of spending time. I often share a coffee with people while building the new stories of how to make a better world. Perhaps the new culture I'm promoting is 'Cut Consumption and Chat'.

1243 days later – the Pyramid of Power

April starts today and Melbourne's autumn is in full swing. When we bid farewell to Schumacher College with its inspirational teachers and delight-filled kitchen, autumn was ending in the russet tones of the soulful English countryside. This morning, the bay's cooler waters sent a shiver up my spine to remind me of that autumn decay and nature's cycle of life. It also reminded me of the continued lie that rests at the heart of society. The system our society is founded on has an insatiable thirst for never-ending growth. Yet nature holds up the example that all life flows in cycles of growth, maturity, decay and rebirth, not endless straight-line progression. We're blind to it and choose to ignore the lesson, but will only be able to do so for so long. As many previous human societies have found to their detriment, if you don't live in balance with the local ecosystem capacity, the ending is evitable, regardless of money and technology.

At Schumacher, we discussed the urgent need to relearn community economics. In community, people are risk-minimisers not profit-maximisers. However, we've strayed from this fundamental wisdom which has sustained humans over thousands of years. My 'baby boomer' generation has fostered a more self-centred society, yet everyone on Earth can only exist in relationship to other life. The unholy combination of bloated debt creation, accelerated fossil fuel extraction and sophisticated psychological marketing, has seen much of the planet's natural wealth converted into a veritable cornucopia of transient man-made riches soon to be waste. In pursuit of mindless money-making we've created scarcity at what should be a time of great abundance. As Gandhi said, 'There is enough for everyone's needs, but not enough for everyone's greed.' Now, our challenge is to evolve our outlook from being ego-centric to eco-centric.

All human societies have tended to build structures of power that created fealty to a leader or god to control the masses. The Egyptian pharaohs built pyramids to have their position revered as deities and their power reinforced. The daunting monoliths instilled awe and fear to keep the system going. Today our Pyramid of Power reveres Profit, the single-minded obligatory goal of our global business institutions. With their sophisticated systems and golden resources, they enchant the population and grow ever bigger. This effectively has enshrined money as the ultimate deity in the land. And while money sits at the apex of the pyramid, locked inside are the workers, including the CEO's and directors, who have no permission to raise their sights from the Sisyphean task of building the pyramid ever higher.

As companies expand their reach across the world, it is easy to understand how we are all inextricably woven up in the arrangement whereby the pursuit of money is more important than anything else. Global companies like those with which I was intimately involved during my business career now dominate world trade. Society may pay lip service to the idea financial wealth is not the most important thing in life, but it has become our prime organising system. Can there be any greater folly to contemplate on 1st April than this pathological system at the heart of human society. It's not supporting human wellbeing and I feel sure we will soon call it out for what it is and bring change. For now I'll take my notebook out and jot down a few April Fool's Day thoughts. (These appear in the Afterword.)

1,369 days later – back on the track

It's 5th August 2014 and we're back at Land's End. Debby and I are ready to set off on another long walk. We're going to walk across Britain again. This time, from its most westerly point to the eastern extremity on the Suffolk coast at Lowestoft. We're going to follow the Mary Michael Pilgrims Way and investigate an ancient concept for understanding the land. This particular route is thought to follow a pair of interwoven earth energy lines which over thousands of years have attracted many people to create spiritual gathering places. So, we'll once again explore Britain and tap into more sights and sounds of the country from which I've sprung. And if such esoteric concepts as earth energy lines sound fanciful, that's in part why I chose this adventure. I've no knowledge or experience of things such as ley lines and their ilk, but I figure nothing could be as far-fetched as the heights of consumerism to which we're in thrall. So, this is our small way of making a statement to ask people to stop and think about what they consider to be real in today's world.

I'm wearing my favourite 'brand' of clothing today. In 2010 I had a lightweight merino t-shirt in my favourite shade of green. Unfortunately some moth larvae took a similar liking to it and ate a couple of holes. I found them when we stayed with a family friend and Margo, her 90-year-old mother. I mentioned I'd have to get a new t-shirt and Patricianne said her mother would darn it for me. I didn't want her mother inconvenienced at her great age and dismissed the offer. Patricianne looked at me quizzically and quietly explained I'd misunderstood the situation. Her mother was an accomplished darner and at this stage of her life constantly looked for ways to feel useful. To let her darn my t-shirt would not be a chore, but a welcome opportunity. I was dumbstruck. Here again was my modern world interpretation of a situation unravelling.

Margo went on to darn my t-shirt and the beaming smile when she proudly handed it back to me was a joy. So, my favourite top is back in use and those small darns are now the brand I wear with most pride. There is no way the story of human endeavour and joy which lives in my t-shirt could be bettered by any brand fabricated by a marketing organisation to sell fake stories to millions. So brands can still stand for something and have real meaning in a world often considered to be devoid of it.

I set off today in hope. Hope that more people will come to see the falsehood of our sterile marketing-fuelled consumption life-styles. I know a change is stirring in many ways. It's bubbling up through blogs, in community gatherings and in the social and more traditional media. Of course, the sheer size of the global system can be intimidating. It's easy to feel frustrated with the status quo yet incapable of contributing anything that could make things better. I used to feel that someone with my humble beginnings couldn't help a planet of over seven billion other humans and hundreds of millions of non-human species? However, I'm convinced this is the single biggest barrier holding us back. Like the bogs of the Pennine Way, these thoughts can take hold, sucking energy and squashing potential. But I've learned that in the web of life, every single life has a role to play.

Every time someone takes a deep breath, steps back to see the folly of the system and says 'Enough is enough! I'll change my life to live more sensibly and support others to do the same,' it has an impact. We are never alone and our actions reverberate in ways we cannot understand. All that's necessary is to pay attention to our part of the web. It may seem hard to understand all the details of how the system can change, but as Martin Luther King said: 'I have a dream...', not 'I have a plan.'

People of all ages are beginning to embrace change and look for better ways to live their lives and help heal the planet. Us 'greyheads' may have created the mess, but we're beginning to own up to it. We're the Baby Boomers who grew up as a rebellious generation, rejecting authority and creating new music with flower power. It's still in our genes to bring, nay demand, change. We became fascinated with money and appearances, but are coming to understand the marketing sham and planetary destruction our society has created. We're ready to help. Younger generations are already adopting greener, healthier lifestyles. They look for organic food, go to farmers markets and are interested in having more free time for family and friends, rather than simply making more money. They're increasingly spurning traditional employment options and the often tired promises of the corporate and political world.

In all these ways life is working to reconnect and repair the web of life. As I discovered, the secret of life is life itself, and all I need to do now is to help life flourish. I'll do that with love for the diversity and unique attributes every life form brings to the web of life and the joy and inspiration they contribute. And with laughter, to help me hold my passion lightly in the face of so much I cannot understand and to remind me of my imperfections. So, off we go again, taking Love and Laughter to Life, the three L's, my new 'Holy Trinity'.

Afterword

This may be April Fool's Day 2014, but it's the everyday way of life in our consumer society that now seems a farce. I think it's time we looked for a new story of how to organise ourselves to help accelerate a move to a saner, more sustainable world. I once wrote down in an English pub a vision of an adventure I had no idea was possible. That story changed my life, perhaps it's time to take the pen out again...

Connection with Countryside

At Schumacher, I listened to Fritjof Capra explain how ecosystems achieve stability and resilience through the richness and complexity of their ecological webs. Greater biodiversity builds greater resilience. We're now dramatically reducing biodiversity, so the planet's resilience to cope with humanity's expansion is undermined. It's apparent we humans are increasingly withdrawn from direct experience with the natural world and largely unaware of the damage we're doing. I hear only one in four American children have climbed a tree by adulthood for instance, and such statistics are now common. Increasingly we're city dwellers and it's no longer common for our offspring to establish a sense of their place in the rich web of life they're born into. Technology is becoming ubiquitous and young people now often gain their appreciation of nature through TV and computer screens. Such experience though is empty of the vibrancy of relationship we share. It does not provide any sense of the very real obligations and reliance that we have for other life.

The best chance we have of improving a person's respect for the planet is through building a connection with the countryside. It's only when we are in direct contact with other life we can begin to understand its importance to our life and vice versa. Immersed in nature we can get a sense of its mystery, of something much bigger than our day-to-day existence, and from that can grow a lifetime commitment of respect. It enables us to pull into the forefront of our minds the instinctive love we carry for it deep in our bones. Once we've developed a connection with nature we are more likely to understand our place in it and advocate in support of more sustainable policies that permit all life to flourish.

Perhaps it's time to reinstitute a new form of National Service. What a change it would bring to people's lives and the way they relate to the world if everybody between the ages of, say, 18 and 25 spent a year doing 'Natural Service' – living on the land for a year and carrying out projects to facilitate wilderness, while being able to foster a lifelong bond with the web of life they're enmeshed in.

Corporate Charter

It has gone largely unchallenged for the past 40 years that big companies are the most efficient way of creating benefits for society. Jobs, a greater choice of material goods, and monetary wealth for the population are all said to trickle down from company activity. And the best way to stimulate the process is to free markets up to trade. During my business life restrictions on the activity of companies and the flow of financial capital across international borders have relaxed. As a result, companies have gone overseas in search of lower costs. Leaders are criticised as being badly-intentioned, but they're simply caught in a complex system beyond their control. Their duty to their shareholders is to find the lowest cost resources and cheapest labour regardless of whether that means lower safety and environmental controls. Company directors and senior managers are asked to operate ethically and do the right thing by people and the planet, yet they can't. They're also expected to pay the company's fair share of taxes, but if they can legally avoid them, it's their duty to avoid them. Company managers operate within a rigid legal straightjacket to maximise profit. The root problem is the system itself. That's what's bringing our society undone.

The feature that makes companies chasing profit to the exclusion of all else so destructive is their marketing of ever more unneeded consumer goods. They have made the folly of consumerism, whereby we buy more and more stuff that's engineered to fail or quickly become outdated junk, seem thoroughly normal. People in business and politics argue we need consumption and GDP growth to employ people, lift them from poverty and create wealth. Well, let's reframe that comment. The current system was not designed to keep people employed or to lift them out of poverty, and there is plenty of evidence to suggest it's not achieving either.

There is a whole array of confident arguments that human ingenuity and technological prowess will still save the world. Yet our ingenuity and technology are in thrall to global companies where skills are deployed to increase profits at the expense of the planet, not to save it. Technology converts more of nature's resources into must-have gadgets and forever works to do so at lower cost to maximise the quantity sold while increasing the ensuing damage. In the same way, climate change is now embraced as simply another business opportunity. In a world where 'more' is feted, the concept of reducing or conserving energy is rarely discussed. If consumerism has reached this level of futile excess, how much further down Alice's rabbit hole can we possibly go in search of finding enough?

In the race to build ever bigger businesses we have been seduced into thinking top executives need to be treated almost as different beings to most employees. It used to be considered abnormal if senior managers received pay in excess of perhaps 20 times the lowest waged in the company. Nowadays, that multiple can be 200 times or more. We convince ourselves by paying vast amounts that we're recruiting people of unparalleled ability, the superheroes of our old comic books. We must dispel this imagery and recognise these people are only human and as fallible as others. They seek to reassure society the system is in safe hands, but the results of these sprawling international corporations prove otherwise. Disasters, irregularities and write-offs are a routine part of the complexities of a globalised corporate life that's become too single-focussed to be resilient.

We must be careful to see companies in their true light and not be taken in by the gloss of world-leading success they seek to portray. Companies are in business for one thing and only one thing, to maximise the monetary return to their shareholders. This is the flaw set right at the heart of the system we live under. While people think companies are run by bad people, it's the system that's at fault, not the people. We all have some interest in seeing our planetary home preserved and communities thrive, yet we've created and unleashed a psychopathic institution that's expressly forbidden from targeting such outcomes.

Companies may well try to promote the good they do in the world, but the plain fact is that they are not in business to do good. Everything they do, whether it be donating to communities or implementing more 'green' ways of operating, is to improve their potential for more sales and profits. When they take the logical step to move to tax havens or base their operations in less-developed countries where the controls on them, and hence costs of operation, are lower, all these are completely aligned with their directors' overriding responsibility to make their shareholders more money. This is the vital truth we must acknowledge.

We've been naïve to think we can unleash these massive organisations to scour the globe with the single objective to make money and expect great benefits to flow to society. It is the corporate structure that has outlived its use-by date and must now be reimagined. From an obligation to simply grow financial capital, we need to rethink the approach that tries to shackle companies with restrictions and penalties. Companies are now often larger than countries. Walmart has a bigger economy than Australia and two thirds of the top 100 world economies are companies rather than nation states. Companies have transcended national borders and are no longer subservient to any one country, but are typically operated by very able people with some of the best systems and resources available. We need to widen the corporate motive to free these people and resources to bring profit back into service of people and planet.

It is the obligation to maximise shareholders financial returns right at the heart of the corporate charter that must change. Perhaps setting a regulated maximum financial return above central bank interest rates, say an annual five percent premium, would work. This could be a financial 'cap and trade' arrangement, society's bargain for continuing the limited personal liability that is conferred by corporate personhood and keeps managers and shareholders immune from responsibility for so much of the collateral damage perpetrated by their companies. Whatever we do, a fundamental shift in the way the capitalist system works is inevitable and urgently required.

Custodianship of Property

A third change to the broader society where money is feted, would be for real property ownership to be reimagined as custodianship. We can understand at some level that as our lives are finite, so too our ownership of land and property is transient. It has become common in large cities for massive apartment complexes to be constructed which investors buy with no intention of ever occupying or letting them. Sometimes called 'lock-boxes in the sky', they are an abhorrent waste of resources and provide graphic evidence of the ridiculous excesses to which our money-centred system has gone. Instead of land and houses being owned simply as a store of monetary wealth, it would be better for society if property owners were required to recognise their obligations to those people who may follow on the land and those that live in the surrounding community. There is only a limited amount of land on which life can flourish, so it's important that property should only be created to be lived or worked in. Ownership should come with some responsibility for all life on and around that property now and in the future.

Civic Charter

One final change that could benefit society would be an initiative that strengthens all citizens' duty of care for their society. It is common wisdom for people to pay the least tax they can while criticising governments for their waste and ineptitude in spending the taxes raised. Perhaps we should abolish all income taxes and introduce a Civic Charter contribution. Under this every citizen would subscribe a share of their labour for the local, regional, national and international services necessary to develop the type of infrastructure needed for all life to flourish in their society. People need to be re-engaged in civic duty and contribute to its development and maintenance. People could perform services or pay amounts calculated in a similar way to income tax on a sliding scale. I well remember marginal tax rates as high as 97% when I studied for my accounting exams, and while I do not suggest they rise that high, we need to acknowledge the benefits of contributing to pay for the civic society we expect and deserve.

A positive extension of our civic duty could be the obligation of a parting gift to the society that has supported us in life. This gift could resemble death duties and help people regain a grip on their mortality. There is something obscene about the endless focus society creates around building personal financial resources. It's even more bizarre when people keep striving to increase their wealth even as they age and have more than enough money to live out a flourishing retirement. Society should not encourage people in their later years to continue to conserve their capital and worry about making more money when they already have plenty. Perhaps if we introduced an obligatory civic gift equivalent to a 100% death duty, then people would let go of the need to focus so intently on money in the later stages of their lives. Again, any such measures would help to undermine the pernicious effect of money sitting atop the Pyramid of Power.

So, there we have it – four initiatives to disrupt the system and set the scene for a more balanced and meaningful world. While I'm at it though, I think we'll need a strong set of values to support change:

Values

- Compassion, because most people do not understand the state of the planet and like to think they're doing the right thing.
- Collaboration, because none of us have all the answers to what is an immensely complex situation and we'll need to harness everyone's talent.
- Care, as in the end only if our capacity to care for life on our planet is greater than our desire to consume will we survive.
- Communication, to promote better understanding of the unhealthy systems we live with and to share new stories of how all life can flourish on Earth.
- Consciousness, of the complexity of our situation and the web of relationships in which we are all embedded.

– Community, remembering we're all connected in a web of life, citizens of planet Earth and so need to build community and not demonise or build fear of others.
–Comedy, because we need to laugh and remain light of spirit as we tackle confronting situations.
– Contemplation, to appreciate the beauty which nature bestows freely upon us every day to feed our spirits and remind us of the gift of life we enjoy.

All these values begin with the letter 'C' like the change initiatives. This is to remind me to try to 'see' issues clearly. Just as I've been used to framing the way I see life according to the system I inherited, so I'm in danger of not seeing the world as others do. So, every time I look at my list, I hope I'm given a healthy jolt to try to see more clearly.

Acknowledgements

No venture of the size of our walk can be undertaken without the support, encouragement and generosity of spirit of many people. I have now come to understand the writing of a book is no different. In particular, I now appreciate the creative process is one fraught with fragile confidence and benefits greatly from supporters who can nurture the spirit that lies behind the author's vision. I am fortunate that my life is filled by many inspiring people who have been willing to lend their energy to my work and provide encouragement when self-doubt threatened to swamp me.

In particular, I know none of this would have happened without Debby. During the five years it has taken to bring these words to the page she has hauled me through mires of questioning as deep as any Pennine Way bogs, patiently giving me the time and space away from family life to write, and been resolute in her willingness to listen to me read the seven rewrites. I hope you feel this book now does justice to your efforts to complete the walk, type the blog and have our story told.

The book has been a family project in many ways and within its pages walk the ghosts of those who have helped make me the man I am today. I hope my mum and dad would have been pleased with this tome and not consider I've reached too far from their soundly grounded values, and that Barbara would be happy to know she will always live on as part of my character. I know she would be proud of James and Ed. Our sons are fine young men and both have made their own contributions to the birth of this book, as have Matt, Kate and Tom the step children who grace my life. Kate &

her husband, John and Matt even brought energy to our endeavour by spending a week on the track with us.

At the end of the walk I had no serious thoughts to write this book, but many people had other ideas. One in particular has been instrumental in getting me through it. Patricianne is a dear family friend, but more than that she is someone who can see through me, my guru. Anthony took on the challenge to convince me to get the book started and we hope it might find an audience to help fund The Rescope Project that is dear to us both, but it was Patricianne who had the wisdom to know the book also needed to be for me if it was to be completed. She knew how to challenge my purpose and then give honest feedback as she read every page in draft. Beyond that a small group of people have urged me along and provided wise counsel, Morag (the ultimate blog groupie), Diana (with able support from Geoffrey) and SueDoll. And Ree, who did not make it to see this book finally in print. Your spirit is cherished and your light sadly missed from a world that badly needs more bright colours.

As a first time author, I needed professional help of course and that came through a suitably serendipitous encounter. Satish Kumar who has inspired so many, organised the Resurgence 50th anniversary conference at Oxford University in late 2016. We attended and joined a commemorative walk from the source of the Thames to Oxford during which I met Fern Smith. As we walked along a muddy riverbank she told me who my editor should be. Her advice was spot on and over the past year I feel I have been on a creative writing course under the wise and witty tutelage of Charlotte du Cann. Certainly she cannot be held responsible for any literary shortcomings in this book, it would have been far worse without her. And Tim, it all started with your advice on structure in a Melbourne café and ended five years later under Mark's proofing eye.

Probably the best bits of this book are not my words, but the wonderful artworks which I hope you enjoy as much as me. Sarah

McConnell is a young woman blossoming into a fine artist. She produced three watercolour paintings, anyone of which would have graced the cover of better books than mine. In the end, the picture we chose seemed to capture both the vagaries of the British landscape and the turmoil walking through it stirred up inside me. When it came to developing some interior sketches to launch each chapter, I appealed to a very talented young man who I've watched grow up. He does not call himself an artist but is a natural creative and Jason, thank you for going so far beyond the brief. The simple set of mud maps I envisioned have become beautiful distinctive pieces of art.

Other people who were friends or became so as the book evolved offered advice and brought more of the specialist skills I lacked. Thank you to Row in England for gently helping me into the world of writing and to Ed for donating the book title, which I consider worthy of your award-winning cryptic crossword brain. And to Jean and James for gently extricating the by-line out of me, while Clifford & Louise and Francesca and the Grumpy Swimmer bookshop team have been so gracious to answer all my publishing questions. From my beloved swimming group, Roger, Warren, Paul, Rob, Peter, Greg, Russell and Peter have all provided insights and assistance, while Jacques and Alan did the same at OASES. There are too many others to mention, but Mark, Tessa, Fiona, Biddy, Craig, John & Fiona, Greg, Bobby, Annie, Norm, Carol, Jan, Margaret, Maria, Alistair, Jenny, David, Vicki, Len & Pauline, Kes, Lynchy, Bobbie, Glenice & Duncan, Jane & Peter, John & Jane, were all urging me on. While Genevieve set me up as a writer-in-residence at Kyneton to finish the first draft, Heather & Peter put up with my writing drama in Bermagui and Mikey brewed great coffees after head-clearing swims in the Blue Pool.

And then there are a host of well-wishers and supporters, each of whom played central roles at the time they were needed to help us pull this great adventure off. In terms of the walk, no one did more than Phyllis and Colin ('Mum & Dad') who were our peerless logistical support team, but so much more. And Steve, where would we have been without your maps, or Lance, without your yoga instruction?! From the moment we landed in Scotland people opened their homes and their hearts to us, sometimes joining us for a walk. A special mention goes to Di who joined us from Australia for a walk and fought her vertigo through some shocking conditions for three weeks down the Pennine Way. But there were so many more: Robert & Rachel, Linda & Robert, Shona & Gerry, Kay, John & Sarah, Susie & Matt, Jason & Wendy, Chris & Wendy, Dave, Mike & Dorothy, Mary & Lance, Angela & Alan, Richard & Dot, June & Ilt, Liz & Chris, Sheila & Andrew, Yolanda & Phil, Tim, Mary & Jack, Megan, Jill, Sue & Derek, my thanks to you all.

About the author

Keith Badger is a company director, philanthropist, mentor, writer, speaker, and a year-round ocean swimmer. Born and raised in a working class family on South London council estates, he spent 25 years as Finance Director and Chief Executive Officer for global organisations, travelling throughout Europe, Africa and Asia. He lived in Paris and Lagos before settling with his family in Melbourne, Australia.

After losing his first wife to illness, Keith started a new chapter of life with his second wife, Debby, as they brought together their five teenage children in an old Victorian home. As a founding director of The Rescope Project, he now works closely with various organisations and individuals to shape a more sustainable world.

LANDS
END
2010
NEW YORK 3147
JOHN O'GROATS 874
ISLES OF SCILLY
LONGSHIPS
END TO END 2801 KM
5TH NOVEMBER

Route Map

ORKNEY
ISLANDS
ISLE OF LEWIS
MORAY FIRTH
SCOTLAND
N O R
U N I T E D
K I N G D O M
NORTHERN
IRELAND
REPUBLIC
OF
IRELAND
IRISH SEA
WALES
ENGLAND
CELTIC
SEA
ENGLISH CHANNEL

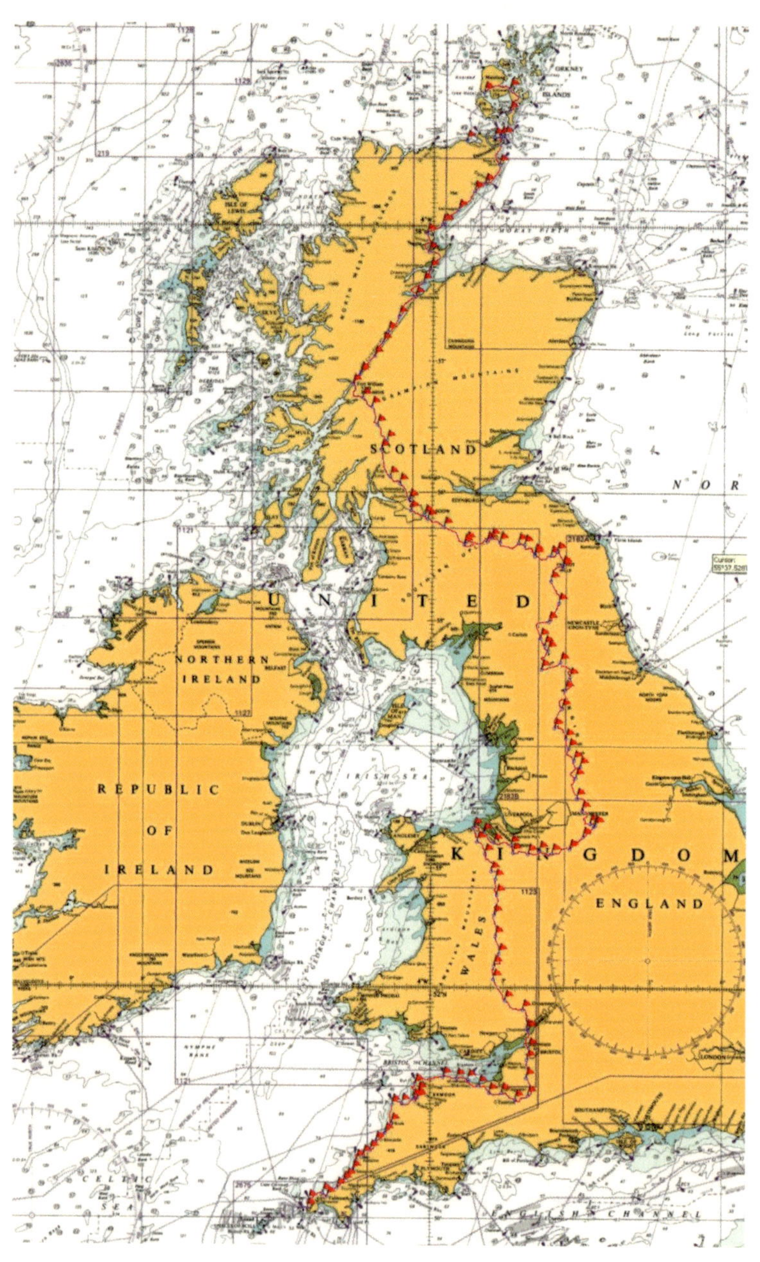